THE CREATIVE MYSTIQUE

THE CREATIVE MYSTIQUE

From Red Shoes Frenzy to Love and Creativity

SUSAN KAVALER-ADLER, Ph.D.

ROUTLEDGE
New York & London

Published in 1996 by
Routledge
29 West 35th Street
New York, NY 10001

Published in Great Britain by
Routledge
11 New Fetter Lane
London EC4P 4EE

Printed in the United States of America on acid-free paper.

Library of Congress Cataloging-in-Publication Data

Kavaler-Adler, Susan.
    The creative mystique: from red shoes frenzy to love and creativity /
Susan Kavaler-Adler .
        p.   cm.
    ISBN 0–415–91412–4 (cloth) — ISBN 0–415–91413–2 (pbk.)
    1. Psychic trauma. 2. Object relations 3. Creation (Literary, artistic, etc.)
— Psychological Aspects.   I. Title.
BF175.5.P75K38   1996
153.3'5'082—dc20   96-26074
                                                               CIP

CONTENTS)

DEDICATIONS)

To my husband, Saul Adler, for his love and patience during so many hours when I communed with my computer.

To my psychoanalyst, Dr. Mark Grunes.

To my friends and students.

To my patients.

To all of those who have joined with me in bringing the Object Relations Institute to life, during the times when I was also giving psychic birth to my two books on creativity and object relations theory. I was pregnant with the books, the Institute, and the Institute's curriculum during the same years. They are all expressions of my "love-creativity dialectic," but also of my "compulsion to create."

FOREWORD)

It is a pleasure and a privilege to write a forward to this book. It is a book written with passion and a powerful sense of conviction, rare in a profession that takes special pride in scientific objectivity. Furthermore, the basic idea that animates this book is, to the best of my knowledge, an original one.

That every poet owes his creativity to a muse is an idea that goes back to ancient Greek poetry. Hesiod, whose authority was second only to that of Homer, who was the first to suggest that the poet receives from the muse his scepter, voice, and knowledge. Throughout history, the relationship between poet and muse was a benign one, reversing gender roles. It is the muse, a woman, who makes the poet fruitful, able to give birth to his creation. I know of only one modern poet, Robert Graves, who, in his book *The White Goddess*, published in 1947, described his relationship to his muse with a complexity reminiscent of the author's description of the relationship between creative women and their demon lovers.

Unlike the male poet, whose relationship to his muse was usually a desexualized one, the creative women described in the pages of this book are both inviting and struggling against the intrusion of their demon lover's. The demon lover, in Dr. Kavaler-Adler's conceptualization, is "immune to a loving contact." The creative woman yearning for him desires "erotic intensity and bodily completion." This "hard, phallic demon lover enters her as a rapist would." If the demon lover becomes a dynamic internal object, he will "haunt the woman in her interpersonal world and within her creative work." Once this fatal union is established, the creative work becomes for the woman artist an addiction, driven by manic intensity. At times death itself can be experienced as a demon lover leading to suicide. I can well imagine a number of feminist readers objecting to this emphasis on the father and his phallus. However, in the author's view this demon-lover-father obtains such immense power only because the mother image and her psychic representations are for various biographical reasons too weak to offer a counterforce.

In some cases, as in the relationship between the sculptor Rodin and Camille Claudel, and also between the choreographer George Ballanchine and Suzanne Farrell, the demon lover relationships become interpersonal relationships between an aging master and his particularly gifted young woman disciple. Far from solving the problem, such externalizations of the demon create for the woman artist a new kind of suffering.

Dr. Kavaler-Adler is an ardent object relations theorist and a Kleinian. Therefore, the inability to mourn plays a central role in the understanding of these women. All the major Kleinians—Winnicott, Bion, Hannah Segal, and Otto Kernberg—play a significant role in this book. However, the author is not a narrow Kleinian. The work of Ronald Fairbairn, Loewald, and Margaret Mahler are also valued. She has learned much from contemporary psychoanalysts such as Ogden, Sheldon Bach, and others. As I already indicated, she is passionate in her beliefs and convinced that had some of the heroines discussed in this book, such as Anne Sexton, been treated by an object relations therapist, their lives might have been saved. In my own experience, new schools of treatment always tend to idealize their own discovery. However, many of them in time have to reach the more difficult realization that the new model they espouse can cure some, but remains beyond the reach of other patients. It is exhilarating to encounter this powerful optimism, but readers like myself, who may not share her belief will also find her book enriching.

To my ear, the demon lover has a strong mythological quality. Freudian psychoanalysis attempted to explain mythology by analogy to the dream—making the dream a private myth and the myth a collective dream. By contrast, Jung brought myth back into his psychology. His concepts are closer to the myth itself, as is also the author's demon lover. It is not meant as a disparagement that the shadow of C. J. Jung hovers over this interesting book.

Professor Martin Bergmann
Clinical Professor of Psychology
New York University Post-Doctoral Program
in Psychoanalysis and Psychotherapy

ACKNOWLEDGMENTS)

I would like to thank all those I thanked in my acknowledgments for my first Routledge Book, *The Compulsion to Create*. All of you have inspired and supported the writing that has led past the *Compulsion to Create* to *The Creative Mystique*. In addition, I would particularly like to acknowledge Dr. Althea Horner and Dr. Jeffrey Seinfeld for their commentary on the original manuscript. I wish to thank Sandra Indig for her acquisition of the Paris biography of Camille Claudel. I would like to thank Dr. Marvin Hurvich for some pertinent comments on the Anne Sexton manuscript. I wish to express gratitude to Marilyn Miller for her incisive and clarifying editing, and to Maureen MacGrogen for her encouragement as senior editor at Routledge.

I wish to thank those psychotherapy patients who consented to allow me to use aspects of their treatment process for clarification of critical theoretical and clinical issues related to the themes of this book. My debt of gratitude is greatest to them.

I would like to thank Marc Wayne, colleague, friend, and Object Relations Institute faculty member, for his vivid understanding of the themes that join *The Compulsion to Create* and *The Creative Mystique*, ones that touch on profound clinical issues I have benefitted from and enjoyed discussing with him. I would also like to thank my Object Relations Institute co-director, Dr. Robert Weinstein, for his continuing support of my theoretical and clinical work, and for his enthusiasm about me presenting all my work, particularly that related to my writing, to the Institute faculty; and to the candidates, affiliates, and guests.

I would like to thank Louise De Costa, the ORI chairperson of Education (until 1995), faculty, and supervisor at ORI, for her passionate appreciation of the road I am traveling in my studies, which overlaps with her own road of interest in educating those who work with performing artists. In addition, I want to thank Dr. Joseph Reppen, Dr. Joyce Mc Dougall, Dr. Desy Sanford-Gerard, Dr. Albert Brok, Dr. Richard Alperin, Dr. Connie Levine-Schneidman, Rosemary Masters, Art Baur, Harriet Wald, Audrey Goldich, and Audrey Ashendorf. I'd like to thank Dr. James Masterson for his inspiring enthusiasm for my first book, *The*

Compulsion to Create. All of these colleagues have encouraged me to continue to pursue my studies.

I wish to thank the members of the private teaching seminars I have conducted, who have inspired me through their response to my theories and readings, among whom are Dr. Anita Katz, Dr. Aracelia Pearson-Brok, Dr. Marvin Hurvich, Colleen Konheim, Dr. Robert Weinstein, and Jonathon Block. I thank all my Object Relations Institute (for Psychotherapy and Psychoanalysis) candidate students, as well as my former students from the Postgraduate Center for Mental Health, the National Institute for the Psychotherapies (NIP), the Brooklyn Institute for Psychotherapy and Psychoanalysis, and the Institute of Developmental Psychology for their role in encouraging my thinking. I extend my gratitude to all the members of the nine-year weekly writing group, currently including Rollene Saal, Roger Rosen, Valerie Bryant, Bo Niles, Gerry Alpert, and Susan Kornfeld. Although I lead the group and don't present my own work, I find the courage of all the group members to expose their extremely personal struggles with the creative process to be a source of continuing inspiration for me.

My thanks and regards to George and all his staff at the Park East Restaurant, which has been the cafe I most frequent while writing and editing my psychoanalytic and literary work. Thank you for your cappuccino. I specifically want to thank Lucy, who has been my long-term friendly waitress.

My thanks to all those at the Park Heights Stationers who have photocopied my work through the years. Thanks also to those at MailBoxes on Flatbush Avenue.

PART ONE)

Theory

1)

PATHOLOGY AND HEALTH OF CREATIVITY

*Compulsion and Mystique
or Dialectic*

THE COMPULSION TO CREATE

Artists express the vitality and meaning of their lives through creative work and the creative process. I would propose that this is not all. At some psychic level, I believe artists also seek emotional healing through their creative work. Perhaps this is one reason why creativity and the process that gives birth to it has often been idealized (see Kavaler-Adler, 1993a, on Kohut's idealization of creativity). Indeed, the creative process has been seen as totally positive for psychological growth and well-being, while its pathological aspects have been virtually overlooked.

In an earlier book, *The Compulsion to Create* (Routledge, 1993), I showed how the creative process can become the captive of pathological forces. This occurs when early trauma lives psychologically within the individual and disrupts the development of the internal psychic structure necessary for critical mourning and reparation to be processed within the artist's creative work. With early trauma, a closed internal system is created (see Fairbairn, 1952) that perpetuates the repetition of the trauma in the theme and process of the work and perpetuates an unconscious fantasy marriage to a demon lover figure—the demon lover can be experienced as an omnipotent homicidal intruder and rapist. Both the content and process of the work, then, manifest as an unresolvable demon lover theme.

The demon lover figure leads the alter-ego characters of a number of major female artists to their death. In each extensive study in the *Compulsion to Create* and in *The Creative Mystique,* I describe how the demon lover becomes death itself, with death taking on an erotic and seductive form. At this point symbolic self-fragmentation occurs, with human part-object forms regressing, often into insects and rodent forms, thereby becoming object fragments that cannot be empathized with.

As the demon lover theme of self-disintegration and fatal despair within the creative work of the artist becomes increasingly evident, the artist's life dissipates. With such developments, creative work fails to be the scene of successful mourning and self-integration. This combines with a striving to heal and mourn that compels the artist, who is trapped in an internal closed system, to be obsessed with modes of pathological mourning, symptomatically symbolized by the demon lover theme. The desire for repairing the inner world and for creating whole and good love objects not only fails, but is continually frustrated. Creative productivity is idealized into a magic radiance, and muse figures who personify that radiance are sought through the creative work. Artists may thus become hopelessly caught up in a cycle of aborted mourning, with death and self-deterioration as possible denouements. The female artist in such a predicament is drawn deeper and deeper into a psychic marriage with demonic figures within her work. Therefore she moves further away from interpersonal relations in daily life. The originally impaired interpersonal capacities then show a fatal decline, simultaneous with a fatal decline of self-integrative capacities in the work. When there is no nurturance for the work from interpersonal love and intimacy, and no nurturance for interpersonal life from affectively alive resolutions of internal world relations within the creative work, both psychic spheres oppose and obviate, rather than nurture one another. This self-destructive process is enforced by the closed-off system of the sealed and traumatized inchoate self under the pressure of demonic themes. As the creative work dissipates, and its symbolized characters fragment, the artist (writer) moves away from the interpersonal world rather than towards it. The artist, in response, either resorts to seclusion or suicide.

In *The Compulsion to Create*, I demonstrated how Emily Dickinson, Emily Bronte, and ultimately Edith Sitwell withdrew into seclusion and into psychophysical regressions, whereas Sylvia Plath committed suicide. In *The Creative Mystique* we will study the suicides of Virginia Woolf, Diane Arbus, Anne Sexton, Katherine Mansfield, and the seclusion and literal imprisonment of Camille Claudel. All are led away from life by their pathological compulsions to seek a rescuing merger with an omnipotent muse through the medium of their creative work, and by the obstruction of any healthy psychic need to realistically heal the self through mourning. Seeking to psychically marry a muse, these artists end up wed to the demon lover. Self-fragmentation, rather than generative children, is the result. The female artists' withdrawal from men and intimacy in the interpersonal world, and the breakdown of the modes of narcissistic alliances they have formed, lead to psychic and literal death.

THE DEMON LOVER

The demon lover is a chimerical figure. He is so psychically real that his domination of the woman's core capacities for love and creativity can extinguish all hope, leading to deep despair and often to literal death. Because he operates in a sealed-off self, the demon lover as internal object can lead one away from the world. Called the "Nightwind" by Emily Brontë (Kavaler-Adler, 1993a), the demon lover is a dark instinctual and masculine force for Brontë who comes only in the night, when all direct visual facial contact is suspended. Emily Dickinson too wrote (Kavaler-Adler, 1993a) of "peeping in parlors shut by day," as she sought in the night the dark side of her father. In the process she became an incestuous voyeur, who ended up perpetually assaulted by her demon lover. Marriage to the demon lover can be fatal, and to marry the muse god, the omnipotent father who seems to hold the keys to artistic expression, and who is experienced as operating outside of the realm of the female artist's own self, is to marry the demon side as well.

To marry the muse is to psychically merge with the expressive powers of some split-off part of the self, which has been identified with the father, and with those symbolic representatives who carry the father projection. This marriage is fatal because it is a marriage to a part-object representation of the father, which has already been merged with a split-off core of the woman artist's own self. The marriage is not only incestuous, but in terms of psychic structure, it is a marriage to a part of the self, which always has its backlash reactive projections against the victim part of the core or central self. The central self is fragile and lacking in self-agency, as it is an arrested infantile part of the self, whose feminine aspect lacks the nurturance of an adequate mother identification.

Yet every muse becomes a tantalizing and eroticized demon, when the female artist's desire cannot be contained within the body self, nor through the medium of sustained intimate personal relations. When whole-object ties cannot be sustained, and the paradox of love and hate collapses into a monotone of mirroring subjective objects manifesting as a narcissistic hall of mirrors, the possession by a demon lover within is inevitable. Both the compulsion within female creativity, and the creative mystique that can accompany that compulsion, are addictions based on the possession by the inner demon.

The demon lover may seem psychically real, but is he fact or fantasy, instinct or psychic internalization? The answer can only be both (see "Heathcliff as mirror or man," Kavaler-Adler, 1993a). Possessing intense eroticization gained from fusion with split-off self parts of the woman's psyche, the demon lover is also the personification of "cumulative trauma" (Khan, 1974). When hostile intrusions characterize early mothering, or when severe detachment or literal abandonment occurs during the first few years of early self formation, the capacity to sustain a positive image of the other is continually disrupted or is obviated all together.[1] The demon lover is the devalued, poisoned, spoiled object, the idealized muse turned black with the evil of hostile aggression and unmodified primitive hatred.

Why does a female artist yearn for a masculinized demon lover? Is she yearning for her father or for something more primitive or for both? At first the female artist yearns for an inspiring muse.

The muse-demon lover possesses the allure of the grandiose self, an expectation of being fused with greatness. To wish to marry the inspiring muse is an oedipal-level psychic wish, but with those female artists who have had pre-oedipal psychic trauma and arrest, such a wish is enacted through a primitive psychic structure that only allows merger, not marriage. The symbolic metaphor of marriage collapses into the "thing in itself," (see "symbolic equation," as opposed to true symbolism, Segal, 1986), or into a psychophysical fusion, without symbolic representation. The would-be marriage turns into an eroticized fusion, which gains its intensity through the mirroring of the fused self or grandiose self structure. The creative work of the female artist can then serve as a transitional object, a mirror, or a sensory self-extension constructed from protosymbols, rather than from true representational symbols (see Wright, 1991; Segal, 1986b). This happens when the female artist lacks self-agency and lacks the capacity to be an "interpreting subject" (Ogden, 1986), who can consciously reflect on the meaning of her connections. At the level of narcissistic fusion, or symbiotic merger, there is no potential psychic space for the woman to reflect on her own experience, and she is not conscious of a symbolic level of meaning in her connection to the muse-god turned demon. She is therefore not able to be an interpreting subject who understands the level of subjective desire in her merger. She just needs the connection and fuses psychically with the split-off part of the self that is represented in her creative work as a masculine muse-demon. Through the collapsed oedipal marriage (see threeness collapsing into twoness, Ogden, 1986), manifesting as narcissistic fusion, the grandiose part of the self, which cannot tolerate being ordinary, joins with the god-demon.

However, the demon lover is also an instinctual force: he can fill a psychic longing for erotic body-based completion that the artist's psyche converts into the form of an "image object" or narcissistic image. The less psychic fulfillment that occurs through good-enough object relations (originating in early mothering), the more intense the craving for the hard phallic power of the demon lover force. The woman resists the demon lover who enters her as a rapist does. He is like a phallic intruder. The woman who is unable to yield willingly to the other, because she is locked inside a closed psychic system that walls off connections to her own body, cannot in real life be either penetrated or even ravished. Unconsciously she believes that she must be raped—(an actual rape would be as abhorrent to her as to any woman). The demon lover rapist, the seducer and abandoner, is recreated repeatedly in the female artist's work. The potential passion becomes a repetition compulsion. But the passion should not for this reason be overlooked. Although the demon lover is devoid of tenderness and touch, and is immune to loving contact and affect connection, he is craved for erotic intensity and body completion. It is this sadistic quality, his hard intrusion and his implacable resilience that is so desired. The more the woman artist suffers from a sense of a void within her psychophysical self, the more she hungers for the demon lover. When early abandonment trauma leaves a core void in the self (see Masterson, 1976, 1981), her own evolving erotic desire is mixed with a craving to be plugged up and completed. But the only true resolution is through feeling the pain of the void and becoming aware of her own murderous attacks on the object.

True reparation involves feeling the anguished grief that is associated with the realization of void, longing, rage, and love. To face the anguished grief, and the murderess attacks, the presence of another is required, particularly the consistent presence of a psychotherapist, to allow the pain to be tolerable. To grieve this primitive mode of grief on her own generally leads to failure for the preoedipally arrested artist. The attempt to mourn turns into pathological mourning, and the themes of the work reflect this in evoking the images of the repetition trauma.

Liberation through mourning (Pollack, 1975, 1977, 1982) seems only significantly possible for the female artist who has internalized a whole-object mother, and has navigated through separation-individuation to oedipal levels of experience.

Nobody with preoedipal trauma can tolerate the developmental mourning experience without the holding environment provided by an object relations therapist who is attuned to the mourning of both loss and guilt. Cases showing this kind of treatment will be discussed later in this book.

They are included to contrast the situation of artists who become possessed by the demon lover within and the related creative compulsion and mystique. The sad tales of the female artists who have critical early trauma, and who have no access to treatment—or like Anne Sexton had access to an inadequate treatment—illustrate that, without a painful abandonment-depression mourning process the inner void within widens. The desperate drive towards the demon lover intensifies over time. It is often experienced as a paranoid terror of rape (see Emily Dickinson, Kavaler-Adler, 1993a) or an obsession with rape (see Virginia Woolf study), or as a fanatical subjugation to an omnipotent god—(see Sexton, *The Awful Rowing Toward God*, Middlebrook, 1991: 366,). The rapist can also be experienced as a vampire whose teeth are hard phallic implements (Plath, 1994).

A more extreme form of the craving to fill up a psychic void with a phallic demon is that of the schizophrenic's psychotic area manifesting as a black hole (see Grotstein, 1989). In James Grotstein's theory of the black hole (personal communication, 1994), the craving for the demon lover is a craving to have an infinite inner void be plugged up, when it cannot be filled up. The demon lover figure is psychically experienced as a hard cork that will plug up the infinite void that annihilates any sense of self. According to Grotstein, the black hole is more extreme than feelings of emptiness—because it can never be filled. The black-hole phenomenon implies that there is no psychic sense of a containing body. Without a body for containment, there is no possibility of bringing the psychophysical or biological dilemma to an emotional level of felt psychic experience. Without such conscious and healing experience, there is no mourning. Without a psychic container within the body self, there is no filling of the black hole through contact with a sensory sense of void, nor the object-related contact that allows the comprehension of this experience. Therefore, the black hole can only be plugged.

THE CREATIVE MYSTIQUE

The pre-oedipal artist is often compelled to create in order to merge with the lost primal object. This lost primal object can be described as the original mother dressed in the personality characteristics of the father, and often of the father as perceived at a preoedipal level, but invested with oedipal-level eroticism. This primal mother object can also be seen as D. W. Winnicott's omnipotent internal object, a diabolically intrusive figure, who is promoted by the failings of the external-environment mother (see Ogden, 1986). In Kleinian terms, the primal mother can be seen as two split and omnipotent figures, that of the persecutory part object (demon) and that of the idealized part object (muse). But the Kleinian terminology doesn't allow us to sufficiently take into account the failings of the real external mother, for all are described as having this omnipotent and persecutory force within them to begin with. Those trapped by the vicious cycle of yearning for the parent as muse, but who are unable to tolerate the affects necessary to connect with the need for the parent who is lost, are trapped in a state of pathological mourning in which the parent fantasy as muse is continually destroyed and replaced by demon lover possession.

There is also a narcissistic image addiction that is part of the state of possession. The artist who experiences a powerful compulsion to turn away from external others and to seclude herself in her own private world, or in a community apart from the world, can become possessed by addictive and narcissistically tantalizing images of the self. This is particularly true when the internal world has been sealed off by critical early trauma, prior to the completion of core self-formation and before adequate separation has occurred. Such an artist can marry a demonic father on an instinctual level, and then become addicted to the demon psychic fantasy. Furthermore, she can become addicted to the image of intensity created by manically driven work. The intensity of such work resonates with a narcissistic longing for vivid recognition that can come to substitute for a healthy longing for a good object. We may view such an artist as trapped in a hall of mirrors, in which the reflected image of the self through the powerful affective intensity of the creative work becomes what I would call an "image object." The image object substitutes for real external objects in the interpersonal world. The myth of the Red Shoes, described in a later chapter, catches the essence of this solipsistic drama, where the male muse captures the creative power of the woman, and in so far as she strives to be a "star," allures her away from the world of heterosexual love and interpersonal intimacy. Fears of erotic instinctual desires, as well as limited body containment of those desires, due to early trauma, contribute to the addiction to an idealized self-image, that is to the image of being a star or being "great." The female artist who's vulnerable to the substitution of narcissistic desire for object desire can easily be exploited by her male muse. From the moment the psychic or actual figure of the male muse seeks to possess her, rather than just to fertilize her talent, he can tantalize her with her fantasy of being great. He is then felt as demonic in his tenacious hold on her, as he uses her subverted erotic desire to tantalize her with her passion for greatness, and to lead her away from eroticism and love in the interpersonal world.

The "creative mystique" is the idealized image that is substituted for the desire for a live and available object. For artists possessed by the creative mystique, the wish to be desired is substituted for the capacity to own and feel desire. For to own one's desire, which is the only avenue to having an object, as opposed to an image, brings the pain of loving. To own one's desire involves the depressive pain of guilt as one hates who one loves. The hate is also often related to shame. There is shame originating in the consciousness of needing the other, which can feel too profound and overwhelming. Unconscious shame and guilt both resonate within us all, but in persons with early traumatic disruptions in mothering, cumulative trauma abounds. Therefore, the terror of persecution is so great that guilt anxiety and depressive pain cannot be tolerated. Because it can't be owned and integrated, aggression must be split off. Aggression also remains split off when it is based on identifications with intrusive, abandoning, abusive, or sadistic parents. Then there is Fairbairn's "internal saboteur" (1952) or "anti-libidinal ego," which assaults and seals off the victim child-self within a closed off internal world. This is another view of the demon lover, as the actual demonic parent, who is perpetually taken in and used against the internal child-self, when it can't be defended against with an idealized external object (or muse figure).

Split-off aggression blocks mourning and creates instead a pathological mourning state. The demon lover is the personified internal dynamic structure characterizing the blocked pathological mourning state. In this state, primal objects can never be assimilated into the psyche, and so all object experience in the external world is converted into the same split-off aggressive intruders, following from the unassimilated blueprint of objects from within. This might be thought of in terms of Bion's failed alpha function, where beta elements in the psyche remain undigested.

PATHOLOGICAL MOURNING VERSUS HEALTHY DEVELOPMENTAL MOURNING

In *The Compulsion to Create* (1993), I spell out the critical role of mourning as a developmental process and as a healing process. Melanie Klein (1940) in her papers on "Mourning and Manic Depressive States" was the first to speak of mourning as both a critical clinical and developmental process. She followed Freud's "Mourning and Melancholia" (1917). Freud understood pathological mourning to be a depressive melancholia, in which hate for the love object is turned against oneself, against the self containing the object, and against its image within. Freud writes, "The shadow of the object falls upon the ego," and we have the first view of object relations theory, and its place within the context of comparing healthy and pathological modes of mourning.

Psychic health relates to degrees of self-integration. Since I consider the necessary increments of self-integration to be critically dependent on the capacity to mourn, and to thus tolerate sadness in love that is always mixed in with one's hate, the theme of the capacity to mourn within creative work is of prime interest to me in studying artists. Therefore, blocks to mourning and persistent modes of pathological mourning are at issue in all my studies—both those of the artist in creative work and those of contrasting treatment cases. My thesis extends beyond the artist to all those engaged in a striving for psychic reparation whether conscious or unconscious. An unresolved demon lover theme is the object relations symptom of pathological mourning that is a state in which neither the grief of object loss, nor the depressive pain of guilt, can be tolerated by the subject. The demon lover theme remains unresolved, when the split-off phallic rapist or murderer does not get repaired into a whole object form in which capacities for tenderness, love, and creative generativity are seen. The failure to produce whole objects is related to developmental deficits and to the splitting off of aggression, which oppose the conscious suffering of one's hatred in psychic fantasy form.

In Charlotte Brontë's novel, *Villette* (see Kavaler-Adler, 1993a), the demon lover is a differentiated male figure, who is transformed through love into a tender loving man, after having been a hostile and chauvinistic man. Charlotte Brontë demonstrates capacities for whole object relations and for psychic reparation as she transforms her male figure from a more malevolent male figure into a loving one. Charlotte Brontë stands out as a comparative study in relation to the woman artist who suffered primal trauma in her self-development during infancy and/or separation years. Her demon lover theme never turns into a demon lover complex, in which the part-object demon turns into the image of increasing degrees of despair, self-fragmentation, and death. Charlotte Brontë was able to mourn through her work, and was able to own both her hate as well as her love, rather than depositing her hatred into a male figure. She stands in contrast to the women who lost their mothers in infancy, such as her sister Emily Brontë (Kavaler-Adler, 1993) or who had detached or abusive mothers. Whereas Emily had lost her mother to disease and death during the critical toddler stages of separation-individuation, Charlotte had been able to reach the age of five. Charlotte lost her mother only at the oedipal stage, when core self-development had already been completed. Emily Brontë, like Emily Dickinson, Sylvia Plath, Edith Sitwell (Kavaler-Adler, 1993), and many of the women artists to be studied in this new volume, suffered a primal loss of the mother which harshly influenced the way the father was internalized and deployed in the internal world. Given such primal trauma with the early mother, split-off aggression takes the personified form of the mother's phallic blueprint dressed in the father's personality. Furthermore, the father's image is galvanized by the erotic desires for the father at the oedipal stage.

The father-mother combination that generally characterizes the literary theme of the demon lover in the work of women writers, as well as characterizing the demon lover figures in their lives, can be compared to a particular psychic fantasy described by Melanie Klein. This is a fantasy in which the father's penis resides within the mother's body. In this fantasy the father does not exist as a separate whole object. He is a part-object phallus grounded within the primal-object mother, a primal object from whom one has not yet separated, and who therefore exists as an intrusive force within the psyche, not having been digested or assimilated.[2] The demon lover figure, as psychic fantasy and artistic image, is also a part-object phallus grounded in the primal object that has not been separated from, nor assimilated into the self. This figure can be endowed with magic power, and then takes on the mystique of a manic and tantalizing muse. Then the creative process, which can be felt to be born as the artist's baby, becomes the emblem of the creative mystique. Since the muse-demon lover is an idealized part-object figure, and not a realistic whole object that can be remembered and ultimately loved and assimilated into the self, he must always become malevolently intrusive and disruptive. Yet he becomes the source of the female artist's addiction as both preoedipal cravings and oedipal passions combine in the focus on this figure. The splitting off of aggression and eroticism, which can not be contained in the female artist's body self, invests the demon lover with its malevolent instinctual powers. This can clearly be seen in the case of Emily Brontë in *The Compulsion to Create* (Kavaler-Adler, 1993a). This disowning of instinct and the depositing of it into the psychic fantasy object, through projective-identification,[3] creates the possession by one's own passions, so that the creative process becomes a compulsion, and a natural developmental need to mourn becomes compulsive as well. There is a natural developmental need to mourn one's objects, so as to assimilate them into the psyche. However, the ability to mourn is obstructed by the incapacity to sustain love for one's objects. This is true in those with developmental deficit or arrest. The internal attack on the object keeps turning the object bad. Furthermore, such a psychic attack interacts with any actual bad-object internalization.[4] Therefore, the preoedipally arrested artist becomes stuck in the pathological mourning state in which the anguish of the need to mourn and to love is felt, but persecutory terror is met up with instead of love. A female artist paralyzed in pathological mourning arrest encounters a malignant phallus, not a whole object or whole father. This can be seen in Edith Sitwell's portrayal of the image of an atomic bomb mushroom cloud as an inverted malignant phallus (Kavaler-Adler, 1993a). This phallus may be dressed in the personality traits of the father or brothers (Kavaler-Adler, 1993a), but it is static and is the source of decay and suicidal themes. This phallus produces death, not babies. It produces disease, not symbols. In Bion's terms (1989), it is a Beta element that cannot be digested. The Alpha function in the arrested woman is undeveloped. This is the function which assimilates external life into internal symbols with affect connection. The psychic structure for Alpha is missing, as the primary loving connections with a benign mother are missing. Thus love, which is the necessary feeling state for the critical object connection in mourning, cannot be sustained.

In healthy mourning, on the other hand, one has progressive moves towards grief and sadness, with regressions to defense and omnipotent rage. Psychic memories of the real object are experienced, as are psychic fantasies of the object from the inner blueprints of instinct life (and its deep structure, see Ogden, 1986). The pain of loss is felt as one remembers love for the object, and the pain of grief is felt as one's own spoiling attacks on the object are remembered. Mourning also involves memories of one's lost opportunities to connect with the love object and to express love and gratitude. In healthy mourning, one's very real need for the object is felt, and is acknowledged to the self. The spoiling attacks of envy are diminished, as one's need is acknowledged. Guilt towards the other is processed, and manic reactions subside as depressive pain can be tolerated. Persecutory fear of the other is lessened, since the goodness of the object is retained and touches one's own capacity to love. In loss, love is felt, and in love loss is felt. Very real hostile aspects of the object can then be faced and assimilated, rather than being denied, disavowed, split off, and dissociated.

LOVE-CREATIVITY DIALECTIC

Love and creativity come from the same place. They come from core-object relations psychic structure, which encounters the external world and assimilates that external world through the core-object relations blueprints from early infancy. Therefore, when one is engaged with internal others in the internal world, through the creative process, one has withdrawn from the interpersonal world of love relations and intimacy. However, one world cannot exist without the other. When one world is engaged, the other is a background, or exists as a latent level of consciousness. This is like the dialectic of Freud's conscious and unconscious minds described by Ogden (1994) where both side of the dialectic define

and negate each other simultaneously. The subjectivity of the self can only
be experienced in one arena at a time. Yet, the subjectivity of oneself in
the interpersonal world is a necessary background and latent shadow for
the subjective self in the internal world as it emerges into the transitional
world of creative work. Likewise, the world of external and interpersonal relations is a necessary background and shadow for the internal world
relations contacted within the process of creative work. Unless the internal world is an open system that can be nurtured by interpersonal relations, the internal world and the creative process drawn from it will begin
to fragment. When someone withdraws into extreme seclusion, as did
Emily Dickinson (Kavaler-Adler, 1993a), the self-disintegration is seen in
the work. The demon lover theme symbolizes the decline and leads to
images of death and self-fragmentation. In *The Creative Mystique* we will
see the decline and symbolized self-fragmentation in the work of Virginia
Woolf, Katherine Mansfield, and other female artists, who failed to evolve
into whole-object love relations. However, we will also see the artist who
can successfully use her work for mourning and self-healing, an artist,
who like Charlotte Brontë, had good-enough preoedipal development.
Suzanne Farrell, of the New York City Ballet, was able to commune with
a paternal male muse for inspiration, without turning her muse into a
demon. Furthermore, we will see clinical cases of evolution towards
whole-object love relations, and thus towards the love-creativity dialectic through the creative women's willing participation in an object relations mode of psychoanalysis in which developmental mourning could be
contained and processed.

The journey from the pathological dynamics of creativity, described as
compulsion and mystique, to that of the love-creativity dialectic is a
painful and courageous one. This journey and the obstacles to the journey are the story of this book.

2)

"THE LOVE-CREATIVITY DIALECTIC"

A Theory of Psychic Health

PSYCHIC HEALTH AND THE PHENOMENOLOGY OF THE
LOVE-CREATIVITY DIALECTIC

What is psychic health? What is cure?

I believe that the first step in defining psychic health and cure is to describe a state of consciousness I would call the phenomenology of the love-creativity dialectic. I define that state as a relatively free capacity to move back and forth between internal psychic life and external reality. Or it is when there is a free dialectic between a person's affect connection and internal objects and a person's affect connection and external objects (those in the interpersonal world). When I speak of internal object relations, I am also referring to thoughts and feelings varying in developmental levels and differentiated forms. I am speaking of internalized moments of encounter between one's self and another. And I am speaking about the psychic fantasy dimensions of those internalized encounters. Are these internal objects found or created? Are they instinctually derived from deep structure blueprints within the psyche, or are they actual perceptual encounters with external others that have been internalized? I think I might leave this question, just as Winnicott does when speaking of an infant's encounter with its external transitional object. Perhaps, as in relation to the infant, the question should never be asked.

Yet, it is a question that affects one's metapsychological perspective. As such, it should be addressed. Therefore, I would say that both sources always apply to internal object relations and their internal world dynamics. There is always some combination of internalized object relations, from early and later reality relationships, and a deep structure form that stamps these experiences (see Ogden, 1986). The universal deep structure aspect might be compared to Jungian archetypes or instinctual drive derivatives. The more differentiated the internalized relations, the less molded by the stamp of archetypical form or any kind of apriori psychic fantasy, the less molded is the internal object relation (see Kavaler-Adler, 1993).

In terms of the state of consciousness I call the "love-creativity" dialectic, moving to one's internal object connections. represents moving towards the creative process. I believe that it is through these internal world relations that a person enters into the state of imagination that is the essence of creativity, a state of vision within the mind, which is removed from touching and doing in external reality (see Wright, 1991). Moving into this inner realm is moving into a state of meditation that has its own mode of apex and denouement. When one engages with one's internal world in such a way that a creative process fully unfolds, there is a natural ebb and flow that opens one to re-engagement, once it has run its course, with the interpersonal world of external object relations. Such ebb and flow can be related to a free psychic state of love-creativity dialectic, in which the internal and external worlds speak to each other.

This is not true when, due to preoedipal trauma, there is a sealed-off self state within the internal world. I define preoedipal trauma as developmental arrest, in that a core differentiated, separated, and integrated self has failed to form. With such early trauma, self and other representations are not completely formed. Part-object imprints cause impulsive reactivity, because there is no intermediary interpreting subject or reflective activity of the mind.

A fully formed core self has integrated modes of love and hate, as well as integrated modes of autonomy and interdependence. For a core self to form, early internalization of a blueprint for mutual interaction is required. This blueprint allows for a dialectical interplay between self and other within the internal world, promoting a free interplay between a conscious focus on internal life and a conscious focus on external world relations. Through the ebb and flow of concentrated meditation on the internal imaginary world (also the world of thought) symbolic art forms are created. The love-creativity dialectic also encourages an ebb and flow of external world relations to accompany the internal imaginary life. This natural course of psychic events makes it possible for the artist to complete a piece of creative work, and then return to engagement with interpersonal relations. Also, when there is an interruption of the internal world engagement for creative work, an artist who has evolved to this level of love-creativity dialectic can have the capacity for tolerating the interruption without turning it into disruption, temporarily re-engaging in interpersonal relations while concentrating on creative work.

In contrast, when the self is sealed off due to traumatic disruptions of bonding with the early facilitating mother, the possibility of open dialectic between internal world relations (the essence of creativity) and external world relations is blocked by an internal barrier, often called the schizoid barrier (Ogden, 1986). One example of an artist with a schizoid barrier is Emily Brontë, whom I wrote about in *The Compulsion to Create*. Brontë lost her mother to disease and death during the critical separation-individuation phases of development (Mahler, 1975). In her poetry and one novel, *Wuthering Heights* (see Kavaler-Adler, 1993), Brontë divides the world into an internal world and external world. The two worlds are neither interactive nor engaged in mutual dialectic. Rather they reflect the schizoid barrier of impenetrable demarcation. Emily Brontë writes of her compulsion to choose the internal world over the external world. But in secluding herself from external world relations, she sees herself as betraying the external world by allying herself with the powerful archaic and undifferentiated forces of her internal world.

THE PHENOMENOLOGY OF TIME

The "love-creativity dialectic" is a state of mind in which there is a sense of flow, realized by a letting go of time as an impinging internal force or a restrictive element. But, in the background of the mind, there is still the sense of the limits of time, which provides a necessary tension and intensity for motivating creative work. In such a state, the artist lets go of the possession of time and of time's possession of herself. As any personified image of time recedes to the background of consciousness, the stage is set for a frontal focus on the essence of imaginative engagement with her internal objects and for self-expression. Time takes on a holding quality through an inner embrace by the artist's soothing internal objects. Time is felt as evolving into a spiral of self-expression, rather than as limiting and confining. This self-expression has the subjective feeling of an inner voice, and of a fluid flow from the heart. There is a psychic unfolding, rather than a psychic doing from one's head, and parts of the self in process of synthesis. Time is no longer a warden omnisciently guarding the artist's prison cell, but is transformed into part of the inner sequence of expanding thought.

The free mind state characterizing the love-creativity dialectic can partly be viewed as a state of organic time. Linear time is suspended and replaced by a sense of internal rhythm. Organic time as it is experienced has an ebb and flow all its own. Through freeing up the artist's attachment to a linear thought, the experience of time as sequential diminishes. The whole linear approach to reality in fact is lessened. We might think of this as suspending left-brain linear thought and relying instead on right-brain modes of perception. In this mind state, a healing mode of deep concentration becomes possible. Within this mode of concentration — something like a meditative state—the artist feels an internal freedom to focus. She exercises a deep internal sense of control, coming from the core of psychophysical connection, the sense of control can be felt as being in the stomach, guts, or vagina through strong affect experience of that body center (see "The Vaginal Core in Women and the Demon Lover Part Object," Kavaler-Adler, lecture, 1991), but with room for one's internal vision (or internal eye) to focus on concepts in one's mind. In this state of mind, an artist can maintain a steady stream of concentrated thought, or a central focus, such as on a theme for a paper. Thoughts can then be free-flowing as well as focused, with associations to the theme of a project being preconsciously selected. Other potential thoughts may never rise to consciousness, as they are outside the frame of focal attention. Or miscellaneous thoughts may pass through the artist's mind and be selectively screened out as they are observed not to fit in with the project. In sum, differentiated thoughts, free-floating attention, and free-associative thinking go hand in hand. Alternatively, when thoughts focused on the project are perpetually blocked out, there may be split in the psyche, because of a sealed-off self, or repressed areas of mental life.

The following are two examples of time experienced as holding and containing. The first is a recollection of my own of a psychotherapy marathon, at a time when I was ripe for an intense experience of grief. In a marathon, there is a suspension of all the usual limits of therapy sessions and of life in general. The illusion of endless time is created by having a twenty-four-hour period for basically nonstop interaction between participants and the therapist leading the group. What I recall from this particular experience is hours of feeling sadness and grief and crying, followed by a huge eruption of wailing grief and sadness from within me. I was responding to feelings expressed by people in the group, and then to one particular comment expressed by one woman, about how her mother always came down hard on her, but her father was always behind her. Years of grief for the loss of my father who died of cancer erupted inside. I opened up from what I can only describe as my deepest gut-wrenching psychophysical core. My wails could be heard as an infant's cry or as merely the most poignant wails of a woman in mourning. I let go from some primal level where an ultimate mode of release gave way. Yet, at the very moment when I was totally relinquishing all constricting head control and yielding and surrendering to the greater forces of love and grief and longing within me, I was also completely, and more deeply than ever, in control. The kind of control I experienced was totally organic. So just as someone reached out to me, with the comment, "I feel your pain, Susan!," I could suspend all the intense affective expression of grief and sorrow, and could turn towards this woman and verbally respond. All my conceptual powers of differentiated thought and communication were immediately at hand. The relinquishment of self-conscious modes of head control had freed me to have access to each part of myself, clearly and directly in the moment. Also, I was capable of being immediately in touch with everyone in my interpersonal environment. Here was evidence of the love-creativity dialectic at its height, in terms of the eternal now moment, when some ultimate scene of internal integration is achieved.

And how was it achieved? It was achieved in the most clear object relations mode of connection, in which love for one's primary others is contacted through the experience of anguished sadness in grief. Time seemed suspended. I was held by my internal love connection, which could alternately extend to present external object connections and to interpersonal communication, and time became a vessel of love, as opposed to an impinging force. Time still existed in the background in the form of limits that would need to take their measure again, but the sense of time as constricting was fully relinquished at that moment, that "One Moment in Time," as the song goes....

I need add, however, that it was only when I later participated in the even segments of multiple weekly sessions in psychoanalysis was I able to contact and differentiate the myriad meanings that lay behind that intense feeling. Afterwards time needed to be used in a very different way, with regular segments and limits, which allowed me to come up against the longings in the context of a normally paced human relationship. My usual modes of resisting such opening from within to direct interpersonal contact could be repeatedly experienced and made clearly vivid. But whether time's limits are lengthened or shortened, the ability to allow those limits to be in the background, and to contact a holding presence within oneself, which then can merge with the sense of time, seems to be a necessary prerequisite for moments of love-creativity dialectic, in which both internal relations and external relations are flexibly available for loving contact. This free interplay gives birth to the evolution of self-expression.

The second example is not firsthand, but read through the journal of a deeply moving writer, who died in the ovens at Aushswitz. The source of this historical anecdote is a book entitled *An Interrupted Life* (1983), written by a young Dutch Jewish woman, Etty Hillesum. The book is the author's diary before and during the Nazi invasion of Holland. More mature than Anne Frank, and consciously engaged with her creative struggles and the horrifying context of her time, the author reaches out from the most intense spiritual and emotional inner reality into the external reality of the pages of her diary. At the time she was struggling to be a writer and did not want to use the increasing restrictions and diabolical environment of her time as excuses to avoid her creative process. Of all the miracles of her evolving consciousness during this critical historical period, one particular incident stands out. To understand its meaning in the context of the love-creativity dialectic, the reader needs to keep in mind that the writer lived in a town that was being transformed into a prison by the Nazis. First, Jews were asked to wear yellow badges and had daily restrictions put on their activities and whereabouts. Day by day these restrictions were increased. Then there was the inevitable orchestrated dislocation of Jews from their homes to camps and places unknown. Ultimately this young and talented woman, who aspired to be a writer of fiction, was to be quoted as writing a note on the train to a death camp, "We go to Aushswitz singing!" Her spiritual communion with God, which she wrote increasingly about, was at its height.

The day I recall from her diary, however, was one among many. It was a day when embarkations for death camps were nipping at her heels, and the daily restrictions on all Jewish activities in Holland were imprinting each moment. In the midst of all this, Etty Hillesum speaks of her ecstacy while washing herself with lilac soap in her bathroom. She knew that this might be her last chance to do this simple daily act. Any time might be the last. There was no way to predict the erratic pace of the Nazi juggernaut. Was she to be in her home another week, month, day? Nobody knew. What she did know was that each day there were more and more limits on what she could buy at any drugstore, or even on which drugstore she might enter, if any at all. This made her cherish the cake of lilac soap she held in her hands more than ever. She relished the use of it, the moments of having it and feeling it, the sensuous pleasure of its touch and smell. Washing herself with the soap, she felt the most stringent and sadistically impinging time limits of all, the very real persecutory thrust of murderous impingements on the length of life. Yet this homicidal tread of time stayed safely and neatly in the background for her as she washed with her lilac soap, just as it did when she wrote in her diary. The reality of the limits of time, when most impinging, were transformed through the love-creativity mode of connection with time. This was possible because one's relationship to time is based on one's relationship to internal objects (others or object representations). For the author of the diary, time was maternally holding, when most limited by real-life circumstances. The amazing capacity of this young woman to be that lilac bar of soap, to inhale its fragrance, and to appreciate its worth at a time when the soap, and all that it represented, could be taken from her is an a powerful demonstration of psychic health. It is a demonstration of the mind poised in readiness for the dynamics of the love-creativity dialectic. Arlow and Brenner write of the *Mind in Conflict* (1982), but here the mind was in a state of quiescent incubation. This Dutch woman had the psychic capacity to make her moments with the bar of soap the eternal now. The same capacity enabled her to continue to write, to pray, and to reach out to others at that nightmare time, expressing mature interpersonal relations throughout. For example, she attended to the needs of both adults and children who were on the verge of being shipped off to concentration camps.

THE PHENOMENOLOGY OF SPACE IN THE LOVE-CREATIVITY DIALECTIC

Just as the psychic sense of time changes in this state, so does the psychic sense of space. Inner space seems expanded. External space reverts to the background of consciousness, rather than being experienced in the foreground. In this state, intrusive thoughts and internal persecutory demonic objects are laid to rest. We are in adequate enough contact with our inner self to maintain a secure boundary in which our inner life feels both contained and accessible for self-expression, either through creative work or through interpersonal love relations. Space seems to expand because we can symbolize internal-object experience—which constitutes the sense of self—and the sense of thought into symbolic messages, verbal or otherwise (musical notes, for example). This experience seems to relate to D. W. Winnicott's notions on "potential space." Potential space can be space for play, for transitional objects that substitute for the mother, or for symbol formation. Potential space is space that is not impinged on by the needs of the other. It is created by having the presence of the other as an environment rather than as an object with needs. This is Winnicott's "absent presence." An example of the absent presence can be seen in Virginia Woolf's novel, *To The Lighthouse*, Woolf's alter-ego character, the artist Lily is momentarily relieved of her impulse to throw herself off a cliff or pinnacle by the internalization of a mother figure. The moment Mrs. Ramsay appears beside her at her easel, she can begin to paint. Although this is an example of a desperate cry for a mother—of the life and death need for a mother's presence—it also shows that potential space for creative work is psychically dependent on the mother's presence. When the maternal presence has been internalized, the mother need not be literally present, as an external object. The sense of potential space is created by the internalized presence of mother, which allows both time and space to have a holding quality. Within the container of both space and time, differentiated symbols, objects, or characters can be created. Thus, there is not only the presence of the holding environment mother, but also of the mother as an object. The father can be a third observing object, who through his separate perspective, may help the artist give birth to differentiated symbolism (see Wright, 1991).

MEDITATION AND DIALECTIC

The love-creativity dialectic is not primarily characterized by "creative ecstacy," which is like an orgasm or apex of desire connected to creative work. Such ecstacy can be part of a love-creativity dialectic process, but if craved too strongly it can become addictive, and foreclose the underlying meditation necessary for potential space in creative work and love relations. As indicated, the love-creativity dialectic is a meditative state, in which self-healing is felt through concentration. Generally, the love-creativity dialectic brings a powerful sense of awareness and of emotional contact with one's inner self. To maintain such a state, a person must have internalized a good-enough "holding object" (see Seinfeld, 1990, 1993). In addition, there must be a developed capacity to mourn. Mourning involves conscious grief about the lost love objects and memories of them. Mourning also means to suffer and endure the depressive grief related to the recognition of one's attacks on others, who have either their dynamic or representational form as internal objects. Both modes of mourning are necessary to modify hostile and disruptive aggression.

Some believe, with Freud, that aggression is an innate drive. Others, such as Steven Mitchell (1993), suggest that aggression, particularly in its more primitive hostile form as rage or retaliatory rage, is based on psychically pre-wired reactions triggered by early primal frustrations, which then in turn get recycled and reenacted as current stimuli, retriggering the response to original objects in current object relations. (I don't know how such theory would explain the spoiling operations of unconscious envy, except by developmental failures and frustrations that don't seem to do it justice.) Either etiology, it seems to me, calls for the modification of archaic and generally spoiling modes of aggression. Therefore, the affective process of mourning, which I see as a developmental process is required throughout life. Mourning is a prerequisite to letting go of rage and the impulses that are on route to becoming compulsions. Mourning renews and regenerates the capacity to love. Therefore, it also creates and recreates the internal environment that can allow memory, symbol formation, digestion of new modes of object relations, and the letting go of old and redundant modes of object relations. With such letting go, self-integration can occur continuously in an open system. To speak of neu-tralizing aggression, in the language of drive theory, as ego psychologists have done, doesn't quite capture the affective phenomenology of modify-ing our own hostile impulses. Nor does it address the modification of hos-tile aggression from internalized "bad objects," that is, from primitive introjections of parental hostility. It doesn't capture the existential state of grief and regret involved at an experiential level nor does it capture the heartfelt love characteristic of the grief, nor how love and loss are always intertwined, as are love and guilt. The object relations view of develop-mental mourning that I have hypothesized (see Kavaler-Adler, 1992 and 1993) does capture all this. The essential need to face the grief of one's own regrets (Kavaler-Adler, 1992), in order to renew love and be capable of new modes of psychic integration seems more personally related to us all than mechanistic drive language, which makes us sound like motor-bikes or mere chemical substances. In stating my position, I am ever aware of the debt I owe Melanie Klein, who in her papers on "Mourning and Manic Depressive States" (1940) first proposed that mourning was a crit-ical developmental and clinical process, a suggestion extending beyond what Freud proposed in "Mourning and Melancholia" (1917).

Mourning allows for a self-integration process, as we own our love and prepare the inner container for symbolizing new modes of self-experience. This process is intricately related to the capacity for psychic dialectic. In the captivity of a split-off bad object, as referred to by Fairbairn (1952) in relation to pre-oedipal primary trauma, we are sealed off in a closed sys-tem that neither allows for loving relations nor for being in touch with any innate loving capacity within the self. Therefore mourning is impos-sible. What is sealed off are primary parts of the self, in conjunction with the splitting off of those object experiences to which those parts of the self are attached. Consequently, there is no free dialectic between different parts of the self. This subverts the creative process, which cannot occur without a free dialectic between the part of the self that might be able to attain degrees of meditative concentration for creative work and other parts of the self that engage with people and their needs in interpersonal relations. Sheldon Bach (1985, 1994) speaks about narcissistic character pathology in which a person is unable to psychically move back and forth between one's own subjective experience, and the interpersonal area of being in touch with another's needs, feelings, and subjectivity. For people with such pathology, a reverie-like meditation might be possible, but the object-related aspect of such meditation for creative work is generally compromised, and certainly the avenue to others is obstructed (as by a schizoid barrier or sealing off of self part). However, these people can be in touch with others, and even the subjectivity of others if they are forced to relinquish contact with their own inner selves or subjectivities, which in turn closes the door on creative self-expression.

Bach is, therefore, describing preoedipal character pathology in which the love-creativity dialectic cannot be obtained. His narcissistic character cannot be affectively connected simultaneously to her inner self and to the inner self of the other. Creativity that is based on internal object relations must be developed at the expense of external interpersonal relations, or visa versa. In my view, this is also a state of pathological mourning, in that the individual is addicted to some form of archetypical part object, such as a demon lover, and is not interactive with whole objects either in the internal or interpersonal worlds. Without internal loving connections to whole objects (those one can love or hate), there is no capacity for grief and mourning, since the grief of sadness and loss must be generated by a loving connection. Pathological mourning and obstructed dialectic go hand in hand. The capacity to mourn and to love goes hand in hand with the capacity for all forms of intrapsychic dialectic, including that of gestational creative states in dialectic with interpersonal modes of love and intimacy. Mourning opens up potential psychic space. Pathological mourning, with its modes of demon lover addiction and sealed-off potential space, results in continual repetition in art and life of themes related to early trauma.

DEVELOPMENTAL ACHIEVEMENTS NECESSARY FOR THE PSYCHIC STATE OF LOVE-CREATIVITY DIALECTIC

There are certain developmental prerequisites for reaching the psychic health capacity for love-creativity dialectic. In terms of psychic structure, there must be an interactive set up between self and object structures within the "central ego" (Fairbairn, 1952). The interactive self and other components in the central self core must have been formed from differentiated experience with objects. These structures can serve as psychic blueprints of others, blueprints not overly distorted by alien and omnipotent intrusions (Winnicott, 1974), which are necessary for all dialectical relations. For such differentiated and interactive structures of form, certain modes of self and object separation must have been completed. Specifically, a child needs to have nontraumatic disillusionments with the primary other. These disillusionments allow, in Winnicott's terms, for the externality of the other to take shape in the mind of the infant. This is one avenue by which a blueprint of the other can be attained, a blueprint that is not overly distorted by alien and omnipotent intrusions (Winnicott, 1974). Non-traumatic disillusionments relate to a child's experience during the transitional period,[1] of gaps between the experience of infant needs and the meeting of those needs by the mother. Following a period of primary maternal preoccupation, there is a natural gap created between the child and mother by the mother's temporary absences, by her separate activities and relationships, and by her natural shortcomings in bringing immediate stop-gap relief for every infant need and craving. As long as the emotionally responsive mother doesn't stay away for too long, a transitional-stage child can tolerate the gap between need and satiation of need. The child can fill in the gap with transitional objects that have qualities like the mother, and which temporarily substitute for her, or for the imagined fulfillment through her presence. Such transitional objects can be a primitive form of symbol formation, akin to protosymbols, in which there are body-felt sensual and visceral connections to the images described, as opposed to differentiated and abstract representational symbols. However, if the space between the infant and the mother, based on her distance from the infant and its needs, is not felt merely as a temporary gap, but is instead felt as an endless void, then there is a traumatic lapse of connection with the mother. This in turn causes a collapse of the balance between the dialectical poles of imagination and reality, or between the imagined mother created and the real mother found. Then, "unthinkable anxieties" (Winnicott, 1974), will cause a closing off of the self. The self recedes behind an adaptive veneer of the self, called by Winnicott a "false self," or it recedes behind a false grandiose self, in which the illusion of omnipotence becomes a rigidified system of narcissistic defense.

As the mother changes from a "subjective object," which is believed to be created by the infant to meet each and every need, to that of an objective other, and ultimately to a separate other, whose subjectivity is felt as external (rather than as an alien otherness), her separate subjectivity is internalized by the child. If the mother is in tune with the child to the extent of allowing gaps, but not voids in her attention, her responsiveness is felt. When the subjective perspective of the child's self has not been prematurely or intrusively exposed to the perspective of the other, a dialectic can naturally emerge between both perspectives. The separate perspective at first comes from the mother, to the extent that the mother can hold off from providing immediate responses and can observe the child as the child feels her needs. However, more distinctly and profoundly, the separate perspective comes from the father, to the extent that he remains outside the mother-infant dyad, as opposed to being a substitute mother. If both the mother and father are responsive to the spontaneity of the visceral aliveness of the child, as in Winnicott's parental responsiveness to the child's own "omnipotent gesture," there will be some harmony between what the child experiences as inside and outside. Therefore, a true self subjectivity can be developed. Such true self experience occurs in contrast to a divided self or false self, in which spontaneity is sacrificed to adaptation to the directive demands or "gestures" of the other. The experience for the child of externality, without the trauma of abandonment or continuous impinging intrusion by the demands of the other, allows for the development of the other as a relatively benign observer. To the extent that this development is facilitated by the parents, the child need not be possessed by persecutory, alien, and perpetually omnipotent forces that may have archetypical blueprints within the psyche. The benign environment can contain the persecutory aspects of the psyche through repression and need not have split-off core parts of the psyche merging with persecutory fantasies or persecutory object representations[2] to form malevolent internal objects.

I would add to Winnicott's view formulations about the development of an observing ego within developing psychic structure. However, gradual disillusionments about parental and self-omnipotence are not enough to explain why others come to be experienced as external to oneself (in Winnicott's terms, as beyond one's own omnipotence.). Disillusionments by themselves fail to explain why the subjectivity of the other comes to be appreciated. For this to occur, there is a need for empathy, not simply for recognition of otherness. The desire and ability to be empathic is related to a capacity to love, and in Winnicott's terms, to the capacity for concern. Winnicott was aware that the capacity for concern comes from being able to contain guilt, but he didn't appreciate, as Klein did, that suffering and grieving, as well as the witnessing of our realistic and tolerable guilt towards others, whose motivational base is love, allows for concern. One must mourn the losses of connections to those we are attached to if our potential capacity to love is to survive. As Melanie Klein observed in "Envy and Gratitude" (1957), we must mourn our psychic and actual attacks on the needed other. This mourning involves a growing awareness of the spoiling operations of our own envy, often acted out through devaluing thoughts and comments about the other. Only through the mourning of losses of loving connection by which we have related ourselves to the other, and through owning our attacks so that reparation can be offered, does one come to feel the affective bond to the other being sustained through and within the gap of separation. Disillusionment of one's idealized expectations of the parental other is not enough. We must also yield to grief, in order to feel the losses that we create through our own active agency and intentionality, as we attack the image and persona of the other, whether in thought or deed. These attacks can go on in the internal world, as described in Freud's "Mourning and Melancholia" (1917), and can be turned against the self as we attack the internal other. But such attacks must be understood as rage towards the other, and also as our own attack on the loving capacity of our own self. This is true in as far as the rage takes the form of devaluing attacks, prompted by envy, in addition to whatever realistic frustrations may exist. Without the owning of such attacks, Freud's mode of melancholia can result, because it becomes impossible to make reparation to the other. Therefore the internal personification or image of the other cannot be made. This result is a perpetual state of depression, as opposed to the mourning of alive depressive affect that is linked to love for the other. This state of depression is generally enmeshed with paranoid thinking, in which the other remains a persecutory force within the psyche. Such a state seals off the inner self from contact with others in the external world, others who might offer love and concern, and who might genuinely care about our own needs. This closed-off state prevents the internalization of care and concern from the other, and thus arrests the development of internal resources and psychic structure.

In her theory of separation-individuation, Margaret Mahler emphasizes the rapprochement phase of separation in which the toddler returns from autonomous adventures to a separate relationship of conscious need of the mother (Klein conceived of such need in terms of the depressive position pining for the other). During this new consciousness of need for the other, which is created by separation, a "low-keyedness" is experienced in the longing for the mother. At rapprochement, the mother is increasingly sensed as a separate object, as the distance caused by the toddler's departure from the mother's sphere begins to feel too wide for him or her, and the toddler returns to the mother. A representation of the mother as a differentiated figure can now be formed within the mind of the child. Although an early symbiotic view of the mother may become repressed, never again, will the child have a conflict-free view of the mother as an extension of the self, or as part of a symbiotic oneness. As separation progresses, the toddler must now relate through words and symbolic communication. Such need to feel the gap of contact associated with verbal communication contributes to depressive pain, which includes an awareness of need for and love for the separate mother.

In its mildest form, this depressive pain is seen as Margaret Mahler's behavioral description of "low-keyedness." Mahler is referring to an early (two-year-old) stage of developmental mourning in healthy children, in which the affect of loss is felt, without any sophisticated understanding by the part of the child about what that loss is about.[3] The memory of the mother is sufficient at two years old (or eighteen to thirty-six months) to induce this affective mode of yearning and beginning grief. However, if the mother has not been in adequate contact with the child throughout the separation-individuation stages, then the internal container for feeling and tolerating grief will not have been formed, for it is created through internalized engagements with the affectively present mother. This internal container is necessary for more sophisticated forms of cognitive processing that accompany the affective experience of grief, which is a capacity that develops throughout life, as long as the self remains open to new psychic internalizations, and is not barricaded behind a sealed-off self system (as described by Ronald Fairbairn in *Psychoanalytic Studies of the Personality*, in speaking about childhood abuse, 1952).

RAPPROCHEMENT AND DIALECTIC

Margaret Mahler's view of the separation-individuation process culminates in the rapprochement stage. This is a critical time in development, eighteen to thirty-six months, when the child, now a toddler, needs to come together with the mother in a new way. The question of whether the child and mother fit at this point, in terms of attunement to one another, is a separate question from whether they fit together at the earlier time of mother-infant harmony, which Mahler sees as a unity in the earlier symbiotic stage. The coming together at rapprochement occurs after a period of the child's autonomous "love affair with the world." According to Mahler, following critical and primary phases of differentiation, the toddler moves away from the mother, and out into the world, during a practicing period. The mother needs to allow this to happen. She needs to stay attuned to the child, who plays at a distance. She needs to be emotionally available for "refueling," providing affection, hugs, food, and so forth. But as Winnicott argues, such moments of refueling must be initiated by the toddler, not by the mother's needs or gestures. Benjamin (1988) has pointed out that the mother needs to be in a state of receptive recognition of the child, even during the child's play at a distance during the practicing period, not just at rapprochement. However, according to Mahler, it is at the critical rapprochement phase that the mother truly begins to join in the child's independent activities by allowing the child to share her[4] activities with her. The mother needs to sustain an emotional connection with her toddler as her toddler comes and goes. The mother must communicate that she is ready to allow her child to share on the child's own terms. James Masterson (1976) has described the parental behavior needed during this period as "communicative matching." Communicative matching implies that the mother is tuned into the child's exploits as they are shared with her during rapprochement. This attunement requires the mother to be emotionally available. A dialectic emerges through this availability, which is primarily child-focused at this time, but as the mother responds to the independent initiative, or in Masterson's terms, to the child's "self-activation" (Masterson, 1993), the child internalizes her capacity to respond to the initiation of the other. She then comes to respond to the initiation of the mother, so that a mutuality of response to the autonomy of the other comes about.

Masterson's view of the child's self-activation and of the parental "communicative matching" can be compared to Winnicott's view of a child's "omnipotent gesture," which involves being responded to before she can adopt to the gesture of the mother. If the mother is unable to allow the spontaneous omnipotent gesture of the child, true self-development is curtailed and a premature adaptation causes false self-construction.

What is later to become the capacity for love-creativity dialectic can begin here, or can be sabotaged. The collapse of potential dialectic into modes of compulsion can occur at this time. If the mother is unable to allow her child to move away from her, into her own "love affair with the world," or if she turns away from her daughter in retaliation, the child is torn apart by her divided loyalties. On the one side is the child's loyalty to her own developmental thrust towards autonomy and true self-development. On the other side is her loyalty to stay with a mother, who forces her into a regressive symbiosis to avoid the mother's own separation terrors. The pull to cling to the mother is the force of the child's own abandonment terror. The mother withdraws when her child takes her own direction, and then the child is faced with a terrifying void within the self. There is no gap of potential space in which to create interactions and play that can become psychic internalizations. There is no gap of potential space for the image of the mother to form in the psyche, nor for later representational symbols to form these also. Instead, the gap is a void, as the child is forced into the "unthinkable anxieties" (Winnicott, 1974) produced by a mother's emotional abandonment during this stage, at the point when the mother is threatened by the child's autonomy. Generally , this is due to the mother's own abandonment fears, often accompanied by narcissistic injuries. The child is then forced to cling in a regressive mode of symbiosis to the mother. This stifles any differentiated and true self-development, for she collapses into pseudo-adaptation. Or the child is thrust into the black void of unmarked space without mother—a space that because it is not mediated by the mother's image, is felt as infinite and endless. In extreme cases, it is perceived as a "black hole."

For example, one patient dreamed of falling endlessly down the side of a cliff. She couldn't believe that no one caught, stopped, or rescued her. Terror followed, with the feeling of infinite black space before her.

The potential image of the mother is aborted by the mother's precipitous abortion of emotional contact. The inner child is torn apart. To have herself is to lose mother, and to have mother is to lose herself. There is no choice in the rapprochement crisis (Mahler, 1975; Masterson, 1976)when it turns for the child into an experience of profound suffocation and/or abandonment. There is only a jumping-out-of-her-skin feeling or physical and psychic eruptions from within. Terror is bypassed by conforming to the mother's mode of operation. This occurs whether the mother is borderline or narcissistic. A borderline mother clings to meet her regressive needs, having her toddler cuddle when she feels the need, and opposing her child's autonomous moves away from her. The predominantly narcissistic mother demands her child mirror her own self-image or her own grandiose self. She may, therefore, respond to the child only when the child is performing or achieving. For a child to surrender herself psychologically is a developmental achievement, once separation is reached, but first she must have a secure separate and subjective self, not merely a self that operates as a reflexively reactive object to the mother. To the degree that the child at this critical separation phase is a pawn in the pattern of the mother's own infantile need compulsion, the child's formation of a whole and subjective self is sabotaged. Potential dialectic collapses into a two-sided compulsion, since an earlier symbiotic oneness cannot be achieved. Compulsive adaptation of the child to the mother substitutes for it. This can be the beginning of the "compulsion to create." The child's only way of contacting subjective states in the self is through art forms, in which she uses the creative process as a substitute mother. In the whole sphere of external object relations, or the higher level of whole-object relations in interpersonal life, those who turn to the creative process for maternal functions that have not been adequately provided at the critical separation phases, are crippled. Their compulsion to use others as they have been used, or to repeat the other side of the collapsed dialectic by being used by some omnipotent other, results, in their enmeshment in part-object relations. Either they use others as subjective objects, or they serve as self-extensions for the other.

For example, Edith Sitwell's chief biographer, Victoria Glendinning (see Kavaler-Adler, 1993), notes that Sitwell had no avenue to a state of "being," as opposed to compulsive doing, other than that of writing poetry. Glendinning compares Sitwell to the ordinary human being who can, through simple activities like gardening, find internal rest in a state of being. For Sitwell, this was never possible. Neither could she achieve such a state through swimming or making love. Late in life, Sitwell regretted that she had never experienced physical love. Her inability to connect intimately with a man can be traced back to her earlier life with her mother and father. She could be a muse to stimulate the artistic vision of a highly narcissistic man, such as her idealized love, the painter Pavlick Tchelitchew. But she could never be seen for herself, particularly if that meant having her faults visable, as well as her achievements. Nor could Sitwell have sexual intimacy with Tchelitchew. The painter reserved sex for homosexual relations. His idealized form of love for Sitwell had to be carried out solely at a distance, through letters. For Sitwell, there was no internal maternal matrix (Ogden, 1986) to return to within her body and psyche. She never had an adequate experience of coordinated dialectic with her early mother to achieve that. In her poetry she could narrate subjective states, thus providing for herself some relief and mirroring, but she herself did not connect with her own vulnerability in these subjective states, for she walled herself off in a grandiose self, which in her poetry took the image of a prophet. Thus, no conscious identification with the walled-off child self within appears in her work.

The intensity of her engagement with the split-off, injured, and more malevolent parts of herself remained and surfaced in her poetry as images depicted from the lofty superior pose of a prophet. Her intensity could tantalize with its own allure, leading her into an addiction to her own creative mystique. We see this also in the case of Sylvia Plath (Kavaler-Adler, 1985), who wrote of herself as her goddaddy's "golden girl." Plath portrays herself as intensely vibrating to her father's dynamic. She heralds him as her "Lord of the Mirrors" (Kavaler-Adler, 1986). Plath rages at her father and her husband Ted Hughes, who carried for her the father's projection. Both the father and Hughes became part of Plath's "creative mystique intensity." Insofar as she was dealing with them as an extension of an early mother, (as well as an external oedipal object), her father and the target of father projections—the husband, Hughes—were to rule her psyche as her demon lover. Her father became the king who proffered upon her the narcissistic emblem of the creative mystique. She could identify with his narcissistic requirements for her to perform for him. For their part, both her mother and father could cling to her from their omnipotent position of demanding a reflection of their own grandiose selves (the achieving self with all faults and shortcomings hidden). She had incorporated a mother-father fusion. During rapprochement, Mrs. Aurelia Plath may have been too much there for her daughter, for the mother lacked boundaries (see Bennet, 1990), and lacked a separate Self that could have its own internal dialectic, between Self and Symbolized Other. The father then too was also too much, seeing his daughter as the golden girl performer. For example, Plath recited polysyllabic Latin terms to her father's friends when she was five, and performed when she was eight for her father each night as he lay dying from a gangrene infection that his grandiosity prevented him from getting timely medical treatment for. Sylvia resonated to a pattern of response to her as a performer, not as a child with vulnerabilities and emotional needs. Plath mirrored and flattered both parents with the grandiose mirror of the creative mystique. As a child she was compelled by their mode of selected narcissistic attunement, trained to flatter, rather than to face them. Her adult poetry gave her a format for the eruption of her rage. This rage did not emerge as a communication, but as an elegant performance, combined with the impulse of retaliatory assault.

THE SUCCESSFUL DIALECTIC EVOLVING AT RAPPROCHEMENT:
IMPLICATIONS FOR PSYCHIC STRUCTURE AND SYMBOL FORMATION

When a child is lucky enough to have a mother who has successfully formed a core whole self and is therefore capable of whole object relations, a healthy interaction between mother and daughter is possible at rapprochement. This can become the basis for internalizing a dialectic of mutual responsiveness that will serve to build a structure for all psychic dialectics, including that of the love-creativity dialectic.[5] The mother of a rapprochement-age child can facilitate the child's internalization of a blueprint for life by being emotionally available to her child, as the child returns to share the outer world with her mother and by being emotionally responsive to what she shares. To substitute her own program for directing the child's needs and actions at this point would violate the dialectic of the child's experience. Shortcomings on the mother's part in meeting the child's invitations to share the outer world (failure to meet what Winnicott has called the omnipotent gesture of the child) allows a tolerable gap to form. This gap is distinguished from a void. Within the space of the psychic gap, the child can miss and want the mother. The child can then find, build, and sustain images that represent the mother within the psychic space provided by the gap of response. Building such a representation of the mother depends on nontraumatic disillusionments about her ability to respond. Such representations, in part, come to replace the mother's actual presence; they are similar to an external transitional object that carries her qualities. If the mother is too intrusive,—

that is, not abandoning, but neither permitting enough of a gap, nor responding to the initiation of the child's gesture towards her, a more omnipotent mother is internalized. This mother may be too traumatically possessive to be adequately represented in an image. Such a mother impinges as a visceral force within or as a mental force felt as obsession or compulsion. When the formation of psychic representations is in this way disrupted, a paranoid-schizoid mode of psychic operation becomes more prominent than a depressive position mode. The paranoid-schizoid mode of operation is characterized by the lack of an objective view of one's self, or of another. The individual has no awareness of her own perceptions of self and other, as mediated by an interpreting and observing part of the self, separate from the raw tactile experiencing part of the self (see Ogden, 1986, on the "interpreting subject"). This can create an artistic form of creativity that features forces which omnipotently do things to and against the self. Out-of-control impulsive and reflexive reactions are also characteristic. In the paranoid-schizoid mentality, the self is possessed by the object, and the object is possessed by the self. The result is not interaction and dialectic, but a primal state of impulses, operating like forces without a mediating intellect between part objects. The self can appear as a reactive part object and the other as a compulsively driven sadist. Only imperative dynamics exist in this paranoid-schizoid mode of operation. There are no spontaneous or exploratory seeking gestures.

When representations do form sufficiently during the rapprochement period—or when a gap, rather than a void, is created—critical psychic structures and symbolic modes of communication develop. These permit a healthy love-creativity dialectic to operate in adult life.

Initially the child's representations are direct perceptual images of that other, and of another in interaction with herself—so that the other's own self-image is implied. However, as developments proceed from rapprochement to the oedipal stage, the child's representations move beyond eidetic images and eidetic memory into more abstract representational forms. In his book *Vision and Separation* (1991), Wright has elaborated on this developmental process. He delineates transformations from transitional objects with literal qualities like the mother, and which in literature overlap with protosymbols (visceral and sensory body experience expressed in words) to that of representational symbols. Representational symbols are differentiated from the actual qualities of the mother or others who they represent. Unlike a soft toy or blanket serving as a transitional object to signify "mommy" in sensual form, representational symbols, like the letters of the alphabet "mother," symbolize the mother and stand for her as a whole person, not as a sensual extension of part of her, such as her softness. For their representational meaning to be sustained in the mind of the artist or person, her interpreting and observing self must operate in a separate mode of function from that of an experiencing self. For this to occur, adequate developmental separation from the mother is required (see also Loewald, 1988). Another developmental process helps make representational symbolism possible: the perspective of a third party, generally the father, who by deferring an alternate view from the primary self and other, sustains a gap that may otherwise collapse into concrete operations of touching and doing between mother and child. The father's view—when it is not too alien or intrusive—can provide a critical observational perspective which mirrors and interprets interactions between the mother and child. This third view allows for a triad of psychic functions to develop, which Ogden (1986) has described in terms of the symbol, the symbolized, and the interpreter. The interpreter applies and uses the symbol to represent the symbolized concrete external other. The triadic interpersonal relation of father, mother and child, with the father representing a more separate viewpoint and a more differentiated perspective, allows for an "interpreting other" to be internalized such as Ogden (1986) describes in his work on the "interpreting subject." The concrete other who the child finds in the holding (or "symbiotic") mother, and subsequently discovers in others in the world, can be transferred into the object that is symbolized rather than touched. This can only occur following sufficient bonding between mother and child, which, in turn, is modified by developmental frustrations, as well as by the separate role of the father (as an external object, rather than a subjective object). Transitional objects and protosymbolic word forms draw their qualities from direct sensory likeness to the mother, but the symbol itself need not be intimately attached to the sensory experience of the mother. The new representational symbol can simply be a word adopted in consensual agreement with the social world, as that world employs language symbols based on consensual validation of abstractly assigned meanings.

The interpretation of how the symbol matches personal experience comes from the developing child, who now attaches mutually validated concepts to word symbols. The self-and-mother interaction—internalized during rapprochement—can become an inner blueprint for the dialectics of self, other, and the object to be shared, which becomes the symbolic other. For artists, the thing shared becomes the artistic medium, to be played with through symbol formation. The interpretations of this primary rapprochement mode of sharing then become appropriated by the father in his role as the third. As the separate observer, he becomes integrated with the interaction between mother and child. The ability to play with representations of others (through symbols that show patterns across objects) allows for a form of engagement with external others and internal objects, in which transformation through interpretation is more powerful than possession through incorporation of something concrete. The child with adequate rapprochement attunement no longer needs to depend on transitional objects that substitute for the primal object because of a sensual similarity. Once the child possesses the object through a concept, and can communicate its relation to that symbolized object through either representational art forms or through language in interpersonal exchange, she develops into someone equipped to travel back and forth on the path between interpersonal love relations. The transversal of the route can become the essence of progressive creative work. When representational symbolism is not reached as a primary mode of both thought and interpersonal language communication, the artist can still express herself, but the work has quite a different quality, with the dialectical route back and forth between love and creativity obstructed and/or obviated. Then creative-process relations can become imprisoned in the sealed-off sphere (mirroring the sealed-off self) of the creative work, manifesting as the compulsion to create, and as any idealized image addiction to the compulsion's intensity, as seen in the hall of mirrors of the creative mystique. Alternatively, a person who is not in contact with her artistic capacities, as an avenue to self-expression, can become trapped in the sealed-off sphere of external love relations and become a love addict. Love addicts are generally unaware of and disconnected from their potential creative talents. In general, they also lack a sense of their abilities. Rather, they are enmeshed in seeing themselves through the image of the other, who they addictively love. They are possessed and absorbed in the other to the point of excluding their own potential development.

In this book, I discuss artists, who prolifically create under the force of compulsion, and in contrast to them artists who can navigate the avenue of the love-creativity dialectic. Artists working under this compulsion may vividly portray subjective self states but be unable to relate to others as separate objects, either in their work or in the interpersonal world. Emily Dickinson is an example (see Kavaler-Adler, 1993).

Today, she is considered by many to be America's greatest poet. Yet during her lifetime, she lived in total obscurity. In *The Compulsion to Create* (Kavaler-Adler, 1993), I showed how Dickinson displayed the power to capture vivid sensation based on experiences in the immediacy of the moment. She also had the power to move from poetry which is visceral and immediate, and which often captures urgent oral and genital body cravings, to metaphors which demarcate between herself and her own sensations, so that a symbolized likeness is created, such as in the line, "I felt a funeral in my brain," (c. 1861, #280). If Dickinson instead had written, "I felt a funeral" or "I felt my brain," her poetry would reside in the area of concrete sensation where words are protosymbols (visceral extensions of the body self), as opposed to representational concepts. When she selected the word "funeral" and inserted it as a feeling in her brain—she created a metaphor, something she herself recognized and felt ecstatic about. A metaphor, as Wright (1981) so elegantly explains, offers a fine line between the subjective experience and the conceptual observation of it, or what I would call, in line with Ogden, the interpretations of it. Dickinson was a genius in manufacturing metaphors. But her developmental shortcomings are also visible in the arena that these metaphors occupy. The arena is the arena of the self, where only an alien, obscure, and anonymous other is implied to exist outside the solipsistic self's domain. A clear example appears in her well-known "Master letters," which are reflected in her love poetry. In these letters, and in her poetry, the man she speaks to, the man she cries to and pleads with, even remonstrates with, has no identity. In fact, he does not even possess a differentiated form. As the female poet articulates her emotional state of longing for him and her emotional state of despair reactive to losing him and to his always essentially eluding her, he exists in a vacuum. Dickinson's own subjectivity is vivid. One might even call it radiant. It is this radiance that if she experienced it, could addict her to her own creative mystique. Yet, in object relations terms, her subjectivity is basically all we get! This phenomenon can be viewed as a collapsed dialectic, or as an unrealized dialectic. It can be seen within the framework of the poet's creative work, but this work also mirrors the poet's life. Within her work, there is no self and other interaction, and in her life she cannot share in intimacy with another who she loves. Instead, the self is repeatedly thrown back upon itself, just as the poet's writing of her self is repeatedly thrown back into the internal world to produce the transitional world of the creative process. The lack of a dialectical pathway between self and other, within the creative work and its process, reflects the lack of the psychic structure for that avenue within the internal psychic world (central ego) and also the lack of an avenue for dialectic between internal and external object relations. Thus, the love-creativity dialectic is thwarted and the compulsion to create is perpetuated.

This example demonstrates that the level of symbolism in creative work relates to the capacity for free psychic dialectic between object relations within that work and object relations in the interpersonal world. Even if representational symbolism is partially formed, as in the creation of metaphor, representations of self states still rely primarily upon proto-symbols and transitional object forms. They fail to attain the graduated form of representational symbolism applied to a differentiated other. In Kleinian terms, we may say that those who create in the paranoid-schizoid position are still within the realm of the self. Only upon entering the depressive position[6] does the object become focus for conscious yearnings for a needed other and for the awareness of the subjectivity of the other. According to Melanie Klein, the affective process of mourning, or of grieving our regrets over attacks on the other, is also necessary to bring the subjectivity of the other alive. Mourning requires an inner psychic dialectic of self and other. It also requires an "interpreting subject" perspective to appreciate the object relations meaning embedded within the experience of depressive pain.

THE LOVE-CREATIVITY DIALECTIC IN RELATION TO OTHER OBJECT RELATIONS THEORISTS

Explaining the concept of the dialectic, and of the love-creativity dialectic in particular, in developmental terms brings up conceptual formulations from Ronald Fairbairn, D. W. Winnicott, and Melanie Klein, as well as other object-relations theorists. In order to describe the nature of the love-creativity dialectic in relation to an observing ego structure, it is necessary to describe what the observing ego is not. This allows us to have a contrast in object-relations terms between healthy and pathological developments.

Ronald Fairbairn (1952) has written about a pathological psychic structure in which split-off parts of the personality act as a consolidated internal saboteur. This internal saboteur is an incorporated aspect of one's early parents. These incorporated but unassimilated parents have been experienced as bad objects, due to severe frustration during the infant stages of self-development, frustration that has often reached traumatic intensity. The internal saboteur—the consolidation of many bad object experiences—acquires its dynamic and assaultive quality through its fusion with a split-off part of the self. The fusion of the bad object and self part acts to oppose any true self-expression, self-activation, and self-agency. It also opposes any modes of feeling connected to external others. In his later writings, within his collected papers of 1952, *Psychoanalytic Studies of the Personality*, Fairbairn called the internal saboteur the anti-libidinal ego, because of its fusion with the rejecting object aspect of the parent. The anti-libidinal ego is the part of

the self that has identified with a traumatizing early parent, whether the
parent is abandoning, detached, or assaultive. In one way or another,
the extreme infantile dependence on an exclusive parent figure results in
identification. The more unavailable the parent is as a responsive, emotional human being, the more the child's identification is at a primitive
level of fusion and incorporation. The incorporated bad parent, or bad
aspect of the parent, acts in the internal world as the parent had reacted
to the child in the external world. The internal saboteur continuously
engages in opposition to the libidinal ego (Fairbairn, 1952), or in opposition to what Jeffrey Seinfeld (1990) has called the "dependent self."
The traumatically frustrated needs of the child continue to be perpetually frustrated in a closed system based on split-off parts of the self and its
primitive incorporating mode of identification with the bad parents.
The libidinal self splits off from the central ego, which is in contact with
others besides the self, but which often may only be in touch mentally,
as in the schizoid. In its split-off state, the libidinal ego operates in a
sealed-off internal world in which the anti-libidinal ego (internal saboteur) continues to torment or deprive it. The anti-libidinal ego's aggression becomes an internal assaultive energy, sealing off the libidinal ego
from contact with needed others in the outside world.[7] It operates in a
dissociated state.

I would suggest that such a state of affairs, as Fairbairn describes, represents a pathological state of mourning. The child has not been able to
mourn the original love object. Therefore, she has not been able to move
on to others who may be more adequate objects, in terms of meeting her
developmental needs. This inability to mourn is, of course, related to a
lack of primary psychic structure. The child can develop psychic structure, as discussed, only through adequate self and other connections during infancy and separation-individuation. Without primary separation
and developmental mourning, which in its early and simplest terms can
be described as Margaret Mahler's low-keyedness, the mechanisms of psychic assimilation and integration cannot be established. Without them,
the child cannot emotionally connect to parental behaviors. Without such
affect connection, it is impossible to transform painful experiences into
conceptual memories and associations. Parts of the self dissociated to dis-
avow these experiences consequently remain unassimilated into the core
and interpersonally related self. Instead, the parent remains toxic, or, in
Fairbairn's terms, like a demon who needs to be exorcised, or a "bad
object." This would be Fairbairn's explanation of the demon lover phenomenon.

Winnicott has referred to the phenomenon of the omnipotent mother in the psyche, which he suggests originates from the actual behavior of an early mother. This is the internalized mother who is too intrusive in her control of the child. Because such a mother places her own gesture (Winnicott, 1974) before the omnipotent gesture of the child, she is experienced as omnipotent and unyielding.

Klein speaks of a persecutory internal mother, a persecutory object who is seen by the child as a primitive superego. The primitive superego is both punitive and assaultive, which distinguishes it from Freud's oedipal stage superego. A mature superego (see Ogden, 1989) provides prohibitions and limits, rather than retaliatory punishments (although Freud also spoke of castration threats initiating the formation of a superego). Loewald (1962) has written about the necessary mourning process for the development of a superego at the oedipal stage. I believe there are varying forms of mourning related to the formation of a mature superego. We must mourn the loss of omnipotence in the face of the opposite sex parent competitor, which involves mourning or disillusionments with the self. When we speak of mourning disillusionments, I mean consciously suffering the loss and grief of giving up idealized images and fantasies. We must also mourn disillusionments with the parent, as our own capacities to bypass the parents' competencies make themselves known in adolescence and adulthood. This view is along the lines of Loewald's later paper on "The Waning of the Oedipus Complex" (1979). In this paper Loewald was aware of the lifelong struggle with oedipal issues, which are never just resolved at the oedipal stage of development. To even see this lifelong struggle one must understand the importance of the mourning process. Such thinking complements that of Melanie Klein, who also saw the depressive position mourning process as a lifelong struggle, a struggle, I would add, which humbles us all, for in it we continually confront our infantile omnipotence.

OBSERVING EGO

In contrast to the internal saboteur type of internal object stands the integrated internal object, which is partly experienced as an observing ego. With nontraumatic parenting and developmental mourning, the observing ego should be able to form. This is a benign internal object, which we are mostly aware of through its editorial mode of functioning. To have an internal observing ego, the child must have separated from objects sufficiently for the experiencing part of the self to have become differentiated from the observing part of the self. The observations of the observing ego must of necessity be highly motivated by the observational view of the parent. The parent's view of the child's self allows an intimate vantage point for a concept of the child that highly determines the child's own self-concept as it develops over time (see Wright, 1991). However, as mourning and separation proceed, a separate view of one's self can be formed, which can be influenced by the view of others outside the parental sphere. How closely the observations of the observing ego match the subjective instinctual and visceral experience of the core experiencing self will depend on the role of parents and others, who reflect back their view of the child (Winnicott, 1974, "The Role of the Mirror," in *Playing and Reality*). When the view of the parent is so critical and rejecting that it is annihilating to the child's sense of identity, the parent's view will manifest as aspects of an internal saboteur or anti-libidinal ego (called "anti-dependent self" by Seinfeld, 1990). Such a parental view of the self will not contribute to the constitution of a relatively benign observing ego structure.

I would add to Loewald's view of mourning and superego formation that not only the superego, but also the observing ego is formed through mourning of disillusionments with the self as well as of the two parent objects involved in the oedipal triad. In becoming separate from the parent, we give up our fusion with an omnipotent object, and gradually accept the limitations of both oneself and one's parents. The benign quality of the observing ego depends on the mourning and disillusionment process, as well as on the more benign characteristics of the real parent. As any Kleinian knows, the parent may be relatively benign and still be perceived as persecutory. The persecutory view is engendered through psychic fantasies related to the frustrating effects of separation that result in the formation of projected villains who personify the frustration experience. The persecutory view is also related to guilt for our own aggression towards the other, which requires grieving over our own created losses, and the conscious owning of our aggression to be resolved. Frustration and guilt are quite sufficient to create a persecutory image of the parent. We need not resort to the metapsychology of the death instinct to explain the paranoid mode of psychic fantasy formation.

Why is it necessary to speak of the observing ego in explaining the nature of the love-creativity dialectic? The love-creativity dialectic is based on an open psychic system, in which self-integration, transformation, and transcendence can occur, in contrast to possession by a personified demon within a closed system. To the extent that an internal saboteur dominates the psyche, the love-creativity dialectic is blocked or obviated. An observing ego is a sign of an open system in which one can move freely back and forth between internal objects and external object relations. Beyond being a sign of healthy psychic structure, the observing ego also operates in such a manner as to facilitate the continuous building of psychic structures that can provide open pathways between a subjective self in the internal world for creative process relations and the subjective self in the external world for interpersonal love relations. As the observing ego assimilates data about our own subjective self-experience, and joins with our symbolic capacities to formulate it, artistic modes of communication are facilitated, as are interpersonal modes of communication. The benign quality of the observing ego refers to its visions and evaluations as potent formulations that can be contained in concepts, as opposed to hostile critical assaults that are spoiling and devaluing. With critical spoiling operations, characteristic of the internal saboteur and of the persecutory object of Klein, symbolic modes of conceptualization are assaulted. The very capacity for symbol formation and thought is attacked. Another way to look at this phenomenon is that concepts cannot serve as psychic containers if their deep structure molds within the psyche are too dominant. When this occurs, primitive modes of omnipotent idealization and omnipotent demons are generated prolifically, while metaphors that integrate self-experience and reality perceptions are attenuated. The creative process then becomes captive to the compulsion to create and to the creative mystique, syndromes in which there is an addiction to the highlighted primitive forms from an unmediated deep-structure consciousness. The interpersonal process becomes captive to this primitive mode of consciousness, too dominated by innate psychic fantasy or archetypcial mental organizations. On a manifest level, part-object relations are seen. Schizoid detachment results, or love addictions develop based on part-object relations, in which the subjectivity of the other is denied. Love addictions then mirror the part-object relations of the compulsion to create, in which self and other relations fail to evolve into interactions, mutuality, and intimacy.

WILFRED R. BION'S ALPHA AND BETA ELEMENTS

Wilfred Bion (1967) describes psychic contents as Beta or Alpha elements. Beta elements are undigestible psychic content, which I would compare to incorporated aspects of the other. They operate like part objects projected into the psyche through modes of projective-identification.

Alpha elements, by contrast, are digested psychic contents. Such Alpha elements relate to object experience that has been integrated into the self through metabolizing processes—these processes give conceptual meaning to experience with external others and with the external world. Others are experienced as whole objects, as opposed to part objects or bad objects (which must be part objects, because nobody is all bad, to the extent that they operated from understandable motivations and comprehensible states of ambivalence).[8]

The love-creativity dialectic operates to the extent that Beta elements can be processed into Alpha elements, or into symbolic conceptualization that gives meaning as concepts are connected to affect experience. Precocious conceptualizing capacities do not provide meaning integrated with affect experience. Developmental mourning allows for the integration of affect and concept, of memory and present desire. If we undergo developmental mourning and good-enough parenting, we develop conceptual abilities to process those alien forces and things that enact their drama upon our passive psyche. Through such processing, which is part of mourning, we can transform alien forces and alien things into interactive experience, in which our own motivation is understood to interact with the motivation of another. With such links between affective and cognitive processing, the individual is not a victim of the paranoid-schizoid position. Also, depressive pain tolerance can bring awareness of our own motivations as shaping the behavior of others. This awareness allows us to conceptualize motives of another in the same way we conceptualize our own motives. Conscious feeling states are necessary to provide such meaning. Mourning and disillusionment processes allow an open system of affect and of self-affect-object connection to provide meaning. This becomes the basis for the metabolizing process of the psyche, which transforms Beta elements which are forces and things in the external world acting upon the self, into Alpha elements.

When this metabolizing process unfolds on a continuous basis, creative work can reach a sustained level of personal meaning. We see this in Charlotte Brontë's novel, *Villette*, which is extensively analyzed in *The Compulsion to Create* (Kavaler-Adler, 1993). The narrator of *Villette* has a conscious psyche. She functions with an observing ego and with a conceptual system that can assign meaning to human motivation. When this sustained level of personal meaning is attained in creative work, the creative work interacts with the internal world sufficiently to provide psychic fulfillment. Such fulfillment can be defined as an adequate response to the existential psychic need for meaning. This level of fulfillment allows the artist to relinquish her creative work, just as sexual fulfillment allows us to relinquish the immediate sexual experience. This can occur because there is potential space for movement into the external world of interpersonal relations. As the subjective self finds meaning, interactions with others come about in the interpersonal world, particularly through modes of intimacy. The interpersonal experience can then be freely relinquished for a new journey into the internal world through the transitional modes of creative work. This journey is based on interactions with internal objects, and on memories of engagement with those others from which such internal objects and their representational forms were derived. Consequently, the fulfilling love-creativity mode of creative work is never just the externalization of an internally formulated process, but rather is a constant dynamic interaction between the experiential subjective self and the observing ego, through engagement with an artistic medium. The artist thinks and creates during the process of writing, not just ahead of time. In fact, if the artist attempts to only put down on paper or canvas what she has already formulated in her head, creative blocks can form. She may, for example, continuously discard paper or canvas because what she has placed upon it does not match up with her mental image (Safan-Gerard, 1994, personal communication). The artist has to be able to surrender to the transformation of internal thought and image while in the process of engaging with a transformative medium and its symbols. She must separate, say good-bye, and essentially mourn each inner mind's blueprint that can never be realized in its embryonic form, but which must be distorted by transformations gained from interactions with the external world. This phenomena would, in Winnicott's terms (1974), be a confrontation with the real world as existing beyond one's omnipotent gesture, providing degrees of disillusionment. Birth involves transformation. To preserve the embryo, one must constantly abort.

FORESHADOWING OF THINGS TO COME

The studies within begin with the myth of the Red Shoes, which highlights the tragedy of the creative mystique. This is a tragedy in which the female artist's intensity in art becomes an addictive craving to perform for a father-god muse. When an female artist seeks to compensate for an early void in the self, created through preoedipal trauma and unresolved loss, by hooking her grandiose self into a male muse, her potential capacity for whole-object love relations is suffocated, and she becomes sealed off in a hall of mirrors. In this sealed-off state, performing incessantly to be the god muse's "star," her muse must inevitably turn into a demon. The demon lover is created, who tantalizes those unable to be ordinary with their own projected images of greatness. Life is extinguished, as all hopes for intimacy are extinguished. Some, such as Sylvia Plath (Kavaler, 1985, 1986, 1993), Anne Sexton, and Diane Arbus, commit literal suicide. Others, such as Camille Claudel, Emily Dickinson, and Emily Brontë withdraw into modes of seclusion from the world that result in a living death that is a form of emotional suicide. Others, such as Katherine Mansfield, die from the inability to care for the self in the face of disease.

The Red Shoes is a story of part-object love. It is a story in which death comes because of an inability to successfully mourn and separate. Next, I discuss the specific case of Camille Claudel, the nineteenth-century sculptress, who personifies the narcissistic pathology of most of the artists described in this volume. Camille Claudel hitched her wagon to the star of the male sculptor Auguste Rodin and ended up losing her artistic identity as she merged her visions in with his own.

Next we separately discuss the photographer Diane Arbus, the writers Katherine Mansfield and Virginia Woolf, and Freud's Anna O. For all these women, as with Camille Claudel, we see a clinging to the father and father substitutes, in reaction to critical failings in early mothering. The father's narcissism stimulates both the use of him as an idealized muse, and as a "Lord of the mirrors" reflector for these artists' own grandiose self-performance.[9]

The incestuous desires of Diane Arbus for her father were intricately enmeshed with her preoedipal yearnings for a mother who could be a subjective object or her other half. These yearnings were transferred to her husband, and then to her creative work. The manic frenzy of Red Shoes creativity began most distinctly when she suffered the loss of her husband, which triggered the primal loss. She tried to fill up a void that was too huge to be experienced and mourned, with photographic images of those who reflected split-off and dissociated parts of herself.

Katherine Mansfield also sought to substitute the father and father figures for an environmental mother—or subjective object—whom she lost too traumatically when an infant. Even though her oedipal hopes collapsed with the pressure of her preoedipal cravings, she kept seeking father figures to guide her and to inspire her.

In the case of Virginia Woolf we see a father fulfilling a mothering role,[10] when the detachment from the actual mother is overwhelming. The image of a black void continually appears in the work of Woolf, as the demon lover continually usurps the place of the longed-for father-mother figure.

Anna O. is also an artistic female, although she never actually becomes an artist. She is presented here as both an historical figure in psychoanalysis, and as a representative of a woman whose creative pursuits also extended from an attachment to an idealized male muse.

Anne Sexton is the fulcrum of this book. For it is through Anne Sexton that we make the transition from female artists with preoedipal trauma, who suffered their fates without the aides of modern psychotherapy, to those who did receive treatment, as we know it today. Anne Sexton illustrates the creative mystique, in that she became addicted to her own intensity. She did seek psychotherapeutic treatment, but it was inappropriate. She never received the object relations treatment that would have helped her integrate the primary split-off parts of her self. In my study I explain why.

I have included Suzanne Farrell in my book because she stands as a sharp contrast to the other tales of female artists presented here. Farrell was able to ally herself with a paternal muse without sacrificing her core self-identity. She was able to surrender without merging. She was able to maintain boundaries and to be separate. Unlike the other artists, she was never sacrificed on the altar of the creative mystique. In her own words, she could take the Reds Shoes off!

Following from Anne Sexton's failed treatment are psychotherapy cases that have been treated with a knowledge of object-relations theory and of psychic structure. These cases focus on two women. one of the cases was treated by me, and one was treated by a male psychoanalyst in supervision with me.

These clinical cases form a dialectic with the biographical tales of female artists presented within this text. They each show successful mourning and movement towards the psychic health state of love-creativity dialectic. In contrast to the tragic tales of artists paralyzed in a pathological mourning state, the analysands in these clinical studies were able to form connections with their analysts that enabled them to modify both creative compulsions and love addictions. They were able to develop whole-object capacities that substituted their own creative mystique for whole-object love. Love and creativity became interactive and mutually nourishing.

PART TWO

Tales and Traumas of Women Artists

3)

THE RED SHOES MYTH
AND THE STORY OF
CAMILLE CLAUDEL

In this chapter I discuss the myth of the Red Shoes, which reflects the symbolic theme of this book. Following my description of the classic Red Shoes theme, I will then present the tragic tale of the sculptor Camille Claudel. Claudel's biography offers a vivid view of the psychological dynamics of the Red Shoe theme as it applies to a woman artist who is becoming increasingly well-known. Camille Claudel substitutes creativity for love, after a tragic loss in love, just as does the movie heroine of the Red Shoes. Both mythic female figures end their lives in suicidal despair, as the moorings of love for a flesh-and-blood man turn into a morbid fixation on a demonic muse, an internal object derived from the split-off dark side of the father-muse man. All sense of agency is lost. Early trauma related to maternal detachment and malignancy is suggested in both cases, as each woman artist loses touch with body and feelings. This is the inevitable demise, once the binding merger with a male muse figure becomes the haunting possession of an internal male muse-demon. The muse turns possessive in fact and fantasy, and transforms into the symbolic manifestation of early trauma seen in the demonic image.

The Red Shoes can symbolize feminine power and sexual passion, but the frenzy of the Red Shoes dance implies an addiction to an internal object that merges with creative inspiration to become creative compulsion. The Red Shoes can also symbolize an addiction to the artist's narcissistic image and its manic intensity, as it is reflected in the eyes of the male muse and becomes the Red Shoes, the image of the star or genius. Another meaning of the Red Shoes is that of a passion for the oedipal father that is split off from the central self, due to the lack of integrated

self-connection to the primary mother. The part of the self represented by
the Red Shoes acts as an alienated drive impinging on the subjective psyche from without. The internal father takes possession, and all sense of
self-agency is lost. All these meanings of the Red Shoes symbolism will be
discussed.

The myth of the Red Shoes captures the theme of this book. Initially a
tale by Hans Christian Anderson, it was made into a film, entitled *The
Red Shoes*, (1948) by GB Productions. The film depicts the syndrome of
the creative mystique, the theme of addiction to the narcissistic image as it
becomes linked to the creative process, culminating in a manic intensity. It
also illuminates the demon lover syndrome that accompanies the creative
mystique (see Kavaler-Adler, 1993a).

In the film version of the Red Shoes, the heroine is a young ballerina,
Ms. S., who vies for a position in an internationally reputed dance company. She and a handful of other female dancers win highly coveted spots
in the dance company. Once abroad with the company, Ms. S. dances in
the corps. The director of the company soon recognizes her talent, and he
offers her a big chance for a solo star role. This occurs at the critical point
when the former ballet corps star affronts him by choosing to get married. Like a jealous father, who feels betrayed by his daughter when she
loves and marries another man, the ballet director emotionally disowns
his prima ballerina, who had trespassed upon his idealization of art by
placing love before art. The director bans her name from his vocabulary
and defies members of the company to speak to him of her. His actions
illustrate that the director lacks the psychic ability to navigate past his
rage in order to mourn the loss of his spiritual daughter. Instead, he
replaces his lost object without mourning, designating Ms. S. to play the
lead role in the company's production of *The Red Shoes,* while seducing
her (not physically) with his charm and sense of privilege.[1]

Ms. S.'s talent has certainly paved her way to this role, but she could
not have obtained it at this early stage of her career without the power of
the thrown behind her. The male master's point of his baton had given her
the chance at a challenging role and at the tantalizing allure of stardom.

Once chosen for her part, Ms. S. is courted by the director. She is to be
Galathea to his Pygmalion, an extension of his own lust for talent and creative activity, perhaps an extension of his own idealized image of himself.
After a few rehearsals, the director takes Ms. S. out to dine. But on the
set, another romance is brewing. The composer of the production, a
young musician with an abundant talent of his own, is supporting Ms.
S.'s efforts, slowing down rhythms to meet her pace, or speeding up to
guide her pace. The meeting of their rhythms, and the tender meshing that

takes place, can easily be seen in terms of sexual innuendoes that flesh out the course of a romance.

Once their rehearsals end and the first performances begin, Ms. S. comes into her own power. Both lord ballet director and her romantic lover, the company's talented young composer, remain in the background of her own incandescent glow. She stars in the dance narrative which predicts the agony of her own tale, as mapped out by Hans Christian Anderson. In the ballet an innocent young woman is seduced by an old shoemaker, who represents the dual-edged—magical and demonic—power of the Red Shoes. The shoemaker's motives are dubious, if not devious, as he woos Ms. S., in her role of diva and little girl, the owner of the Red Shoes. The shoemaker's seductions can easily be likened to those of the dance company's director as he tantalizes Ms. S. with the allure of the Dance. The shoemaker invites her to be the one, the chosen one, who assumes the tantalizing power engendered by the Red Shoes. He seduces her through the young girl's projections of her own view of herself as possessing the magical aura of the dancer, regal with beauty. He stirs up an insatiable desire in her that becomes focused on the red dance shoes, a symbol of feminine power and sexual ecstasy (the color red). When the young woman appropriates the Red Shoes held out to her by the shoemaker, her initial engagement with the shoes is transformative, and perhaps transcendent. She reaches the heights of her own creative powers as she puts on the shoes which inspire her and lift her spirits. The Red Shoes are not just transformative, they are also magical. They are possessed! When the young girl reaches the point of exhaustion from all her dancing, she wants to go home, but she is no longer free. The shoes compel her to keep dancing. She has become possessed by the power of her own sexual eroticism, as unrecognized sexual desires are now projected onto the shoes. The compulsion to keep dancing is felt as a compulsion to create.

The Red Shoes never let our heroine go. She is possessed both within the interior play of the ballet and in the external play of her biographical life. She is forced to dance till she drops and dies. Her wish to gain radical creative power and sexual allure has turned fatal. Lust for creative self-expression has turned to being possessed. Potential transcendence has turned to being possessed. The malignant father figure—the shoemaker, or the shadow side of the dance director—has helped give life to her creative talent, but for her the price is very high—the loss of all the love relationships that sustain her in the world. Both in the ballet and outside it, Ms. S. is in flight for eternity. Cut off, she is sucked (oral level) into the black void of death, the darkest shadow of the demon lover father figure.

The young girl is possessed on stage and off by the demon lover, who nurtures her talent at the expense of her soul. The tragedy is a serious counterpoint to the culmination of all life's aspirations. In the dance narrative "The Red Shoes," Ms. S. reaches that culmination as she reaches the creative ecstasy through her magnificent performance of the ballet. In her offstage life, she is falling deeply in love with the company's orchestral composer. The other elements related to her triumph are stardom, which resonate with her grandiose-image self, and the confirming adoration of her paternal director. The peak of triumph is fragile and quickly collapses. At a birthday party held for one of the male members of the company, the paternal director learns that Ms. S. is no longer available to him. She is out with the composer, with whom he is told that she is in love as is the composer in love with her.

Ms. S.'s period of bliss with her new lover is cut short by her father figure's wrath. The director fires the composer, banishing him from the company. Ms. S. is forced to make a choice she does not wish to make. She can either marry the man she loves and separate from the company, or she can remain with the company and the father figure who nurtures and mirrors her talent but who also has tried to figuratively castrate her lover. Faced with this choice, she decides to marry the composer, and to give up her position as prima ballerina, and no longer dance the role that has brought her fame. If it is truly the art and process of dance she loves, she can continue to take her dance lessons, and dance with a lesser company. Ms. S.'s need for a true interpersonal love is evident in this choice. She needs the love of a man who sees her for herself—beyond the aura of her creative talent (which is given full reflection on a stage) and beyond the dimension of her art. She also needs a man who could allow her to love him and know him in everyday moments of intimacy, as a person in the world, beyond the dimension of his talent and art. All this is implied in the film. Yet, after a relative short time with her new husband, Ms. S. becomes restless listening to him practice the piano every night. She takes a train to visit her family and on the return trip encounters her old ballet master. Their passion for each other is rekindled. Earlier she declared her freedom: she had been capable of separation from the demonic spell of a muse-demon father figure. Yet on meeting him again, she seems not to have the power to make the separation once again.

Upon her second encounter with the director, following the consummation of her marriage, the director's allure (and all that he represents) overcomes her need for love in the interpersonal world. After assuring the director that she has never stopped dance lessons, she comes back with him to his company to once more perform "The Red Shoes." She is re-endowed with the costumes of her stardom, and re-encased in the magical

Red Shoes. Before her performance, her husband arrives furious that she has returned to the director who he now considers his enemy. He declares that he will leave her if she goes through with the performance. Distraught and desperate, Ms. S. begs her husband to wait for her till after the performance. Enraged, he refuses and walks out on her, leaves her to be psychically wed only to the director and to the compulsion and mystique of her art. Ms. S. is unable to let her husband go. Her need for love must overwhelm her as she runs after her husband. The movie of *The Red Shoes* ends on a melodramatic note as Ms. S.'s ballet slippers take off on their own, propelling her over a balcony as she runs in the direction of her husband. Despite the melodrama, the Greek tragedy plays out its dark destiny, and the symbolism of the Red Shoes echoes its poignant message.

What is the message? There is an obvious parallel between the internal play of the ballet "The Red Shoes" and the external play about the ballerina herself. In the end of both, Ms. S. is dominated by a passion that breaks her bonds with those she loves and with those who can love her. She is caught up in a desire for marriage to a male muse—as symbolized both by the internal play's shoemaker and by the external play's director—which propels her beyond her limits. Spiritually tied to the male-muse father figure by her art, she loses a loving bond to a man in the interpersonal world. She is without a home and without a body. Without a loving bond within the interpersonal world, she entirely loses her center. She becomes driven beyond her limits to the point of extinction.

How does the film highlight a mythic struggle endemic to our psyches? In what way, does it portray the creative mystique?

The heroine of *The Red Shoes* movie is a ballerina, who is inspired by a male-muse father figure. She is unable to successfully separate from this father figure, while still retaining the dynamic power of creative inspiration. In attempting to separate through love and marriage to a non-incestuous figure, a flesh and blood man, the heroine loses the fabulous mystique of her former days as a star ballerina for a major international ballet company. Although she could dance in other companies, the allure of reflecting the glory of the paternal and god like ballet director tantalizes and magnetically compels her back to the ballet director's company. Only when she returns does she feel that she is truly a star, a "great" ballerina. Only in her paternal muse's company does she possess the incandescent intensity that glows as a reflected glory. Only in her muse's company is her creative talent reflected in the eyes of her father-god-muse. She merges into a spiritual communion with the muse who, as a psychological vampire, feeds off her for his very life. Yet, without love and sexual intimacy with a man, with whom she could live in the interpersonal world of external object relations, the heroine of the Red Shoes loses her moorings in her body. She is then driven by the Red Shoes, in contrast to being connected to her artistic and expressive powers through her body self. She loses all sense of agency.

Disconnected from her body and from any core feeling self that could live through interpersonal intimacy with an external man, she becomes addictively wed to the internal father demon represented by the ballet master—the incestuous god-father. Her spiritual merger is a merger with an image of herself reflected in her god-muse's eyes; she becomes addicted to the intensity of her own image in the creative act, rather than a true connection to her core body and feeling self. To remain connected to herself in her creative work, as opposed to deriving her resources from an addictive merger with a reflected star-image intensity, she would need to sustain an interpersonal relationship to an external male who could offer sexual love and intimacy. She loses this connection when her husband walks out on her, and without having an early internalization that would adequately connect her to herself, the loss of interpersonal love leaves her in the power of the male muse, who wishes to possess her. Her muse father, made omnipotent by her own godlike projection onto him, cannot relate to her as an external other, with her own subjectivity and agenda for a separate life. The implication that the ballerina lacks an adequate internal environment mother from infancy (see Winnicott, 1964), and an adequate mother of separation from the separation period (see Mahler, 1975), is only alluded to in the *The Red Shoes* movie, where we see the only mother figure, the aunt, as a woman who co-ops the company of artists through her power as a rich socialite. Such a figure might be too narcissistic to be truly maternal. Perhaps she is only interested in the welfare of her niece, at least as far as supporting her creative work and achievements.

Broader than any one developmental circumstance, however, is the meaning we can find in the the Red Shoes symbolism, when the Red Shoes are seen to reflect the power of all our internal objects, in that they exist as internalizations of object representations that can take on a power of their own as they merge with alien, or split-off, parts of our selves. The power of the Red Shoes, and of internal objects in general, becomes demonic specifically because this power is split off and alienated from our central selves, or in Fairbairn's (1952) words, from our central egos. Yet the symbolism of the Red Shoes extends beyond the meaning of an internal object per se. The Red Shoes symbolize a particular constellation of psychic pathology. This constellation is based on a part of the self, which could potentially manifest as feminine power and sexual ecstacy in interpersonal relations, but which has instead become wedded to a worship of our talents. Such parents often have a basic narcissistic disregard for our primary emotional needs and a disdain for our human faults and vulnerabilities. When someone in the external world resonates with the projection of such an internal subjective object (Winnicott, 1974, or Klein's part object), he or she becomes a powerful magnet, often an idealized mirroring other, whose aura and attraction is supercharged by a primal infant-mother, child-parent intensity. For many artists, as for Ms. S., at least one primary parent served as the powerful mirror who reflected their talents, while disregarding the basic human needs for whole-object love. For such a parent these needs threatened to interfere with the expression of the special talents of the child that mirrored the parents' narcissism—providing an idealized glow reflecting back from the potential artist child towards the parent. For the female artist, presented by the symbolic representative Ms. S., the father is often the primal parent who played the role of an adoring and admiring mirror, sometimes in contrast to a hostile and belittling mother, and sometimes in contrast to another side of the father that was possessive, mocking, or indifferent. Once this father has been internalized in his mirroring role, any other future males whom the female artist becomes attached to will often play out the role as a narcissistic mirror. Each new male reflector will be experienced as an inspiring muse, or an impinging demon by the woman. Each of these men will possess enormous power over her. Since yearnings for love with such a father must often be split off in terms of the incestuous aspects of their erotic lust interwoven with this love, the power of the lust can also be a profound component of the creative drive that the woman brings to fruition with the resonating role of the mirroring-muse father.

The ballerina's Red Shoes symbolize the profound primal psychic tie to a father, or his muse representation, who mirrors the artistic talent and the criticized image of the female child. However, they also symbolize the manic intensity of a passion for that father, which impinges like a drive, from an alien part of the psyche. This manic intensity gives an incandescent glow to the creativity of the female artist. Sometimes the artist comes to mistake the manic intensity itself for a manifestation of creative ability and creative process. Many manic depressive artists wait for their manic highs. For many artists with "borderline" and "narcissistic" psychopathology, this is particularly true. Foremost, Sylvia Plath (Kavaler-Adler, 1985, 1986, 1993a), Anne Sexton (Kavaler-Adler, 1989), Diane Arbus (Kavaler-Adler, 1988), Emily Bronte (Kavaler-Adler, 1993), and Emily Dickinson (Kavaler-Adler, 1993a), as well as the case of Freud's "Anna O." (Kavaler-Adler, 1991) show this pattern. Plath and Sexton are two of the clearest examples. As they both become addicted to their own intensity, they relinquish the more classical poetic forms (Silverman and Will, 1986), as well as the holding environment of writing workshops and interpersonal connections that had grounded and contained them.

Often, artists mistake intensity for creative process. The addiction to the intensity can become a manifest symptom of an internal-object addiction, in which the varying levels of libidinal and erotic ties to an internal parent are encapsulated in the manic mode of the creative process.

THE RED SHOES AND THE CREATIVE MYSTIQUE

The Red Shoes are a symbol for an addiction to an internal parental object that manifests as a manic compulsion to create. They also become a symbol for the creative mystique, which is the external manifestation of the internal situation. The term "creative mystique" refers, as mentioned, to the theme of addiction to a narcissistic image (the "star"), as it becomes linked to the creative process, culminating in a manic intensity. Another way to speak of this is as an incandescent aura of god-like specialness that the male god-muse confers upon the creative artist. The male muse confers this specialness by means of reflecting an image of her greatness, which obviates the female artist's own sense of agency and creates a grandiose image self. Without having an adequate holding mother internalized, which can connect the female artist securely to her body self, she becomes split off from her body and from emotional attachments with external objects, and ends up living in a hall of mirrors. The male muses who confer this mystique enact the same psychic function (tending towards the pathological) as narcissistic parents who mirror a child's talents, because they mirror the artist as a special figure, while often neglecting the female artist's emotional and object-related needs (needs for interpersonal love and intimacy), as well as ignoring personality characteristics that don't fit neatly into the mold of living like a star. Frequently, the narcissistic parent even fails to see the child's talents, seeking instead to have the child mirror the parent's own idealized self-image by performing in artistic ways unrelated to the child's own personality and talents (see Kavaler-Adler on Edith Sitwell, 1993a). This was true of Edith Sitwell's father who tried to force her to play the cello or zither but ignored her talent as a poet. In fact, he even forced his daughter to read *his* favorite poets, rather than her own.

When an artist grows up with these kind of narcissistically mirroring parents, and then is greeted by fans and audience and by male muses who mirror them in the same manner, the addiction to the grandiose image attached to creative ability and creative process is repeatedly reinforced. The relationship that has been internalized from the mirroring parent is triggered by the new external audience, and the deep (libidinal) erotic ties to the primal parent reinforce the addictive tie to the mirroring audience that the artist must repeatedly win over time and time again, by living up to their performance of the mystique. The child in the artist who first desired to express her true nature through an art genre, and its particular form of creative process, is now competing with her own compulsion to perform repeatedly to the resonance of an image. For example, Red Shoes are symbolically transformed from ballet slippers, in which one truly connects to the emotional life in one's creative work, into compulsive spirits formed from internal self-images, which are tied to the energy of the muse's reflected view of the self. This happens when a part of the self, which is absorbed in the natural rhythms of the artist's creative process, becomes possessed by internal objects (primal blueprints for any new external muses). These internal objects are energized by split-off primal-self parts, and these primal-self parts contain oral and genital body cravings, which galvanize them into a state of intensity. When these oral and genital body cravings are not at least partially satiated through interpersonal love relations, they lead the artist to seek satiation through the assumption of a narcissistic image and all its hope for magnetic appeal to part-object external mirrors (see Kavaler-Adler, 1992 and 1993a, on Anaïs Nin).

CAMILLE CLAUDEL

The tragic tale of Camille Claudel's life captures the essence of the Red Shoes myth. She loses connection to the flesh-and-blood interpersonal relationship with her male muse, Auguste Rodin, and ends up addicted to the internal male muse, as she constructs him from a negative afterimage of Rodin. She becomes possessed by the image of her own intensity, as formerly reflected in the eyes of Rodin, and turns to her creative work with an exclusive absorption that secludes her from the world. She fights against the experience of loss with her creative mystique intensity, not being able to mourn on her own, and her work repeats the trauma of despair and lost love, which probably stems back to early infancy, as well as back to the critical loss of Rodin himself. Camille Claudel's intensity increases with the loss of Rodin, as she cannot mourn. She becomes both manic and paranoid in her state of pathological mourning, repeating the theme of despair and loss in a creative enactment, in the sad condition of those she sculpted. Trying desperately to rid herself of Rodin's influence, she becomes increasingly possessed by him as an internal object that she is addicted to hating. Her powerful yearning for Rodin, as her ideal male muse and father figure is converted into a frenzy of Red Shoes intensity in creative work.

As Claudel isolates herself from the world, losing even minimal contact with external interpersonal relations, her compulsion to create reaches suicidal proportions. She locks herself away in seclusion to do her sculpture, and then she smashes her sculpture and sits alone in the rubble. She attempts to seal off her studio from all outside influence, to the point of sealing doors and windows so that even the outside air will not enter. The fate that follows is living death in an insane asylum. She is never unlocked from either her external or internal prison. The potential developmental mourning, which could have unlocked her—mourning for the primary love for Rodin, who has come to represent the bad-object mother of her infancy, after having been the father-muse ideal when she was with him—cannot be done through sculpture alone. There is no connection with the primary sources of her love or hate. The symbolic displacements only become an insatiable number of substitutes for the primal figures who she cannot mourn, and to whom she therefore remains addictively tied through the internal-world figure of Auguste Rodin.

Reine-Marie Paris has written a biography of the French sculptor Camille Claudel (1864 to 1943). A film has also been made of her life. The film was produced by DO Productions (France: Annon Films), and was made in 1988. In both the written biography and the movie are haunting testaments to the tragic obscurity that overcame one of the most talented sculptors of all times, turning her bright light into a faint shadow hidden behind the monumental renown of the male sculptor Auguste Rodin. Paris (1984) writes:

> Posterity has yet to make amends to Camille Claudel for her misfortunes. At the end of her solitary and miserable life, she left a spare and nearly forgotten body of work, some resting in the shadow of Rodin's, the rest scattered and neglected in small provincial museums, in storage or perhaps in private and uncatalogued collections. Several of her works have disappeared without leaving a trace; unless they resurface by chance, the loss seems all the more poignant, considering how very briefly she worked and how very little she left us. (p. x).

The work of Camille Claudel attests to the desperate effort of the disciple who tries to escape the influence of the master not so much by a break or a disavowal but by a deeper and more concentrated form.

But while she was straining to achieve this and creating her purest masterpieces, Rodin, her teacher, rejected her and forced her to make the break. The effect of Rodin's abandonment on Camille Claudel's life can be compared to a huge geological split that swallowed up her creative sources. It was as if, all of a sudden, her inspiration had been denied her. Doubting more and more in herself, her art, art itself, she withdrew into silence—not a silence of mockery as did some of her contemporaries but a silence of unreason." ...before darkness totally engulfed her, Camille Claudel modeled only disembodied hands and feet. (X–XI)...

...There was no artistic environment that would lead her to L'Ecole des Beaux-Arts or—and why not?—to the Prix de Rome. All of that was closed to a woman. Provincial and without connections and support, she could not help but become completely dependent on her teacher in exchange for the gift she made of herself. This exchange was the secret of her genius. When it dissolved everything crumbled. (XI).

The biographer's observations are conveyed through plot. In the movie, the film first presents the brilliant sculptor as an adult. A background of maternal rejection is implied by the harsh rejections in the present, but the maternal rejection never assumes a foreground position. The realities of Ms. Claudel's childhood are muted and opaque.

The Camille Claudel first shown in this film is a woman who rises before dawn to search the mountain slopes for clay for modeling. Claudel grasps at the clay in the rocks like an infant grasping a maternal finger. She clasps the piles of clay as an infant hungers for the breast and its milk. From the first moment of initiation and impulse, she is hungering for her ideal of aesthetic verisimilitude. This ideal image or object can more closely be compared to the infant's hunger for the "environmental mother" (Winnicott, 1974), the mother behind the breast, the mother as a holding and continuing presence. The movie about Camille Claudel, as well as Paris's biography, suggest that Claudel's artistic ideal is often not the classic equilibrium of form and mode, but rather the ideal of the authentic. Thus, her sculptured shapes and forms come to express, increasingly throughout her life, her personal agony and anguish made universal through the instinctual symbolism of the organic body. Her anguish, as it appears in the forms she created, is, I believe, comparable to the verbal poetic forms that women writers, such as Sylvia Plath Katherine Mansfield, and Anne Sexton use to express the authenticity of their internal life—the interiority of their anguish. It may also be compared to the photographs of Diane Arbus, photographs which echo the horror of the grotesque in human attitude, which emphasize interior pain, and which implicitly view the narcissistic ideal as false—as an intrusion from narcissistic parents, a suffocating mold.

After this opening image, and a scene at her studio with Rodin visiting to inspect her work, we see the sculptor with her mother. This relationship impinges on us as it must have impinged on Camille herself. The mother is cold, brittle, rejecting, and even hating towards her adult daughter. Yet, viewing Camille Claudel as an adult, in the biographical film, we see her mother's effect muted by the relationship configurations and the implied internalizations, that exist so prominently in respect to the sculptor's father and brother. These other family relationships distort the profound impact of the mother of the past, as the current mother recedes into the background. In other words, the primitive mother symbolically recedes into the background due to the foreground emergence of oedipal strivings, connecting the daughter to the father, and due to incestuous longings, to the brother as well. The movie conveys the adult Camille Claudel separating from her mother by entering into the more benevolent arms of the men, when faced with the envious "demonic" mother.

The film offers no insights into the particular nature of the mother's demonic effect. But the biography, to the extent that it is historically correct, allows us to surmise something about these demonic roots. Perhaps because the mother remains in the film's background, she haunts the viewer just as the biographical subject may have been haunted to the point of taking in the bad object to control it (see Fairbairn, 1952). If this did occur to Claudel, the part of the self that contained the internal bad object must have been split off from the central consciousness and from the self that related to external others in the interpersonal world. As core-self parts were split off, higher level aspects of an oedipal level self were drawn to the interpersonal world through heterosexual erotic desire—the psychic incest with father and brother motivating intense modes of relational engagement.

Consequently, the film and the biography show us Camille Claudel casually bypassing boundaries. She cuddles on top of a bed with her brother and charmingly flirts with him. This disregard of boundaries foreshadows her relationship with the paternal and adoring Rodin, a renowned sculptor.

Claudel's relationship with her father continually echoes the intensity of that between a daughter and a seductive and oedipal father, who, while more maternal than the mother, is also powerful as an autonomous bourgeois male. The daughter is chosen as "special." Her artistic talents are supported as well as particularly co-opted by the father's narcissistic image of his daughter: her "special" artistic talents mirror his own narcissistic yearnings.

In such a father-daughter relationship, the father's ideal self can be reflected through his daughter's creations as they take their shape and power in the world. However, his erotic longings for his daughter are reflected in his fascination with her artistic talents as well. Libidinal longings find expression through narcissistic strivings, in both father and daughter. Unlike Edith Sitwell's father (who by this showed his extreme narcissism), who strove to push his daughter toward the artistic pursuits he chose, which were alien to her true nature, the father of Camille Claudel, like the fathers of Sylvia Plath and Emily Brontë, appreciated the actual talents of his daughter—part of her true self. To this degree, his narcissistic absorption was normal and healthy; it positively motivated his daughter's creative development. Even so, his narcissism was capable of turning impinging and possessive—and ultimately demonic—to the extent that while cherishing Camille's talents, he disregarded her broader span of emotional needs. How susceptible Camille Claudel was to such negative behavior depended on her early mothering—particularly the mothering at the "basic fault" level referred to by Michael Balint (1979), the level of mother-infant holding environment influence that forms the core self, and which allows or disallows that self to connect with the interpersonal world, rather than to split it off (Fairbairn, 1952). According to D. W. Winnicott, effective early mothering needs to have a sustained aliveness of contact that is not intrusive (1965). This combination permits the infant's "capacity to be alone," that is, alone with the nonimpinging environment mother. In other words, the infant's sense of "going-on-being" (Winnicott, 1974) depends on such an interaction. Next, during the transitional stage modes of separation-individuation (Mahler, 1975), the mother must remain attuned to the child's needs to pull away and return to the maternal orbit. During rapprochement, the mother must be able to engage interactively with her child's separate self. She must be able to allow the child a new conscious dependency (Melanie Klein's depressive position), without shaming and humiliating the child for her dependent needs.

Why is mother's "absent presence" necessary during the first stages of self-formation? Her ability to allow space for the child's unique "idiom" (Bollas, 1993, *Psychoanalytic Dialogues*, Vol. 3 (3)), while still being available as an "object mother" for instinct expression and gratification is necessary. The mother's presence during separation, as during the transitional stage following holding (in Winnicott's terms), must be one of an alternating availability—present to defer any traumatic sense of absence and void, but not too satiating. Otherwise the creative development of an initiating self that must struggle to strengthen itself by facing frustrations and losses is obstructed. The dangers of an internal void in the self are ever-present until the maternal contact has been sufficiently internalized for "object constancy," signaling the good-enough alternation of presence and absence. Abandonment and/or intrusive engulfment are the two harbingers of trauma that must be avoided. When the mother of separation is psychicallly disconnected from her child, the humiliation that the child can experience when needing the mother during rapprochement is a horror. But even worse is the experience of being abandoned to such a degree that the child is left without interiority or containment in the self, since the connection with the mother has not been adequate during infancy and during critical separation-individuation phases of development, to provide an internal container within the child's psyche. Instead, the sense of a void or black hole is experienced when the sealed-off traumatic self is faced. Clinging and manic activity are symptoms of the internal void that resembles what Christopher Bollas' has called the "unthought known" (1987), something beyond the limits of conscious conception. The predisposition to the frenetic Dance of the Red Shoes begins here. So does the fatal seeds of father-daughter psychic incest. The silencing of the female voice—of need, of desire, of artistic manifestation—begin here.

What do we know about Claudel's actual maternal environment? According to Paris, Camille Claudel's mother, Louise, was hard, cold, demanding, envious, critical, and self-pitying. Paris reported that she had children out of a sense of duty, a calculated, cold sense of matriarchal principle, based on her martyred submission to her role in society. This excluded warmth and genuine love from her contact with her children. Such a mother as Paris describes, and as conveyed in the biographical movie, would hardly have allowed her infant daughter to have nestled into her skin or to feel held and secure. Such a mother was bound to be impinging and intrusive in her mode of duty-bound physical care. Such a mother would hardly have been "the absent presence" (Winnicott, 1974) envisioned by Winnicott, who can be present as a holding environment. Such an environmental mother is required for the development of a child's "true self" or innate "idiom" (Bollas, 1993) to emerge fully into an interpersonal context, where it could be fully supported in its development. Perhaps the self would have been left as a "submerged personality" (Wolff and Kutash, 1991), a potentially active, initiating unique self that has been sealed off and split off from interpersonal life. Such a personality must be expressed, but when it can't be expressed through the normal developmental connections in the interpersonal field, it may get expressed through the artist's work, as fully as it can. But even here it must be nurtured by some interpersonal form of psychic holding. Camille Claudel's kind of mother must have been caretaking enough to allow her daughter's artistic talents to emerge as a personality from within. Yet given the mother's inability to maintain a state of emotional contact, support, and "going-on-being" (Winnicott, 1974), the disruptions in connection between mother and infant, and the trauma to the self during times of separation, must have been severe. Adequate internalization of an early relationship of self and other cannot be made under such circumstances. The developing child is left with a more profound sense of emptiness and void within than appears in normal separation stress. For once the infant leaves such a mother during the toddler years, she is left out in the cold, remembered only as she fits into the mother's pretty picture of the child.

THE AFFAIR WITH RODIN

How did Camille Claudel find her way to Rodin? As a young woman sculptor, she was destined to fit into a patriarchal mold. In Victorian society no avenue to legitimacy existed other than through apprenticeship to a male artist. When Camille Claudel sought this with Rodin, she sought through this "alliance" the literal stamp of approval that would bring her legitimate recognition in the world. In 1881, the middle-aged Rodin (he was forty) had a reputation as a sculptor and teacher when the nineteen-year-old woman approached him. He already had the aura of the creative mystique, being an internationally renowned artist, whose artistic acumen had become a public myth of glamour and brilliance. His fame was to grow through the years. Yet the source of this mystique, the original creative process from which its products emerged into social consciousness, was drying up. The inspiration was gone. According to the film version, Rodin was on the verge of becoming a mere technician. He was in danger of re-articulating without new meaning. Not surprisingly, his emotional connection with his work was fast waning. His focus had turned to instructing young male and female art students in how to put together the massive forms creating his work. His forms were becoming bigger and he was producing more, but the quality of these new works was eclipsed by a lapse in primary self-connection. Indeed he had to store his works in warehouses which Camille Claudel, in her claim that he was an industrialist, not an artist, later called factories (taken from the film biography).

When Camille Claudel came into his life, Rodin was seeking a muse to arouse his dying inspiration. According to Paris's biography, as well as the film, he was at a point at which his inner life was dissipating. At the time, Rodin was working on a group sculpture called *The Gates of Hell*. He was not yet famous as he was to become, but he had large studios, where he employed students and workmen to help him.

Claudel was young, fresh, and arrogant. She was filled with her own inspiration, which she had since childhood. Intoxicated with her own talents, she had forced everyone in her family to pose for her (Paris, 1984). She had been discovered by older male artists, such as Alfred Boucher and Paul Dubois, who found her somewhat alien, but also fascinating. Boucher, believing that her work resembled Rodin's in its emotional motivation and force, introduced them.

The coming together of Claudel and Rodin must be imagined in terms of the intensity of the interior psychodynamics that seem to have compelled them both. To look only from the outside would not capture the essence of their idiosyncratic mating, nor the mythic constellation of the Red Shoes that immortalizes the nature of their compulsion.

Claudel was filled with the emotional resources that Rodin had lost, but she needed his help in becoming legitimate in the world. Rodin, in turn, needed the dynamic of her interior life to resurrect his creativity. But one additional factor was critical. Camille Claudel was willing to risk everything. She did so without being aware of what she was doing. Given early trauma with her mother she had been self-encased in a cocoon, such as that of a narcissistic shield or grandiose self (Modell, 1975, 1976). She possessed an arrogance, split off from the darker forces within her. She expected everything from the world, just as she had expected everything from her father. Her sense of entitlement became linked to her talent. She thought of herself as special as her father's daughter and as her brother's intimate. This arrogant self-ascendance shielded her from the dark interior life that was haunted by a primal hatred that she carried from her mother, Louise Claudel, and also from her younger sister Louise. But even this dark hatred could work to her advantage as long as she was shielded in her cocoon of arrogance and narcissistic pride, that is, as long as she was shielded from this hatred by a special link to her father. The dark interior anguish, related to primal hatred and primal rejection, could be a source of unlimited inspiration for her—a dark malicious stream under her shield of grandiosity—quite fitting for Rodin's figures of the damned in his composition, *The Gates of Hell*.

Claudel and Rodin merged with one another. Through they never lived permanently together, they comingled, without differentiating definition, in their joint artistic work. One might say they wed through the creative process, but Camille was left unanchored to the world beyond. Interpersonal life was to be replaced by a love that had its manifestation in art, through creative work. Eventually, for Camille Claudel, interpersonal modes of love and sensual intimacy would entirely be replaced by creative work.

Camille Claudel modeled for Rodin. She also composed sculptures within his work. For example, she skillfully crafted hands and feet of his figures. But she also created heads and larger statues. In exchange, he gave her a legitimacy in artistic society as his pupil, and proposed her name for exhibitions and newspapers, and designated her works as hers to certain parties that might help her, although he might have signed the sculptures as his (Paris, 1984, p. 19). What remained hidden from the world was that it was her genius filling up his molds and going in new directions in art that he could not find on his own. What was more blatantly displayed to the world were the implications of their sexual liaison. Paris (1984) has spoken of Camille Claudel as Rodin's muse. Yet Claudel shaped and molded Rodin's works more than he shaped and molded her. Still the intense passion of their mental union drove her. To some extent Camille Claudel was both Rodin's Pygmalion and his Galathea. She posed for him as his Galathea, but she also composed for him and thus created him in her own role as Pygmalion. The relationship becomes even more complex when this question is asked—whose inspiration was it when she posed for him? It is suggested in the film and biography by Paris, that Claudel composed herself as she posed for Rodin. Thus, while she was his muse perhaps his presence inspired her as well, and she was inspired to sculpt a bust of him in his absence. He served as her male muse. All their mutual passion poured forth into mutual works they jointly created. Yet few sculptures were signed by Claudel. Her talent poured into the pores of Rodin's marble casts. In fact, according to Paris, she, not he, was the one skilled in the execution of sculpture in marble. Clearly she was a genius. Rodin himself acknowledged this in speaking of her to friends. He was not her equal. But Rodin never confessed this to the world, and as his fame began to grow, he incorporated Claudel's ideas, the inspiration of her presence through modeling and her own composition, and even her finished works into pieces of artwork signed by him.

Despite the bitterness this practice ultimately created within the mind of Claudel, Claudel and Rodin were lovers for fifteen years. The first years especially were filled with the positive power of their mutual passion. They were merged both in sexual terms and in the undifferentiated way they worked together. The two artists excluded all others from their intimacy, even Rodin's common-law wife, whom Rodin continued to live with. (Rodin actually married his common-law wife during the last year of his life. Yet, on his death bed, when he called for his wife, and his legal wife was brought to him, he protested, asking for "the other one," referring to Camille Claudel [see Paris, 1984].)

For Camille Claudel, perhaps even more than for Rodin, the relationship was symbiotic, because she had very few friends, and even these were more like acquaintances. Only Rodin knew her intimately, as her brother once had. Because of her hostile relations with her mother and sister, she was never close to women, although some admired her and tried to keep in contact. In fact, she may have flaunted Rodin's attentions before the world, hoping to induce envy in other women, since this was the politics of her own family.

Rodin lusted after Camille Claudel for both her talent and for her beauty. According to Paris (1984), Rodin was quite enamored with Camille, missing her powerfully when he and she were separated. Still, he never relinquished his living situation with his common-law wife, Rose Beriet (Paris, 1984, p. 14), nor did Camille leave her family home, until years later when she lived and worked on her own. Camille and Rodin would steal time away to be with each other, totally alone in the country. Their first years were joyous, according to Paris.

In these early years, Claudel's art was known in France through the influence of Rodin. Paris writes (p. 218):

> Until 1903, with only a few rare exceptions, Camille Claudel exhibited at the Societé Nationale des Beaux-Arts. Each year the newspapers mentioned her name more or less at length. In 1891, probably thanks to Rodin, Camille Claudel became a member of the jury.

However, Paris also writes (1984, p. 219):

> From 1888, when she was only twenty-four years old, to 1905, the name of Camille Claudel appears frequently in the press. As long as she remained with Rodin, however, she does not seem to have held the attention of the great critics. Her name is mentioned with indulgence—the kind that second-rate, near-sighted critics with timid judgment reserve for a skillful young artist, who does not deserve a classic cursus honorum.

Ultimately, the tragic denouement of the Red Shoe myth was to mark Claudel's form of union with Rodin, and was to permanently obstruct her future. The fate of the Red Shoes heroine, as you may recall, is sealed by the transformation of potential transcendence into possession by her male muse. The male muse's act of possession is destined to turn him into a demon, unless the woman is able to separate from an exclusive tie with him that seems to have served as a psychologically symbiotic bond and bind. For the young female to be possessed by the rescuing male muse, with the consequent loss of self and connections to the outside world, she must have had certain psychic vulnerabilities.

Camille Claudel had these psychic vulnerabilities to an extreme, just as did other women artists whose tales will be told in this volume. She gave up her artistic and sexual self to Rodin, seemingly without even feeling the love that might possibly justify such self-surrender. For according to Paris, Claudel was not as emotionally attached to Rodin as he to her. While he was able to feel enough attachment to Camille to grieve their separations, Claudel was, according to Paris, calculating in her attitude toward him. This gives us an interesting clue to what led to Camille Claudel's demise. She appears to have had the character traits of a narcissistic character who merges her ideal self with that of another (generally an idealized male father figure), but who is unable to internalize the real other as she cannot truly experience him through emotional and psychic connection. The narcissistic character cannot feel and mourn loss, and therefore cannot truly separate nor connect. Claudel used art, just like she later used alcohol, to numb the pain of loss that could not be tolerated. She seems to have suffered like the poet Edith Sitwell, who wrote a poem called "Still Falls the Rain," (see Kavaler-Adler, 1993), in which endless tears fall in the form of the unconscious image of rain, because the ability to truly cry and grieve is arrested and sealed off. Those with preoedipal self-trauma, which manifests in the psychic structure form of narcissistic character traits, are generally unable to truly give themselves in a way that allows their soul and self to be reborn through the communion of spiritual and sexual love. Without such true communion, merger can never provide enough for psychic satiation. For it is impossible to become organically nourished on ideals and images, which substitute for true emotional communion between two separate self-centers. These narcissistic compensations obviate the confrontation and working through of separation and loss. They prevent psychic internalization and self-integration.

Camille Claudel gave all she had to Rodin, and she ended up feeling as if she had been robbed. She ended up feeling emptied out, not renewed. Given her family history, and the probable lack of a primal body communion with her mother, her inability to take in Rodin emotionally is quite understandable.

Not only was Camille unable to trust a merger due to her primal experience of mothering, but she was also inflamed, as discussed, by a passionate oedipal desire which had been aroused by her adoring father. Camille's oedipal longings must have been intense. Her father had focused a special idealizing form of mirroring on her, arousing her at a genital level, but encouraging her to express all excitement and through her creative work. Her early needs to touch another were obvious in her sculpture. There, her tactile desires served to shape and mold clay and marble. However, such primitive tactile needs never stand alone in a fully developed women. Beyond the primal craving for touch is the genital level of arousal for the oedipal father. This craving must be either mourned, sublimated, or acted out. For Camille Claudel, it appears, they were acted out in her sexual engagement with Rodin, but they also shaped the agonizing guilt that she seems to have portrayed so movingly in *The Gates of Hell* sculpture (currently in the Metropolitan Museum of Art as a work of Rodin). There she created herself as one of the damned. Later she created many figures in states of emotional starvation and tortured agony. Levels of guilt may have combined in her—guilt for her hatred of her mother and for the psychic incest with her father, which she may have unconsciously viewed as actual sexual incest, as she became a father figure's lover. Given her hatred of her mother, to the extent that Camille was an oedipal victor with her father she was sure to be overcome by intense guilt. The intensity of the Red Shoes creative-process dance is driven by this guilt. Also, the Red Shoes dance is driven by the compulsion to ward off loss of the love object. It is an attempt to deny loss by merging with the idealized muse object who can never die. However, the muse inevitably turns to a demon and leads the woman to her death.

The female artist's longings for an object that she can emotionally contain can be even more basic, however, than this guilt. Claudel had been starved of an adequate internalization of a primary object. Therefore, she substituted images of herself and images of another for the emotional intimacy she had missed achieving. Emotional starvation must have driven her, for she was bereft of the basic psychic structure of self and other that needs to be built during infancy through the emotional contact that comes from the care of a mother. Because of starvation, Claudel must have been tantalized on two basic levels, one in relation to the primal mother, and the other in relation to the oedipal father. Her mother had been unattainable as an emotionally responsive caregiver and her father had tantalized her with the promise of "specialness." In her yearnings to merge with Rodin she must have been seeking the unfulfilled promise of both parents, yet, even prior to Rodin came the art itself, the transitional stage objects of her own creation, the images, the contact with her clay, and the initiating power of her creative abilities. Camille Claudel's wish to compensate for emotional lack with a self reflected through art in the world must have made for a powerful drive and creative compulsion. The father's validation and reflection of this artistic self was also critical. Once Claudel put on the Red Shoes and "danced" in the orbit of Rodin, she could not take them off. Rodin tantalized her on levels both of her deprivation and of her erotic yearnings. In addition, his narcissism—his need to have her fulfill him—aroused her psychically and genitally. She gave her all to him as long as the route to her own recognition in the world was of necessity through him. As an accepted sculptor, and in a male-dominated society. Rodin must have seemed to hold the keys to her own future as an artist.

Without an understanding of Camille Claudel's susceptibility to him, we have only Rodin's narcissism to blame for the outcome of her life. Feminists who have unearthed the tragic tale of Camille Claudel have targeted Rodin as at fault. However, Rodin was transformed from muse to demon in Camille Claudel's mind for reasons that extended beyond Rodin's own narcissism. Camille's need to feed narcissistically on images as a substitute for the nurturance of emotional love must also be distinctly taken into account. Only from such a psychological perspective can Rodin's narcissism, just like her father's, be viewed in perspective. Claudel was like Sylvia Plath—longing for a "Lord of the mirrors" (to be seen in a later chapter), a father who inevitably turns into the dark daddy of the demon lover theme. She is like Emily Dickinson who submits to the mammoth god or "Nobodaddy" (see Kavaler-Adler, 1993), because she feels helplessly in need and powerless, only to become tormented by the figure of a tormenting and sadistic demon lover god. When Camille Claudel gave herself up to Rodin, her psychic vulnerability must have been stressed beyond the limit of endurance.

And what precisely did she give up to him? Paris informs us that she relinquished formative years of her creative life, her inspired ideals, as well as her talents, crafts, and skills. Besides these Claudel surrendered her status as a lady in society and both her budding and mature sexuality. She also may have had to separate from several children that were born to her from Rodin. According to Paris, her sculpture suggests this and that she may have undergone at least one abortion. For example, he notes a sculpture of a bereft woman having to relinquish a child. He also describes secret journeys to the countryside where births and abortions were performed. Claudel seems to have been helpless in such circumstances. She hardly had any power of her own as an unwed mother in Victorian France, especially when the children's father, Rodin, had a reputation to cultivate, playing the role of a gentleman and of a reputable artist in the world. Realistically, Camille Claudel had no legal grounds to claim that which was hers. She was living in a patriarchal culture, one in which she had a psychological sense of power only through merging her talents with the mystique of a renowned male artist. Further, Rodin's wish to have her while not marrying her certainly made her a victim in such society. Their fifteen-year love affair culminated in disaster when Rodin's refusal to marry became increasingly explicit.

Rodin's fear of marriage, Paris suggests, may not have entirely related to his narcissism nor to his living with Rose. The biographer alludes to Rodin's fear of what he sensed as Claudel's growing madness. Whether or not Claudel's "madness" could be fully assigned to her state of social and political powerlessness, as two feminist critics have theorized about other women artists in *The Madwoman in the Attic* (1979), the madness that manifested later, in flagrant delusions of persecution, may well have been growing when she and Rodin were together. It is easy to understand why Rodin would have been scared by such a state of mind. However, should not Claudel have been mad, after giving up what she had to a man who seemed to have all the power to make or break her legitimacy in the world?

We may wonder why Claudel could never break up with Rodin, why she could not emotionally separate, and create the psychic opportunity to be with another man. Instead, she turned to alcohol to fill up her inner void, one that could no longer be filled with images of greatness through the consecrating adoration and admiration of a man. Can we ever tease out which came first, the madness or the victimization? Obviously, they must have interacted, for in some ways Camille Claudel was a victim. She depended far too greatly on Rodin to bring her out in society, not only as an artist, but as a legitimate wife. Without Rodin's approval or his name, she was left without any power to claim her work or her children in a patriarchal society. Still, the seeds of her madness seem to have been sown at the beginning of her life. Her situation was even more desolate because there was no doctor at the time who could treat a borderline psychosis, a pathological condition triggered by the inability to tolerate early life loss in the form of an abandonment depression. Such an abandonment depression, generally related to early separation stage trauma, could easily be triggered by loss of her merger with Rodin, who had provided her with a sense of identity. Claudel lived in a society where one was either sane or insane, and once classified as insane one's rights and voice could be extinguished forever. Paris writes of the law of 1838 (Paris, p. 70), still in existence today, that made anyone who entered an insane asylum languish there until the institute's doctor decided that release was advisable.

Paris writes of Rodin's anguish at Claudel's mental state. I believe her biography allows us to view that anguish so that it defeats any black and white judgment of Rodin. Although he became the chief demon in Camille Claudel's mind, he must be seen as a victim as well as a demon. His involvement with Claudel must have been based on a complex array of yearnings and needs. Even if his desire for her may have been more passionate than hers for him, he could not face the consequences of it anymore than she could. They both invested in Camille Claudel as an extension of Rodin. They both participated in allowing her art to be appropriated by Rodin, and they both enjoyed Rodin worshipping her as an emotionally highly strung, beautiful woman. Further, Rodin seems to have tried to have supported Claudel as an artist in the world by referring to her in private as a genius. Whether, however, Rodin would have promoted Claudel openly as such, when he was craving increasing recognition for himself, is certainly doubtful. He did, however, promote work of hers that was signed by her. While Claudel believed that Rodin wished only to possess her soul and her work, appropriating all for his own prestige, Paris notes that he did propose Camille as an artist in her own right for projects, expositions, and academic art societies. Even after they parted, he seems to have continued to advocate on her behalf. And, ultimately, when all was lost, and she withered away in an insane asylum, he secretly made contributions to her asylum fees. At that point, her family prevented Rodin from making any other kind of support, and the asylum fees he paid would also have been rejected if Camille's family had found him out. He had been by then too repeatedly cast in the light of "the monster" (Paris, 1984) to her family by Camille herself.

What was the spell of the Red Shoes that overtook Camille Claudel and made her ultimately dance a dance of death? What made her turn against herself so brutally that she began to sculpt at a manic pace, only to end up repeatedly over the years smashing and destroying her work and her self? What inner demon possessed her, which she projected onto the pompous, image-seeking, and depleted Rodin?

The whirling dervish image of the Red Shoes fits Camille Claudel sublimely. Her fanatic pace came from within her. It was ignited by her lust for Rodin—at least for the image of Rodin—and it grew suicidal when cut off from Rodin. Camille Claudel worked intensely throughout her life. I don't believe she was capable of less than that intensity. According to Paris, there were constant creations for Rodin, very few of which were

differentiated from her own. She succeeded at opening up the middle-age
Rodin as well. Rodin might have remained lacking in imagination if he
had not met Claudel. He might have remained ignorant of the artistic tra-
ditions and movements which he began to follow through her enthusi-
asms. She had been influenced by Florentine art, Japanese art, and
indirectly by the Impressionists. Yet, all the influence was given dramatic
life through the emotional poignancy of a soul simultaneously seized by
passion and emotional starvation. While Rodin grew increasingly lyrical
in his work through his love for Claudel (Paris 1984), Camille set the
stage for a whole new direction in his art. She injected an acute interior
life into Rodin's facades and molds, at a time when he increasingly
became a technician who directed others to do his work. By contrast,
Claudel was all interior life, without social, interpersonal, or other modes
of external support. Like Emily Dickinson's breakdown poetry (see
Kavaler-Adler, 1993), Camille Claudel's sculptures captured the moment.
Claudel made the moment vivid through her human figures and forms.
She made the interior life of the moment speak and tremble. She was
capable of showing tenderness and sadness, agony and malevolence.
Rodin, with the support of the world given to him, could provide a haven
for the lost soul in Camille Claudel, the soul that lived in the moment of
affect and authentic inner life, but which was profoundly disconnected
from interpersonal relations and from any society or community.
Claudel's soul had never found a place in the world.

But as we have seen, the psychic haven Camille Claudel found with
Rodin came at great cost. With Rodin, who gave her money and brought
her gifts, there was only the illusion of materialistic gain, for in truth she
acquired little of real financial value from their association. Also, the psychic haven rested on illusions of a union perpetuated by summer week-
ends in the country or by placating titles bestowed on Claudel as "Rodin's
pupil." Ultimately, the lack of a commitment within the broader society
had to be faced. Although Claudel thumbed her nose at society when she
paraded at receptions with Rodin, her power to feel triumphant and
immune to rancor was based on the frail thread of Rodin's grand image
and on the illusion that he was hers. Once robbed of this illusion by
Rodin's refusal to marry her, and by his continuing live-in life with another woman, who came to hate her, Camille Claudel lost all defensive
arrogance, all grandiose pride, all of her insular psychic cocoon. She compensated for psychic collapse by a manic pace of creative work. No longer
did she join Rodin when he invited her to public receptions. No longer
did she accept his offers to buy her clothes. She claimed she had no adequate clothes to go to receptions. She made her break from Rodin while

Rodin still overtly longed for her presence. In fact, according to her biographer (Paris, 1984), Rodin continued to long for her presence until the day he died.

Camille Claudel never had cultivated friendships. Adversely effected by her negative relations with mother and sister, she failed to sustain friendships with women, although the movie shows her to be friends with one woman who had to return to America. Also, no men other than her lover Rodin were constant friends. In addition to her lifelong emotional starvation, her psychic traumas from infancy, her loss of many years in which she could have created her art for herself, her isolation from others—often consciously chosen by her as a state of solitude to do her artistic work—left her more vulnerable than ever. At a time when her illusions of a future life with Rodin were crumbling, and her artistic merger with him had to be acutely severed, she was left with no supports. Her family was alien to her—her father disappointed by her affair with Rodin, and her mother aghast and fanatically condemning. Her one support, her brother, had left Europe and rarely visited France. Her social and artistic contacts were all contaminated by her role as a pupil to Rodin and by her merger with Rodin's work. Left alone, she lived on her own, and withdrew increasingly from the world. Tendencies towards seclusion climaxed into the arid and manic life of a recluse. She then had only alcohol to fill the void, and occasional letters to her brother in which she grew ever more paranoid about Rodin.

Formerly, during the years with Rodin, she had poured all her capacity to love into her creative strivings, but at least she had an intimate relationship with another person. Once severed from Rodin, there was no love relationship to counteract her manic tendencies in relation to her creative work. Sealed away in an apartment, a state mimicking the psychic sealing away that my have been her fate during infancy (as with Emily Dickinson and Emily Brontë, see Kavaler-Adler, 1993a), she exploded with frantic creative activity until evasion of any route out towards the world left her turning more and more upon herself. Claudel's compulsive and bitter comments about Rodin increasingly alienated anyone who sought to help her, among them those who might exhibit or publicize her work. Furthermore, she also avoided opportunities, blaming an ill state of health. Paris writes of an opportunity for an article and an accompanying display of her work in newspapers. Her self-sabotage was blatant. She contaminated her new contact with bitter comments about Rodin, claiming that he was constantly creating conspiracies to rob her of her work and to claim it as his own. She also resisted responding to the interviewer's comments, and reacted with hostility to this inquiry which might have brought her recognition. She seems blind to her self-sabotage, or else out of control. She wrote not only of resenting the reporter's inquiry, but also of remaining in bed sick for much of the time. Her depression seems to have been overtaking her, and her early life neglect may well have been psychically repeated in her debilitated state at this time.

It is painful to read about Camille Claudel's increasing degrees of self-destruction. She began to neglect even basic modes of caretaking, house-keeping, and cleaning for her own custodial needs. She failed to leave her apartment, even declining an exhibition in Prague. The opportunity she saw as an insult, for she was to exhibit next to Rodin. She interpreted such a chance to exhibit as a maneuver to have her work claimed and once more co-opted by Rodin. Having refused a last opportunity for recognition in the world, she seals off her apartment as if she were creating a self-made tomb, or a perverted womb that has no permeability. She sealed off windows, doors, and any avenue to contact with others. She festered in the filth within. But even more heartbreaking than all this is the nadir point, the ultimate psychic death, when Camille began annually to smash the very artworks of her own that preoccupied her mind's every waking moment.

The smashing of Claudel's hammer against the marble and clay resounds with piercing nightmare tones through the sensibilities of the viewer, who watches the biographical film of Claudel's life. In Paris's biography, her many radical displays of self-destruction are also reported. Her behavior is a frightening testimony to the mind gone mad from lack of relationship, and from lack of a primal internal relationship that could provide the route to current relations, and through that to healing. Camille Claudel had lived her whole life in the pursuit of her artistic talents. She had been shielded from loss and rage that she could not tolerate—stemming from a primary maternal hatred—by the arrogant possessiveness of her own talent and vision. Now she had no more shield. She had given up years of her inner life and creative expression for symbiosis with Rodin. As Paris remarks, there was no way for Claudel to reclaim those years, those ideas, and those daily artistic gifts that she had showered on Rodin. She could not face nor tolerate the degree of loss, which was at a traumatic level. She did not have enough psychic internalization and structure from infancy to make mourning of such loss possible.[2] Her grief may have showed in her work, but she could not bear to behold it from an objective perspective that would have required emotional awareness of her loss. Unable to tolerate loss and grief, she destroyed herself. The only thing she had left was her retaliatory rage against Rodin. Blaming him for everything was a diversion from the anguish of her loss. Her portrayal of him as a thief and psychic murderer kept her from remembering him, his love and her own work. Surely it was a turning against herself, this very primitive rage she cherished toward Rodin, which made her smash herself by smashing her sculpture. Leaving herself with nothing but rubble, she claimed that Rodin's secret pals had robbed her apartment, seizing her art for their own display. To smash the very works she had lived for when nothing else was left to her, became part of a manic Red Shoes intensity gone wild. The tantalizing behavior of her muse father, Rodin, had inspired her. Now in her belief that his abandonment meant a conspiracy of evil against her, she lost all reason, all separation from him. She turned him into a demon, in her mind, one that was perennially abandoning her, and was stealing her ideas and work. Now Camille Claudel truly gave up her power to Rodin. She made him omnipotent in her mind, maintaining a steadfast belief that he could see all in her life and had the power to destroy it all.

When Paul Claudel was summoned by his mother to witness his sister's wreckage, it was too late. His father had just died. His mother wished to be rid of Camille, who she viewed as a burden. Paul was pressed by the mother to certify his sister insane. From that day forward Camille Claudel lost all rights and became a vegetable in an insane asylum.

The last part of Camille Claudel's life constitutes the most horrendous tragedy to befall any woman artist I've read or written about. Even women artists who committed suicide did not have to endure the living death that Camille Claudel experienced. She was taken by force from her home and put in a local insane asylum in 1913, eight years after her affair with Rodin had ended. Later, she was transferred to another asylum, from which she was never to leave, staying there until her death in 1943. For thirty years, she rotted in a cold, damp castle of an asylum. She refused to ever sculpt again, and she froze through seven-month winters, with hardly ever a visitor. Even letters were kept from her at her mother's request. Paris writes of his view of Camille's mental collapse, reading into her subjective state, lending it the form of reason where only paranoid delusion was actually encountered. Paris states: "to see the man whom she had inspired with her own talent advance toward fame and glory while she was being swallowed up by darkness must have been too much for Camille's proud and solitary spirit. Her reason collapsed. From 1905 onward, her obsessions, her anguish moved from fixations to psychosis" (Paris, p. 65). From 1905 until her entrance into the asylum in 1913, at the end of each year, she smashed all the sculpture she had produced. "The idea that her works were being copied," Paris writes, "obsessed her," (p. 66). There was some truth to her fears. Paris observes that her sculpture, *The Gossipers*, created a sensation in the Beaux-Arts circle. Many artists really did wish to imitate her. But Camille's fixed belief that her imitators and imagined imitators were agents of Rodin, led all who encountered her to understand why her family and the doctors of the institution where she was eventually interred believed that she had a "persecution complex." By 1913, she was armoring herself with a nail-spiked broom in order to chase away the devils she thought were trying to enter her studio at night. She believed these devils were models who worked for Rodin. It was soon after, following the death of her father and the failure of her family to notify her of his death, that she was dragged off to the insane asylum by two muscular male nurses. The combination of her paranoia and her style of living in filth and sealed-off isolation had compelled her brother, under the pressure of their mother, to do something! The internment began on March 10, 1913. She was just forty-eight years old at the time (Paris, p. 148).

Even when the doctors at the asylum were willing to free her, in 1920, just seven years after her incarceration, her mother Louise protested that she could not bear to have her daughter outside of the institution, let alone at home with her. Possibly to quell her guilt, Camille's mother constantly sent her parcels of material goods and food. But she remained Camille's most fanatical jailor. Perhaps it is was a repetition, a mirror reflection of the past, of Camille's childhood, that her mother substituted material goods and physical care for any emotional contact, empathy, or object-related concern.

Letters reproduced by Paris portray how Camille begged her mother to allow her to come home. She swore to her mother that she would be tranquil and pliable after having been forced into a living death that had vanquished any rebellious fire. No pleas swayed her obdurate mother who, more rigid than any plaster cast, refused to crumble. The manic tide had been subdued. In Claudel's life, just as in the myth of the Red Shoes, the heroine is compelled to leave home through the manic magic spell of lust for the masculine muse. The masculine muse is fantasized to be the source of her talents and exposition of these talents at a superior level of greatness, where the creative mystique star image is projected outward as her own image. For Camille Claudel, the creative mystique star image could have served as a protection against the paranoid and scapegoating hatred constantly directed at her by her mother and sister. Simultaneously, the crowning of authentic achievement with the star image of the creative mystique was a way of consummating a reunion fantasy (see Masterson, 1976) or symbiotic merger with the father, who came to symbolize the preoedipal mother as well as the oedipal father. Idealizing the father at a pre-oedipal level of psychic fantasy would have made him godlike, and could therefore serve as a magical muse figure in fantasy. Yet, without her real living father to buttress this fantasy muse father, and without a merger with Rodin that would buttress the same fantasy, the internal mother-father muse figure inevitably turned into the demon lover, thundering loner leading her to join him only in the land of death, once her creative work could not sustain and nurture the fantasy. Her state of seclusion, made her the haunted and possessed victim of the internal demon, who she experienced as the personification of Rodin, and surely he had Rodin's blueprint upon him. Without a secure sense of self-agency that could be responded to adequately by the real world, her need for Rodin, combined with her own denial of the need, which prevented her from taking any support from him, became a perverse form of possession. The internal demon lover swallowed her up, and a shell of her former self remained, going through its motions in the insane asylum.

Once far from home, she could never return. For Camille Claudel this might be understood in terms of her mother's obdurate resistance to any forgiveness. She never relented once Camille had taken on the mantel of prostitution in her eyes, by living as much as she did with Rodin.

In reaction to the mother's malignant mode of constant rejection and vilification of her daughter as well as the loss of the father, and his symbolic representative, Rodin, Claudel was propelled into the St. Vitus mode of a Red Shoes dance (akin to the St. Vitus dance of the Middle Ages, in which those infected with the virus couldn't stop moving). It was a dance of sexual ecstasy transformed into mania within the creative work process. The female artist's creative work became unconsciously molded in both point and counterpoint to the fantasized image of herself reflected in the eyes of her paternal muse, taking on the mystique of Rodin's incandescent narcissistic glow, as he shaped his young Galathea into the image in his mind and rejected the rest of her.

What other rejections did this echo for Camille Claudel? Her mother's rejection was pervasive and so was her sister's. After Camille withdrew into madness and was incarcerated, her sister was triumphant. She wished to win Camille's inheritance, and her envy made her relish her sister's downfall. The psychic effect on Camille of these dark wishes from women had only been forestalled by her merger with her brother, who lived far away from her for the rest of her life, and by her father's special image of her. As she disappointed her father's expectations of her, most of which centered around his wishes for her to succeed as an artist, she turned a sense of shame (expressed explicitly by the character of Camille Claudel in the movie) into self-hatred. She psychically allied herself with the internal

hating figures of her mother and sister. All this contributed to transforming Auguste Rodin from a muse to a demon in her mind. A former creative ecstacy, based on a merger with her muse, led to self-hatred and
psychic death, as her muse turned demonic. Claudel became allied with
the malignant envy of her mother and sister and turned against herself,
marshaling their hatred to fuel the self-destruction born out of despair.
And so she smashed her own sculptures!

Her mental collapse was the collapse of her link with the idealized
father and his idealized image of her. Only this link had shielded her from
a primal incorporation of her mother's and sister's hatred. Though consciously she turned her wrath against Rodin, the real psychic thief in her
life was her mother and the maternal extension she experienced in her sister. Their gestures of fake benevolence during her asylum years blinded
her to the true source of her anguish and despair, for she could not sustain an awareness of such female and primal hatred. Hating Rodin was
safer: making him alien was less of a threat than facing the primal envy
of the mother and sister. Perhaps it was Rodin's sexual lust for her, as well
as his very real power over her opportunities in the world of art, which
made Rodin the perfect demon lover for Claudel. It would be easy to forget his tenderness and adoration and to remember only his power, which
easily becomes omnipotent in the internal world of psychic fantasy, with
the loss of the external Rodin and impinging of the internal omnipotent
object. Psychic splitting, which manifests as a dichotomy between an internal blueprint of an ideal muse object, and of a devalued demonic object,
could determine what was remembered and what forgotten. Once the ideal
is lost, only the demons remain, for at the developmental level of preoedipal trauma and arrest, there is no psychic capacity to assimilate the
muse and demon into an integrated whole. Therefore, Claudel could easily associate Rodin with a suicidal demise that came with the loss of him
and of his fantasized preoedipal godlike aura in the image form of a creative mystique. When Claudel was faced with her mother's refusal to allow
her freedom from her asylum, she evaded the full blunt force of the truth,
not only through self-hatred,[3] but once again through displacement of her
bad object onto Rodin. She proclaimed that Rodin had locked her away
and wished to throw away the key forever, with the ulterior motive of
assuring his fame by eliminating her as competition. She believed that his
mystique in the world was more important to him than any genuine
motive to find truth through art. To some extent, her delusion probably
contained some truth, for Rodin too was a victim of the creative mystique.
His evil was similar to that of the old shoemaker who tantalized the young
ballerina with the aura of the Red Shoes in the tale by the same name.

4)

THE STORY OF SUZANNE FARRELL AND GEORGE BALLANCHINE

In sharp contrast to Camille Claudel's story, and to the other women artists studied in this book, stands the story of Suzanne Farrell, the renowned New York City Ballet dancer. Suzanne Farrell joined the New York City Ballet when its great director and choreographer, George Ballanchine, was in his late middle-age years. Suzanne had been a teenage student in the New York City Ballet's school, coming to New York from the Midwest and winning a dance scholarship, several years after her parents' divorce.

The romantic tale of Suzanne Farrell and George Ballanchine highlights how the fantasy of union with a muse can have a sustained success, when early trauma does not turn the muse into a demon lover. However Suzanne's background must be surmised as far as her infancy goes. Her autobiography, entitled *Holding On To The Air* (1990), does give us a picture of both parents. Her mother was an enterprising woman, a nurse by profession, who had the courage to divorce her husband in the days when divorce was severely frowned upon. She also had the independent strength to put her children into ballet school, and then to move them all to New York where she worked out a deal to have her children receive free ballet lessons in exchange for their teaching ballet to younger students. One can only speculate what kind of woman Suzanne Farrell's mother was during Suzanne's infancy. However, her independent spirit, her durable self-reliance, and her sustained capabilities all suggests that she could have been an extremely adequate mother for an infant and toddler. She seems to have possessed a secure inner core from which an infant could feel a solid sense of being held, both during the stages of symbiosis and of separation-individuation (Mahler, 1975). With a secure center, Suzanne Farrell's mother could have been able to relinquish control and therefore to have allowed Suzanne developmental autonomy during phases of practicing and rapprochement. Nor would she have been threatened by her daughter's emotional demands to welcome her back as a separate other during rapprochement.

When Suzanne Farrell and George Ballanchine first encountered each other, she was an awe-inspired student and he was a brilliant choreographer (and former dancer). Suzanne anxiously awaited each time that Ballanchine would enter one of her dance classes. Gradually, the adored father figure began to select Suzanne to try out particularly difficult movements and innovative steps during her classes. Suzanne heard innuendoes and whispers implying that Ballanchine was singling her out. Early in her career, Suzanne was to dance *Meditation*, a romantic "pas de deux," with a male partner, Jacques D'Amboise. In her autobiography, Farrell describes the two figures in *Meditation*, who represent the aging Ballanchine and herself, in the following terms, as she has constructed them in retrospect:

> The two figures begin to move together, quietly at first, then with such passion, tenderness, and reckless desire that if this were fiction it might endure, but if it were life it could not. (Farrell, 1990, p. 9)

In this phrase, Farrell succinctly sums up why she could not later marry Ballanchine, despite the mutual desire they shared through their creation of a vision through dance.

Ballanchine had choreographed this piece explicitly for her. While he was away, he sent her a poem, which expressed what her male partner was supposed to be feeling towards her.

> I can't forget the Blessed Vision
> In Front of Me you Stood My Love
> Like Instant Moment of Decision
>   at retirement—
> Like Spirit Beauteous From Above
>
> Through Languor, through Despair and Sorrow,
> Through Clamor and Through Restless Space,
> I Heard Your Voice From Night
> And Dreamt of Darling Face

The Years of Storm Compel Surrender
Dispel and Scattered Dream of Mine,
And I Have Lost Your Voice So Tender
And Face So Heavenly Divine.

P.S. I hope by now you are thin and beautiful and light in lift.
  See you soon,
  your G.B.

At the time Farrell did not dare contemplate what personal significance the poem could have in terms of Ballanchine himself. But, over the years Ballanchine's attention increasingly focused on her, with the spotlight of his infatuation growing more heated. She, in turn, received more and more dance roles, ultimately becoming a principal performer.

Farrell writes that "in me [Ballanchine] found a body and a mind willing to risk being her," that is, willing to risk being the woman that Ballanchine dreamed of when he told Farrell to have her partner feel like the man in the poem towards her. One way, and not her way, of interpreting the developing Farrell-Ballanchine relationship is to see Farrell as Ballanchine's Galathea, his feminized ideal self, and his adored muse. In turn Ballanchine was Farrell's male muse father, who was helping her create herself through the imprint upon her of his vision of her. At one point, Farrell explicitly surrenders to Ballanchine, encouraging him to make decisions for her about what her creative capacities and dance talent allowed her to take on. Farrell asks, "Which came first, the chicken or the egg?" Who created her as a woman, herself or Ballanchine? She has no answer. The chicken and egg question that Farrell must leave open is the same one Winnicott (1974) asks, when he reflects, "Does the infant find or create the breast?" Winnicott concludes this is a question we never should ask the infant. It must be left open. In her inquiry into the origins of her fate, Farrell continues:

> What is indisputable is that in *Meditation* Ballanchine prophesied the future. I don't know how he could have known so much of what was to happen. Since I was the story I couldn't see it; I just danced it. It was only an eight-minute pas de deux, and it was everything. (Farrell, p. 12)

Ballanchine instructed her for *Meditation:*

You just hold on to the air when you're up there [on point]," he said, "You're riding on the air. (p. 13)

Farrell was overwhelmed by this instruction, based on Ballanchine's ethereal vision of her. She explains to the reader:

living motionless on stage is far more difficult than the more obvious tricks of the dancing trade. (p. 13)

Farrell couldn't follow Ballanchine's instructions in rehearsal, but she felt that he had faith in her. He trusted her to become his vision. He never threatened to back out or to remove her from the role.

Every little girl has the aspiring yearnings of oedipal stage love and oedipal stage narcissism. Every little girl can yearn to be her father's muse as well as yearn for her father to be her muse, inspiring her to reach to dimensions seemingly beyond herself. She may strive to be a part of her father, particularly when earlier separations from her mother have been incomplete. But even when such separation has been relatively complete, the unconscious yearning to be a perfect image by being part of her father (Stolorow and Lachmann, 1980, "I'm perfect because I'm part of you.") can be profound. When unconscious, it may lead to hazardous tendencies to merge with paternal figures. When accompanied by early disruptions in self-development, it can lead to terrors of self-loss or to actual loss of identity that threatens the psyche. However, when early development has sustained a whole, integrated, and separate self, unconscious longings to become part of the father figure, by creating a self that resonates with his own idealized image, can create powerful motivation for creative work. Whether the intensity of this striving turns to the manic escalation of the Red Shoes phenomenon depends on early development, and on the degree to which the father or father figure is narcissistically possessive. When the father figure isn't that narcissistic, he can allow a mutual dialectic between himself and his daughter in creating her image. His own voice and vision may not have to crush the creative woman's own voice as she grows and develops. When the young girl has developed a significant degree of true and differentiated self, through separation with the mother, and with the oedipal father as well, she need not merge with her paternal muse in an undifferentiated symbiosis, as Camille Claudel did with Rodin. Rather, she may aspire to an active agency in creating her own image within a resonating field of dialectic with her father figure's vision. It is a myth of early infancy that the narcissistic striving to be part of another in order to be perfect is anonymous and indiscriminating. Once a young girl successfully navigates separation-individuation with the early mother, she becomes quite discriminating in her yearning for psychic union, entering a more mature dialectic with her father and with later father figures and male figures. When Suzanne Farrell was awe-struck with Ballanchine, she was quite selective in the agency and direction of her object-related and yet narcissistic desires. She did not want to fulfill any male image. In fact, her own father had been a disappointment. He probably lacked comple-mentary resonating oedipal stage passion for her oedipal years. At least he was remembered by her as generally distant by the time she was ten and her parents divorced.

Ballanchine's vision of Farrell as the perfect female can be captured in the following comment, made in response to her showing him a flaw in her foot, "Oh, dear, but you know, if it was a beautiful foot you'd be per-fect," (p. 42). For Ballanchine Farrell was too close to his idea of perfec-tion to resist, but he also was continually creating his idea of perfection, as he choreographed ballets for her specifically to perform.

Meditation was Farrell's introduction to being the star in Ballanchine's eyes, the focus of his improvised creations. He choreographed "on her" according to her own expression.

This professional mating must have had sexual and romantic innuen-does for both Ballanchine and Farrell. A romantic coupling had begun, taking its shape through the creative process. It became clear to Suzanne Farrell over the years that Ballanchine identified with the male role he had choreographed for Jacques d'Amboise to partner with Suzanne during the heart-felt engagement of *Meditation's* pas de deux. Farrell ultimately con-cluded that if Ballanchine had not been so old he would have danced the part himself. And indeed, when he choreographed his dance pageant drama, *Don Quixote*, despite his advanced age, he did indeed dance the part himself for the opening and for occasional performances afterwards. With *Mediation*, which Farrell first danced at eighteen, Ballanchine did what was second best to dancing himself. He had D'Amboise put grey in his hair to indicate that he was an aging man who was falling in love with a young girl.

At the time that Ballanchine choreographed *Don Quixote* a magnifi-cent sublimation unfolded. For years, Farrell had resonated to Ballan-chine's beat. Luckily, they were not both dancers. Because he was a choreographer, Ballanchine was more differentiated from her than if he had been a dancer. Yet his dancing the role of Don Quixote himself, with Suzanne Farrell as Dulcinea, was a magnificent culmination of what had been developing between the psyches of Farrell and Ballanchine. From Farrell's viewpoint, Ballanchine had waited years, almost a lifetime, to put his dramatic vision of Don Quixote into effect. He had declined to do any producing of this story until he had found his Dulcinea. In Suzanne Farrell, he saw the young peasant girl whose spiritual aura revives Don Quixote's aging spirit, and brings his interior dream life into manifest form in the world where he creates through his imagination. Farrell writes movingly and compassionately of Ballanchine's vulnerability during his dancing with her in Don Quixote. She writes of his trembling humility, in which she sensed his love and desire, as he knelt at her feet and worshiped her. She reports that tears streamed down her face, as on stage, before a live audience, she danced the pas de deux with Ballanchine. The audience sensed the passion that lived between them and became electrified. It was like magic!

Was what occurred merely genital passion channeled into the physical catharsis of dance and sublimated into symbolic forms? Or was it that two individual souls had found their completion through object connection in the passion and compassion that they shared? It appears that an artist with an integrated self like Farrell could successfully sublimate. The dance between her and Ballanchine could give life to the deepest erotic affects and longings, as long as their individuated selves were integrated enough to sustain it. Unlike Camille Claudel, or Anne Sexton (as will be seen), Farrell could feel the fulfillment of her longings, both to have Ballanchine and to be Ballanchine's ideal, through the ballet and pas de deux. Although she and Ballanchine appeared as a couple at parties after performances, and were seen festively toasting together and sharing the limelight of their company's attentions together, Farrell was not compelled to act out their passion and union in sexual form. Nor did she deny her needs for sexual intimacy and decline an opportunity to marry another when the time came. Because of her degree of self-integration, she could have an emotional intimacy with Ballanchine without the sex act and marriage, despite both the powerful romantic form of love that existed between them, and Ballanchine's tantalizing courtship of many years. Ballanchine, on the other hand, found this sublimated bliss much less satisfactory. For many years, before his intentions were revealed and before he had formerly obtained a divorce from his current wife, he yearned to marry her. Farrell, still a virgin, must have felt the tension of her passion too, but she contained it and perhaps mourned it in the weeping she did on stage. Significantly, she seems to have been capable of feeling grief and processing the dynamics of mourning at many stages of her life.

The specifics of this artist couple's togetherness are fascinating. The couple made journeys abroad together, during the New York City Ballet tours. In Paris, Ballanchine constantly dined with his protégé. He ate breakfast with her. According to Farrell, they spent nearly every waking moment together. They slept separately, but they had breakfast and dinner together at his clubs and restaurants. They went to shows. And of course they rehearsed together. In Paris, he was again her guide, and she the willing spirit. But having a solid sense of herself, she did not feel he was robbing her by molding her. She shared in his world. He initiated and she followed, but then each evening, up on the stage, she was the princess, while he was in the audience. In this manner, they straddled a fragile balance of power.

But then the balance was tipped. Beneath the surface magnanimity of the man who wined and dined her, and who continually bought her beautiful gifts, emerged the shadow side of the demon lover male.

Back in the States and just turned twenty-one, Farrell began to see a young man her own age. His name was Roger. Through Roger she experienced her first dates, and her first taste of a more normal developmental progression in heterosexual life. With Roger, she reports, she could laugh. She felt that they were just two kids having fun. Gone was the pressure to use each moment to transform her creative expression on stage into a charismatic presence! Gone was the pressure of creating symbolic meanings, to be transmuted on stage, through her encounters with her male muse! With Roger, she was a young woman, an adored dancer, but not an image beyond her presence. Roger did not carry a mirror for her to reflect her image as George Ballanchine did.

Relations with Roger began to get serious. He gave her a big ring. They began to think of an engagement and marriage. Yet, because of her relationship with Ballanchine, and her mother's support for her exclusive engagement with him, she felt torn apart. She was not ready for a break with either Ballanchine or her mother. Friends suggested she move out of her mother's home to give herself freedom and time to think. She was not ready. One day during a rehearsal Ballanchine walked brusquely across the room towards her, and then pointing to the ring on her finger, barked an order, so unlike his usual manner: "I don't like it! Take it off!" He grabbed her ring and threw it across the room. The jealous and possessive demon had suddenly showed its head like a snake. His erotic desires were not being fulfilled through physical dancing on stage. He surely had struggled to contain them. Now they erupted. Farrell must have been shocked. Terrified of losing all she had of herself and her life on stage under Ballanchine's auspices she temporarily crumbled. Rather than the former feminine surrender to a benign masculine vision and force, she was now forced to see herself in a position of submission. She never claimed the ring, and her relationship with Roger dwindled until he began to date other women.

His departure kept Suzanne Farrell "free" to return to her life with Ballanchine. Her psychic conflict was temporarily put to bed, but not by her resolution, but by what must have felt at some level as a humiliating submission. She still cherished her intimacy with Ballanchine, but she began to take steps away, distancing herself from him. Her autonomy was at stake. She began to decline dinner engagements with him. He responded by becoming depressed, morose, and irritable with his troupe of dancers. Instead of support from those around her for her difficult strivings towards autonomy, Farrell now received punitive reactions. Her mother, who had been thoroughly seduced by Ballanchine, as he had become a father figure in her home, was relieved to be rid of Roger. Her earlier sentiments that Suzanne should date someone her own age were forgotten. Even more distressing to Suzanne, her colleague dancers from the New York City Ballet began to argue that she should not withdraw from Mr. B. She was encouraged to go to dinner with him as usual. No one paid attention to her feelings of discomfort, her growing state of tension. Everyone in her world wanted her to restore harmony by pacifying George Ballanchine, even if this meant her putting aside her own feelings and needs. Her mother even asked, "What's wrong with being Mrs. Ballanchine?" after Ballanchine divorced his wife and declared his betrothal to Farrell in the newspapers.

Suzanne Farrell's ability to find her own way in the face of so much pressure to comply with Ballanchine's wishes must be strongly noted. Although she submitted to his jealousy for a period of time, her own developmental needs were able to successfully emerge at a critical juncture. Even though she was still deeply wedded to him in their artistic work together, Suzanne had not, despite the pressure in her private life, stopped her attempts to separate from Ballanchine. Eventually, as she grew into her twenties, she did take her own apartment. Perhaps this helped her to separate from the pressure of her mother's opinions. Then, there was her attempt to see Ballanchine less frequently. As this countered Ballanchine's arduous strivings to be in her company, tensions between them mounted. His desires for ongoing intimacy between them in their private life were keeping Farrell from having a life of her own. Alone in her needs to separate, Farrell says she frequently prayed in church for guidance from God. Then fate took a hand in her dilemma. She began to date Paul Mejia, a young male dancer from the New York City Ballet Company. Farrell describes the course of their relationship in the heated climate of the ballet company, in which they were constantly being watched. At first, the two shared their admiration for Ballanchine and joy in creating within his choreographic domain. Gradually, however, they grew to love each other for themselves. Farrell writes of her distress on the evening that Paul told her he was in love with her and proposed. She was unsure which way to turn, as Ballanchine's power at the helm of the New York City Ballet was almost omnipotent. The possibility of crossing or offending him made her fear for her artistic life. Despite those fears, Farrell followed her intuition. A risk-taker all her life, particularly in her fantastic leaps of faith on stage, she now took the steps necessary to develop her own life in the world, separate from the shadow of her paternal god-muse. Because of her actions, her muse did not have to turn into a demon in her mind, whatever his objective behavior. Farrell said "yes" to Paul. She told him she returned his love and would marry him.[1]

In contrast to her relation with Ballanchine, with Paul there were no grand artistic visions imprinting her expectations for a future life. But, as Paul was a dancer, he was in sympathy with her artist's passions and creative process. Paul was also close to her age. He could offer her a life of sexual intimacy that was not dependent for its stimulus on the epic romance of the stage. With Paul, she could just be herself. The pressure of multiple mirrors reflecting her image could be relieved, as she engaged in an interpersonal life with Paul that was apart from and yet in a dialectic with the New York City Ballet. Thus, at this juncture, Farrell chose and created her life, reaching beyond the grasp of her male muse's Pygmalion image. She was not captured for eternity by the mystique of George Ballanchine, by the mystique that could accompany the creative process they both shared. Rather, she wished to put a boundary between her life on stage and that of an intimate life with a man. She did not believe that creativity, or the love it inspired within sharing in the creative process, could replace the solid rapport of an interpersonal love between two fully separate beings. But, once she made her decision, she had to face the wrath of her male muse, who despite her continuing surrender within their artistic work, was bound to interpret her decision to marry another man as a betrayal. Ballanchine's paternal yearnings were marked by psychic incest, therefore, his vision of her as his personal goddess, who he could possess and mold into the image of an ideal woman, one he hoped to worship in order to love, were threatened by Suzanne Farrell's decision to marry another!

After her marriage, Suzanne walked a narrow tightrope in her relationship to Ballanchine and his New York City Ballet. She was still dazzling on stage, living up to Ballanchine's most breathtaking hopes.

However, his attitude towards her now turned sharply cool. His attitude changed to icy reserve. No more was Suzanne the princess on whom tons of flowers were bestowed each performance. (She had formerly remarked that Ballanchine sent her so many flowers that she "looked like she had raided a flower shop" on her way home). No longer did she share dinners with Ballanchine or other private moments. Yet, despite the coldness, one night he came to her dressing room to offer her enthusiastic praise for her performance, as he had done so frequently in the past. She appealed to him at this moment to melt his reserve. Pretending all could be as before, she declared, "See, nothing's changed!" The effect was not as she hoped; he withdrew acutely. She then asked him if he wanted her to leave the company. Her marriage was obviously a powerful disappointment for him that created an impenetrable barrier. He said "no" that she needn't leave, but he said it might be better for her husband to depart.

Things were at a stalemate. Then one night Paul was removed from a part that he had always danced for the company. Both Suzanne and Paul were enraged. Suzanne wrote a letter to Ballanchine threatening that they both would leave the company. She soon found out that Ballanchine was enraged by the ultimatums! One day later, both Suzanne Farrell and her husband Paul were out of the program. Farrell's comments at this time capture something of the dramatic change in her internal state consequent to this. She explains that she suddenly felt like a bag lady. From high priestess to bag lady in one day's time. She was out of the company and therefore out on the street—without a job. Ballanchine's power over the full stretch of her life was awesome. No more was Farrell the center of Ballanchine's attention, no more his muse, no more the living culmination of his creative mystique, no more the recipient of gifts and flowers! Farrell's whole identity had developed with Ballanchine—dancing for Ballanchine, feeling his tempo and guidance, feeling his vision as her own inspiration. Without that identity, cast out by her muse father, she began a lonely struggle to forge a new identity even more separate from Ballanchine. She attempted to build a new mode of life in a private daily world that gained its intimacy from the dialectics of a shared interpersonal life. This matrix of intimacy through interpersonal life was a contrast to the artistic matrix of creative process and performance for the reflective eyes of one idealized male other.

For Farrell, her love of Ballanchine, his art, and his creative genius was never tarnished. But she had now aroused the great man's retaliatory wrath when she had challenged him. She could no longer submit. She had grown beyond his Pygmalion image of her, as in Robert Browning's poem about the Pygmalion duke whose created duchess starts to have ideas and tastes of her own, posing a profound threat to her creator. In the Greek myth Galatea is the young girl statue brought to life to fit the image of her male creator and inventor. Pygmalion is a sculptor and King of Cyprus, who fell in love with an ivory statue which he had made and which came to life in answer to his prayer. (American College Dictionary, 1962)

The male muse, who like Pygmalion, looks to his creative woman to be a muse and Galatea for himself, and who can't let go when she builds a life and identity outside of his sphere, is bound to be experienced as demonic. Pygmalion's possessiveness can be felt as the demons lover's sadistic mode of lust. His cravings for control over his lady Galatea can combine with Galatea's own erotic lust for this sadistic aspect of him. Furthermore, as Galatea seeks to fill her own psychic deficits with his voyeuristic intensity and her own manic exhibitionistic response, she can become possessed, as was Camille Claudel. Former spirits merged in artistic transcendence can turn to demonic possession.

However, Suzanne Farrell's psychic and character development was quite different than that of Camille Claudel or of the other women artists described in this book. Farrell did not need a male muse as an extension of herself for developmental reasons. As we have seen, she was not arrested in self-development, and therefore did not require a male muse as a transitional object (see Bach, 1985) as would a narcissistic character. When she left the company and lost Ballanchine, she did not lose half her psyche, unlike an artist such as Camille Claudel who projected out her own psyche, reflecting her psyche back to herself again through her male muse.

Therefore, Farrell was not compelled to go mad or become suicidal like Camille Claudel, Diane Arbus, Anne Sexton, or Sylvia Plath. She was not overwhelmed by a retaliatory rage despite Ballanchine's rejection. She was capable of retaining an objective and empathic perspective towards her male muse, even at the height of her loss. She understood that Ballanchine was jealous and disappointed because of his frustrated desire. In a newspaper interview, Ballanchine stated that he was disappointed in Suzanne Farrell for believing that an artistic and professional decision by Ballanchine about Paul's not dancing a role was personally prejudiced. Suzanne read the interview and persisted, even at such a time, in trying to understand the man behind it, as she had always tried to understand Ballanchine. Her love for Paul did not blind her to Ballanchine and to the hurt feelings he was acting out of. She was not at a primitive psychic level where she needed to split her loved and hated objects. She felt compassion for both her men, despite her own personal suffering. In fact, she increasingly differentiated and made objective the type of love she had for each man. She loved Ballanchine for his uniquely brilliant creativity, and for the love of her he displayed by having inspired her to grow within the field of her creativity. She felt the kind of love any daughter can feel for a father. She also loved Paul as a comrade, dancer, lover, and husband. Like Elizabeth Barrett Browning gaining back her legs from psychic paralysis after leaving her possessive father's house to marry Robert Browning, Farrell could gain a new pair of independent legs if she sustained her loss, and faced and endured the necessary suffering of her break with Ballanchine. Indeed, she was to gain her real independence through the dark night of her loss, but her initial loss was acute and traumatic. Her sense of powerlessness was overwhelming as she left the proverbial "father's house" (see Woodman, 1992) to try and make it on her own. Luckily she had Paul, but both she and Paul were out of work for a significant period of time, never knowing when they would be re-employed. Suzanne Farrell had become so much a part of Ballanchine's world and of Ballanchine's vision, and he a part of her, that despite her psychic independence, her options for employment in the dance world seemed dismal. Nobody in America would hire her for fear, according to Farrell, that they might offend the great George Ballanchine. His rejection of her was equivalent to having a stamp of disapproval on her forehead. She and Paul practically starved! Moreover, everyone in their former social milieu was alienated from them. Suzanne Farrell's own mother remained loyal to Ballanchine and critical of her daughter for not marrying him and for leaving the company. Nevertheless, despite her isolation, Suzanne Farrell was able to retain her sense of humor. She writes with more amusement than bitterness of how she and Paul appeared in the television show "To Tell the Truth," only winning a consolation prize when the set up of "Will Suzanne Farrell's real husband please stand up" was more than transparent. Anytime they could get an opportunity to make a few dollars they took it without pride. Eventually they contemplated teaching dance in the suburbs, even going so far as taking a loan for a house and turning the garage into a dance studio. However, the fire of firsthand creative life blazed strongly within Farrell! She was only in her early twenties. Rather then settle for teaching and for the conservative suburbs, she and Paul renovated an old house in the Adirondacks, sharing in the labor together, a sign of their comradeship—and kept their eyes and ears open for new dance world opportunities. One day opportunity knocked. The famed director of a Belgium ballet company, a theatrical company, Maurice Bejart, made a bid for Suzanne Farrell (not Paul). He offered Suzanne a ballet contract that would involve performing all over the world—particularly in Europe, but even in America. After negotiations about how many toe shoes Suzanne Farrell would have provided for her, she signed on the dotted line. Bejart saw an opportunity to change his predominantly male company and its masculine themes in a new direction by collaborating with Farrell. Being outside of America, he was free of Ballanchine's umbrella, and he could risk his intuition that Suzanne Farrell was a disowned prize to be had. Farrell, for her part, was excited at the prospect of not only dancing on stage again,[2] but also of having solo parts hand-tailored and designed for her. She, in turn, could then yield to a new male muse. Despite the anguish of her disappointment, her capacity to sustain hope in the light of grief allowed her to open to Bejart's newly inspiring influence. Farrell did not submit and become a Galatea. She never lost nor left her core Ballanchine forms, but she did combine them in a new dialectic, as opposed to merger, with the dramatic poses and devices choreographed by Bejart. She also opened herself to new male dance partners. She found another life, and according to her own view, she didn't look back as one addicted, but rather forward as one free to develop from the base of roots of the past. She seems to have adequately internalized her past, so adequately that the internalization was integrated at her core. Ballanchine's ideas and images, combined with her own physical experiments, had become an integral part of her character, her creative process, and her stage presence. She did not have split-off internal objects from her past relations with Ballanchine. Therefore, she was not a victim of pathological mourning. Not having Ballanchine as a demon lover in her psyche, she did not become addicted to intense sadomasochistic engagement that accompanies the demon lover image. She had no need to fill a psychic void (from early traumatic deficits in maternal bonding) with a demonic lover and live within a closed internal system with an anti-libidinal ego structure (Fairbairn, 1952). In fact, Farrell retained and restored a positive internalization of Ballanchine, and lived out in the open in her newfound world. After all had been taken from her, Farrell survived a traumatic separation and recreated a new life of love and creativity. This love and creativity entailed a dialectic between a personal life of intimate relationships and a professional life of creative-process relationships. This latter mode of relationship involved imaginative intimacy with those with whom she shared the creative process.

I conjecture from her capacity to sustain the assaults of adult separation trauma, that original developmental stage separation (of around two years old) had not been traumatic. Her early core personality did not have to submerge itself at that time (Wolff and Kutash, 1991), nor did she have to split the old part of herself off into a malevolent drama with a demonic mother of separation. In addition, she was not compelled to form a primitive idealization of an oedipal father to compensate for this. If she had formed such a primitive idealization of Ballanchine, her involvement with him would have been based on too profound a fusion to allow her the leverage to leave him successfully. Her strength to leave him and yet to retain him psychically as a good object allowed her to move forward with her life.

In the end, Farrell could even return to Ballanchine, her original male muse, with renewed self-worth. This provides a striking contrast to artists who can only return with open wounds, wounds from being torn away from another who has served as a psychic half, a self-extension or transitional object. Five years after working for Bejart, Farrell took another major risk and returned to Ballanchine. While with Bejart, she had danced *Meditation*, the ballet Ballanchine had first choreographed for her. She had been able to do this because Ballanchine had given her the rights to own this ballet. But once tasting the blood of Ballanchine in her dancer's body again, she yearned for more. During her performance of *Meditation* she cried, feeling the old rhythms of Tchaikovsky in dialogue with the forms of Ballanchine. This led to her writing to Ballanchine and then going to see him. Five years after their break, Farrell returned to Ballanchine and hugged him as if they had never parted. They talked. He agreed to have her come back to the New York City Ballet. He also respected her commitment to finish her contract with Bejart. The reunion was harmonious. Yet this harmony belied the psychic changes that both had experienced during this time. They could be so warm and friendly again because Suzanne had managed to live up to the privilege of her newfound freedom by creating a life of her own, apart from Ballanchine. Ballanchine, in turn, had softened over time. Suzanne Farrell had penetrated his being, but he had been able to let her go while letting her imprint remain upon him. He, like Farrell, had shown a capacity to mourn. He had faced his despair and found the capacity to understand and feel grief. He had come to understand that he had been wrong not to allow Farrell her marriage without bitterness and retaliation. When he finally relieved his consciousness of his regrets and self-criticism to Farrell, he was openly sad, contrite, and remorseful, saying that he should have let her have her marriage to another, since she was young and he himself was old. Farrell reacted anxiously to his self-revelations. She still wished to protect him as children wish to protect their parents, and daughters their fathers. "No, no, no!," she protested, as he offered his remorse as a confession. She didn't want him to feel the pain of consciousness. But he needed to truly accept her back as an independent woman, married to another. He had given up the incestuous layer of his desire for her, allowing her to dance the visions in his mind again. She had become a self-extension without being the object of his own oedipal erotic love.

Still, his healing was not complete. Ballanchine never did ask Suzanne's husband, Paul, back to the company. However, even with Paul, there was some reconciliatory rapprochement as he helped him find a position as a choreographer for another ballet company. Perhaps, in doing so, Ballanchine could also pretend that Paul didn't exist for periods of time. Paul was sent to other cities and countries for his work. Yet at the same time there was some realistic acceptance of Paul's place in Suzanne's life. For Suzanne's part, she was able to consciously face her two different forms of love for two different men, Paul and George Ballanchine (Farrell, p. 242).

Farrell was also able to have peace of mind knowing that in, her words, she "could take the Red Shoes off." She made this explicit statement during her work with Bejart. One night she wore Red Shoes, but she was quite clear that "Unlike the ballerina in the movies, I had no trouble getting them off..." (Farrell, p. 210). How should we, as readers of her life story, interpret this statement? This phrase rings out, contrasting Farrell with the other women artists in this book. Obviously, Camille Claudel could not take the Red Shoes off.

Suzanne Farrell could indeed take off her Red Shoes. At no point in her life, despite feelings of loss and rejection, did she feel an inner void from the repetition of some primal abandonment. She always had a self, whatever her losses and disappointments. Her creative work was inspired by her self and by the man she artistically wed, but she never substituted her creative work, nor being on stage, for a sense of selfhood. She always had friendships and relationships that extended beyond the stage. The intensity of her presence on stage originated in a related passion to another, a passion for the male muse who inspired her and for partners she danced with, and for the music she danced to. She showed her love for the music with Ballanchine. It was a force outside her, beyond her. It tempered the tide of passions within. It guided these passions, just as her choreographer's instructions did. She never was consumed by her internal world to the point that her creative intensity became a mania, a mania to exorcise that within. She could face and grieve her internal life, rather than having her internal life take the shape of demons possessing her. She escaped the lust for exorcism and the vomiting up of demonic objects.

Farrell's ability to sustain her positive internalizations is particularly poignant given the unjust possessiveness of Ballanchine. She could view her subjective self, take it in, and objectively observe it. When Farrell lost

Ballanchine, she didn't turn her rejection into an artistic theme of aban-donment and betrayal like the other women artists I describe. Moreover, she also committed to a married life that had its center off the stage of her creative life. She could come and go from stage to marriage, from cre-ativity to the love of an interpersonal matrix and world. She had a sense throughout her life, which she states in her autobiography, that she could and would survive, even though her life seemed to be falling apart at times, particularly when Ballanchine dismissed her. She gained this sense from her mother, who had the strength to pick up and make a new life for herself and her family after her divorce. However, one suspects, as indi-cated, that such learned risk-taking and inner sense of security must have its roots back earlier, during a secure infancy and separation period, in which she could feel psychically held by her mother.

5)

KATHERINE MANSFIELD

A Theory of Creative Process Reparation and its Mode of Failure

THE THEORY OF CREATIVE REPARATION

Writers and artists demonstrate wishes for self reparation in their creative work as well as in the pattern of life that they often weave around their creative work process. However, while they might strive for such self reparation, it is an ambivalent striving that leads to ambivalent dynamics within the course of creative process work. Reparative strivings can be undermined by excessive aggression, which impairs a basic psychic capacity to mourn internal objects, and to integrate internal object relations so that a healthy self integration can take place. Developmental failure, and defensive resistance to mourning disappointments and losses, both play a part in arresting reparative self growth, and in promoting reparative reenactments in the creative work of such writers and artists. In women writers, a demon lover literary theme can serve as symptomatic evidence of unmourned internal objects, which persist as persecutory objects in the psyche.

THE SYMPTOMATIC DEMON LOVER LITERARY THEME

In women writers, a demon lover literary theme can serve as symptomatic evidence of unmourned internal objects, which persist as persecutory objects in the psyche.[1] When the demon lover theme is resolved into themes of three-dimensional whole objects—which involves a general capacity to sustain healthy internal and external object connections—we can see reparative strivings to be at work. This is accompanied by a diminishment of destructive aggression, as seen in symbolic literary form (in terms of characterization, narration, and plot). Such diminishing aggression may be seen after themes of destructive aggression are consciously faced by the artist. Good object experience is seen to survive, which can appear as Klein's "re-creation" of the good after depressive fantasies are faced (Klein, 1940, Segal, 1951). However, if mourning of the original bad objects is not experienced and processed, either in the life or through the work of the woman artist (writer), the artist is vulnerable to a regression into bad object relations and its pathological fixations. With such vulnerability persisting, new disappointments, and particularly traumatic disappointments, will promote a regression into pathological relations with bad internal objects, causing a detachment in external interpersonal relations. Consequently, the demon lover theme will reappear within the creative work of such female artists, and will serve as symptomatic evidence of psychic regression. This can be seen in the case of Katherine Mansfield, the well-known short-story writer and innovator.

KATHERINE MANSFIELD

Born in 1988, in the rough-hewn landscape of New Zealand, Katherine Mansfield passed her first eighteen years in rather lush country, or by the sea, nestled in an extended family in which a grandmother, an aunt, and a group of siblings furnished her constant domain. All was presided over by her large, booming, paterfamilias father, Harold Beauchamp. Her mother languidly presided as queen in the background, controlling with the unseen hand of the invalid, while her husband exerted all the overt control.

Katherine was the third daughter of a young, upwardly mobile couple. Her father, Harold Beauchamp, was a successful businessman, who was invited to the royal court in London as part of a circle of colonial financial entrepreneurs. Harold pictured himself as the provider and protector of his growing family clan. Katherine's mother, Annie Beauchamp, had been married quite young. Although she had four children, she found it easy to withdraw from child-rearing behind the veiled excuse of invalidism. She had some vaguely alluded to "heart condition", which made her dislike for "babies" acceptable (Alpers, p. 3), as long as her mother, Mrs. Dyer, was willing to fulfill her caretaking functions in her stead. Annie Beauchamp's sister, Aunt Belle,[2] also lived with the family. She was later depicted in Katherine Mansfield's stories from a subjective point of view that seemed to engage the author's own adolescent experience of the world. Katherine had two older sisters who snubbed her, and her little brother came along much after she was already the "odd-one-out" in the whole family constellation.

When Katherine Beauchamp (Mansfield) was just one year old, her mother departed for a cross-continental journey, accompanying her husband to England. One of Katherine Mansfield's biographers, Alpers, suggests that the mother may not have been sorely missed, since the grandmother served a nurturing role for the young infant. However, from a psychoanalytic perspective, such a conclusion must be questioned. What role might the mother's detachment from her female baby have played in Katherine's sense of isolation in her family? Katherine wrote about her combined sense of isolation and passionate yearning from quite early on. In fact, Katherine is reported, from quite early in childhood, to have been writing "as if under compulsion" (Alpers, p. 140). During Katherine's adolescence, Alpers notes that "the life and the writing were one" (Alpers, p. 76). From early childhood she began to cultivate her persona as a writer. Her family laughed at her for this early presumption, and one might speculate that her mother played a leading role in this laughter. Such a speculation fits with biographical observations of the mother's attitude of ridicule towards Katherine in general. It is reported that Mrs. Beauchamp's first words to Katherine following a trip abroad were "Well, Kathleen, I see you're as fat as ever." (Alpers, p. 16).

THE TURN TO FATHER

A little girl shunned by a rather cold mother is likely to become excessively fixated on her father. This is particularly true as the erotic passions of the oedipal era inflame the already frustrated cravings for maternal love and acceptance. Although Katherine had nurturance from her grandmother, who she fondly wrote about as Kass's "granny," she did not have a mother who, in Fairbairn's terms, accepted her for herself. The caretaking functions of the mother serve to satiate instinctual needs, but they do not provide the psychological acceptance that is a primary part of mothering. The caretaking mother does not necessarily provide an acceptance of the child's basic love, nor does she necessarily provide acceptance of the child in the child's ambivalent state of loving and hating. The child's subjective experience of self is not necessarily reflected and validated by a caretaking mother.[3]

Without a basic maternal acceptance of the child's self, the child often runs precociously into an oedipal love with her father that fails to be tempered by maternal support and maternal connection. In the case of Katherine Mansfield, her biography suggests that she ran into her oedipal attachment with her father in just this manner. The adolescent pattern that frequently mirrors the oedipal period shows that Katherine's first adolescent romance was precipitous and unmodified in intensity. She threw herself blindly into sexual love, believing her teenage love would last forever, and ended up pregnant and deserted by her lover, Garnet

Trowell. If the impetuosity of her adolescent love does in actuality reflect voracious hunger for her father during the oedipal phase, it is likely that Katherine opened herself to a shame-ridden sense of self injury at this earlier time. Even if her father was accepting of her love, her vulnerability to even minor signs of rejection must have been extreme following the rejection of her early mother. Perhaps this is why the theme of oedipal seduction and abandonment is seen repeatedly in her later literary work, as in her well known tales, "Bliss" and "Je Ne Parle Pas Français". In her life as well, Katherine voraciously seeks the support of father figures, who she then feels betrayed and abandoned by. Later life developments also suggest that Katherine's father's capacity to respond to her with the engagement of oedipal romance was far greater than his capacity to provide support, nurturance, or aspects of self acceptance that she hungered for. During her early thirties, when she had already contracted tuberculosis, there was no support from her father, either financially or emotionally, during her illness. As reported by several biographers, a visit from her father brought only a romantic gesture of picking a bouquet of flowers for her. Even this gesture was marred by her father's accompanying comment in which he addressed her as "the image of her mother all over again" (Alpers, p. 301), seeing only the image of his wife in her.

Yet, during her childhood her father was her more benign parent. Perhaps it is because Katherine's father was less rejecting than her mother that Katherine was free to mock him. When young, she called her father "bottlenose" (Alpers, p. 19), and mimicked his gestures and posture in her self created "mime" performances, staged before her family.

THE DEMON LOVER THEME AND COMPLEX

Wishing for compensatory love from her father, in addition to all the usual demands for erotic desire that a daughter shows a father, it is no wonder that Katherine began to write poetry with prominent "demon lover" themes during her adolescence. During her teenage years, Katherine consciously rejected and devalued her father, contemptuously commenting that he "exudes an undeniable trade atmosphere" (Alpers, p. 39). She viewed her father's manner as gross, and became infatuated with delicate artistic males. In her demon lover poetry, however, she revealed the unconscious desires that she paradoxically had to oppose with her conscious rejection. The following are examples of such poetry:

> When I am with him a preposterous desire seizes me, I want to be badly hurt by him. I should like to be strangled by his firm hands...
> (Alpers, p. 40)

"Leave me alone" said Juliet. She raised her eyes to his face, and his expression caused her to suddenly cease struggling and look up at him dumbly, her lips parted, terror in her eyes,

"You adorable creature" whispered Rudolf, his face close to hers. "You adorable creature—

you shall not go out now…" She felt the room sway and heave. She felt that she was going to faint. "Rudolf, Rudolf, she said, and Rudolf's answer was "At last." (Alpers, p. 38)

An abortion follows, which turns the demon lover rape into death:

She opened her eyes and saw the two beside her. "Ought to join your hands and say bless you?' 'O-o-I want to live,' she screamed. But Death put his hand over her mouth." (Alpers, p. 38)

As the Demon lover turns into the image of death itself, we see a theme seen in the literary work of many well known women writers, writers who suffered from preoedipal failings in mothering. In earlier articles (1985, 1986, 1988, 1989), I have written about this fatal twist of the demon lover theme. The demon lover theme, in which the demon lover turns into death, is reflective of an addictive object tie that turns death into an object image form. The demon lover turns to death in the work of Emily Dickinson, Edith Sitwell, Anne Sexton, and Sylvia Plath. As we see, the adolescent Katherine Mansfield yearned to be hugged with masculine love to the point of suffocation. We can wonder what turned Katherine's oedipal yearnings into early oral cravings that could be fatally passionate. Was the embrace she yearned for from her demon lover a projection of the intensity of her own aggressively-inflamed cravings for love? Was the desired embrace the kind of sensual and psychic embrace she could never get from her mother in infancy? Was Katherine adhesively wedded to her early bad object, as Fairbairn's theory suggests, so that she ended up expressing a death wish that could be seen as evidence of a death instinct by Melanie Klein?

THE LIFE AND THE WORK

Katherine's first published stories were published in New Zealand, after a term of study abroad in England. She returned to her family with an attitude of contempt, characteristic of adolescence, for all that was part of her childhood. Her contempt was most pointedly directed at her father and at her country, the obvious targets for the rejection of an ambivalent love. Yet it was her father who helped her promote her work. Mr. Beauchamp made the initial contact with the magazine editor who published two of her stories. Although her father had no particular interest in the content of her work, her father may have seen her self-proclaimed literary talent as a narcissistically gratifying extension of himself. Also, he may have generally liked to promote success in his children, particularly if it didn't tax his emotional capacities, but merely demanded the kind of practical interventions he was capable of. In any case, Katherine was granted the best payment for her work that she would receive for many years, and it was through her father's effort. Her father also secretly defended her as "an original" when the editor became suspicious that such a young girl could produce such work. During the same period, Mr. Beauchamp also arranged for Katherine to take a tour of the wild New Zealand countryside. It was on this trip that Katherine gained experience that would lead to some of her most unique writing in the future. She gained familiarity with a lush natural atmosphere that would later come alive in the personifications of nature that she depicts in "Prelude" (1918). She also gained knowledge of the native people, the "maori" folk who would be depicted in adult-child dialogue in her story, "The Store."

Her father's role as a benign and even as a "good" object during this period seems significant. Fairbairn (1952) has written about the counterbalancing of an internal bad object with an external object, which is benign merely by virtue of not being all "bad".[4] At this point in Katherine's life, as we can see how the internal situation that had bred the archaic self annihilation of her adolescent demon lover poetry was countered by her real father. Her father's role as promoter, protector, and general all-around benefactor protected her form being locked into the demonic dynamics of a closed off internal world. Later in her life her father would not "survive" as a parental good object in this way,[5] but at this time she could hold her benefactor in contempt with impunity. Her adolescent mode of rejection did not prevent her father from granting her wish to return to England as a would-be writer, nor did it prevent him from making her ongoing stay there possible by providing a monthly allowance of 300 lbs., which she would continue to receive from her father for the remainder of her life.

Alpers (p. 43), the author of Katherine Mansfield's most in-depth biography, has remarked that Katherine Mansfield's whole emotional and creative life revolved around the churning confusion of her love and hate for her country and her love and hate for her father. Katherine's attraction to her father must have led her to repel him as she entered adolescence and needed to separate from him so that she might seek the non-incestuous love of other men. Yet, she was strongly tied to her father, and he would remain in her consciousness as a combined protector and nurturer. When Katherine became ill with tuberculosis and hungered for former paternal care, she imagined her father in the form of a sturdy and enveloping masculine chapeau. He was a chapeau to her in that she wished to be covered by him when she felt threatened and wanted his protection against harm. He was also a chapeau to her in that she wished she could reach into to him to find nurturing financial resources that might sustain her. It is an interesting image, because it is paternally phallic and maternally womb-like at once. The image of the chapeau combines the two psychic levels on which Katherine may have experienced her internal father, a father who was also sought as a compensatory mother when her own mother continued to fail her.

Once returned to England where she had earlier been to school, Katherine flung herself into a love affair with a young male musician, who like herself was still a late adolescent. She followed him on tour and slept with him, presuming that her love was both reciprocated and eternal. She then became pregnant, and was shocked and mortified to find that he abandoned her. Katherine had taken on her boyfriend's family and father as her own. Consequently, her sense of betrayal was harsh when Garnet was advised by his family, and particularly by his father, to throw her off. She must have felt abandoned twice, both by the son and by her surrogate father. Her naiveté at the time seems to reflect the lack of any healthy resolution of her attachment to her father during her oedipal years. Perhaps, her belief in instant and eternal love was also reinforced, not only by adolescent bravado, but also by a need to deny maternal rejection by seeing her father as her life-long unadulterated savior.

Katherine's abandonment by her first male love was quickly followed by a new rejection from her mother. Although her mother had not actually heard of her pregnancy, she heard of some rather passionate female attachments. Perhaps fearing homosexuality in her daughter, Mrs. Beauchamp charged across the ocean and sought to precipitously resolve the situation. When she heard that her daughter had married another man, a Mr. Bowen, who she left the same day as she was wed, Mrs. Beauchamp sought to return Katherine to her husband. When not successful, she took Katherine to a resort in Bavaria, known for its practice of "hosing." In the effete Edwardian era, "hosing" was a common practice of washing off young women with water so that their bodies, as well as their souls, might be kept pure of sexual desire and sexual acts. Katherine's mother's solution was perfunctory, accomplished as quickly and acutely as her immediate willingness to "cut" Katherine out of her will as soon as she returned to New Zealand. The cut was obviously incisive, and probably can be seen as generally symbolic of Katherine's "care" from her mother.

However Katherine could be cutting too, and her contempt could be sharp. She not only dumped a man she married in one day, and declined to sleep with him, but she also became bitter as she resorted to an abortion in the hills of Bavaria. After the abortion, she tried to soothe herself by caring for a young orphan, who she subsequently abandoned without any apparent thought about the effect on the child. Her rage must have been intense for later she claimed that her abortionist used a dirty button hook. In actuality the operation was later discovered to have inflamed a case of gonorrhea, contributing to the body's cultivation of tuberculosis in her last years. With no awareness of her disease, and told by medical men that she had some form of peritonitis for which they medicated her, she returned lame to England.

In London, Katherine performed comic mime acts at society parties, while she endeavored to write. She met John Middleton Murry, who eventually became her husband. This well-known editor, who at that time wished to write himself, could easily be perceived by Katherine as the opposite of her father. He was impractical, intellectual, and literary in orientation. Where her father was protective and dependable, Murry was dependent and sought maternal nurturance as well as financial support from Katherine, who continued to receive an allowance from her father.

Nevertheless, at least in the beginning, Murry was a fairly stable mate from whom Katherine sought rescue. Mansfield and Murry fell together like two Bohemian waifs, attracting the attention of D. H. Lawrence, who became another fickle male in Katherine's erratic life.[6]

Katherine sought continuously to write, but rarely had the time to pursue the kind of short story writing she desired to do (see Tomalin, 1987). Frequently, she wrote serial magazine tales for commercial remuneration so that she might sustain both herself and Murry. Yet, when Murry made money, he declined to share his reserves with her. She and Murry frequently fought, and would repeatedly separate from one another, yearning for the idealized form of the other once having parted. When together they were restless, alternating in their roles of emotional abandoner and betrayer. Often they were itinerant, and Katherine's attempts to do serious writing were hampered by their lack of any real home.

However, there was one brief period of tranquility when Katherine and Murry had some money, and they lived for several months in a villa at Bandol, in France. Even this momentary bliss, which Katherine immortalized in a tale called "Bliss" (1918),[7] was sufficient to bring the artist's natural striving towards self reparation to fruition. Although Katherine and Murry may have failed at interpersonal intimacy, in Bandol they were able to write side by side in relative tranquility. Murry had a job then, and they could have hopes for future comforts.

In such a state of relaxation, Katherine was able to produce her first and primary reparative creative work, a piece that she originally believed might become a novel. The tale was called "Prelude." It was innovative as a short story without plot or narrator. The tale featured character pictures of individuals within Katherine's family. There were also dialogues between the forces of nature, which she had experienced in New Zealand. The characters were three dimensional. They had subjective selves, although the female characters were reflective, while the males were not. Her father was the main male character, and he expanded in this tale with a sense of vitality that her demon lover males all lacked. Virginia Woolf and her husband, Leonard, admired the "Prelude" piece, and they offered to publish it in their Hogarth press collections.

The following is an excerpt from "Prelude" that expresses the childlike vitality of her father:

> The grey mare went very well; Burnell was impatient to be out of the town. He wanted to be home. Ah, it was splendid to live in the country—to get right out of that hole of town once the office was closed; and this drive in the fresh warm air, knowing all the while that his own house was at the end, with its garden and paddocks, its three tip-top cows and enough fowls and ducks to keep them in poultry, was splendid too.
>
> As they left the town finally and bowled away up the deserted road his heart beat hard for joy. He rooted in the bag and began to eat the cherries, three or four at a time, chucking the stones over the side of the buggy. They were delicious, so plump and cold, without a spot or a bruise on them.
>
> Look at those two, now—black one side and white the other— perfect! A perfect little pair of Siamese twins. And he stuck them in his button-hole...
>
> He began to plan what he would do with his Saturday afternoons and his Sundays. He wouldn't go to the club for lunch on Saturday. No, cut away from the office as soon as possible and get them to give him a couple of slices of cold meat and half a lettuce when he got home. And then he'd get a few chaps out from town to play tennis in the afternoon. Not too many—three at most. Beryl was a

good player, too.... He stretched out his right arm and slowly bent it, feeling the muscle.... A bath, a good rub down, a cigar on the verandah after dinner....

A sort of panic overtook Burnell whenever he approached near home. Before he was well inside the gate he would shout to anyone within site: "Is everything all right?" And then he did not believe it was until he heard Linda say? "Hullo! Are you home again?" That was the worst of living in the country— it took the duce of along time to get back.... But now they weren't far off. They were on the top of the last hill;...

It wanted a few minutes to sunset. Everything stood motionless bathed in bright, metallic light and from the paddocks on either side there streamed the milky scent of ripe grass. The iron gates were open. They dashed through and up the drive and round the island, stopping at the exact middle of the verandah.... Linda came out of the glass door; her voice rang in the shadowy quiet. "Hullo! Are you home again?"

At the sound of her his heart beat so hard that he could hardly stop himself dashing up the steps and catching her in his arms.

"Yes, I'm home again. Is everything all right?"...

"Here, half a moment," said Burnell. "Hand me those two parcels." And he said to Linda, "I've brought you back a bottle of oysters and a pineapple," as though he had brought her back all the harvest of the earth.

They went into the hall; Linda carried the oysters in one hand and the pineapple in the other. Burnell shut the glass door, threw his hat down, put his arms round her and strained her to him, kissing the top of her head, her ears, her lips, her eyes. (*Stories* of Katherine Mansfield, pp. 75–78)

Katherine's picture of her father in this narration is refreshing. His love of his life, of his wife, and of his role as paterfamilias in his picture book family comes alive without cynicism. Hints of his immaturity do not mar the vitality of his image here. There is no hint of the earlier demon lover theme. Life, rather than death is evidently triumphant. In Melanie Klein's terms, the good is "re-created" after depressive fantasies have been faced by the artist. The loving capacity is revived as destructive aggression is overcome in a time of a retrospective review of the loved objects from the past.

The bliss at Bandol doesn't last. Murry leaves Katherine to take a job in London, and she feels abandoned. Also, Katherine's brother, Leslie, is killed during his training in the army during the course of World War I. Katherine had just become close to her brother during her stay at Bandol, and his death is crushing to her sense of well-being. Also, Katherine had moved away from Murry when close to her brother, leaving Murry feeling abandoned. His retaliatory rejection of her only leads to her running off to have an affair with another man, a French writer, named Carco. Carco exploits her as an experience, as a story, as a piece of research for his work. She returns to England with the theme of seduction and abandonment reverberating through her, and the theme is highlighted by the war's macabre atmosphere. Alone, with Murry still at a job in London, while she resides elsewhere, unable to mourn her losses on her own. Her internal world seems to turn cold, and her attitude turns bitter, as reflected in her next short story. Entering the self-expressive mode of the creative process again, it is clear that her former reparative strivings have been vanquished by a new sense of despair. Her own rage turns against her in her new tale, illustrating how the loss of the good in her environment commingles with her own aggression to undo the former love and life that flowed forth in "Prelude." Now in "Je Ne Parle Pas Français", we see a pathological mourning state, a fatalistic reenactment of her childhood and adult losses that echoes her adolescent era poetry in its return to the demon lover theme and motif. The following is an encapsulation of "Je Ne Parle Pas Français."

The Frenchman who is central to the piece is a caricature of Français Carco, the Frenchman who abandoned her after a four day love affair. Katherine names him Raoul Duquette. Duquette sits regularly by himself in a shabby cafe, contemplating all those around him with an air of contempt that sustains his inflated view of himself. One day he looks for a piece of writing paper in the cafe, and discovers a piece of blotting paper with the phrase "Je ne parle pas français" written upon it. He is overwhelmed by the strength of his emotional response in reading this phrase and pompously lauds himself with the title of "genius" for feeling so deeply. The author's narration creates the impression that Duquette is continually looking at himself in a mirror as he comments on himself, and in fact there are several scenes in the story in which Duquette is actually before a mirror.

The phrase "Je ne parle pas français" reminds Duquette of a woman named "Mouse," and of the story he has created in his mind as a voyeuristic observer of this woman's fate. In seeing the phrase on the blotting paper, Duquette reflects back to the meeting he had with "Mouse" and with an Englishman named Dick Harmon. As he tells the reader his tale, Duquette elaborates his story with all kinds of pretentious details about himself. As he stresses his plans to be a serious student of English Literature, he reveals that he has so far written three books: "False Coins," "Wrong Doors," and "Left Umbrellas."

Duquette's main occupation appears to be that of a pimp, although he also serves as a male prostitute upon occasion. The story reveals his homosexuality, and his particular homoerotic attraction to Dick Harmon. Dick Harmon, who appears to be the author's portrayal of Murry, is an English writer who Duquette admires and wishes to be accepted by. Despite his lustful attraction to Harmon, Duquette tries to please him by attempting to fix him up with women. Harmon quickly disengages from all these matches with women, and disconcerts Duquette by abruptly leaving for England. Before he does so, however, he drops a photograph out of his wallet, which arouses Duquette's ever active curiosity. It is revealed to be a picture of his mother, reported as a woman of "haggard pride." Her martyred, guilt-provoking attitude towards her son is suggested as an explanation for Harmon's lack of any sustained interest in women.

When Dick Harmon later returns to Paris, he calls Duquette to arrange rooms for him. He brings along a young female waif, whom he refers to as "Mouse." Duquette becomes a salacious voyeur of Mouse's pain as Harmon abandons her rather precipitously. Eluding Mouse on the pretext of writing to his mother, Harmon actually disappears and writes a note in which he excuses himself for not marrying Mouse on the grounds that it would kill his mother.

Left alone with Mouse, Duquette is thrilled by Mouse's pained reaction. He experiences himself as a literary adventurer happening upon a piece of literary meat that he savors for future reference. Amazed at this good fortune, Duquette exclaims excitedly to himself, "These two people are really suffering." Duquette proffers his hand to Mouse, requesting that she confide her inner torment to him. Bereft, Mouse does begin to speak to Duquette, sharing the sense of humiliation that prevents her from returning to England, saying "all my friends think I am married." Then Duquette insensitively asks Mouse if she has "plans" and loses her emotionally. His antennae are alerted, and he says to himself, "I must get her back!" In hopes of doing so, he lures her with the seductive overture that he will come to see her the next day, "to take care of you a little." She accepts because "Je ne parle pas français."

Duquette never returns the next day nor ever after. He himself notes "or else it wouldn't be me."

While Duquette masquerades in a semblance of relatedness and caring, he uses "mouse" as a thing to be observed, alluring and entrapping his victim and then abandoning her. Such behavior in Katherine Mansfield's anti-hero character is reminiscent of Otto Kernberg's description of the pathological narcissist: i.e., as one who exploits another as one would squeeze the juice out of a lemon and discard its remains (see Kernberg, 1975). Such a man can be seen as one aspect of the archetypical demon lover, while Harmon is the more passive-aggressive variety of the abandoning and exploitative male demon. Mouse is seduced and abandoned twice in a day, by two different men. She serves as an archetypical female victim. So it can be seen in this story that Katherine Mansfield returns to the villain/victim split of her adolescent "demon lover" poetry. Once again sadism triumphs over the vitality of love and life.

Katherine's use of the creative process here might be characterized in Melanie Klein's terms as an attempt to face "depressive phantasies," phantasies in which aggressive forces within the author override any positive strivings towards love, self-healing, and mourning of lost love objects (see Segal, 1952). However, even though the author may be attempting to face her own destructive aggression, she is also engaged in a retaliatory defensive reaction. She is most consciously identified with the female victim, and seeks to indite the men she feels victimized by. Also, as Duquette represents an aspect of Katherine's own self, we see Katherine encased in the manic defense attitudes of contempt, control and triumph, (see Segal, 1964) which forestall any ability to feel the actual anguish of her pain. Without conscious awareness of her pain, Katherine cannot feel the sadness of her losses, and she cannot mourn. Her anger, which is also fundamental to the mourning process, is also shielded by her manic mode of cynical satire. She externalizes her internal bad objects in her work, but she fails to face them in failing to feel them from within. As she runs from the affects of her anger and her aggrieved despair in loss, she fails to surrender herself and to yield to her anguish. Her guilt seems to block her as she unconsciously identifies with the sadistic male, who is a part of her as much as the victim child-self. In failing to mourn, she fails to repair herself, and she perpetuates a blocked anger that is disguised in masochistic modes of self-destruction. This can be seen in her actions in her life as she becomes ill with tuberculosis. However, both her life and her creative work continue to express the ambivalent striving to repair herself that she defeats with her defensive attitudes and her internally directed aggression.

Katherine sends her father a copy of "Je Ne Parle Pas Français." Her father is filled with disgust and contempt. He throws the story behind his fireplace in a rage, and declares it to be "not even clever" (Alpers, p. 313). Why did Katherine send him this particular tale? Although the story does come to be seen by literary critics as a technical masterpiece, it also is filled with perversion and sadism to such an extent that she might expect

it would repel her father. Although consciously seeking approval by send-
ing some of her work to her father, it appears that she was more unconsciously seeking punishment for the anger she would not consciously
allow herself to feel towards her father. As she became ill with tuberculosis her father failed to aide her. Her husband also failed to aide her—not
only financially—but he refused to be with her when she had to move to
the Italian riviera for a rest cure. Her masochism can be seen in her refusal
to enter a sanitorium, as well as in her behavior towards her father.
Katherine's anger towards the "father figure" men in her life was building.
Both her life and her work reflect the battle between this anger and her
wishes for self repair and paternal forms of support and affection.

Katherine's creative process shows the ambivalence of her struggle.
Following "Je Ne Parle Pas Français," Katherine returns to the form of
writing she began with "Prelude." Again in "At the Bay" her father
appears as a subjectively alive character. Yet, now he is more infantile.
The male here is no longer a villain, but he is a bit of a buffoon. He
expresses infantile reactions to his wife, turning his wife into a mother.
The father's vitality becomes overshadowed by his inadequacy. We can
see this as a regression in Katherine Mansfield's internal world from the
time of "Prelude." However, we also see some attempt to recover the three
dimensional human characterization that was lost much more fully in "Je
Ne Parle Pas Français." Interpersonal dialogue reappears, whereas it was
mostly lost in the perpetual narcissistic self reflection of "Je Ne Parle Pas
Français." The author is attempting to regain the life and heart of
"Prelude," but her insecurities and anger show themselves to be as powerful as the love that she seeks to regain and to repair herself with. Her
failure to mourn through her work shows itself in these effects, symptomatically shown in the character of her father, as he appears in "At the
Bay":

> Stanley was half-way up the path before he saw Linda. "Is that you,
> darling?:
>   "Yes, Stanley."
>   He leapt across the flower-bed and seized her in his arms. She
> was enfolded in that familiar, eager, strong embrace.
>   "Forgive me, darling, forgive me!" stammered Stanley, and he
> put his hand under her chin and lifted her face to him.
>   "Forgive you?" smiled Linda. "But whatever for?"
>   "Good God! You can't have forgotten," cried Stanley Burnell.
> "I've thought of nothing else all day. I've had the hell of a day. I
> made up my mind to dash out and telegraph, and then I thought the

wire might not reach you before I did. I've been in tortures, Linda!"

"But Stanley," said Linda, "what must I forgive you for?"

"Linda!"—Stanley was very hurt—"didn't you realize—you must have realized—I went away without saying good-bye to you this morning? I can't imagine how I can have done such a thing. My confounded temper, of course. But—well"—and he signed and took her in his arms again—"I've suffered for it enough to-day!"

"What's that you've got in your hand?" asked Linda. "New gloves? Let me see."

"Oh, just a cheap pair of wash-leather ones" said Stanley. "I noticed Bell was wearing some in the coach this morning, so, as I was passing the shop, I dashed in and got myself a pair. What are you smiling at? You don't think it was wrong of me do you?"

"On the contrary, darling," said Linda, "I think it was most sensible."

She pulled on one of the large, pale gloves on her own fingers and looked at her hand, turning it this way and that. She was still smiling.

Stanley wanted to say, "I was thinking of you the whole time I bought them." It was true, but for some reason he couldn't say it. "Let's go in," said he. (pp. 132–133, *Short Stories*)

The author captures an aspect of her father here that is appealing in its vulnerability, but which also shows an insecure and immature nature. It is obvious to any reader familiar with Katherine Mansfield's biography that Stanley Burnell is Harold Beauchamp. Katherine paints her father in "At the Bay" as less like a husband and more like a small boy who seeks constant reassurance from the mother he seeks in his wife. Katherine's current disappointments with her father may have slanted her vision of the man in this direction, as her internal father is redefined and recreated in the "transitional world"[8] of her creative work. However, Katherine may also be finding an aspect of her father here that she longed for in her own husband as Murry continued to fail her as someone to depend on. Her father's enthrallment with his wife, although he idealizes her, and may not see her at all realistically, does demonstrate a capacity to care in a day to day living situation. Such caring may be the author's contrast to the lack of care she felt from her husband, Murry. Murry could idealize her from afar, and after her death eulogized her continually as a great author. Yet he was unable to stay by her side when she needed him, and this was most apparent as she became ill and needed to stay abroad in Italy. Katherine imagines what it would have been like if Murry did come to the continent with her, in a story entitled, "The Man Without a Temperament." She sees her husband as detached and elusive throughout this tale, his emotional abandonment being prominent when he attempts to be physically present.

Katherine returns to the demon lover theme again in her reaction to her husband's abandonment. In her letters to Murry, she writes a poem entitled, "The New Husband":

> Someone came to me and said
> Forget, forget that you've been wed
> Who's your man to leave you be
> Ill and cold in a far country?
> Who's the husband—who's the stone
> Could leave a child like you alone?...
> Ha! Ha! Six months, six weeks, six hours
> Among these glittering palms and flowers
> With Melancholy at my side
> For my nurse and for my guide
> Despair—and for my footman Pain
> —I'll never see my home again. (Meyers, pp. 192–193)

Again Katherine portrays herself as a helpless child victim here as she waits for male rescue, only to be vanquished by despair, and ultimately by death. Perhaps unconsciously she is returning to an early childhood abandonment, with a maternal and paternal abandonment intermingling. The abandonment feelings from the past are triggered as she looks to her husband for both emotional and financial support, both of which he fails to offer her. Katherine's rage at her husband and at her father combine, as seen in the letters she writes to her female friend Ida Baker (also called L. M.). She writes of her husband's failure to offer even her car fare from a medical operation (Meyers, pp. 195–196). To Murry himself, she writes of her father's abandonment: "We shall not get another sou out of Father" (Alpers, p. 301).

Feeling abandoned by her father, and taking some relative's comment to mean that he even regretted rendering her her normal allowance at this point in her life, Katherine withdraws into a "long and painful silence" (Alpers, p. 301) in relation to her father. During her silence, unable to write to him, she nevertheless expresses her anger in her characterization of her father in her writing. Although "The Stranger" was written two years prior to this particular silence, it illustrates how Katherine devalues her father, going beyond the infantile quality in "At The Bay" to that of a more narcissistic figure. She herself writes that her portrayal of him in this tale is an expression of her "hatred" (Alpers, p. 350). One of Katherine's biographers, Meyers, writes the following of Katherine's portrayal of Harold as John Hammond in "The Stranger":

> In 'The Stranger' (1921)—Katherine's version of Joyce's 'The Dead'—John Hammond, wealthy, successful, self-important, pompous yet terribly insecure, waits impatiently for his wife's ship to dock in New Zealand. He is desperately eager to regain and possess Janey, and childishly jealous of her friends aboard ship, of the doctor and the captain, and even of his children's letters to their mother—of anything that distracts her attention from himself. (Meyers, p. 214)

Consumed with her anger, portraying a negative view of her father, Katherine cannot repair herself. She is left desperately longing for her father's love. Her solution is to turn her anger against herself as she seeks communication with her father again. She writes to her father, asking him if it is true that he begrudges her allowance. Her father is insulted by such a suspicion and responds sharply to defend himself. This leaves Katherine even more threatened. Seemingly seeking to assuage her father's anger, she pleads for his love, calling herself a "black sheep" and recriminating herself for being "an extraordinarily unsatisfactory and disappointing child" (Alpers, p. 349). Katherine now comes to speak of her adolescent rejection of her father as a sin, becoming overcome with guilt. In Fairbairn's terms, Katherine employs a "moral defense," accusing herself of being the guilty party to protect her image of her father, when the loss of him would seem intolerable.

Katherine declines deeper into the disease that is consuming her from within at this point. Her creative work is failing to be an adequate container for her grief, for no mourning can proceed as long as her hatred is outweighing her capacity to love. Her work becomes increasingly marked by destructive inner forces and by the manic defense of cynicism, reflective of her unspoken despair. Perhaps we can speculate here with Joyce McDougall (1980, p. 346) that the person vanquished with the disease of tuberculosis has failed to open inwardly to the experience of grief, and instead opens their lungs to the ingestion of tubercular bacilli.

Without loving connections with others, Katherine's loving capacity declines, so ultimately she cannot truly mourn nor genuinely repair herself. Unable to mourn and repair, Katherine is left seeking magic solutions, or what Klein calls manic reparation. She engages in a frantic search for idealized father figures from whom she can seek rescue as her own father fails to "survive" as a "good-enough" figure within her. As she begins, in Alpers (p. 350), terms, "gathering up her father figures," she wanders from one quack doctor to another. During the time when there is no communication between her and her father, and she feels most abandoned, she turns to the infamous charlatan, Manoukhin (Alpers, pp. 350 and 358), who promises to cure her of her tuberculosis by irradiating her spleen. Murry is detached and ineffective in his attempts to stop her. She ends up debilitated to the point of breakdown, listening to her heart pounding in a now fragile and burdensome body that she cannot sustain:

> It's pretty frightful—the loneliness, the noise of one's heart pounding away—and the feeling that this is ALL there is. I can't master it. (Meyers, p. 192)

The sicker she becomes, the more she is compelled to write. Her failure to mourn through her work leaves her with a compulsion to express whatever she can while time is short. Yet, her compulsion results in reenactment as mourning fails to be tolerable. Although her last stories have been lauded, they are colored by bitter despair. They recreate the demon lover theme that is so characteristic of her failed reparation, and of her original internal bad objects. She begins to write about herself with the metaphor of "the-fly-in-the milk jug," and creates a story entitled, "The Fly" (late 1921). The fly has no power against the arbitrary and malignant forces in the world and gets helplessly squashed. This victimized self image becomes on ongoing motif, and she quotes Shakespeare's "As flies to wanton boys are we to the gods;/They kill us for their sport" (King Lear, IV.l) and from Blake's "The Fly": 'For I dance,/And drink, and sing,/Till some blind hand/Still brush my wing,'..." (Meyers, p. 234). The "fly" in Katherine Mansfield's internal and transitional worlds can also be seen as a female who is squashed in her story by a large male bank manger, who can be seen as analogous to her father, her persisting internal masculinized demon.

Katherine was becoming too ill to write, but she writes a last story, called "The Canary" and a last poem, called "The Wounded Bird." The story speaks of death, as she writes about a lonely woman's dead canary. The demon lover's theme of movement into death as a subjective persona can be seen to be carried over into thoughts about loss, death, and loneliness in those she sees as fragile and helpless. Her own death was approaching. In "The Wounded Bird" again there is the theme of a helpless and yet special winged creature being struck down. There continues to be no mourning resolution, no recreation of self through loving connection—

only the unresolved loss of psychic wounding that becomes physical decay.

Despair conquers Katherine Mansfield. She is left split internally between self components that are like Fairbairn's victimized libidinal ego and self components that are akin to Fairbairn's anti-libidinal ego, or "internal sabateur." The "exciting and rejecting" objects that she is drawn to continually lead to a new sense of disappointment, as her own way of relating remains fixed in a closed system of seeking male rescuers as she once sought her father's rescue from her mother. Within her writing we continue to see the basic victim/villain drama of the demon lover theme. As masculine demons subjugate and annihilate the female self victim components within her, Katherine's writing resonates with the demon lover themes of Sylvia Plath's *Ariel* poetry, written just prior to her suicidal self annihilation (see also Anne Sexton, Kavaler 1989).

Increasingly ill at thirty-four from both tuberculosis and the attempted magical medical cures, Katherine is about to succumb to suicidal despair when she has one last urge to grasp onto a father figure for rescue. His name is Giurdieff. He is a Russian eccentric, with spiritual and philosophical teachings, who is in the process of establishing a communal living situation for his followers in England. Katherine has yearned continually for a father figure to trust. Her own father left her alone in her illness, so that she was condemned to spend much of the precious time left to her, not on her art, but on the writing of serial magazine stories so that she might survive and pay her medical bills. Guirdieff was the opposite of her father in many ways. He was careless about money, and he offered her pragmatic advice with spiritual inspiration. He encourages her to "live in her body again." She helps in the kitchen, watches others dance, and is told to breathe in the scent of cow dung each day as a curative measure. Although his advice was far from curative, he did offer Katherine some hope during the last few months of her life.

Katherine Mansfield dies on the day that Murry comes to visit her at the Guirdieff institute. Filled with false hopes that she is becoming healthy, she runs up a flight of stairs and encounters her last and fatal wound, the bleeding hemorrhage of uncured tuberculosis. She dies at thirty-four, in 1922, just as many legitimate medical doctors had warned her. They warned her that she had only four years to live if she did not go to a sanitorium, and she would not put her writing aside to go to such a sanitorium, particularly without her father's financial and emotional support. She had found a French doctor who indulged her wishes and advised her to not enter a sanitorium on the grounds that she could not live without her writing. Her choice to follow such advice was fatal, and again it was symptomatic of her wish to idealize male father figures who always were bound to fail her, particularly as she used them not only to reenact an internal psychic drama, but also to avoid the truth about herself and her life. She endowed her father figures with manic magic powers, and failed to face realities that could have led to limited but to true reparative developments in her life. Her work reflected her failure to face such realities, to truly mourn the losses involved, and to achieve self repair. Her work also became idealized, being seen as a source of paternal love that she could never ultimately acquire. She paid the price of dying in four years rather than taking time out for a sanitorium and possibly living longer.

After her death, Murry "forgot" to pay the costs for her burial and her father had to complete the deed. Her father also, within a short period of time, made a large donation to the arts in New Zealand with Katherine in mind. If he had spent even a fraction of this donation on Katherine, herself, during her period of illness, his daughter might have been spared the frantic desperation of her last years, and might have been able to write and to live more. Both Katherine's husband and father made grand gestures in eulogy of her after her death, but these gestures were marred by the nature of the defensive idealization involved. Their grand gestures of recognition were symptomatic of the lack of true understanding of Katherine as the woman that really existed behind any image. As in "Je Ne Parle Pas Français," Katherine's writing revealed the fatality of viewing oneself and others through images rather than through true affective contact. She herself lived much of her life hidden behind the persona of a writer when she could not face the realities of relationship within her life. Yet, stories such as "Prelude" and "At the Bay" were attempts to get beyond images and to come out in the open. She never got the support from the men to whom she looked for love to be able to follow through on this, and originally she never got such support from her mother. In light of her own struggle to use writing to become real and whole, it is ironic that Murry publicized her after her death as a "genius," which only belittled her actual accomplishments and revealed Murry's love for a reflection of his own idealized image rather than for Katherine herself. D. H. Lawrence criticized Murry for creating a mockery out of Katherine's genuine talent by casting it in grandiose dimensions. Regarding these events, the precipitant causes of Katherine Mansfield's demon lover literary theme appear to have continued even after her death.

SUMMARY

Katherine Mansfield is one example of a female writer who ultimately fails in strivings towards self reparative integration through the course of her creative process. Her failing is symptomatically seen in the emergence and reemergence of the demon lover theme within her literary work. The demon lover theme is both a literary motif and a psychodynamic complex. As a psychodynamic complex it is a manifestation of splitting processes that continually disrupt whole object assimilation, causing villain/victim dramas to be enacted both in the life and the work of the female writer. Such enactment, which may be precipitated by new disappointments, is proposed to be colored by reenactments of early preoedipal and oedipal internal object relations, with the preoedipal and oedipal levels being combined.

6)

THE GENIUS AND SORROW
OF VIRGINIA WOOLF,
PART I

Virginia Woolf lived her real life within the realm of her creative work. Her life outside her work was impoverished, as she proclaimed repeatedly in her volumous diary writing and letters. Those interpreting her diary and letters are many. Chief among them is Shirley Panken, whose psychobiography (1987) of Woolf offers a penetrating in-depth analysis of her creative work.

Woolf's inner life, as expressed in her work, was rich, complex, visionary, and yet filled with the most profound despair. Nevertheless, until her suicide in 1941 at the age of fifty-nine, Woolf had many brilliant and productive years.

But throughout, her compulsion to express her inner voice was a dual-edged sword. This compulsion led to the extraordinary effort and craftsmanship that brought realization to the life force within her, a force which she experienced as procreative, pregnant, and gestative—barred from biological pregnancy by the circumstances of her life. Yet it also led to the creation of a private world that displaced communication and contact with those she so desperately needed, disrupting her potential ability to sustain an ego-related self through interpersonal life.

VIRGINIA WOOLF AS A GENIUS AND SURVIVOR

Virginia Woolf has left behind a rich body of literature that haunts readers with questions about the essence of identity, the meaning of life, and the many-sided nature of love and death.

Woolf was born in 1882 into a distinguished literary family. The novelist William Thackery was her uncle. Her father, Leslie Steven, a well-known English intellectual, was the compiler of encyclopedic volume of biographies for the Dictionary of National Biography. Her mother, Julia Stephen, wrote and published stories for children. But (while their position in English cultural society was secure) their marriage was a troubled one—for Woolf's mother had never mourned the death of her first husband. Perhaps because of this inability to mourn, she withheld her love from her second husband, who, possibly in retaliation, often dominated and bullied her into comforting and appeasing him. Despite such chafing frictions and underground hostilities, Virginia's parents presented a united front in valuing literary pursuits. Dinnertime usually became an occasion for sharing quotations and reading aloud passages from literary texts. This intellectually welcoming environment allowed Virginia's potential genius to develop. The psychological environment proved more difficult to navigate. Against a background of maternal tantalization and, simultaneously, emotional unavailability, which has been extensively documented by biographers (DeSalvo, 1989, Bond, 1988, and Panken, 1987), Woolf honed her literary craft until she felt ready to emerge from a cocoon of silence. Her nine major novels[1], essays, such as "A Room of One's Own," prolific diary entries, and letters attest to the power of her yearning to find a voice, and to create an identity that she was unable to develop in her interpersonal relations.

In Woolf's daily life her communication with the people she wished to be most intimate with was, for a number of reasons, blocked. Direct contact and communication was particularly blocked by her inability to process her aggressive impulses. Woolf was, therefore, compelled to reenact failed patterns of connection that had begun during toddlerhood. In the Victorian nursery where she spent her childhood, she was famous for her "purple rages." Although they may have been her way of controlling others, these rages also seem to have been in reaction to the impotency she felt as a younger sibling mercilessly teased, ridiculed, and scapegoated by her older siblings—Vanessa and Thoby. Because Woolf failed to contain and communicate her aggression towards them, it apparently remained at a primitive level, in which articulation is blocked by overwhelming murderous rage. This generally occurs in cases of developmental arrest—as its moves towards autonomy and individuated authenticity of self are blocked through lack of support during critical separation phases of development.

Numerous biographers describe a childhood fight between Thoby and Virginia. In the midst of it, Virginia suddenly put down her arms and let Thoby pummel her with his fists. The biographers have interpreted this response as signaling the early development of a masochistic pattern.

Woolf writes in a diary note that she said asked herself at the moment, "What's the use?" In the interaction, then, she let all the aggression—her own and Thoby's—be turned against her: similarly, within her own internal world, throughout her life she actively turned her aggression against herself.

By adolescence, Woolf was well-schooled in the suppression and repression of her aggressive impulses. When her aggression did surface, it consequently erupted as part of psychotic episodes and manic reactions to depressive self-suppression. Her mother's death in 1895, when Virginia was thirteen, precipitated the first of her so-called "breakdowns." The second was in 1915, which she referred to as her "madness." During them, she heard voices and hallucinated. Her usual frenetic style became a florid mania, imbued with uncontrolled rage. She didn't seem to even believe she could communicate directly what the rage was about. Especially during her breakdowns, her writing offered the only means to express it. But her family responded to her unstable condition by following the advice of doctors who recommended she undertake pragmatic tasks, be closely supervised, and spend very little time alone. The precious solitude that allowed her to find herself—to the extent that she could within her inner life, through creative work—was, during this period, totally closed to her. It was at this period that Woolf was encouraged to live in the background of other people's lives. The time following Woolf's explosive reaction to her mother's death became in other ways as well a time of forced compliance to regimented suppression. For example, she was expected to accompany her older half-sister Stella on daily errands, and to be Stella's chaperone during her engagement to Jack Hill.

However, unlike Stella whose whole personality was compliance, Virginia Woolf's compliance became a mere false veneer behind which she lived a life of active imagination. Although her opposition to those who tried to control and direct her behavior was sometimes expressed in manic and psychotic episodes—when repressed yearnings and aggression could no longer be contained by a fragile self—these explosions were not her only route of escape from a family and patriarchal society, that denied emotional communication. Her other route to self-expression was modified and designed by her intellectual capacities. Even though her solitude was restricted after her breakdown, eventually she was permitted greater freedom to write. The written language became her vehicle for expressing her yearnings, her self-articulation, and the realities of her internal conflicts and predicaments. At least in part because of her genius, Woolf did not end up like her half-sister Stella, who died shortly after marriage, or like her other half-sister Laura, who was placed in a mental institution when the family perceived her to be emotionally unmanageable. Virginia Woolf, like her sister Vanessa, who became a painter, was a creative artist. For Woolf, art became the scene of an internal battle between the part of her that yearned for connection in the interpersonal world and her defensive and aggressive forces that fought against such connection because it threatened a fragile sense of autonomy. Without this avenue of communication for her differentiation and aggression, her intense need to connect with others would always remain a threat to her.

Woolf's blocking of interpersonal communication is revealed in a multitude of incidents reported by biographers. In *Who Killed Virginia Woolf?*, Elma Bond pinpoints one episode in which Woolf denied her anger at her sister Vanessa by flattering and colluding with Vanessa's rejection of her, a verbal repetition of her masochistic collusion with Thoby when he hit her. Virginia never criticized Vanessa because she needed to idealize her to avoid a feared separation with a transferential mother figure, a tactic she must have learned with her real mother. Because she could not express her anger directly, murderous rage fantasies appeared in her work. Thus, at the cost of keeping outwardly intact the interpersonal connection with her sister, Woolf compromised herself internally. More specifically, she sacrificed her potential for differentiation and for healthy developmental mourning, the two processes that could allow an individuated self to emerge into the interpersonal world.

Panken (1987, p. 204) has interpreted Woolf's pursuit of Vanessa as a craving to be suckled at the breast. Both Panken and Bond report innumerable occasions when Virginia sought substitute mothering from Vanessa after her real mother or a transferential mother (husband or female lover), became unavailable. Vanessa always failed her—distancing when Virginia most craved her presence. (Julia was her mother too, and Vanessa had her own reasons for detachment.) But what is striking is how Virginia sacrificed her feelings in order to idealize Vanessa, clinging to an image of her sister as a potential "earth mother." Virginia humbly writes to her, after Vanessa has been unavailable, "You very nearly had me on you; and then what a curse you would have found it! ... your perfect globe would have been smashed" (Bond, 1987, p. 104). Bond argues that Virginia is self-deprecating and masochistically self-denying in order to merge with Vanessa's viewpoint, when she can't merge with Vanessa. By never risking an open expression of anger and instead defending against her frustration with idealization of Vanessa, Woolf's sister is experienced as the object of all her hungers—for affection, primitive nurturance, feminine identification, and for pregnancy.

But her rage is not totally repressed. In her literary work there are abundant examples of oral aggression and of cold, stony, and rejecting mother figures. But even in her work, she fails to successfully face her aggression. Yet, she does give voice to the sources of her vulnerability and to those unifying connections that allow her to build and rebuild a sense of self despite the massive onslaught of her split-off aggression, with its internal bad object situation.

EARLY DEVELOPMENT

For her biographers, Woolf's early infancy has become a source of controversy. Bond, whose psychobiography is influenced by the theories of Margaret Mahler, argues that Woolf had a sensually resplendent and highly fulfilling engagement with her mother during the first five months of infancy, the stage Margaret Mahler has described as symbiosis. Bond maintains this notion despite acknowledging that Woolf's mother stopped breast feeding Virginia at ten weeks. Julia Stephen did so with the approval of her husband who wanted to spare his wife. Another biographer, Louise DeSalvo (1989) speaks of the probability that Julia was suffering from a postpartum depression. In addition, Bond as well as other biographers suggest that Virginia Woolf was not a wanted child. Not only was she an accident, but she was born to a mother who, if she desired a child, hoped for a boy.[2]

DeSalvo, Bond, and Panken note Julia Stephen's generally depressed state as she compulsively drove herself to serve all the needs of the other. First and foremost, Julia Stephen served her own mother. Then came her first husband, whom she adored, and who was perhaps a replacement for the father. Her father had been far away from the family for seven years, from the time Julia was two to the time she was nine. She defended her pathological mourning with a renewed sense of obligation to serve her new husband, as well as to minister to the sick children of the community's poor population. Frequently absenting herself from her own home, she visited these families on an ongoing basis. This was the mother whom Woolf called "The Angel in the House." She was a mother who served the needs of others, as a way of maintaining a symbiotic tie to her own mother from whom she had only minimally separated.

Despite Julia Stephen's depression, an opportunity for symbiosis with an infant may have brought her alive. Bond is emphatic: "When the symbiotic period is joyful (as seems certain in the couple of Virginia and her mother) the infant and mother have close body contact and bonding. This prepares the child of four or five months to follow normal developmental processes that lead away from mother." As support for her interpretation, Bond (p. 24) refers to Woolf's image of her mother in *Moments of Being*:

My mother would come out on her balcony in a white dressing gown. There were passion flowers growing on the wall; they were great starry blossoms with purple streaks and large green birds.... If I were a painter I should paint these first impressions in pale yellow, and silver, and green. Everything would be large and dim; and what was seen would be at the same time heard. (1967, quoted in Bond, p. 66)

This does indeed sound like a lush memory or the vivid radiance of a mutually rewarding symbiotic enthrallment. But, the visual enthrallment could also be a substitute for direct body contact, a displaced form of a visually ingesting mother, when responsive and visceral holding is minimal. Bond's argument for an enthralling symbiosis, in which she views the infant author, Virginia, as intoxicated (p. 24), would be more convincing if similar memories and images appear in Woolf's writing. Instead, in novel after novel there are vivid images of oral rage and insatiable oral cravings.

For example, Panken (1987) notes the many examples of split-off oral aggression that surface in dissociated eruptions throughout Woolf's work. In her first published novel, *The Voyage Out* (1915), the paranoid terrors punctuate heterosexual interludes between Terence and Rachel. While sharing a moment of intimacy with Rachel, Terence imagines her throwing him off a high cliff into the sea. Rachel, in turn, visualizes Terence and her aunt Helen as two parent figures who threatening strangulation and suffocation. In *Night and Day* (1919) and *Between the Acts* (1941), there are images of stabbing oneself or another with a knife. In *The Years* (1937), a man suddenly bites his own thumb in a fit of rage. The oral quality of such murderous rage is even more evident in *Between the Acts*, in which Woolf writes of characters who "gobble in the gutter" (1941, p. 3). (At the end of her life, in 1940, faced with the loss of her literary audience, Woolf starts to gobble down her food (Panken, p. 259), thereby yielding to an intense and insatiable oral craving that she had rebelled against with anorexia after her mother's and father's deaths in 1895 and 1904). An image of a snake attempting to swallow a toad in *Between the Acts* (see Panken, pp. 246–247), is another such image which will be addressed more specifically later on.

Her oral rage imagery suggests that Woolf experienced her weaning at ten weeks as traumatically abortive, and, in actuality, it may have deprived her not only of a maternal breast, but of all nurturant holding, as the nursemaids she was left with for feeding merely propped up a bottle for her, and removed themselves (DeSalvo, p. 116). How enthralling were

her first five months in light of this? Panken (1987, p. 256) and Louise
DeSalvo (1989, p. 102) speak of Woolf's one ecstatic memory of lying in
her mother's lap in the nursery at the family's country home in Cornwall,
and hearing the waves of the ocean. It may have been a screen memory
of earlier ecstasy. This memory stood out for Woolf, DeSalvo suggests,
precisely because she was relieved to feel safe and secure, when normally
she felt unprotected. But, this same memory later appears in Woolf's writing colored, not by ecstasy, but by terror (Panken, 1987). Woolf's placement of this ecstasy memory with one of terror, Panken asserts, could be
related to a primal scene fantasy based on Woolf's hearing noises from
her parents' bedroom. But I think Panken may be wrong here, as De-
Salvo's descriptions suggest that the terror was even more primitive and
pervasive in Woolf's early life. Woolf's novels seem to me to be filled with
self-images of dissolving, being washed away, of having no substance, of
being open to perennial attacks. All this calls into question Bond's theory
that Woolf's five-month symbiotic phase was pleasureful. Still her mother's allure may stem from this stage, causing Woolf to crave throughout
her life merger experiences with Vanessa, at one time with Leonard, and
at alternating times with her female lover, Vita Sackville-West.

The differentiation phase that occurs at five months, Bond notes
(1989), probably presented serious difficulties for Woolf. During this
phase, she may have felt held back by a clinging mother. Bond bases this
idea on Woolf's description of Mrs. Ramsay in *To The Lighthouse*, who is
based on Julia Stephen and loves to carry a baby in her arms. Woolf even
describes Mrs. Ramsay as signing with disappointment at the thought of
her children growing up. From this, Bond deduces that Woolf's mother
must have clung to her, attempting to hold her back at the point of differentiation. Woolf then felt compelled to fight her mother's clinging. Her
practicing period, therefore, was characterized by a manic frenzy of liberation. Woolf's difficulties with differentiation are expressed in her novels, in which she dwells in detail on self-definition and basic differentiating
characteristics. *The Waves* is her most evocative novel about the strivings
and conflicts of the differentiation period. Woolf writes (p. 83):

> How curiously one is changed by the addition, even at a distance,
> of a friend. How useful an office one's friends perform when they
> recall us. Yet how painful to be recalled, to be mitigated, to have
> one's self adulterated, mixed up, become part of another. As he
> approaches I become not myself but Neville mixed with some-
> body—with whom?—with Bernard? Yes, it is Bernard, and it is to
> Bernard that I shall put the question, Who am I?

Woolf refers to each of the novel's six characters as an individual wave. Kelly (1973) writes, in *The Novels of Virginia Woolf, Fact and Vision*:

> So most of the six characters, who have begun to discover their individual identities, have reached that point of selfhood at which they can begin to have some effect on others.... The six characters, too, are concentrating on self-definition and are not yet ready to form a harmonious pattern with others. This period of separation, as we have seen before, is necessary if the individual is to learn to build visionary unity in a disordered factual world. Unless one is aware of division, how can one hope to create a union? So the scene of beach and garden, having emerged from the unity of unconsciousness, has splintered into distinct segments. Inside the house, whose rooms represent the furnishings of the individual mind, everything is still softly amorphous, as if the china of the plate flawed and the steel of the knife were liquid" (*The Waves*, 194). The first step into reality is an awareness of the otherness of the world that surrounds one. Then comes an understanding of the self. (Kelly, p. 157)

Bond's assessment of Woolf's early mothering relies largely on the loss and disappointment she believes Woolf experienced during the rapprochement stage. Woolf's difficulties with differentiation and her inability to effect a full ecstatic release into a "love affair with the world" at the practicing stage, made for a crisis in the rapprochement stage, for here, Woolf returned home to mother, only to find "nobody" there. Expecting to crawl back into her mother's lap, Woolf discovers her baby brother Adrian has appropriated this space. Her mother seems distracted from her, without any interest. Woolf is then caught between the normal need of a child at this stage for autonomy and her fear of the anguished isolation independence would bring because it would mean the loss of all support and nurturance from her mother. Following this line of thought, Bond views Woolf's depression as largely reactive to her mother's unavailability. But what Bond does not remark on is that the unavailability continues. Woolf confided in an abandoned autobiographical piece, called "A Sketch of The Past," (reported by De Salvo, p. 117) how she never had a moment alone with her mother without finding it disrupted by some intruder. In the novels, Panken observes this is reflected in aborted moments of intimacy, such as that between Ralph and Katharine in *Night and Day*:

When Ralph and Katharine, after revealing their secrets seem more intimate then ever before, we are confronted with one of Woolf's karate chops, a strange eruption from her unconscious. As the lovers' discourse is interrupted by the maid who announces that a woman, refusing to give her name, has come to see Mrs. Hilbery, Ralph fantasized that the anonymous woman was a "black hunchback provided with a steel knife that she would plunge into Katharine's heart." (Panken, p. 97)

The murderous rage evoked by disruption between the lovers who represent Leonard and herself may be due to Woolf's own guilt about being with a man. This kind of oedipal stage rage is projected onto the mother, as represented by the "anonymous woman" fantasized by Ralph to be a Black Hunchback. But all of Woolf's biographies articulate that it originates in an earlier stage, when the unity with her mother was fundamentally disrupted. Katharine and Ralph's relationship, in *Night and Day*, demonstrates the mismatch between Woolf and her mother, within the earlier mother-child dyad, which Bond has suggested may have began during Woolf's infant differentiation period and then manifested most profoundly during rapprochement. Panken writes:

> *Night and Day* shows subtlety and skill in portraying the emotional swayings of two mutually detached individuals, Katharine and Ralph who wished to share their solitude. Their flickering connectedness, frequently obliterated, requires almost emergency like measures to fuel and sustain it. Interestingly, Woolf here delineates a reciprocal responsibility for the lovers' difficulties, perhaps a communication that the problems between herself and Leonard were mutual. (Panken, p. 96)

MOTHER

Panken and DeSalvo find overwhelming evidence in Woolf's writing of early maternal deprivation and ongoing maternal unavailability. We also discover references to an alluring symbiotic mother (see Woolf and Kutash on *The Submerged Personality* (1991). Indeed, although Woolf herself refers to the mother who was the "base on which life stands," (Bond, p. 21), her mother figures are consistently as alluring as they are unavailable (Mrs. Ramsay in *To The Lighthouse)* or alluring and homicidally possessive (the aunt in *Voyage Out*). Mrs. Ramsay is an idealized mother, more attentive to her children (see Panken) than Julia Stephen ever was. But even the attentive mother is a distracted mother, as Mrs. Ramsay often seems far away, lost in her own dissociated vision. Nevertheless, the portrait of Mrs. Ramsay suggests Woolf's own residue of yearnings for symbiotic period unity.

In contrast, the other fictional mothers Woolf created, like Mrs. Flanders, the mother of Jacob in *Jacob's Room* (Panken, p. 106), and Mrs. Hilbery, the mother in *Night and Day* (Panken, p. 93) are critical and intrusive. In *Voyage Out*, the admired aunt Helen first becomes intrusive, then murderous. In *Night and Day*, Elizabeth's mother, Katherine is controlling, possessive, and intrusive. The movement away from the mother, towards heterosexual love with a man, is highly conflictual for Woolf and for her alter-ego female characters. This would follow from the failure to have internalized a good-enough mother as a primary object.

In this context, it is interesting to note that in *The Years* when a mother dies, nobody in the family feels any genuine grief. Julia Stephen's last words to Virginia before dying were "stand up straight Goat"—a rather critical and distancing remark, and a frigid farewell. This mirrors Woolf's own guilt about her inability to mourn her mother. Possibly, Mrs. Ramsay represents an attempt to exorcise the ghost. But if she is attempting by this creation to truly mourn, Woolf fails. By idealizing Mrs. Ramsay and so converting Julia Stephen into a symbol of motherhood as a unifying force—true mourning eludes Woolf. The real mother, who can arouse genuine grief, is lost when defensive idealization blocks actual experience. Thus, Woolf's attempt to mourn is not only the result of split-off rage at her internal mother, but is derived from infancy and rapprochement failures.

Nevertheless, Woolf did have enough of her mother during infancy to allow her to take in her father's form of mothering. It is in her relationship with her father that I believe Woolf really gained a mother. Panken's (1987) psychobiography makes this most clear, as does Quentin Bell's portrayal of his aunt Virginia (1972). For example, Bell describes how Virginia and her father walked together at St. Ives during her childhood summers:

> This was the time when Virginia could walk out with her father to the fairyland of great ferns which stood high above a child's head, or to Halestown Bog where the osmunda grew. (Bell, p. 34)

The more negative traits of Leslie Stephen's character have been recorded by Woolf's biographers, such as DeSalvo (1989) who focuses on the adverse effects on Woolf of the Victorian patriarchal system. But her father's benign and nurturing attitude are evident during Woolf's pre-adolescent development. Like Bell, Panken is aware of the powerful tie between Leslie and Virginia. While Julia Stephen was preoccupied with Virginia's younger brother, Adrian, her husband turned his attention to Virginia. Panken records Woolf's early affection for her father. Apparently, he responded to it warmly.

Moreover, while Julia Stephen was visiting her ill mother, or the sick and the poor, Leslie was usually at home. He generally seems to have engaged more with his children than did his wife, although Julia assumed the stressful caretaking when they were sick. Panken observes:

> A considerable part of his correspondence consists of letters to his absent wife, describing the activities, development, and unique sayings of his children, an unusual reversal of roles in the Victorian period. (Panken, p. 27)

She adds:

> With their mother away, tending to the poor, sick, or needy, governesses, or older siblings took over. Their father also took part in their lives, drawing for them, telling them stories, reciting his favorite poems, though Love suggests he was 'at his worst' with mother absent (215). Woolf recalls that her father once recovered her toy boat which sank in the pond. On this occasion, her mother made new sails and her father rigged the boat, which points to an occasional sense of harmony in Virginia's family life. (Panken, p. 28)

Leslie's involvement with his children was particularly noticeable in relation to Virginia:

> Writing Julia when Adrian was born, Leslie indicated his decided pleasure in Virginia's affection and physical demonstrativeness; she sat on his knee, said "kiss" and laid her cheek against his. (Panken, p. 27)

The affection between Leslie and Virginia, Panken suggests, obviously flattered Leslie, and was catalyzed by Leslie's and Virginia's exclusion from the Julia-Adrian symbiotic dyad. Most importantly, given Woolf's talents, would have been her father's attentiveness to her educational needs. Specifically, Panken describes Virginia as "soothed" by his reading to her. Here his involvement suggests a stronger maternal component than what she received from her mother. Woolf recalled her father's interest in her development. He inquireed into the nature of what she chose to read, guiding her inquiries and suggesting books for her. Since she often experienced her reading as oral incorporation and digestion, his involvement with it takes on the coloring of maternal care and of basic nurturance. This nurturance played a role in helping Virginia to internalize a positive identification with her father as a writer and intellect. Such identification filled a void, summarizes Panken:

> Critical in Virginia's development, her father from early on favored his younger daughter who resembled him physically. He took great pride in her verbal facility, offered her the 'tools' she needed to write and enjoyed her obvious attachment to him (Hill, 351–352). Acutely aware she was the child most responsive to and identified with his literary bent, Leslie encouraged her writing skills, and provided a solid grounding in history and biography, which he thought necessary in understanding literature. He assigned and then discussed specific areas of study with her: 'She takes in a great deal and will really be an author in time' he wrote his wife; 'through I cannot make up my mind in what line' (July 29, 1893; Berg).... In as much as Julia felt 'inept with words, 'there is reason to think she was threatened by the closeness between father and daughter.
>
> Though fathers customarily propel the oldest son to follow their professional orientation, Leslie chose Virginia instead, as evidenced in a letter to Julia when Virginia was 11 and Thoby 13, telling his wife that Thoby had "just the good sound brains that tell at Cambridge; some say he might be Lord Chancellor but I don't want him to be an author. That is a thing for ladies, and Ginia will do well in that line." (Aug. 3, 1893; Berg). (Panken, pp. 30–31)

Woolf responded to her father's interest by showing avid interest in her education, learning quickly from him. This behavior sharply contrasts with her earlier learning at the side of her mother. According to several biographers and psychobiographers, including Panken and Bond, Woolf didn't talk until the age of three. Her late development may have been caused by Woolf's wish to please her mother, who she believed always wanted to carry a small baby in her arms.[3] But it may also have been a retaliatory form of oppositionalism—a rageful withholding of what her mother expected from her. Woolf may have simply refused for a year to talk to a mother who was not there for her. Given the role reversal in the household, it is not surprising that Virginia recalled her mother in phallic terms. For example, she equated the mother, Mrs. Ramsay, with the lighthouse in *To the Lighthouse*. Also, she remembered her mother, not as a soft holding body, but as a figure adorned with cold, hard jewels. She recalled her mother as wearing rings, one diamond, one emerald, one opal, and twisted silver bracelets (Rose, *Woman of Letters*, 1978, p. 9).

As Panken noted, this dynamic of father-daughter closeness, characterized by mother-daughter alienation, most probably took a powerful toll on Woolf's psyche. Woolf was haunted by unconscious guilt towards her mother, because of closeness with her father. Her incestuous fantasies in relation to her father, which she later acted out with Vanessa's lovers, probably contributed to this guilt. These feelings may have perpetuated oral rage and oral incorporative hunger towards the mother, interfering with Woolf's capacity to mourn her mother after early disappointments and after her death.

LOSS AND TRAUMA

Virginia Woolf's life was overwhelmed by loss and trauma. Her mother was lost to her both physically and emotionally during her toddlerhood. The mother's actual death left Woolf, at thirteen, terror-stricken and guilty. Another source of guilt towards her mother, besides the inability to mourn, was Woolf's feeling that she had killed her mother by preferring her father (see Panken, 1987). In addition, Woolf harbored so much anger towards her mother that her unconscious experience was of repressing murderous rage.

From the extensive study of DeSalvo (1989), we now know still another source of Woolf's rage: she was sexually molested by both her older stepbrothers, Gerald and George Duckworth. As early as the age of six, Woolf had her genitals fondled by Gerald, while she was placed on a dinner tray on a window ledge. The horror of ridicule she subsequently lived with, throughout her life, seems at least partly to be related to her helplessness and humiliation while Gerald molested her. Woolf was forced to view herself in a mirror during the molestation. For the rest of her life she was phobic about mirrors, while seeking compensatory mirroring from her literary audiences. This episode occurred during a time of excruciating vulnerability, following her recovery from a lengthy period of whooping cough illness, an illness which had become so severe it was nearly fatal (DeSalvo, p. 107). The death of both her parents, first her mother when Woolf was thirteen, and then her father when she was twenty-two, brought more incestuous abuse, this time from her half-brother George.

Woolf's literature reflects the threatening view she developed of male sexuality. Woolf's response to the actual molestations, added to her experience of Leslie Stephen's tantrums during her adolescence (raging at

Vanessa about household expenses), and her intense neediness, imposed by her father on the women in the family (Julia, Stella, Vanessa) may well have congealed in Woolf's mind. Her allusions to Mr. Ramsay in *To the Lighthouse* reflect this male oppression: "But he'll be down on me any moment, demanding—something she felt she could not give him" (p. 223). For most survivors of incestuous and sexual abuse, and Woolf was no exception, the greatest pain is the pain of keeping the secret, protecting the assailant while forfeiting all potential protection for oneself. Woolf blanked out her own memory of the molestations until late in life, when she began to recover her horrors in an aborted piece of personal writing, *Sketch of the Past*. Although silenced by shame, Woolf was able to share her memories of sexual abuse with her sister Vanessa, for Vanessa too was the object of George's amorous and salacious midnight advances. However, Vanessa was probably spared the molestation at six years old. All the repressed rage under the silent void demanded an outlet!

THE TRANSITIONAL WORLD OF CREATIVE WORK

Woolf had been eased into her art by her father's hand. Despite his needy, possessive, and intrusive demands that overwhelmed the household after Julia's death, Virginia had already internalized him as a good object. Through his sharing of literary interests and creative work, Leslie Stephen offered a lifeline to his daughter whose despair first erupted into psychosis following her mother's death period. After Julia Stephen died, Leslie wrote the *Mausoleum Book* (1895, cited by Panken, p. 20). By using the creative process to mourn, he set an example for Virginia. Already writing a novel at the age of eleven as well as a family newspaper, the *Hyde Park News*, Woolf was to look thereafter to her creative work as a way to find hope in the face of repeated trauma and continuing loss. In fact, writing was to become the well she dipped into for all her needs, particularly those that were highly frustrated in other areas of her life. Ultimately, defensive processes undermined the psychological reparation of the creative process, but, initially, she found, in the psychological function of the creative process, her salvation. Writing became Woolf's route to body feelings that eluded her in sexual relations. It became the route to both masculine and feminine self-experience. It became the route to a form of identity that she could hold in her hand just as she held a piece of paper. It became the route to vision, and moments in which she experienced fleetingly a sense of harmony and a unifying self-cohesion. It became the route to asking the questions that haunted her about the meaning of life. These questions and their answers made comprehensible the covertly enraged murmuring of disconnected voices that impinged inward upon her during her erupting manic psychosis. It became the route to recapturing the lyrical feelings experienced when walking with her father in the lush countryside of St. Ives. It became her rhythm, a rhythm that temporarily linked a sealed-off inner world to the world without, so that her inner sense of terror could be, at least for a while, reduced. When she lived, while writing, in the rhythm, when she lived in the lyric, when she lived in the resonance of visual sensuality and physical body sensation, she felt a wholeness that escaped her when hemmed in by the black pits and blocked walls of her interpersonal life. When she lived in this lyric she had her good father again, and with him she salvaged some memory of an early good mother who could join her in harmony. These moments could feel like an "eternal now," even though imminent disruptions, too powerful to contain and describe directly, always followed.

Kelley's view of Woolf's work, which she sees as of a striving to integrate vision and fact, allows the outsider to grasp how moments of vision transformed Woolf's "shocks" of reality and temporarily healed her. Woolf may have substituted an infant's sense of viewing her mother for the yearned holding that her mother failed to adequately give. In this process Woolf created her own form of holding, perhaps based on a projective-identification process, in which she took in her mother and projected her out again through visual grasp. This infant vision became a lifelong method of grasping the resonant world around her through a synthesizing view that made the world a mothering force. This synthesizing view perceived the world as a unity for moments that became externalized into a mystic union of self and other, where subject and object become one.

TRANSITIONAL TRAUMA

In 1904, when Virginia Woolf's father died, she reacted by having her second psychotic break. This psychic eruption of manic psychosis was more florid than what she experienced following her mother's death. This time, Woolf jumped out of a window and heard birds singing to her in Greek. Her suicide attempt was obviously a cry for rescue, for she made sure to fall from not too high off the ground. Leaping out a window can be symptomatic of a feeling of jumping out of one's own skin. We jump out of our skin when the terror of losing all connection with others is so intense that it cannot be bodily contained. Woolf must have felt that her internal locus was lost forever when Leslie Stephen first grew detached following his wife's death, and then died. Without him to bind her, she was in tumult. In general, losing a father involves not only a literal loss, but the loss of a fantasy of paternal protection. In our unconscious, it is the father who provides a haven from the world and its dangers. Leslie Stephen had failed to protect Virginia and her sisters from dangers inside her and his own home, such as the direct sexual abuse of her half-brother and the vicarious torment caused by a mad cousin's sexual attacks on her half-sister Stella. Nevertheless, for Woolf he had the symbolic radiance of the archetypical paternal protector. This death left her feeling extraordinarily unprotected. And despite his failures, it made her actual situation even more precarious, as George Duckworth's advances towards the Stephen sisters now became more frequent and intense. His access was easier because Virginia and Vanessa found themselves living in a home dominated by their stepbrother George.

Virginia and Vanessa were under the societally approved social tutelage of the same stepbrother who haunted their room as a demon lover late into the night. George Duckworth demanded that Vanessa and Virginia dress formally for dinner and negotiate the tea table at mid-afternoon. He actively courted Vanessa and took her to the theatre. For Virginia, his impingements were felt on the home front. Now she developed a social phobia and was afraid to enter a drawing room. She feared, in a highly paranoid fashion, the caustic judges of the social arena (Bell, 1972). "She went through agonies of embarassment, miserable humiliating evenings when she couldn't find a partner ghastly meaningless conversations which got bogged down and left her blushing and wordless." (Bell, p. 77)

Woolf's quote form Swineburne in her last novel, *Between the Acts*, may have been an indictment against George for his molestations in the night. Isa, Woolf's alter-ego female character repeats the poet's lines: "'Swallow my sister, O sister swallow'" (Panken, p. 247). Was this the memory of forced fellatio? Woolf's moments between men and women in her novels, always punctured by dark eruptions of violence, suggests the theme of demonic male sexuality, and suggests the archetypical demon lover theme. Once her mother died, she was essentially unchaperoned, for her half-brother, who might be seen by society as her male protector and chaperone, was actually the demon lover who molested her, as well as her sister, at night. Her own instinctual eruptions could be captured in his image, as well as her own split-off and uncontained desire. His dark shadow was a malignant way of filling the void within her.

Because both Woolf's aggression and her sexuality were split off from consciousness, as they had not been integrated during the critical rapprochement stage into an autonomous integration of intentions that she could use for interpersonal relations (see Bond, 1989), Woolf could easily become the unprotected victim that she did become. The feeling that she was this appears in her fiction. Rhoda, in the *Waves*, sees herself as an unprotected child, an insubstantial being. With Woolf's father gone, and her own split-off impulses returning as invaders rather than as passions, her older stepbrother could haunt her bedroom with impunity.

Virginia must have frantically searched for possible ways out. She sought refuge in her room, where, during the day, she found some peace. Fending off doctors who forbade her the sanctuary of reading in her room, Woolf entered a world of books. She marveled at the division between this inner world of thought and imagination that so comforted her, as had her father's reading to her, and the outer world which was empty, yet so dangerous. To survive in the outer world, she put on her false self, a compliant facade to ward off attacks or intrusions. Woolf writes of her false self in generalized terms; everybody in society is seen as wearing masks and speaking nonentities. Up in her room she breathed as she read. Here she was free, but at the price of becoming disconnected from all the people around her. Without a shift in such circumstance, Woolf's life could have taken on the same imprisoning mode of seclusion as did the lives of Emily Brontë and Emily Dickinson (see Kavaler, 1990, 1993). But unlike them, she had some reprieve. This reprieve, in the shape of the man who became her husband, fertilized her creative work. But first there was the move from her stepbrother's domain to the intellectual commune at Bloomsbury.

In 1904, Virginia, Vanessa, and their brothers (Adrian and Thoby) left their half-brother's house, where her father lived as an eccentric and distant figure after her mother's death, and moved into a house in Bloomsbury, 46 Gordon Square. Virginia was twenty-two, and she had suffered many years of George's roving advances following her mother's death when she was thirteen, not to mention the years of Gerald's molestations, from the time she was six.

When the Bloomsbury circle of intellectuals and artists began to take shape, she had, for the first time, a social life she could connect to. Thoby's friends from Cambridge visited. So did Vanessa's artist friends. In this new location Woolf met Aldous Huxley, Bertrand Russell, and Lytton Strachey, among others. Lytton proposed marriage, only to withdraw his offer the next day. He later encouraged Leonard Woolf to make a pitch for Virginia. Leonard's appearance on the scene radically changed and molded Woolf's life. When Virginia said "yes" to Leonard Woolf's proposal of marriage, she imagined a life in which she would have it all. She told Leonard what she wanted, a literary career and marriage and children. Just before their wedding and honeymoon, she wrote to a friend that "By next year I must have a child." (Panken, p. 64). Woolf's chance for marriage clearly brought with it wishes for motherhood. Yet life was not to be as she predicted. There was a sudden twist!

MARRIAGE AND BARRIERS

Following her honeymoon, Woolf wrote, "I find the climax intensely exaggerated," (Panken, p. 65, from letters, Sept. 4, 1912). Soon all of Bloomsbury knew that the newlyweds had failed to achieve sexual union and sexual pleasure, although they had gone through the motions. Leonard Woolf was very inexperienced sexually (Panken, p. 64–65). But on his and Virginia's return from their honeymoon, what came out of discussing their sexual relations with Vanessa and her husband Clive Bell, was that Virginia became the one seen as lacking. Virginia agreed. In her usual fashion, she turned all expected and projected ridicule, along with her own frustrated aggression, against herself. Thus, she developed the myth of her sexual flaw. Perhaps, by this stratagem she avoided facing the pain of the actual barrier she felt when her body went numb in the face of possible sexual intimacy. Only when thoughts and images crowded in her mind did her body come alive. Panken, following another critic, notes how the men and women in Woolf's novels pass in and out of each others minds, not in an out of each other's bodies. This seems particularly true of Ralph and Katharine in *Night and Day*. In their relationship, clear outlines of the Leonard-Virginia relationship are visible. As with the Woolf's, exultation is part of the early relationship, but it is an exultation of the mind, not body. This is how Ralph (Leonard) views Katherine (Virginia):

> Sitting alone at home, forcing himself to imagine Katharine as she really is, not as his dreams have created her, he is overwhelmed by a sense of her presence.... They seemed to pass in and out of each others' minds, questioning and answering. The utmost fullness of communion seemed to be theirs. Thus united, he felt himself raised to an eminence, exalted, and filled with a power of achievement that this sense of unity is love and that love is a force that can reconcile opposites. (Quoted in Kelly, p. 58)

What little intimacy Leonard and Virginia share appears to be of this nature. Such moments were those of mental vision, the mode of love that was possibly an outgrowth of Woolf's infancy. They occurred when some reality of the other was grasped without idealization blocking the view. Such union through vision allowed Virginia Woolf to believe in love. It allowed her to survive the sexual disillusionment of her marriage and to remain with Leonard. It also gave life to the relations between the fictional characters, she created. In this way love and creativity could both be interactive avenues to feeling alive, despite her body numbness and affect blocks.

But what did Virginia do with the anger she must have felt when Leonard allowed her to be the target of the discussion about sexual failure? Or her anger, when he infantalized her as a mental "patient," who might always be on the verge of falling ill?

And what did she do with her longings when Leonard withdrew totally from sexual relations, causing her to write of her character, Clarissa Dalloway, that she was like a "nun who had left the world.... The sheets were clean, tight stretched in a broad white band from side to side. Narrower and narrower would her bed be." (Panken, p. 65, Woolf's diaries) Shortly after their marriage, Panken notes, she had written to Leonard that her "flanks and rump are now in finest plumage" (Panken, p. 65). She was waiting for him, but he did not return to fulfill her desires upon his return. Instead, he returned with an authoritative air of judgement along with a paternally protective attitude. He watched over her obsessively. His vigilance offered her the attention she craved. It also gave her the sense of protection she had lost when her father died. However, Virginia retaliated against the regimen of isolation and of forced entrance into a nursing home with another suicide attempt which Leonard did not totally avert (Panken, p. 71). Leonard's sexual withdrawal and his willingness to view Virginia both as a patient and as a woman without feminine sexuality must have been devastating enough for Virginia, but the most malignant blow to her trust of Leonard came when he refused to have their children.

Leonard and Vanessa joined forces to forbid Virginia her much-longed-for experience of being a mother. Vanessa, who had three children, from both her marriage to Clive Bell and her ongoing living arrangement with the bisexual painter, Duncan Grant, was determined to bar Virginia on account of her mental health from motherhood. Together, Leonard and Vanessa consulted doctors. They were the same kind of doctors who, adapting the usual medical approach of the day, had proposed bed rest and eating,[4] and who had prohibited her books and pen. When Virginia became psychotic, suicidal, and despairing following their marriage and honeymoon (in 1913), Leonard probably did not want to see the part he played in bringing about her despair. This is mirrored in Woolf's fiction, when Woolf's character, Rezia, in *Mrs. Dalloway*, did not want to see her role in her husband's (Septimus) mental breakdown, and subsequent suicide (Panken, p. 130). Leonard was probably most comfortable seeing his wife's illness as disconnected from his behavior. He would then not have to face his own fears of sexuality and of fatherhood. He willingly took Virginia on as his child instead, submitting to her dominance in many ways, while retaining the upper hand by controlling many aspects of her life. But what led Virginia to suicidal despair so soon in her marriage? Panken suggests her suicide attempt after their honeymoon was Virginia's only way of striking back at Leonard for his sexual withdrawal and his rejection of her feminine potential, both as lover and mother. In her split-off rage, Woolf struck blows at Leonard by injuring herself, a mode or response just noted in her nursery room fight with Thoby.

Eventually, such a response would kill her. But for many years, Virginia was able to stave off suicide through the genius that allowed her to bring her creative work to fruition. Although she could never openly confront it, her split-off aggression had some opening for expression in her work. Perhaps even more importantly, Virginia could experience her yearnings, body aliveness, sexual sensations, and reproductive emergence in the psychophysical experience of her own creative process.

PREGNANT WITH CREATION

What was the connection for Woolf between writing and craving a child? Panken cites many examples that show how conscious Woolf was of her own connection between creative work and the natural processes of gestation, pregnancy, and childbirth. Thus, Woolf describes her next work as "impending in me; grown heavy in my mind like a ripe pear." The birth of an individual baby is the experience and expression of giving "the moment whole" (Panken, p. 187). Elsewhere, Woolf writes about her own writing: "so I have something instead of children" (Panken, p. 182). Because creativity feels to her like childbirth, Woolf has hope and can therefore write. Her work flows in waves with an organic rhythm, a rhythm approximating primal connection with a preverbal mother. In the outside world, the connection Woolf made took the form of competition with her sister Vanessa. Woolf compared her work to Vanessa's pregnancies and to Vanessa's nurturing of her children (Panken, p. 187, *Diary*, vol. 3, 1925–1930 (1980), Jan. 4, 1929). This view of creativity as providing a feminine mode of experience which she lacked in her own life was an evocative one for Woolf. It allowed her to defend against experiencing the loss occasioned by Leonard's refusal to have children. It also allowed her to use the creative process to fill in a part of her identity that she felt lacking.

Closely allied with Woolf's view of her creative process as reproduction and hence a natural process is her experience of creativity as a source of physical and sexual sensation. Such sensation brings a numbed body alive in a way that Woolf only on rare occasions experienced outside of the creative process.[5] What was the effect on Woolf when she did, at last, have a real sexual relationship? During the period when Woolf found some sexual excitement with a woman, her friend, Vita Sackville-West, she claimed, according Panken (p. 172) that "she no longer wants children since ideas possess her" (*Diary*, vol. 3, July 7, 1928). Ideas remained her children, her mind became her womb, as long as she could adore Vita physically, something she had never done with anyone else, including Leonard. Thus, she was able to write with great directness and vitality to Vita: "I like your energy, I love your legs. I long to see you." (Panken, p. 169, "Letter to Vita," *Letters of Virginia Woolf* (1977), vol. 3, 1923–1928, Aug. 22, 1927).

Such sexual arousal, which made her feel pregnant with ideas, was related to an earlier level of fantasy connection with Vita. After having spent some time with Vita, Woolf observed that she felt satiated like an infant drinking sweet milk from her mother's breast (Panken, p. 188). But if Woolf could imagine herself as a baby, she could also imagine herself as a mother, giving birth to ideas and words through a creative process that allowed her, after years of envying Vanessa's supposed reproductive joys, to devalue and discard the "physicalness of having children" (Panken, p. 170). Because of the sexual connection, everything became "green and vivified" (Panken, p. 189, *Diary* vol. 3, June, 23, 1929) when she thought of her work.

Woolf "notes her reliance upon 'spurts of thought, coming as I walk, as I sit, things churning up in my mind and so making a perpetual pageant,'" (Panken, p. 119) providing Woolf with her happiest moments. The work sexually arouses Woolf and through it she also gains sexual release (Panken, p. 155): "Then her thought which had 'spun quicker and quicker, exploded of its own intensity.' She felt 'released' (40–41 [*To The Lighthouse*]."

Also, in *The Waves*, there is, in a description of the fluidity of the sea, a sexual lyric that allows a creative ecstasy akin to sexual ecstasy (Panken, p. 162O). In *To The Lighthouse*, Woolf writes of Lily: "the ecstasy burst in her eyes, waves of pure delight raced over the floor of her mind and she felt it is enough" (pp. 99–100).

From Panken's descriptions, it appears that various levels of sexual arousal appear in the creative moment. Woolf observes that "her hand quivered with life" (Panken, p. 156). When she writes, Woolf explains that she loses consciousness of "outer things" (Panken, p. 156). She steps out of a poorly fitted and fragmented identity in the world. She becomes soul and rhythm, without a differentiating identity: "The rhythm she acquired sustained her efforts" (Panken, p. 157).

In converting body process and sexual arousal into creative process, Woolf felt she could control and contain these sensations in a way that she was unable to with male sexuality. Performing her creative work, she did not have to numb herself as she had to when with a man. When her artist alter-ego, Lily, paints on a canvas in *To the Lighthouse*, she experiences phallic modes of sexual arousal:

> "Lily now took the plunge: 'with a curious physical sensation as through urged forward and at the same time held back, she painted her first, quick, decisive stroke.'" (quoted in Panken, p. 156)

Describing Lily's creative process, Woolf observes: "achieving a dancing rhythmical movement she synchronized pauses and strokes" (quoted in Panken, p. 156). Wanting to reach behind appearances to shadows and essences (Panken, p. 156), Woolf assumes masculine sexual qualities of phallic penetration and finds hidden subjective states in herself which she casts onto characters, as, for example, in *The Waves*. In this phallic mode, she bypasses the false-self personas that she associates with the social realm of experience, which for her, as for Rhoda in *The Waves*, is a barrier rather than an interactive area of connection.

UNION WITH THE OTHER

Lily feels Mrs. Ramsay's presence with her at the creative moment in which a unifying vision emerges allows inspiration for her art (Panken, p. 157). But rarely absent, even in such moments, is her terror at being an orphaned soul and losing the connection nonverbally established between her mother and herself during earliest infancy.

Woolf's adult couples, such as Ralph and Katharine in *Night and Day* (1919), reflect early levels of connection. (Panken, p. 96) Ralph and Katharine communicate nonverbally. Only on this level do they feel connected to each other. On the verbal level, Ralph is the "bad mother" who intrudes with unwelcome criticism. When he truly desires to convey love for Katharine he doesn't speak. Woolf suggests that if Ralph told Katharine that he loved her it would trivialize his feelings. Therefore, Woolf has him send a nonverbal message. He brings Katharine flowers. Because Katharine understands this gesture, they are able to share a "vision" of life that unites them with each other and with all of nature.

For Woolf, as for Emily Brontë with whom she identified, nature is the unifying mother of all.

Woolf, as Lily, describes the creative moment as a moment in which she stood alive on a "windy pinnacle; exposed without protection to all the blasts of doubt" (Panken, p. 156). She creates a maternal figure in Mrs. Ramsay who provides a form of spiritual holding where intimate physical holding is lacking. Mrs. Ramsay sheds light. She has a radiance of vision. However, she is phallic like a lighthouse, and she lacks any quality of feminine yielding. Her radiance is spiritual. She sheds light and seems like a split off idealization of a mother, who in bodily form is seen as "predatory" (Panken, p. 163).

According to Panken, Woolf creates her mother into a work of art. Her father appears much more realistic. He is both tender with Woolf, who appears as a child in the character of Cam, and is intrusive and sexually threatening with Lily, who appears to be Woolf as an adult daughter. He is too demanding and too rationalistic, but he also joins with his wife to allow sensibility. Mrs. Ramsay is much more untouchable. Her presence is only felt as fertilizing Lily's creativity when she is at a distance, a foreign presence viewed after death. When alive, she grates on Lily, arousing her to intense cravings for merger, while simultaneously eluding contact with her. Then she preys on Lily—Woolf as an uninvited matchmaker. Yet, at a distance, Mrs. Ramsay is created and perhaps remembered by Woolf as a spiritually holding source. Sometimes verging on a madonna, she symbolizes an early spiritual connection between mother and child. The creative moment is pregnant—not only with much craved physical sensation—but also with a spiritual connection felt at a nonverbal level between mother and infant.

Woolf's split between interpersonal communication and artistic communication suggests that she could not connect both with her inner life and with another person and their separate subjective perspective, through direct verbal communication. In contrast, her interpersonal connections, experienced as fleeting, were always felt on a primitive nonverbal level that was much more elusive and undifferentiated. A gap is left then for Woolf between the false-self mode of verbal connection and the deeper nonverbal connection which she could express in the rhythm of writing, but not in direct verbal communication. This gap always was felt as a black abyss across which her creative work provided a tightrope or lifeline. The abyss of a black hollow self was to widen by the time she wrote *The Waves,* and is reflected in this novel. However, at the time of *To The Lighthouse,* her preverbal connection with Leonard and her primitive sexual experience with Vita supported her to face the "naked soul on the pinnacle," through which she gives voice to in the character of Lily. Both Leonard and Vita mirrored Woolf by applauding her writing, and although the inner blueprint for such an appreciative other was fragile and evanescent, her father as a mirroring other had been built into her psyche, and her mother had occasionally responded to her writing as well. Thus, Woolf could get a glimpse of a "good mother" presence in her fiction. Mrs. Ramsay is the "absent presence" identified by Winnicott (1965). She is mother who can be present in her absence because she has to some degree be internalized. When Lily feels Mrs. Ramsay's presence (Panken, p. 155) as she paints she survives the terror of being a "naked soul on a pinnacle" (Panken, p. 154), and plunges into self-expression. As long as Woolf could find a good mother in the symbolism of the process of her work, she could be a mother to her work and remain pregnant with life or creative inspiration.

7)

THE GENIUS AND SORROW OF VIRGINIA WOOLF, PART II

Vision and Art

Before looking at the dark side of Woolf, which became all too pervasive as her life went on, it is necessary to look at the life force that was able to emerge through her genius, despite overwhelming trauma and loss. Based on her study of the major Woolf novels, Kelley (1971) argues that hope survived and, indeed, sometimes thrived in Virginia Woolf. Through her genius, Kelley believes, Woolf was able to grasp that art was an integrative tool, and use it accordingly, despite the deep psychic division within her.

Her resilience was always precarious. If we use Stolorow and Lachmann's (1980) criteria for healthy narcissism, she rarely achieved it. Constantly shifting self-images, erratic mood states and eruptions from split-off self-components ("the unthought known" of Bollas, 1990), and unconscious fantasies threatened her cohesion. The coloring of her self-representation was rarely positive. Often it was the blackness of depression (Panken, p. 26, on "black trees"). Because her view of herself was decidedly unstable and shifting, each of her characters can only represent an attempt to capture a fragment of her self-image. With so much unneutralized primitive aggression split off in her psyche, for Woolf to have any sustained body-mind integration would have required intensive clinical treatment.

Woolf was never to receive such treatment. Nor was she to avail herself of the rudimentary psychoanalytic treatment of her day (even though her brother Adrian became a psychoanalyst). Rather, she used her genius, as indicated, to employ the creative process as an integrative force. Within the creative act, she struggled with the dissonances within her. This often involved facing the enigma of how factual and visionary experience could be made to coalesce.

Woolf knew that anyone lost in a pure visionary world could not survive. This understanding was most clearly enunciated in her portrayal of Rhoda in *The Waves*. Rhoda is a fragile being. She feels empty and sees herself as substantial as seaweed. But she is extremely intuitive and empathic. She sees into the shadows and roots of things as Virginia the artist would have wanted to do herself. Yet for all her virtues, Rhoda is buffeted by fate and fails to form interpersonal contacts. Feeling that life is a cascade of fluid that will dissolve her into nothingness, she experiences herself as "not existing." Rhoda ultimately looks toward suicide as the only way out of a world in which she cannot sustain connection, a world in which she is socially phobic, even with her closest friends, a world from which she feels divided and apart, and which evokes highly volatile feelings of envy, hate, and love she cannot contain. According to Kelley, Rhoda is Woolf's archetypical example of a being who exists purely in the realm of vision, purely in a spiritual mind realm, so that reality is experienced as if it were intruding like phallic rape into a shadow existence lived in a dream or fantasy. Rhoda has no grounding in reality or "fact," because she is disconnected from her body. Reality continuously shocks her. She experiences the world as though she had no skin, or everyone else is in her skin, and she often needs pain to provide her with boundaries. Without these boundaries, she could dissolve. Thus Rhoda must press her toes against the bed rail at night in order not to lose all contact with physical reality (Kelley, p. 152).

In contrast to Rhoda is Jinny, living fully and sensually in her body, but never going beyond the realm of concrete physical reality. Jinny is imprisoned within her body as Rhoda is imprisoned outside it.

In Woolf's fiction, male characters, such as Ralph in *Night and Day*, also become representative of fact without vision. But through his capacity to love Katharine, who has a large visionary scope, Ralph is able to bridge the gap. Afterwards, he has fleeting moments in which factual reality interacts with his visionary spiritual ideas, thereby creating for him and perhaps his creator a sense of self-wholeness and connection between the self and the universe. In contrast, Richard in *Mrs. Dalloway* is a purely factual man who Clarissa Dalloway, fearful of a more intense and genuine love-hate affair with a man of visionary character who truly understands her, chooses out of a desire for security. Septimus is another purely visionary character in *Mrs. Dalloway*, who can't live in the human world. Specifically, he is unable to face homoerotic feelings for a dead friend, a man who was the only human link to his heart. The price of denial is high. Septimus rejects his wife and goes mad, rebelling through suicide (Panken, p. 127).

As an artist, Woolf sought to combine the factual and visionary parts of her own being through finding unifying symbols. She used themes, images, and characters in the service of this quest. Ultimately, her search for a body-mind integration failed. However, there are moments of integration which she achieves by bringing vision into the world and making it factual through the use of symbol. An example is when Woolf writes of Lily, in *To the Lighthouse*, who paints concrete forms of furniture, but then unites them through a visionary theme that materializes as pattern, rhythm, and radiance. "I have had my vision," Lily says (Panken, p. 158). Afterward, she is at peace. But her reprieve is temporary. Soon she has visions of throwing herself from a cliff. I can speculate on why the inability to sustain the peaceful state derived from artistic vision can be seen in terms of Woolf's deficit in early internalization of primary-object connections. Woolf can temporarily re-connect with a early symbiotic holding mother through the creative act. In other words, the vision of the artist Lily, who represents Woolf in her work, is the vision of the early holding mother.

However all too quickly the negative maternal image of her constellation of her traumatized early life can take over. Then a repetition of a developmental disruption kicks in, displaying a vicious cycle—a backlash of negative visions rather than positive ones. Always images of suicidal self-destruction and disillusion emerge following the brief reproduction of peace. This reenacts the early abandonment trauma of Woolf's early separation years threatening a loss of self when the object turns malignant, indifferent, or disappears. Without an emotionally related mother of separation in the internal world, the cycle from symbiosis to separation remains unresolved. In the black void of the early holding mother's disappearance, all new connections that are regressively based on an early symbiotic bond are disrupted.

Without a vision like Lily's, the feeling of "death in life" permeated Woolf's physical and emotional existence. Yet to be entirely in the grips of visionary experience could leave her ungrounded and tragically isolated. Nevertheless, Kelley selects passages expressive of hope in Woolf that are based on reaching a vision. In each, a vision of unity survives despite failed interpersonal connection and communication. When all else fails such visions of unity can be found in patterns of nature.

In *The Years*, faith glimmers in the midst of increasing despair:

> Bernard in *The Waves* continually approached the moment when his phrases seemed to weave into a perfected story, only to watch sensation blunder in and shatter this increasing sense of harmony.

The characters in *The Years* also experience the frustration of count-
less interruptions of their dreams. But in both cases, these momentary conflicts of fact and vision create a pattern of endeavor that
leads to an ever-growing understanding of life's meaning. So if Rose
makes 'a great effort to tell her [Eleanor] the truth; to tell her about
the man at the pillar-box' (42), only to be interrupted by the
entrance of her nurse, she will grow to see that such obstructions in
the road to truth serve to strengthen the soul and so to bring the
seeker closer to his goal. If German bombs shatter Eleanor's train of
thought, 'as if some dull bore had interrupted an interesting conversation,' (288) or if her message to others is cut off by the roar of
a car engine (308), the hour will come when her vision will near
completion and her thoughts permeate the minds of those who need
to share her insights into the meaning of existence. (Kelley, p. 206)

At this stage in Woolf's work, fact and vision are no longer combined
in human character or human interaction. But there is hope, nevertheless,
for vision surviving an onslaught of disrupting fact. The main character,
Rose, expresses faith in a unifying life force in nature as she speaks of
observing synthesizing patterns. Their existence allows her to believe her
effort to endure and strive will pay off:

> The thought gave her extreme pleasure that there was a pattern.
> (quoted in Kelley, p. 221)

> Yet immediately after this thought, obsessive doubts haunt her: But
> who makes it? Who thinks it? Her mind slipped. She could not fin-
> ish her thought. (quoted in Kelley, p. 221)

Rose's hope often appears as denial:

> Things can't go on forever, she thought. Things pass, things change.
> She thought, looking up at the ceiling. And where are we going?
> Where? Where? (Kelley, p. 213)

Whatever their forms,

> these glimpses of the natural world serve as a reminder of the imper-
> turbable cycle of days that rolls beneath the clutter and flatter of
> society. (Kelley, p. 204)

But in *The Waves*, faith and despair alternate. The expression of hope is immediately followed by this description:

> A veil of mist covered the November sky; a many-folded veil, so fine meshed that it made one density.... Wounds coming through the veil.... Sounds coming through the veil—the bleat of sheep, the croak of rocks—were deadened. (quoted in Kelley, p. 204)

Bond views the writing of *The Years* as Woolf's self-destructive act, arguing that it caricatured Woolf's former faith in vision and perhaps, as part of this, purposely was written without her usual rhythmic flow. I suggest that *The Years* reflects Woolf's increasing disillusionment. The cause was twofold. She was disillusioned because of failure to mourn losses in her life, and to resolve the internal bad-object situation. For Woolf, these failures resulted in the repetition of loss by promoting the split-off destructive enactment of her aggression. Woolf turned her aggression against herself or others, consuming herself in the process, rather than using it constructively for communication and contact.

Woolf saw, not only her characters, but the artist as a visionary. In *To the Lighthouse* and in *The Waves* this notion becomes clear through abstracts, which are used to unite split parts of the self. For example, in *To the Lighthouse*, Lily's painting combines the literal fact of Mr. and Mrs. Ramsay with their symbolic representations which are assigned universal meaning through abstract concepts of identity provided by the author (Kelley, p. 163). The mother figure of Mrs. Ramsay, symbolized as a lighthouse, is an image meant to enhance the factual realities of death and life; the spiritual connotation of a light beam gives a transformative quality to the mortal body, which, for Woolf, is always disconnected from its soul.

In *The Waves* Bernard is the artist who comes closest to enlarging fact into vision, rather than, as Rhoda is, being swallowed up by vision:[1]

> So too he must reject the detached exactitude that he admires in Louis and Neville, for rigidity is anathema to anyone who attempts to build stories around life and so catch the vision. Because his phrases depend on factual reality for a base, Bernard can create only in the presence of others; for his words do not describe on ideal dream world but instead preserve the essence of reality. 'The fact is,' he says, 'that I have little aptitude for reflection. I require the concrete in everything. It is so only that I lay hands upon the world. A good phrase, however, seems to me to have an independent existence' (222). Once he has extracted the substance of a fact and set it

in a phrase, that phrase assumes a reality more powerful than the object it describes.... So already, Bernard is assuming the visionary role of artist. (Kelley, p. 163)

Although this task of translating fact into vision is necessary for all Woolf's artist characters, it is also impossible for them to achieve. For they are each isolated in monologues of subjective experience. Therefore, even when they supposedly come together in the outer world where they have no intimacy, they hardly interact. They do not respond to each other. They never engage in direct emotional communication, which connects separate selves. Rather, each character observes the other. The only way they do come together is through their primal fears which are conveyed by Woolf's mirroring imagery of birds. For Woolf, birds frequently serve as soul representations of people. This is how, according to Woolf, people can also find unity in a collective symbiotic vulnerability:

> In the garden the birds that had sung erratically and spasmodically in the dawn in that tree, on that bush, now sang together in chorus, shrill and sharp; now together, as if conscious of companionship, now alone as if to the pale blue sky. They swerved, all in one flight, when the black cat moved among the bushes, when the cook threw cinders in the ash heap and started them. Fear was in their song, and apprehension of pain, and joy to be snatched quickly now at this instant (225). (quoted in Kelley, p. 164, Woolf, 225, *Waves*)

But note, using the birds as a metaphor, Woolf is saying that all human joy and self-realization are fleeting. When faced in *The Waves* with this reality, Rhoda and Bernard (Woolf's alter-egos) react differently. Rhoda retreats into her world of dreams, whereas Bernard survives by accepting that any vision is momentary and must be continually remade (Kelley, p. 169):

> At times too when alone, he watches all his images slip from him for without someone to share them with he loses his creative urge. But it always returns. The artist who is fully aware of the depth and complexity of life recognizes with Lily Briscoe that the vision must be continually remade.

According to Kelley, as Bernard represents Woolf, faith is always renewing vision. Panken attends to the themes of disillusionment that come with the growth of an individual separate self. When Percival, a figure used as a symbolic representation of factual reality (Thoby) dies, Rhoda experiences Percival's death as a shock that threatens to dissolve her for good in "eternal formlessness" (Kelley, p. 179).[2] Rhoda-Virginia then grasps a meaning from his death in listening to music. Here Woolf's capacity for vision is realized. Rhoda finds a pattern in music that gives life meaning:

> Percival, by his death, has made me this gift, let me see the thing. There is a square; there is an oblong. The players take the square and place it upon the oblong. They pace it very accurately; they make a perfect dwelling-place. Very little is left outside. The structure is now visible; what is inchoate is here stated; we are not so various or so mean; we have made oblongs and stood them upon squares. This is our triumph; this is our consolation (Kelley, pp. 179–180)

Rhoda wins a moment of freedom, a moment of vision without dissolution by this discovery. Fact and vision combine for her as Percival's factual life now becomes a symbol as she hears and sees the pattern in music. Art is Woolf's unifying and integrating mode of vision.

Kelley writes (p. 180):

> From Rachel Vincace's piano-playing to Lily Bristol's painting to Bernard's phrases we have seen the power of art to combine fact and vision. Here music, the most visionary of the arts, unites these two worlds for Rhoda by presenting fact in its most abstract, intangible form as geometric shapes. In this way Rhoda can understand that her world of vision and the world of fact that Percival embodied when alive are not contradictory but can be intermeshed through careful effort.

Death is imagined to be an integrated state that Woolf has failed to achieve in life, except during moments of integration through art:

> Bernard realizes that even after death Percival exists somewhere, is part of the unbounded universe that includes action and contemplation, fact and vision. One way to capture this unity of life for a moment is in art, as Rhoda's experience at the concert has indicated. (Kelley, p. 181)

DISILLUSIONMENT

Some repeated themes throughout Woolf's diaries, letters, and novels are, as we have indicated, disillusion and despair. Despite the artistic development of her work, there is no successful emotional connection in the work that could allow transformation of such themes of despair into themes of hope, life, love, and self-agency. As Winnicott (1971) has written, the artist's work, no matter how artful, cannot replace a primary spontaneity of self necessary for everyday life:

> If the artist (in whatever medium) is searching for the self, then it can be said that in all probability there is already some failure for that artist in the field of general creative living. The finished creation never heals the underlying lack of sense of self. (p. 64)

If the primary creativity of everyday life is missing, the art becomes only a compensation that, like drinking alcohol[3] must be repeated, to overcome the sense of inner emptiness. As Panken comments (p. 266), Woolf insatiably sought the dramatic and sensational to overcome a numbness, just as an alcoholic seeks drink to inflate a grandiose image of the self to contrast the numbness of internal depression or disconnection.

Woolf's major despair stemmed from her childlessness, the feeling that here was an "unlived life," and her perpetual obsessions with suicide and death. Even as she was claiming (and so issuing a competitive challenge to Vanessa's motherhood) that *The Years* represented a "long childbirth," Woolf bemoaned her barren state and associated it with an unlived life (Panken, p.208).

Also contributing to Woolf's despair was the failure of love. Love appears in her earlier work, *Night and Day* (1919), but even here passion is fleeting, quickly quelled and tamed. In order to sustain a relationship with Katharine, Ralph draws up an unwritten contract of restrained friendship, in which no emotional risks are allowed. Rationalizing that they both need independence, just as Leonard and Virginia Woolf must have frequently rationalized their mutual distancing, Ralph contracts with Katharine that they be free to be alone, to not have feelings that would bind them to each other (Panken, p. 94). By the time of *Mrs. Dalloway* (1925), Woolf's despair has deepened and passion has become something to avoid. Clarissa Dalloway thus turns down an emotionally alive relationship with Peter, choosing to resign herself to a detached marriage of convention to the promiscuous Richard. Panken asks whether Woolf realized that "this is what a live relationship is about" when she made Clarissa leave Peter because she could neither tolerate the intensity of the feelings between herself and Peter nor the conflicts such passion aroused.

In her next novel, *To The Lighthouse* (1927), love is seen as once again as an abstraction, in terms of a symbolic representation of the other, not as an interpersonal communication. The author's vision is presented through the eyes of Mr. Ramsay, as he visualizes his wife in the image of the lighthouse and its beacon of light. After Mrs. Ramsay's death, the beacon of light becomes a beacon of hope for Mr. Ramsay, symbolizing his wife's spirit. Symbolically she has become the lighthouse shedding light.

The Ramsays do engage in interpersonal exchanges, but they are through sadomasochistic interchanges which Woolf probably based on her parents' relations. But because their aggression is never direct, they do not understand their effect upon one another. The Ramsay's aggression towards one another is almost ritualistic, as most sadomasochistic maneuvers including that of Woolf's parents ultimately are.

To the Lighthouse is followed four years later by *The Waves*. For the first time in her works, there is now no defined theme of love. All the characters are consumed by a self-conscious appraisal of their own mode of perception. This appraisal becomes the means by which each character strives for identity, but the struggle is played out in monologues. Sometimes these monologues are seemingly shared with another character, yet they remain monologues nonetheless. The lack of emotional response between characters is a glaring absence that makes interpersonal experience essentially unavailable. Although Bernard is attracted by Susan and her supposed oneness with nature, there is never any responsive interchange between them that can lead to interpersonal connection, let alone sustained love. In a work that many have viewed as showing Woolf's creative powers at their height, a unification through vision is sought because of the total breakdown of interpersonal relations. The good mother is sought, but a symbolic vision of unity appears instead. There is no felt good mother, no emotional or tactile mother to respond directly to the subjective state of the child. Symbolic representations of unity echo yearnings for a primary holding mother to replace the lack of a separate mother. Without the interpersonal, Woolf's continuous view of herself leading an "unlived life" is certainly understandable.

The sadomasochism of the Ramsay's marriage is that characteristic of Woolf's parents marriage. Sadomasochistic dynamics also reflect the reports by Panken (1987) of Woolf's own marriage. Woolf's description of her own marriage as "too close, but not close enough," (Panken, p. 256) becomes a blueprint for her view of all marriages. Panken reports that Leonard knew the intimate details of Virginia's menstrual life. There was no space or boundary between them. Using the excuse that his role was to

take care of Virginia, and so keep her from a breakdown, Leonard intruded into every crevice of his wife's personal life. Virginia must have felt
Leonard under her skin, for he made daily notes of her physical and mental condition. This lack of boundaries certainly impaired any potential
erotic feeling between them, even if Virginia had not been numbed to heterosexual physical attraction.[4]

Leonard compensated for his intrusiveness by giving his wife something tremendously important—support for her creative work. Having
long put aside his own ambitions, he focused his energies on developing a
publishing company to publish Virginia's work. As the Hogarth Press
grew from a private press to a major publishing house, Leonard published
and publicized all Virginia's books. He also served as a consistent positive mirror for Virginia, reading her work, and commenting on it. By
adoring her work, he also presented an attitude of adoring Virginia, as
indeed he had when they first met, for her work was felt by both to be her
essence.

In this role, Leonard served Virginia, even when having an occasional
sexual affair with another woman. Panken believes that Virginia may
have known about Leonard's affairs. She may have experienced rage at
such transgressions from their symbiotic orbit—as evidenced by Clarissa
Dalloway's thoughts of self-annihilation on learning that her husband
Richard had "lunch" with other women. Yet such suicidal notions probably passed, as Leonard remained strongly bonded to her.[5] However, after
Woolf had completed *The Years*—the same time when she was losing Vita
and Vanessa—Leonard may have become more seriously involved with
someone else. Bond (1989) has stated this as fact, proclaiming that
Leonard fell in love with another woman. The identity of the woman is
unknown. Virginia became emotionally bereft, and consumed with rage
she could not face, process, or communicate.

Leonard's enormous transgression would have been enough to make
Virginia experience a dramatic reduction of support and of narcissistic
sustenance. The emotional loss set in motion by Leonard's adultery was
perhaps even more damaging. Bond chronicles the loss of his responsive
mirroring and applause, as well as his use of deceit as he freed himself
from his nurturing role. The deceit Bond refers to is shown by Leonard's
false representation of his critical responses to *The Years*. Quentin Bell
has written of an incident in which Leonard flatters Virginia rather than
honestly accessing her work. Perhaps Leonard tended towards this in the
past. He was, for example, overtly positive to her about *Jacob's Room*
(1922), while telling others that the characters seemed like insubstantial

beings buffeted by fate (Panken, p. 105). Bell reports, Leonard's thoughts in relation to a fear that his wife would kill herself if he told her the truth.

> The book was a failure—but it was not so much a failure as Virginia supposed. (Bell, Vol II, p. 197).... It would therefore be possible to tell a lie, if he told her the truth he had very little doubt that she would kill herself. Suddenly he put down the proof and said, 'I think its extraordinarily good.' (Bell, p. 196)

Bond's assessment of this incident is that Virginia must have felt Leonard had betrayed her, as she was unconsciously probably very well attuned to him, and, therefore, to his duplicity. Following this episode, Leonard was openly critical of Virginia's biography of Roger Fry. He was so overtly hostile that Virginia described him as lecturing to her in such a way that she felt "pecked at by a strong hard beak." Bond downplays the effect of Leonard's aggression, seeing the earlier deceitful commentary as more likely to have induced a feeling of betrayal. Nevertheless, Leonard was no longer the admirer of Virginia that he once was, and for someone as narcissistically vulnerable as she—Woolf, for example, had felt relief at Katherine Mansfield's death because her friend had aroused her envy—Leonard's withdrawal of admiration must have been a terrible blow.

In Woolf's last novel, *Between the Acts* (1941), she shows her sense of betrayal quite overtly. Her main female character, Isa, is an alter-ego. Isa's husband Gile basically ignores her, and goes off with another woman. She does nothing to stop it, but rather like Clarissa Dalloway, on learning that her husband lunched with other women, Isa turns her aggression against herself. Isa is far more self-aggressive than Mrs. Dalloway is. In a retaliatory gesture against her husband, she picks up a knife and imagines shoving it into her own body. She never communicates her rage directly to him, thereby vindictively stabbing the internal object that she associates with her husband. In real life too, Woolf had turned inward her rage against Leonard. Her suicide represented the culmination of a lifelong pattern of suicidal despair and gestures. In this way, Woolf maintained her idealization of her husband, and split off her aggression, obtaining unconscious revenge through the attack on herself.

The failure of love—to experience the other as a whole object that one can ambivalently love—is seen in both Woolf's work and life, the work echoing the internal despair of the emotionally degenerative life. Woolf's failure is the direct correlation of her failure to move in and thereby renew the organic modes of creativity that had sustained her. The failure in love then parallels Woolf's failure to successfully mourn through her work, each disastrously impacting upon the other.

FAILED SALVATION THROUGH CREATIVITY, FAILED REPARATION

What did Virginia Woolf mean by constantly lamenting an unlived life? As the years passed, bringing increasing disillusionment, her cries of anguish became more acute. When the war isolated the Woolfs from former friends, so that Virginia lost the audience that had provided an echoing response for her work, she wrote about her despair in *Between the Acts*:

> "Thank the actors, not the author," he said, "or ourselves, the audience." (*Between the Acts*, p. 203)

What a poignant pain can be sensed from such a negation of the author's significance! Woolf's lifelong pursuit of identity and love through her creative work left her looking at her work from a detached and disconnected distance.

After publication, Woolf disconnected from each fictional work—she never wanted to look at it again. Ronald Fairbairn (1952) has theorized about this kind of artist, who he labels schizoid. The schizoid artist cannot sustain connection to his or her work after others have it in their possession. If others view and find fault with it, it is spoiled. If it is not in the artist's exclusive possession, it is spoiled as a symbiotic self-extension. Failing to sustain a connection with the inner life of one's work is similar to losing the connection with the inner life of those one loves. To not keep one's creations and real-life objects inside, to not sustain an internalization of them, means one is alone and isolated. Then one only sees from the outside. As Bond says, this is the state Woolf was reduced to after she had completed a work—alone without her characters. Her life became diminutive, represented by the external forms of the books, without a sustained connection to the spiritual life within them.

The war, as indicated, increased Woolf's isolation. For one thing, Leonard was Jewish. Together, they made a suicide pact, pledging to asphyxiate themselves with gasoline fumes in their garage if Hitler should enter England.

The war had increased her isolation in another way. Besides no longer having Leonard to serve her as a positively mirroring "subject object" (Winnicott, 1971),[6] Woolf was now bereft of a more general audience, and the war had ended her connections with publishers, critics, and markets for her work. Because of those two losses, Bond sees Woolf as losing her "echo," her outward validation of an existing self. The double loss was devastating. She had always craved recognition. She did not simply decry her unlived life and "little books," she also wrote that it was not enough for people to read only one of her books (Panken, p. 237). They needed to read all of them. Otherwise, she had no identity. Woolf speaks of losing any wall of protection that she felt around her prior to the war. She also notes losing her audience as a death to her soul. In her diary, at this time, Woolf observes that her writing "I" is gone. Without her audience, there is no "private stimulus, only this outer roar" (Panken, p. 257).

Woolf needed an outer audience to give her a sense of being. Her "I" had disappeared because she had never internalized enough of a good holding mother to sustain a sense of self within.

Woolf's wish for identity through recognition from others became a tragic quest that was impossible to fulfill. How many people were going to read *all* her books? Very few. Of course, many critics and biographers have subsequently done just that. But in her lifetime, Woolf had no way of knowing this would occur.

Woolf's wish to have all her books read to feel alive, to feel her life was "lived," to feel that she had an identity, is typical of the wishes of many artists. But the artists it most reflects are those, who like herself, could not be known to others through direct interpersonal engagement. For the artist whose dilemma emerges in her work—which tells the story of why she or he can't communicate to people—the work becomes the only avenue to self-expression. This, as we have seen, was true for Woolf. Her interpersonal relationships, as noted with Vanessa and Leonard, were basically sadomasochistic after the model of her parents. Bond (1989) sees Virginia as playing the masochistic role with Vanessa and the more sadistic role with Leonard, although her marriage certainly represents an interplay of sadomasochistic dynamics. Even more sensationally sadomasochistic is Virginia's relationship with Vita Sackville-West. Virginia definitely played the more masochistic role as Vita allured her and then pulled out just as Woolf's hunger for her was ripe. Virginia was able to at least partially retaliate by confronting Vita with her lack of responsiveness and her limitations as a writer: "Something in you doesn't vibrate." (Bond, p. 139). However, such confrontation, as we have argued, was extremely rare for Woolf. And as her yearnings for Vita intensified, she lost such directness.

A common thread in all Woolf's dynamics is a sadomasochistic seduction and abandonment theme still merged with her primary mother.[7] Woolf lacked the secure sense of separation and individuation which is needed if a person is to form relationships that extend beyond the push-pull dynamics of sadomasochistic desire. Because sustained interpersonal connection remained so limited—her fear of direct communication was a sign of such limits—Woolf was most often left in a disconnected and isolated state. Her literary characters all reflected this. In one way or another, they were all isolated, for example, Rhoda in *The Waves*, Rachel in *The Voyage Out*, and Isa in *Between the Acts*. It is most poignant that in *The Voyage Out* Rachel faints when any closeness occurs, or she goes into a semi-trance (see Panken, p. 84). If the author, who puts pieces of herself into her characters (in a process of borderline projective-identification) was unable to tolerate intimacy to this degree, it is no wonder that she had abbreviated or aborted moments of intimate sharing between Katharine and Ralph in *Night and Day*, and it is no wonder that Virginia often suffered from headaches and had fainting episodes. Panken points out one occasion when Virginia seemed to choose such symptoms as a way of avoiding conflict with Vanessa, who was then angry at her. Avoidance of interpersonal confrontation and communication, as we have suggested, abounds in Woolf's life.

But for Woolf connecting through her work meant connecting with her internal objects as they already existed within her, and her internal relations reflected her abortions of intimacy. This explains why her overwhelming need to find a self-core through a sustained connection with her creative work was constantly frustrated. She found only a few rare images of a good mother that could lend her security.

The experience of the creative act, no matter how sensual and alive in the moment, could not give Woolf a sustained internalization of a good mother. She needed an object-relations psychotherapeutic treatment, which was then unavailable, to accomplish this. This form of treatment would have precipitated much anguish in the mourning and letting go of the negative object ties that so bound her from within. But without such mourning, which would have involved her confronting her resistance to new modes of relating, Woolf could never have sustained connection to a submerged core personality, even if it emerged briefly in the creative moment, making her feel pregnant and rich inside.

Why Woolf's work failed to be her salvation will become more clear as her aborted attempts to mourn and understand herself through her creative process are discussed. It is, however, important to point out that the life-experience of Woolf and many other female artists contradicts John Gedo's theory that through creative work the artist adequately replaces love objects (see Kavaler, 1985, 1986, 1988, 1989, 1991). The creative work reflects the inner world. Although a sense of self-transcendence may be felt during the creative process, as basic ties to a bad internal object

THE GENIUS AND SORROW OF VIRGINIA WOOLF, PART II

are seemingly bypassed and a connection to a good primary holding mother is rediscovered, this sensation is momentary. The artist must return to face the entire internal object situation that emerges in the content of the creative work. Flashes of connection to a good mother do not transform the internal bad object ties from the separation period and beyond, or from the early trauma of having been weaned like Woolf at ten weeks old. Although the transpersonal psyche has some healing powers of its own (Nathan Schwartz-Salant, 1982), the basic intrapsychic ties to early bad objects cannot significantly change in the absence of ongoing work with a containing and supportive external object, that can over time be internalized through a "holding object" transference. The good aspects of this therapeutic object require ongoing work to overcome major resistance, since good-object connection is unfamiliar, and the bad-object sadomasochistic ties are familiar and primal. When Virginia Woolf exclaimed that all that was left of her life were "these little books," she was revealing that she had devalued all her work, as its positive aspects were overshadowed by bad internal object ties that had to be once again blocked out from consciousness, whether by splitting or by repression.

FAILED MOURNING

Panken observes that Woolf sought out dramatic and sensational life situations and images to overcome her internal numbness. In this regard, as well as in her need to defend against internal pain, Woolf's genuine strivings for authentic expression were compromised at the point where they might have become therapeutic—that is, in terms of resolving internal conflicts through self understanding. Because Woolf's work was her major pathway to spontaneity and authenticity, it was also the primary route available to her for potential mourning. Another route remained closed: she never entered psychoanalysis, perhaps in part out of an unconscious recognition that the people she was closest to would probably not have tolerated such affect.

But as we've seen, work was not enough. Themes of depressive despair appear increasing in her life and work, as the issues evoking them do not get resolved. The basic conflicts, Panken notes, remain the same, reappearing in a late novel such as *The Waves* as they had in her first novel *The Voyage Out*.

It is my thesis that such a breakdown into despair results because Woolf failed to adequately mourn in her work. According to Panken who also observed unresolved mourning through studying Woolf's literary work, Woolf's aborted mourning process can be attributed to three factors: a continual splitting off of aggression from consciousness, a continual pattern of defensive idealization, and a basic mode of denial. I agree with Panken.

Panken's in-depth analysis of the literary work has helped me to see in it repeated instances of primitive aggression, some of which have been discussed, that are never felt nor understood by the characters or the authors.

Why does Woolf fail to resolve this primitive mode of rage? I believe that she is unable to integrate its aggressive power into a conscious self which might neutralize it, and thus use it towards self-agency. For, in order for the neutralization and integration of such primitive aggression to occur, a good-enough internal object connection needs to exist, or to be built in. In this way, mourning for the lost good object, which permits self-integration, can occur. Because of the traumatic disruptions in her early mothering, Woolf lacked a good internal object. We see this in, as indicated, the many oral rage images and themes of insatiable hunger which appear in her fiction. We see it too in the repeated references to self-annihilation due to abandonment.

Not having enough good internal object connection to mourn, Woolf is forced to split off and project her rage, or to repress it to the degree that her psyche was capable of repression (which it generally wasn't). She cannot feel enough loving connection to tolerate loss and integrate herself.

But her failure is not complete. In *To The Lighthouse* Woolf forces herself to acknowledge the very real battle that characterized her parent's marriage (see Panken, p. 152). Despite Woolf's wish to show her mother as nurturing, and to laud her father's intellect and sexuality, the truth emerges. Mrs. Ramsay withholds love to combat her husband's power. It is this authenticity that makes for better art than when Woolf attempts to idealize her mother. Unfortunately, the confrontation with such authentic images is far less frequent than the idealizations. Lily Briscoe, Woolf's adult alter-image, is frightened of marriage, but Woolf only minimally links this with any analysis of how the Ramsay's marriage affected Lily. We are told that Lily feared ever serving a man's wishes and needs, as she saw Mrs. Ramsay doing with her husband. However, why is Lily's fear so great whenever she thinks of heterosexual alliances that she fantasizes throwing herself from a cliff or of drowning? The causes which may be found in Lily's childhood are never revealed.

However there is Woolf's description of Cam, a younger version of Woolf than Lily. Cam, like Virginia Woolf herself, enjoys a close relationship with her father as she grows up. Although Woolf does not describe Cam's infancy, it is clear that Cam, like Virginia, is forced to view her mother's adoration of her younger brother as a young prepubescent girl.

Woolf shows the same inability to face reality in her depiction of

Rhoda in *The Waves*. Rhoda frequently feels insubstantial. She also has suicidal fantasies. Yet Rhoda never analyzes her inability to sustain engagement in the world. For Panken, these examples show that Woolf continually experiences herself as containing an inner black void. She is still out of touch with the roots of her depression and despair—her internal bad object situation.

In mid-life, as in *To the Lighthouse* (1924) Woolf attempted to confront aspects of life that she never dared face before. Given the taboo against speaking out by incest victims, DeSalvo praises Woolf for her bravery, especially as she did it on her own. DeSalvo cites Woolf's attempt to remember and describe their sexual and incestuous abuse in *The Sketch of Things Past* (19). Woolf's failure to pursue what she had started, DeSalvo suggests, could be attributed to her reading Freud at that time. Freud was then claiming that formerly labeled memories of sexual abuse were not based on real events, but were fantasies of intrapsychic origin— libidinal oedipal stage desire. If DeSalvo is right, Freud's teachings may have encouraged Woolf to censor herself. Whatever the reason for it, Woolf's retreat had tragic consequences. She regressed to turning her aggression against herself which made her suicidal as she was unable to successfully split off her aggression, for it was at a psychic level where repression fails. Her response allowed her to ward off grief, thereby cutting her off from a more full mourning. She returned also to modes of idealization that prevented her from knowing any truth about her past which could help her mourn. Woolf's tendency to create a barrier against her pain through defensive idealization is most visible in her relation to her mother.

It is in this relation that Woolf had the greatest need to distance herself from the truth, because it is presumably towards her mother that she felt the most guilt. She felt guilt about the special relationship with her father that excluded her mother and possibly aroused her jealousy (see Panken, p. 30). Then there was guilt over her inability to mourn her mother. This is illustrated vividly in *The Years*, in which a mother's death is not only unmourned, but eagerly anticipated. Although Panken believes that Woolf shed some tears along with her other siblings at her mother's, she may not have grieved more fully from within. If her portrayal of Delia in *The Years* (Panken, p. 215–216) is true to Woolf's own emotional life, she may have merely gone through the motions of grief. Heartfelt grief was probably blocked by unconcious rage towards her mother. Without consciously being able to hate, she could consciously grieve (see Melanie Klein, 1940, "Mourning and Manic Depressive States").

Woolf's guilt probably fixated her in a state of pathological mourning for her mother. Pathological mourning is characterized by obsession with the lost object that is a symptom of inability to love the object. Because a person in this state cannot grieve over the objects, letting go of it becomes impossible, unless an object-relations mode of treatment intercedes.[8] The greater the split-off unconscious rage Woolf held towards her mother, the more Woolf had reason to feel guilty. Panken provides extensive evidence of Woolf's guilt.

Woolf acknowledges her obsessive preoccupation with her mother. The writing of *To the Lighthouse* represented an attempt to purge, exorcise, or mourn this obsession. After completing the novel, Woolf believed that she had indeed freed herself. Bond buys into Woolf's conviction. Panken, however, does not accept Woolf's version and neither do I. One example shows that Woolf was still awash in her guilt. In *Moments of Being*, written years after *To the Lighthouse*, Woolf turns abruptly from an image of her mother to that of the lush flowers on the wallpaper surrounding her. Bond has interpreted these images as showing the alluring mother of Woolf's symbiotic period. But an alluring mother can be more the "exciting object" (Seinfeld, 1990, Fairbairn, 1952) than a good mothering object. The exciting object tantalizes, as Ronald Fairbairn suggests, but ultimately unavailable, it is experienced as rejecting. In this example, we can assume that the pain for Woolf in facing the image of the alluring, but rejecting mother may have been too great. She was too imbued with guilt and too full of hatred towards a primary object. Therefore, she tried desperately to preserve her identity through avoiding the traumatic impact of the pain, by switching instead to a description of the wallpaper. Such evasion may have been necessary for Woolf's survival when she had no interpersonal support for grief. But it aborted her potential to mourn and, consequently, to develop psychologically.

Without a psychotherapist, Woolf may have had no option but to avoid what was too painful. Alone she could not contain the aggression, guilt, and loss of the fantasy "exciting" mother, who Vita Sackville-West came to represent. Woolf's failure here to mourn her real mother, even when she attempted to—trying through art in *To the Lighthouse*—shows that genius cannot overcome psychic limitations nor can the creative process—for by itself, the creative process cannot serve as an adequate container or good holding mother.

When Woolf wrote *To the Lighthouse*, her wish to mourn her mother by facing her in symbiotic representational form was at its height. But symbolism fails when its images are too idealized. In Woolf's case her symbols were too far from the negative images of her mother that she needed to face and integrate. They were too far from the reality of her mother's limitations as a maternal figure.

Panken addresses Woolf's tendency, in *To the Lighthouse*, to idealize her mother. Although the capacity to idealize is a sign of some good early mothering, it wards off negative images and distorts the truth in order to avoid genuine affect, and thus mourning. Woolf's portrayal of her mother in *To the Lighthouse* emerges as both phallic and maternal. But the symbolism is used to substitute this relationship. For example, Woolf tries to accentuate her mother's maternal engagement with her children. Mrs. Ramsay supposedly wishes that all her children could stay as babies in her arms. She is described as appreciating each of her children's individual talents. She is absorbed with her son, and empathic to his disappointment in his father. Panken believes that here Woolf portrays her mother as much more engaged with her children than Julia Stephen ever was.

Who then was the "source" of Mrs. Ramsay? DeSalvo (1989) suggests that during Woolf's childhood her stepsister Stella was her only real, consistent maternal caretaker. Possibly driven by her wish to paint a glowing portrait of her dead mother, Woolf took the attitude of nurturing attention she had experienced with Stella and transposed it onto the character of Mrs. Ramsay. In contrast, Woolf's portrait of the father is much more authentic. His moods change. His varying levels of capacity to be a father are depicted. He is loving, tender, and engaged with his children, yet only when in good spirits. When preoccupied by self-doubt, he is very demanding and full of infantile rage.[9]

Despite all Woolf's attempts to create a mother who palpably exists on a day-to-day basis, Mrs. Ramsay ultimately emerges as a symbol. She becomes one of Woolf's visionary presences. For example, she manipulates her knitting needles as if enacting a religious rite. Such imagery is in sharp contrast to Woolf's descriptions (as reported by Panken, 1987) about her mother as a woman whose ideas on what it meant to be feminine were based on cajoling, flattering, and deceiving men with "wiles." In contrast, Mrs. Ramsay is a source of spiritual salvation. She is a fictional mother who Woolf created, contrived, and tailored. She is a mother born out of Woolf's childhood adoration for a very different real mother—an adoration all children experience, an adoration that made her feel uplifted by selecting the jewels her mother wore for dinner.[10] In *To the Lighthouse*, then, Woolf extends the untransformed childhood adoration for her mother into an adult religious awe and reverence. Mrs. Ramsay becomes a god-force, and, in the image of the lighthouse, a spiritual phallus. She sheds mystic radiance, promising Woolf the visionary ideals that would allow her to enter a transpersonal realm where she could overcome the misery of her family's sadomasochistic modes of relating. Many would call this mode of thinking wish fulfillment or wishful thinking.

Denial, Panken argues, is another barrier Woolf erects in her work to ward off successful mourning. Once again, I agree. Defensive denial appears often in the fiction. One poignant example is that of Septimus in *Mrs. Dalloway*. In denying his feelings for a military comrade lost in the war, Septimus grows increasingly depressed, rageful, incoherently mad, and suicidal. Panken notes how Septimus kills himself by denying his feelings for the one human being for whom he had allowed himself to care.

Clarissa, in *Mrs. Dalloway*, is another example of a character in denial. Clarissa rationalizes her rejection of Peter and her marriage to Richard as caused by her need for stability and independence. Two people, she remarks, cannot be as close as Peter and herself are, without intruding on each other. Yet Peter truly seeks to know her. He feels ecstasy in her presence, even though he sees her faults. He is someone with whom she can fight. Therefore, it is not surprising that she feels an absorbing intensity and passion in his presence that is completely lacking in her response to Richard. Nevertheless, she pleases her father by marrying the conventional man, Richard. In effect, she chooses a martyrdom in which she gives up her inner self to fit into an outer or societally conventional mold. When Richard betrays her by having affairs with other women, she thinks evasively of "self-annihilation." Her suicidal thoughts allow her to avoid her rage at Richard and possibly at her father.

These examples indicate how Woolf's defensive maneuvers overshadowed her capacities to face the pain, loss, grief, and rage involved in mourning. These manuevers obviated the processing of powerful psychic states that must be contained for successful mourning to occur. Moreover, her belief (Kelley, 1972) that she could mourn on her own, through the portrayal of universal truths rather than personal self-analysis, ultimately sabotaged her "effort." But Woolf's failure to seek assistance from psychoanalysis is mirrored in her own resistance to really using the creative process and her own capacity for self-expression as psychotherapy. Her idealization of herself as an artist was as one who tries, like Emily Brontë, to heal the division in her universe through the depiction of universal truths. This was but one more idealization that prevented her from facing head on her personal pain and conflict.

FINAL DESCENT INTO DESPAIR AND SUICIDE

Virginia Woolf's last novel, *Between the Acts*, begins with regressive oral and anal themes which reflect Woolf's own decompensating state during this period. The first image is of a cesspool. The image contains "regressive implications of excremental smells; the filth of human drainage and sewage, evocative of the mud and dung of *The Years*" (Panken p. 244). A typical example of oral regressive imagery is the phrase, "gobble in the gutter" (Panken, p. 244). Formerly latent primitive levels in Woolf are manifest and pervasive in *Between the Acts*. Primitive images abound where they had, in her other novels, surfaced only sporadically. The powerful phallic self image of a "race horse" in *The Years* is replaced by images of maggots and rodents (Panken, p. 252). Two swans float downstream in the midst of "dirty duckweed," (Panken p. 244) obviously a reference to the Duckworth brothers.

Indeed, Isa, Woolf's alter-ego, is obsessed with the report of a rape she read about in a newspaper. There are other, indirect references to involuntary sexual acts, such as Lucy's recollection of a fishing expedition with Bart who "forced" her to remove the fish from a fishing hook, her shock in seeing the gills saturated with blood (Panken, p. 245)." The negative phallic images, which have cropped up throughout Woolf's work are here even more violent and obsessive.

Death and suicide imagery are also overt and increasingly pervasive. In describing the lily pond filling with water, and a nightmarish self-image: "in that deep center [black] in that black heart 'a woman had drowned herself for love'" (p. 245), love is equated with self-annihilation or entering a black void. In this void where there is no maternal connection or protection.

At the time of writing *Between The Acts*, Woolf had lost the moorings of her primary relationships, with her husband and with her female lover. Consequently at this time she was left more vulnerable than ever to the deficits of her internal world, in which maternal absence was pervasive and the malignancy of sexual abuse haunted her. Another image of primitive phallic motherhood appears:

> a snake with a toad in its mouth, unable to swallow and the toad unable to die. It was 'birth the wrong way.' (quoted in Panken, pp. 246–247)

Here Woolf apparently confuses reproduction and oral ingestion. Even more striking is how the inability of the toad to die mirrors Woolf's own wish to die and her resistance to death. The description also foreshadows her failed suicide attempt before she drowns herself. When she made her last and successful suicide attempt, she placed a stone in each pocket to keep her under water. This is birth "the wrong way," in that we all come from the water, the water within our mothers' womb, our personal river or ocean.

Isa murmurs her suicidal thoughts: "What wish should I drop into the well? That the waters should cover me" (Panken, p. 247). Accompanying her withdrawal into suicidal thought is her "masochistic" (Panken, p. 247) refusal to accept her husband's conciliatory efforts. Isa's need for punishment and rejection, might obviously reflect Woolf's own needs since she generally used characters as her alter-egos (Panken, pp. 37, 143, 243).

Following Bart's recital of Swineburne's: "Swallow, my sister, O sister swallow," a line evocative of Woolf's oral rape by her brothers, Isa turns her wrath at her husband against herself:

> Picking up a knife she recites:
> 'from her bosom's snowy antre drew the gleaming blade. Plunge blade! she said. And struck. Faithless! She cried, Knife, too! It broke. So too my heart' (quoted in Panken, p. 248)

The split-off cravings for a mother echo. Woolf writes that a cow bellowed: "The whole world was filled with dumb yearning. It was the primeval voice sounding loud in the present moment" (In *Between the Acts,* p. 140).

Miss La Trobe, the writer and director of a pageant in *Between the Acts*, is another alter-ego of the author. She represents Woolf's creativity and her strivings for recognition. Her dilemma reproduces Woolf's own: how to deal with the loss of echo from her audience, as the war closed off her literary market. Miss La Trobe's audience disperses. Her pageant disintegrates. The moment of artistic vision is briefer in this novel than in any of Woolf's previous fiction. As the bad object overwhelms Woolf in her life, self-fragmentation proceeds, with her work displaying a corresponding deterioration. In *Between the Acts*, Woolf's cries have become desperate: "What we need is a center, something to bring us together" (Panken, 1987). La Trobe "'felt her play a failure'" (Panken, p. 249). Still the director tries to hold on to a shred of hope, telling herself that it is in her "giving that the triumph was." In *Between the Acts*, Miss La Trobe has just quarreled with her homosexual lover, just as Woolf had with Vita. Panken reports La Trobe's despair, which like that of Isa reflects Woolf's own:

> Feeling she had 'suffered triumph, humiliation, ecstasy, despair, for nothing' (210), Miss La Trobe, since the quarrel with her lover, felt

permeated with the 'horror and terror of being alone,' felt 'nature
had set her apart from her kind.' (Panken, p. 250)

As the key people in her external life withdrew, their loss exacerbated in
Woolf her internal bad-object situation, the early maternal abandonment.
Ultimately, Woolf's internal situation of inner isolation was overwhelming
her.

So *Between the Acts* expresses Woolf's inner struggle at a time when
her negative internal object situation was vanquishing her. We have spoken of the loss of support from Leonard. It had counterbalanced the internal situation. But Leonard had changed the constellation of their
relationship, breaking free of his old subservient role. As Panken points
out (p. 257), Leonard's hand was for the first time not tied to Woolf's
needs; he was now writing for himself.

It was Woolf's hand which began to feel frozen. Leonard was no longer
participating in the myth that Virginia's creative works were their children—and that his publishing them was helping her through pregnancy
and childbirth. If Bond is right, and Leonard Woolf was in love with
another woman, then his withdrawal from a symbiotic relationship with
Woolf—in which he sired the children she chose and mirrored her virtues
as a mother-creator by applauding her work—is understandable. Perhaps
because of his new distance from her, Leonard failed to save Woolf from
suicide as he had in the past. He ignored the signs of trouble when he
bumped into her on the day she tried and failed to drown. Although she
was drenched, he took no emergency measures. (Panken, p. 260).
Moreover, during the period of his withdrawal, he never attempted to
speak to her about what she was feeling. Losing Leonard must have been
like losing the good father who psychologically fulfilled the role of a
mother for Woolf.

At this time of great vulnerability, she also backed down from any self-
assertion with Vita. Bond (1989) describes a previous time when she confronted Vita. (Panken sees Woolf as having put herself in a subordinate
role with Vita, supplicating her as she had Vanessa. She pursued the
unavailable mother, and the more she did, the more Vita eluded her.)

In the end Woolf did not deviate from idealizing, rather than confronting, those she felt she needed so desperately. She played out the last
act of her internal script. The final suicide missive to Leonard was decidedly protective of him: "If anyone could have saved me I know it would
have been you." To end her life on a note of defensive idealization was to
end herself to protect the love object. At the end, Woolf also idealized
Vanessa and in so doing, once and for all, denied all her sister's rejections.

Her husband and her sister also were projections of Woolf's internal parents while she defended against her rage at Leonard and Vanessa with idealizations of them, her personal writing (Panken, p. 256) contained idealizations of her parents. She remembered "sitting on her mother's lap, of hearing the waves and feeling the 'purist' ecstasy while lying in the children's nursery." Here she exalts her mother noting only briefly her unavailability.

Perhaps Woolf's memory of the sea as soothing led her once again to seek the soothing mother. Was she trying through suicide to escape the demon lover—animus without anima—that had gone beyond haunting to pervading her being? Was she attempting to transform the demon lover back into the muse father by passing through the entrance of the sea and being reborn? Possibly such a fantasy involved substituting a soft and receptive sea mother for her own hard, implacable, phallic, and dissociated mother.

Woolf's capacity to remember the good things about those she loved and needed could, of course, have loaned her strength, if it had not been a memory sustained through the denial of her anger. She must have feared that she was filled with so much unexpressed rage—a lifetime of it—that any acknowledgment would have wiped out all the love she had managed to sustain for her objects. However, the devaluation of herself that came with the idealization of the other left her impotent. Her idealization may have been a psychically determined event, but it turned out also to be fatal.

Woolf's idealization of her parents, and of those who played the psychic roles of her parents in her current life, extended to an idealization of death. Kelley (Page 211) adopts this same idealization by interpreting Woolf's view of death as one in which vision is attained by bypassing the ultimate boundary and relinquished life. For Kelley, Rachel's death in *The Voyage Out* allows her and Terence to reunite and transcend their separateness by sharing vision. Kelley writes (p. 32) similarly of *The Waves*, remarking how Rhoda's yearning for death, which culminates in suicide, represents a broader view of spiritual transcendence (p. 155). This kind of transcendence through death may have been sought by Woolf, but if so, it is the wish of someone who cannot experience closeness with others through affect communication and interpersonal relationships.

In idealizing Woolf's defensive idealization, Kelley fails to appreciate her pain and grief. Kelley is a literary critic, not a psychologist, and can therefore take Woolf's ideas at their manifest level. In contrast, Panken is a psychologist and a psychoanalyst. As such, she is perhaps more sensitive to the intense inner conflict that led Woolf to idealize death. For

Woolf, sinking into the water represented an image of maternal soothing that she turned to when overwhelmed with pain and when out of control. If creativity once meant joining her father and having his child, feeling barren now meant turning to primitive early mother fantasies of an intrauterine life in water. In fantasy, descending into the water could have meant joining her mother.

Woolf's suicide was, I believe, psychologically overdetermined, but I believe it was her idealizing mode of defense that tipped the balance. She feared death. She wished for rescue, as Panken (p. 270) suggests, right to the end, as indicated by her mentioning his "saving" her in her suicide note to Leonard. Even so, Woolf was unable to tolerate the "aloneness" she felt as articulated by her alter-egos, Isa and Miss La Trobe, in *Between the Acts*. Split-off aggression, manifested in sarcastic and indirect accusatory demands, reinforced her isolation and her fears of abandonment. She has Miss La Trobe bravely declare that she has another creative work in mind after the disintegration and abandonment she experiences as her current creative work fails to hold her audience. But this moment of hope, of continued psychic effort in the face of overwhelming obstacles, passes quickly.[11] Miss La Trobe cries out in despair about "aloneness" and the failure of effort and then recedes into the background. Isa murmurs that she and Giles must fight like "vixen" if they are ever to be reunited, echoing Woolf's thoughts concerning herself and Leonard. But fighting, as suggested, is just what Woolf couldn't do. Sarcastic quips at people escaped, but direct confrontation was absent. She, therefore, reinforced feelings of helplessness that must have originated in the very real victimized helplessness she had endured when her mother weaned her at ten weeks and then withdrew more completely during the vulnerability of rapprochement.

Woolf set up a desperate hope for "fighting like vixen" in marriage through the voice of Isa in her last novel *Between the Acts*, which she couldn't fulfill in her own life. Instead, she sank into the mud beneath the water as Isa had imagined doing. I believe that Woolf's suicide represented both an indirect act of vindictiveness against Leonard, Vanessa, and Vita, as Panken suggests, as well as a wish to find a psychic salvation through merger with a primitive holding mother who she fantasizes she can join through death. Her split-off rage, which she turned against herself, and the idealizing defense that reinforced it signed her death certificate. Creativity had not proved a substitute for love; it was entirely dependent on it. Woolf's split-off aggression and her sealed-off, haunted internal world compelled her to recreate a negative internal-object situation in the external world—this preventing her from transforming her rage into the grief of early loss. Without grief, Woolf could not connect with early love and longings for her primary parents. Therefore, she could not channel such primary love into interpersonal life.

8)

DIANE ARBUS AND THE
DEMON LOVER

In the larger analogy that binds many creative women, we find a cross-rhythm of pain, loss, and denial. We find a rush into creative expression, with the manic apex appearing in conjunction with object loss.

Like the poet Sylvia Plath, Diane Arbus suffered early object loss, followed by renewed object loss in adulthood.[1] I have described Sylvia Plath's traumatic reaction to her father's death, as it interacted with her reaction to her mother's psychological fusion with her, in earlier studies (Kavaler, 1985, 1986, Kavaler-Adler, 1993). A combination of childhood object loss and narcissistic relations with both mother and father contributed to a demon lover syndrome in Plath, when attempts to mourn through her work were arrested in longings for a split father-god figure of grandiose and villanized proportions. Similar dynamics can be seen in Diane Arbus. However, the early loss that Diane Arbus suffered was not that of her father. At seven years old, she lost her governess, that very nanny who had yielded her the tenderness withheld from her by her parents. In her teens, she met Allan Arbus, who provided her with the fatherly affection she had longed for. Older than her in years, and more particularly in manner and experience, Allan Arbus set guidelines for her future life which she hastened to follow. For many years, Diane and Allan worked together as fashion photographers, but the near symbiotic cord was broken when their individual artistic desires led them two different ways. Like Ted Hughes leaving Sylvia Plath, Allan left Diane for his own art, as well as for another woman. While Diane wandered around with her camera strapped across her chest, anxiously searching out the intensely authentic and deviant, her solo search left Allan to his new career in acting, and to his new kinship with another woman.

So similar to Plath, Diane's reaction to her husband's abandonment was to take the form of frantic creative efforts, of manic intensity. Like Plath also, some of Diane Arbus's best work was done at this time. She sought out transvestites in circus tents and midgets in sideshows. She was seeking the irregular, the erratic, anything that didn't fit into her mother's pretty and false pictures of the world.

Diane Arbus's parents were not the kind to face loss, or to allow mourning. They lived a life invested in their image. The Russeks department store was the family business, and it served as the family facade as well. Diane's mother, Gertrude, was a department store heiress, whose world was based on being the daughter and the wife of wealthy department store designer-directors. At one point in Gertrude's earlier adult years, she had a breakdown, but she somehow regained, without any insight, the narcissistic defenses that had briefly escaped her. She was glad to be rid of the pain, and quick to flee from any inquiry into its nature.

Diane was not so lucky, nor so naive. Her defenses were not so immaculate. To find the key to Diane's more vulnerable psyche, we must look at the internal father-daughter bond, or bind—the demon binding her from within.

In Patricia Boswell's biography of Diane Arbus, she quotes Diane as saying, at the time of her father's death, that she was haunted by the combination of blind indifference and veiled eroticism, which characterized her father's attitude toward her. She considered herself a prisoner of her yearnings towards this cold, and yet intensely seductive, father. Her tenacious tie to this father drove her to cling to men who both tantalized and rejected her. She was constantly seeking the approval of men like him, and she grew addicted to the mirroring confirmation that they would bestow on her. Without such mirroring, she was bereft, unable to grasp and know herself from within. It was in a period of deprivation of this addictive drug that she did finally kill herself.

Similar to the narcissistic character of Sylvia Plath's father, Diane Arbus's father was self-absorbed, and sought from his daughter mirroring for his own grandiose self. Whatever mirroring he gave was at the expense of the mirroring that he required. Diane felt unnoticed as a little girl by her father. She was unnoticed before and after the loss of her nanny, at age seven. Yet, when Diane grew into her adolescent years, and began to paint and sculpt, her father was quickly to claim her creative talents as a reflection of his own blood rendered legacy. Now, she suddenly became *his* daughter. Perhaps it was partly his own "veiled eroticism" and suppressed incestuality that actually impelled in her the compulsion to create, taking its form in her sculptures of swelling pregnant women. As her biographer notes, Diane did have many overt fantasies of father-daughter incest at this time, graphically imagining how it would be to copulate with her father.

Soon she had Allan Arbus to turn to, and the heightened creative drive seemed to subside, along with her father's approval. Her father saw Allan as a blight on the family name, far beneath Diane. He made every effort to forestall his daughter's plans for marriage to Allan. He tried to enlist the cooperation of one of Diane's male teachers, but he did not have the influence in the private school realm which he might have liked. He forbade Diane to see Allan, but of course the undertone of opposition only heightened the Romeo and Juliet passion of the teenage lovers.

Despite Diane's rejection of her father at this time, she was internally bound to him. No true emotional separation was made. No mourning took place. Within her, her father remained the mirror who reflected her glory in order to proclaim his own. Only a thin sheath of protection was wedged between his combined power as a mirroring self-object and as an eroticized oedipal object; and that sheath of protection depended on Allan, and on Allan's continued literal presence.

Many years later, when Allan left, Diane went on a rampage of combined creative and sexual exploration. The night he acutely cut the knot, and declared that he was leaving, Diane was found by friends inside a circus tent, voraciously sucking in life with her camera, as she photographed a half-dressed transsexual. She denied her rage, and her loss, as she had had to do in the past when her nanny left her. She took flight into an intense, solo search for all things exotic and unusual to photograph. Simultaneously, she made a solo journey in and out of bed with assorted male acquaintances. Wandering itinerant, and lost without a male guide, she sat wailing, like a child in desperation, when one male friend-lover was late to show up at the airport upon her arrival in London. She looked to men for mothering, addicted to an external male mirror, who could give her a guiding reflection of herself, and thus give her a locus, when the internal locus was lost.

Without good-enough mothering from our mothers, Winnicott tells us, we cannot internalize the parental image, and thus we can't mourn and separate, in the Kleinian sense of the depressive position. Given the kind of narcissistic parents that Diane Arbus had, it is likely that neither parent gave her the empathy and nurturance that she needed to tolerate internalization. Thus, the negative images of the parents could not be modified by sustained good images. Diane was left with a negative image of herself, making her continually addicted to seeking an antidote.

What made the father within her so powerful as an internal object? It seems that it was his idealized form in terms of rendering mirroring and confirmation, combined with his oedipal appeal as an eroticized love object. Split from the ideal father was the bad-object, part-object father, triggering the demon lover syndrome. Fairbairn would call it the tantalizing and rejecting internal object, which gets attached to the libidinal ego (James Masterson's pleasure ego). Unable to assimilate any constant internal image of her father, since the splitting process was undermining this, Diane became extremely dependent on external males, who resonated with the internal contours of the split mirror-demon whom her father originally represented.

With Allan gone, Diane's addiction to external male self-object functions led her into confusion and chaos. Running from one erotic entanglement to another, Diane ended up lost and fragmented. At the end of her journey, she latched onto a man who wooed her and refused her, in the same vein as her father had. His name was Marvin Israel. Diane's biographer notes his narcissistic concerns, his erotic tantalization, and his ultimate unavailability. Like her father, Marvin gave Diane recognition through her creative work. He was drawn to her talent, and wore it for apparel as a Roman Emperor wears his fig leaf crown. He also basked in the reflection of his own glory by claiming Diane as his adoring worshipper. Full of bravado, Marvin declared to Diane's mother: "Diane doesn't love Allan anymore, she loves me" (Boswell, p. 242). One can wonder about the impetuosity of such a declaration, and also about why it was necessary for him to proclaim this to Diane's mother.

In the final days of Diane's life, she was shut out by this man who claimed her talents as his glorified reflection. As he remained unavailable to her, she was denied the mirroring he had given her. Being an addict, Diane was then in a state of exacerbated withdrawal symptoms. Marvin's behavior reflected that of her father, who withdrew into the living-room world of bridge playing, reestablishing his bond with his wife, when outside liaisons and seductions proved wearying. Marvin would withdraw into a secluded world that he shared with his artist wife, leaving Diane on the outside of his immured castle, behind the fortress wall, and across the moat and gangplank.

Unable to reach Marvin at all, Diane strained to find little snapshot glimpses of the world forbidden to her. Unable to find him out, and kept securely separate from any news of his life within the marriage walls, Diane wandered aimlessly. Her sense of self was shaken, and she sought in vain for the male self-object confirmation that was so tied in with the demon lover object relations constellation. Due to the nature of the self-object quest, being addicted to male reflection in particular, and to an idealized male at that, no passing approval, recognition, or praise from friends could give Diane a sense of self-recognition. Her image could only be reflected by the idealized male mirror, who glorified her with reflected glory. The self-object power was palpably reinforced by the erotic bond of the oedipal tie. The synthesis of the preoedipal level and oedipal level proved to be a powerful combination, which made the internal father object a structurally intrapsychic mother, which yet possesses eroticized male magnetism. Diane's latest lover was like the demon lover of so many other women artists, a combination of indifference and erotic tantalization, built on the base of yearnings for an idealized self-object figure, an idealized mirror.

Compounding the deprivation in Diane Arbus's case, the deprivation that already reinforced the original developmental arrest, was that of repeated object loss—unmourned in childhood and unmourned in adulthood. Diane deliberately overdosed on pills. Her body was found, but the consternation of her soul has yet to be unraveled. In those days of male abandonment, Diane was at her height as a creative artist. Her photography had become quite well known by that point. The audience of the world was responding. She had many admiring students. Yet the admiration that she sought—as a heroin addict seeks his drug—was the admiration of a man, who was both erotically tantalizing, and also in love with her art and talent. In seeking him, she also sought the man who was indifferent to her needs for contact and understanding, because he was the man who would give her a particular kind of narcissistic mirroring, as her father had, without giving her the object-related empathy of a father. The narcissistic bond with her father made Diane an addict, particularly in light of the insecure self-structure that she retained from the unavailable mother of childhood, and then from the aborted attachment of a caring nanny. Without a continuing stream of mirroring from this idealized, demon lover figure, Diane Arbus could not sustain herself—despite the world itself serving as a mirror. The artistic audience is never enough.

Ironic in this case is the nature of Diane Arbus's creative strivings, which intensified along with her self-fragmentation and self-destruction. As a photographer, Diane sought out the odd, the deviant, the authentic flaw in human subjects. Yet, she herself would never allow photographs to be taken of her. Her camera was a voracious mouth seeking sustenance, but it was also a weapon.

Diane Arbus craved authenticity as she craved mirroring, and she would use her camera to suck up all that was available to her. Perhaps, she was seeking to get behind the false-self walls—the museum facades— of her parents' closed personalities. Yet, people were afraid of her.

Actresses and models were warned to keep her away! She would remove the glamour, the flattering lighting; and she would capture a stark ghost-like shadow. She seemed to seek the hidden shame behind the glamour, and her camera was her vehicle for knocking down the parental walls, and finding the secret within. As such, her camera was her weapon. She ran from others who wished to turn the weapon upon her.

What shame was Arbus seeking so frantically in others? One can only guess. Yet, surely her lust for the odd, the grotesque, and the burlesquely comical was a reflection of her own inner hidden self—perhaps a more true self, but perhaps not. In either case, it was certainly an alienated self. Yet, if she had not been so addicted to seeking the shame in others, and to running from the shame in herself, she might have survived. She might have faced up to her losses; mourned her nanny, Allan, her mother, and her dad. However, with the manic defenses that she employed, compelled to create as a way of escaping the darkness within, she continued to enslave herself to the man with the mirror, and to the flip side of him, seen in the demon lover. Always seeking the antidote to the negative mirror within, she was the prisoner of the idealized men from whom she sought mirroring admiration. From her own father, Diane had received this mirroring in lieu of affection or true concern. She gobbled it up, as a substitute, and ingested the "veiled eroticism" as well. She remained, thus, a love addict, seeking mirroring and adulation from the indifferent, yet lustful, demon lover.

9)

SOME MORE
SPECULATIONS ON
ANNA O.

Demon Lover and
Arrested Creativity

She sat in a rocking chair, by her father's sick bed, looking at the window, and looking away from thoughts that she could never think. While confined to her dying father's room, she began to cough nervously, as she heard echoes of dancing and parties in the streets outside. Suddenly, her two arms changed into the shape of black wriggling snakes. Then her hair, her head, her fingers—all turned into snakes. The sheer terror drove her into frantic prayers—praying to a paternal god in English, so that her earthly father would not hear or understand her words. From that night on she would never speak German, until Dr. Breuer came to hear her prayers through the daily tales she told him.

The conundrum of Anna O. will be with us forever. There simply is not enough factual information to make conclusions. Yet the innuendoes she arouses are multiple. The dark incestual themes haunt us, and the psychic splitting plagues us with divergent diagnostic thoughts. When Breuer saw Anna O., she appeared severed into two halves. She played out the false self roles of a good self and a bad self. Such a split self extends beyond ordinary hysterical dissociation, and suggests borderline pathology: a split that has never healed, and a malignant primary object that is seized up with split off aggression. So we find an intrapsychic situation of pathological mourning doubly compounded with an actual death. Anna O.'s father died during the reported time of fermenting pathology.

What role did Anna O.'s mother play in the acute manifestation of her pathology? The mother threw her daughter into the frey of her father's degenerative illness (tuberculosis), requiring her daughter to be her husband's night nurse, despite the family wealth that certainly would have allowed for the hiring of a professional nurse. Anna O. spent night after night awake in her father's sickroom, at the expense of great social isolation. She would naturally have been erotically stimulated by this nearness to her father, which sometimes extended to bathing him, while she was also deprived of all social contact with peers, particularly deprived of contact with males her own age. She was twenty-one.

Such deprivation must have stimulated Anna O.'s aggression, and conversion symptoms were her only outlet. Eventually, she had to convert so much into her body that her body rebelled and a whole second self formed. This second self was seen as a bad self, as a nasty, irrascible bitch who couldn't be consciously owned.

Anna O. served as the night nurse while her brother was allowed to attend the university. Then to top it all off, when her father finally did die, she was not even allowed to see him. Again, her mother was the agent of her predicament, forbidding Anna entrance to the sickroom, as before she had forced her daughter to enter it. In the end, Anna O. never did say good-bye to her father, a father whom everyone said she adored. Particularly Dr. Breuer, though neglectful of other clinical facts and details, never ceased to record how passionately Anna O. worshipped her father, how her father was the center of her life. First too close, and then too far. Her father was gone, and she did not suffer in silence. Anna O.'s world of daydreams errupted into many years of madness, years spent in a sanitorium after treatment with Breuer and Freud. During these years, Dr. Breuer was to become her new object of passion. Perhaps to keep a piece of him within her, Anna developed a pseudocyesis, a false fetus of which she named Breuer the father. Her doctor then left her abruptly, just as her father had. Again, Anna O. suffered acute father loss, and this followed early sibling loss, as reported by George Pollock (1972).

BERTHA PAPPENHEIM

How did the first woman social worker, Bertha Pappenheim, develop out of all this? For if it is true that Anna O. is truly Bertha Pappenheim, she had quite a life in the world after her earlier seclusion. Some say that Anna-Bertha made her defenses work far better in her adulthood than in her youth. Others speak of sublimation. Was it sublimation when all Anna-Bertha's repressed longings, which had formerly cropped up as conversion symptoms and as a second self, were later channeled into the idealistic social cause of fighting for women's rights within the German-Jewish community? Was it an accompanying reaction formation, when Anna-Bertha's anger was converted into good works, and when her own need for nurturant mothering was converted into being a maternal comforter of forelorn young girls—girls victimized by White Slavery and forced prostitution? Through such modes of defense, Bertha Pappenheim never had to deal with her anger at her mother. In addition, she fought for causes that were close to her father's heart: Jewish Orthodoxy and Jewish practice. She cultivated the Jewish religious practice in her home for unwed mothers, and in her other institutions. Rather than deal with her anger at her father, Anna-Bertha became somewhat like him in her religious beliefs. Meanwhile, she fought against his antifeminist policies, such as keeping his daughter from the university, while he sent his son there. Bertha could never assimilate this, however, and she was in constant conflict between feminism and orthodox Jeudaism, and between education for women and the traditional mother-wife role. Her behavior betrayed the unhealed splits in her character, and what might potentially be experienced as unresolved intrapsychic conflict remained as alternating enactments.

There are others who don't credit sublimation and reaction formation defenses as the tricks behind Anna O's emergence form her cocoon, and into the life of Bertha Pappenheim. For instance, George Pollock, in his articles on sibling loss and father loss in Anna O.'s history (1972, 1973), emphasizes the work of grief done during the therapeutic days with Breuer. Pollock points to the affective processes involved in Anna O.'s "Chimney sweeping", and claims that Anna-Bertha did the work of mourning through the tales she told daily to Breuer, tales that recounted the triggering events behind her symptoms.

How much mourning was actually done at the time of Anna O's treatment remains questionable. Although Pollock may be right to some degree, it does not seem that Anna O. ever came to grips with the immediate parental sources of her rageful grief, and her anguished despair.[1] Guilt and loss remained shielded in tales without immediate and affectively alive transferential reference. The developmental origins were not touched. Anna-Bertha never faced the demons head on. Breuer remained an audience for Anna O.'s tales, rather than being a receptive object for direct transferential yearnings and rage.

What did happen, however, was that Anna O.'s personality did become embedded in sadness. In her *Grief Tales*[2] Anna O. seems to have used creativity to express some of this sadness. She transformed a "bad" self's provocative and largely reactive aggression into assertive activity in validated social causes. The developing person that emerged out of the split between the bad self and the good self was now arrested in unresolved sadness. Anna O. demonstrates the same kind of perpetual bereavement in her own writing (poetry and prose) as shown in the creative work of such preoedipally arrested female poets as Emily Dickinson, Emily Bronte, and Edith Sitwell (Kavaler, 1993a).

We can only guess to what degree true mourning was arrested by the cathartic nature of Breuer's and Freud's technique at that time. Certainly, we could attribute the alleviation of Anna O.'s symptoms more to transference cure than to resolution of intrapsychic conflict through the actual experience of the transferential sources. Dr. Breuer catered to Anna O. The patient controlled and directed her own treatment. Twice a day, Breuer attended her. Often he fed her or gave "body massage". At times, Anna wouldn't talk to anyone else except Breuer. She must have imagined an exclusive bond with him from which she fantasized and somatized his baby. Breuer was a good daddy, who could be adored and idealized, as her real father had been. However, such perpetual idealization defends against the anger and loss that is necessry for true self individuation through mourning. Although it is not clear that Anna-Bertha's real father ever returned her affection and adoration, certainly Breuer did. Sidney Bolkosky (1982) writes of Breuer's maternal concern and responsiveness to Anna O. Breuer's countertransferential absorption with Anna O., as well as his countertransferential anxiety, have been widely noted. The patient's bond with the "good daddy", the idealized as well as eroticized nurturer, could surely be used defensively against a hidden shadow father, a more incestually aggressive and provocative demon lover father (see Kavaler, 1985, 1986, 1988, 1989). I believe that as this split was maintained it reinforced the splitting of the good and bad selves that Anna-Bertha portrayed. Also Anna-Bertha's sexual and aggressive passions remained split off in a life's work that didn't effect intrapsychic development along the lines of capacities for self-integrative creativity and intimacy.

The continuing arrests in Anna-Bertha's development are addressed by Joseph D. Noshpitz, in his essay on "Anna O. As Seen by a Child Psychiatrist", in *Anna O, Fourteen Contemporary Reinterpretations* (ed. Rosenbaum and Muroff, 1984). Noshpitz writes, concerning Anna O. and Breuer,

> He [Breuer] was able to ease a great many of her symptoms; nonetheless, her subsequent years were marked by considerable disability. When she finally did resolve the neurotic and addictive problems, she pursued a life course that raced along the great rainbow of idealism, giving herself to noble causes rather than to specific people. Her poetry tells us of the price she never ceased to pay. (p. 67).

Here Noshpitz refers to Bertha Pappenheim's continuing inability or unwillingness to form intimate relationships. Although she formed organizations, and took a maternal role towards young women, Anna-Bertha failed to have deeply personal associations. Particularly with men, Anna-Bertha kept an estranged distance. Apparently, she allowed men to adore her from afar, just as she had adored her father, but she never developed any emotional or sexual bond with a man.

In her creative efforts as well, Anna-Bertha had distinct limitations. She had an urge to write, and wrote poetry, plays, short-tales, and social treatises. Yet, the level of expression remained ideational and abstract. Her play characters, such as those in *Woman's Rights*, remained stereotypic caricatures, born to express intellectual thoughts, but never reaching beyond a two-dimensional flatness. The complexity of a conflict-ridden human being is missing in her work, similar to the dreams of narcissistic character disorder patients.[3] Anna-Bertha denied her own internal conflict, and turned to external life as an escape, with a consequently limited resolution. Her play, *Woman's Rights*, is particularly interesting to take a look at, because it demonstrates the demon lover theme, a theme of exploitative patriarchal men with women as victims. The male characters are flat villains and female characters are flat victims. Female aggression is only allowed a passive reactive form, in which a woman being victimized by male sexual use and betrayal can self-righteously declare the withholding of sexual favors as a punishment. These are Pappenheim's "woman's rights" in a day when divorce was an unhappy and disfavored solution to actions of male sexual betrayal.

This play seems to reflect the underside of Anna O.'s father worship. As I have demonstrated in many earlier papers (1985, 1986, 1988, 1989), demon lover themes haunt the work of many preoedipally arrested female writers (e.g., Sylvia Plath and Anne Sexton). The work of these women writers reveals that the father is worshipped in the form of a god-ideal, and his power over his daughter turns inevitably demonic as the woman's sense of self is threatened with annihilation. Anna-Bertha's play also demonstrates the constricted internal world of a woman who wishes to use creativity as a means of self-expressive freedom and differentiation, but who is blocked from the necessary developmental components of such a mode of creative process due to split off rage and split off eroticism, which are intrapsychically bound in an unmourned father-daughter bond and bind. An intrapsychic father-daughter bond becomes a narcissistic bind, when preoedipal arrest makes a narcissistic father into an extension of the daughter's self. Without owning and integrating her feelings for her father, who is intrapsychically a combined father-mother for preoedipal women, Anna-Bertha would have been inhibited from having intimate or trusting relationships with men. In addition, her creative development would remain stunted, no matter how prolific. Social causes could be pursued on a more ideational level, which calls for more superficial modes of affective engagement than creativity in its in-depth forms of self-integrative meaning.

Unexperienced internal conflict, and limited self integration seems to have kept Anna-Bertha bound up with an internal father-mother who was still split into ideal and devalued parts. In Pappenheim's work, she could pursue social ideals that would rekindle her passionate idealization of her father. She also fought the demonic and narcissistic elements in her father by turning him into the exploitative demon lover of her *Woman's Rights* play. She fought him through her social work for women: rescuing young girls from male pimps and misogynous husbands. However, without integrating her two male part-objects (both idol and demon), Anna-Bertha never integrated her inner self, and her reaction formation social goodness continued to operate as compensation for an enraged child within her. Anna O.'s inner self seems to have remained sealed off and split off from consciousness. Consequently, this woman's inner self remained sealed off from erotic, intimate, and more deeply creative contact with those in her interpersonal and internal worlds.

ANNA O. AS A BORDERLINE

If one understands Anna O. as a borderline character, it is easier to understand how she dramatically transformed from a paralyzed woman, preoccupied with her own hallucinations, into a fierce social rights freedom fighter. Borderline pathology is suggested in Anna O.'s mother's character, as her mother uses the daughter to care for the dying father, and then allows no process of separation between father and daughter. Critical failures in separation-individuation phases of development might be seen here in terms of the mother's own childhood as she reenacts such failures with her daughter. Also, as the mother pulls her daughter into her service and then pushes her away, she demonstrates the anal-sadistic behavior that is characteristic of the instinctual dynamics of the separation-individuation phases. If Anna O.'s mother treated her daughter like this during her daughter's adolescence, it is likely that she did so during her daughter's preoedipal separation-individuation phases as well.[4]

Once pre-oedipal psychic arrest takes place, as it does in the borderline (see Masterson, 1979), a female child's frustrated desires for empathic mothering will be transferred to the highly arousing father during the oedipal stages of development. Then, not only does the father become the object of erotic yearnings, but he also becomes the object of early oral cravings for nurturance, and a vision of the traumatically lost idealized mother is transferred to the father. Consequently, the father idealization becomes a defensive constellation of images used to ward off the demonic overtones of the early mother. In as far as the father inevitably disappoints the daughter in her complex of yearnings, he is turned demonic within her internal world as well, and his demonic form fuses with that of the early traumatic mother of separation. The idealization of the father will continue to be used defensively to ward off the combined mother-father demon, which has now become eroticized into the form of a demon lover with the erotic desires for the oedipal father coloring it. The father's actual personality will also color the constellation, and his narcissistic traits in particular will feed the intrapsychic images of the demon lover form.

In the case of Anna O., the father would further become demonized following the crushing disappointments of both her father's death and of Breuer's abandonment. The demon lover theme then emerges in both Bertha Pappenheim's literary work, with its social-political emphasis, as well as in her life. The male is seen as a rapist in his own home, and the social abuses of women could certainly be used to substantiate such a view, particularly during that patriarchically dominated Victorian time.

UNRESOLVED BORDERLINE PATHOLOGY

I don't believe that Anna-Bertha ever became as self integrated as George Pollock suggests in his commentaries (1968, 1972, 1973). I would agree that she showed a beginning capacity to grieve, as reported by Pollock in terms of her "grief tales." The sadness reported by such tales suggests that Anna O. may have had some beginning capacity to go beyond splitting to integrative mournful sadness. However, it appears that when Bertha Pappenheim was the patient Anna O., she merely employed cathartic chimney sweeping, which had to be done again and again, on a daily basis. Such daily story telling did not seem to involve a continuing process of self assimilation and self change as true mourning would. In truly reparative mourning the original source of trauma and conflict is re-lived with the formerly untolerated affect.

Pollock minimizes Pappenheim's later difficulties, speaking only of obsessional preoccupations and some bisexual conflicts (*Fourteen Studies*, p. 30). He doesn't mention any remnants of serious pathology later in her life. Given preoedipal trauma and consequent pathology, Anna O. would have had to have mourned her father's death over a long period of time. She would have needed a therapist as a companion, someone who could consistently allow responsive contact so that mournful sadness could be felt and processed. She would also have needed a psychotherapist to serve as a transferential target for her love and rage.

Pollock does not seem to acknowledge the degree of pathology that Breuer's cathartic method could merely have averted momentarily. He does not seem to see the modes of splitting and projective-identification that appear to have gone into Anna O.'s victim women and villain men. In my opinion, when Anna O. repeated her daily "chimney sweeping" tales in order to avoid enacting her bad self behavior externally against others (mainly her mother), as well as internally against herself as persecutory hallucinations (the demon lover snake imagery), she had to do the same story telling repeatedly to keep her internal persecutory objects at bay. This seems more like the kind of repetitive pathological mourning reen-actments seen in the creative work of such borderline level women as Emily Dickinson, Emily Brontë, Edith Sitwell, Anne Sexton and Sylvia Plath (see Kavaler, 1985, 1986, 1988, 1989) than any truly progressive mode of developmental mourning. Yet, Pollock asserts: "This particular woman, maybe a little obsessional, maybe not quite resolved in her own bisexuality, nonetheless was active and contributing in her later adult life."(Fourteen Studies, p. 30)

In contrast to Pollock, I believe a structural view of Bertha Pappenheim confronts us with severe pathology. Anna O. seemed to use a maternal identification[5] as Emily Dickinson used a masculine identification (see Cody, 1971), to seal off a highly vulnerable primary feminine self from contact with rage and traumatic loss that could not be tolerated. Although from an external viewpoint Bertha Pappenheim could be seen as "active and contributing," from a psychoanalytic point of view I believe that she can only be seen as driven by intense compulsion. She helped young women, who she saw as her children, so that she remained in a manic stance of giver (see Klein, 1940), psychically standing above her own pain. In this position, and without the support of contact with an empathic other, she could not tolerate the rageful form of "abandonment mourn-ing" depression that I believe she needed to undergo (see Masterson, 1979). Although Anna-Bertha did have Breuer's support temporarily, Breuer was too controlled by her to provide the ongoing treatment struc-ture that she needed to feel and process the pain behind her "stories." Also, he abandoned her before much could be done, and before he could become the object of her transferential rage.

Pollock doesn't seem to acknowledge the extreme narcissistic patholo-gy and borderline splitting that remained in Bertha Pappenheim. Her greatness in activist social causes for women, admirable as it was in a sociological sense, reflected a psychological failing in developing and sustaining more intimate relations, both within herself and between her and other people. Free of her mother's actual domination, this woman could actively contribute to the social world, but this is reminiscent of many borderline persons who become active in causes, which allows them the illusion that the internal pain is created by villains outside of them. Action is second nature to borderlines, and reinforces their state of denial. Only when prohibited from action, which is also enactment, do they become delusional or generally "crazy," as Anna O. became when confined to her house and to her father's sickroom, under her mother's thumb.

Anna-Bertha's continuing pathology is made more clear when we look at her interpersonal relations. Pappenheim kept an ongoing distance from men, who were seen as villains in her internal world, as reflected in her creative work (*Woman's Rights*). With women, she was also distant, although she befriended them as a maternal figure. She didn't appear to be capable of revealing herself to these women, who she worked so hard to protect. Her personal feelings went into her poetry alone, and if Noshpitz is right, her poety too reflected largely frustration side by side with idealizations. In this sense again, Anna O. reflects the psyche of such interpersonally isolated creative women as Emily Dickinson, Edith Sitwell, Emily Brontë, Anne Sexton, and Sylvia Plath, as well as the photographer, Diane Arbus. The poetry becomes the repository of all that is personal and hidden from others, but it cannot be used to assimilate all this personal data through an affective mourning process if early pathology prevents tolerance of grief and an active intrapsychic dialogue. In the case of Edith Sitwell's psyche, fusion prevents such internal dialgoue need for mourning, so that no dialogue can be seen in her literary work (see Glendinning, 1981). In Anna O.'s case, her schizoid and manic defenses seemed to have continually prevented her from experiencing intrapsychic conflict, and thus from processing intrapsychic dialogue. Consequentially, self-integrative mourning could not take place.

Anna O. displayed no "belle indifference." She was not a neurotic hysteric, but rather, I believe, a borderline character with severe hysteroid symptomatology that manifested at a time when she could not engage in active social causes, and when her idealized father was dying.

10)

ANNE SEXTON'S
TREATMENT, PART I

In the 1950s, when Anne Sexton first showed dramatic signs of mental disturbance, the treatment for emotional disorders was rudimentary in America. Despite the growth of object-relations thinking in Britain, very little of the astute knowledge of Melanie Klein, Ronald Fairbairn, D. W. Winnicott, and Michael Balint had voyaged across the Atlantic. There was no established technique for treating the whole range of borderline, schizoid, and narcissistic disorders.

In New York, the New York Psychoanalytic Training Institute was the only institute for training psychoanalysts in the city. The medical establishment had set up an exclusive citadel in the New York Psychoanalytic, excluding all the Ph.D.'s and all the potential lay analysts who Freud had hoped would provide a rich future for psychoanalysis. Freud looked to the humanities for psychoanalytic candidates, but the New York Psychoanalytic looked solely to a rigid medical establishment, which distilled Freud through Brill, and considered only "classical neurotics" for treatment. Its members remained either indifferent or hostile to the rich mine of information on treating borderline cases that had been contributed by the British object-relations theorists. In fact, they overtly maligned D. W. Winnicott when he came to speak at their training institute. Kleinians who attempted presentations were also the subject of vitriolic assault (from the personal reports of Wolfgang Pappenheim, M.D., June, 1992).

The New York atmosphere was a symptom of a whole medical establishment influence in America. This influence discouraged the major contributions of the British Psychoanalytic Society from being used by psychoanalysts and psychotherapists in America. Only a minority fit into the tight categories of classical neuroses that were considered capable of being analyzed. This minority was a highly coveted population. The acceptable technique dictated that the free spirit of experimentation, which had inhabited Britain, with Fairbairn descending from Scotland to present papers to the Kleinians at the British Psychoanalytic, and with D. W. Winnicott developing his own independent seminars on work with "false self" patients, was squashed in American by the dominance of a psychiatric elite. In Britain, the Kleinians, Winnicottians, as well as Fairbairn, Guntrip, and Balint, were doing in-depth treatment with borderline and even schizophrenic patients.[1] The whole borderline range of disorders, including schizoid, narcissistic, and pre-neurotic patients, were undefined, and techniques for truly working with their serious pathology were notably lacking. Most of those who fell into these categories were classified as "unanalyzable," and were relegated to the non-psychodynamic, and non-penetrating attitude called "supportive therapy." Occasionally, other approaches to these patients were experimented with, but due to the neglect and ignorance of all the defined theory and technique so well propagated in Britain, these experiments were often superficial. For example, we have the instance of Ralph Greenson taking his patient, Marilyn Monroe, home to socialize with his family and their guests. Classified as having a more serious disorder than those labeled neurotic, but without any psychic structure diagnosis that could define what we now call "borderline," Marilyn Monroe could be taken home by Greenson in the name of "support."

When Anne Sexton first resorted to mad suicidal gestures to display a formerly hidden anguish, the treatment available to her was limited. She had been at that time a housewife for two years, living with her husband and two children in the suburbs of Boston. She was embedded in the Massachusetts conservatism that in the 1950s was at its height of sexism. Yet Sexton, with a constant agitation and lability, was never noted as in any way out of the ordinary until she overdosed with sleeping pills. Her first suicidal gesture seemed like an hysterical play. Soon after marriage to Kayo, who became a traveling salesman like her father, Sexton unleashed her frenetic and manic temperament while her husband was on the road. She had brief sexual affairs in which she sought to have her hand held through the night. Being alone was intolerable. She commented that she didn't particularly like having affairs but that she needed "action." She manically defended against an inner emptiness generated by a sealed-off early abandonment trauma. During her husband's regular absences, Sexton would stay up all night, listen to music, drink, and have drunken sex. After Kayo returned from his traveling, she would be temporarily all right. But she couldn't bake a potato when he was away (Middlebrook, p. 36).

One of Sexton's romantic infatuations led to her precipitous wish to leave Kayo. Both her mother and mother-in-law told her to drop her new-found love and commit to Kayo. It was then that Anne Sexton grasped control through masochistic self-destruction. She, who feared her mother-in-law, and who craved the attention of her own narcissistically self-absorbed mother ("Mother always got top-billing in our house" Middlebrook, p. 21 and "Mother doled out her love" p. 37), struck out in the mode of the impotent. Sexton very dramatically took a load of pills and began to vomit. This was her defiant reaction to the two mother figures. Her suicide attempt was impulsive, like a tantrum. It came and went, and she returned to her marriage. But this shudder of rage from Anne Sexton's being was not to be plastered over. This dramatic gesture was to be the precedent for a long line of suicidal acts which ultimately ended in the last and fatal deed.

The family wished to forget, but Anne Sexton's entrance into mother-hood caused new seismic tremors. Anne began to act totally out of control towards her older daughter, Linda. At the sight of Linda putting her feces in the back of a toy truck, Anne blew a fuse and threw Linda across the room (Middlebrook, p. 33). Later, in a fight with Kayo, it would be her typewriter Sexton heaved across the room. Both Linda and her typewriter were extensions of herself, "subjective-objects" (Winnicott, 1971), parts of her, as her mind fused with that outside of her as a means of seeking mirroring for an inchoate self. Anne attacked Kayo by attacking herself, the writer in her who was symbolized by her typewriter. I believe she attacked Linda to disown that recalcitrant part of her inner being that wished to smear shit on her own mother, perhaps the repressive mother who asked her to display her feces to her at the moment prior to flushing them down the toilet bowl (Middlebrook, p. 59). Despite all the years she would spend subsequently seeing therapists, nobody was ever to inquire into all this in an effective way. There was nobody who could understand the process of projective-identification in which Linda became, in a flash, that disowned raging and recalcitrant child within Anne Sexton's own self. There was no one who could understand that Anne's rage at Linda was both a disowning of a part of herself that she would forever split off to protect her mother from it and that Linda was also—at that precipi-tant moment—experienced as Anne's mother. She could rage at Linda like she, Anne, never could have raged as a child, since it would have been too threatening to her bond with her narcissistic mother. If Anne didn't risk revealing her rage as a child, perhaps it was because she feared that her mother would turn away from her with contemptuous indifference. Anne Sexton's terror of abandonment from a mother, who she said had "doled out approval" (Middlebrook, p. 37) and demanded "top billing" (Middlebrook, p. 21), must have been incessant. Early breaks in bonding from such a mother, who used her daughter to mirror her, as Anne herself did with Linda, ("I made you to find me" in "Double Image," Middlebrook, p. 86) must have been followed with critical traumatic abandonments during the separation-individuation phase of "rapprochement," a developmental phase when maternal attunement is most needed for internalization of the mother's presence. Perhaps Anne Sexton illustrates Michael Balint's "basic fault," Winnicott's "unthinkable anxieties," and Masterson's "abandonment depression," as well as Melanie Klein's paranoid and manic defenses against mourning for a lost and needed primary object. Anne Sexton also provides an example of Harry Guntrip's "in and out solution," as she continues an ongoing stream of love affairs throughout her life and marriage. But who in 1950s America could see any of this? In the United States, the psychotherapists—all psychiatrists—were not reading the psychoanalysts from across the Atlantic. "Projective-identification" remained an alien and foreign concept, splitting likewise. The basic fault, and separation-individuation trauma, were to wait for Margaret Mahler's studies to be disseminated. Oral fixation was the Freudian conceptualization of primitive need. Need for internalization of parents as a route to psychic structure self-formation was unknown, except for Edith Jacobson (1954), who began to include internalized introjects in her thinking, while still dismissing most of Melanie Klein's dynamic internal world phenomenology. Who could understand then— in a world without object-relations theory and Melanie Klein—Sexton was an example of the borderline personality? Without Klein's profound understanding of the borderline state and that of other object-relations theorists the most enlightened psychotherapist in Boston was blindly flailing in the dark. In Anne Sexton's case, her enlightened but blinded knight went by the name of Dr. Martin Orne.

THE TREATMENT OF DR. ORNE

Dr. Martin Orne was a clinical psychologist (Ph.D.), as well as an M.D.. As a combined psychiatrist-psychologist, Dr. Orne could establish himself as a respected practitioner in the treatment of mental illness. Although the son of a female psychiatrist, Dr. Brunner-Orne, who had first hospitalized Anne Sexton for her suicide attempts, in 1950, at Westwood Lodge, Dr. Martin Orne did not practice the standard psychiatric approach to hospitalization of those days. Due to Dr. Martin Orne, Anne

Sexton's seven-year treatment stands as a fortunate contrast to that of Sylvia Plath, who received multiple volleys of shock when twice hospitalized. Dr. Martin Orne took over Sexton's treatment in 1956, when she was hospitalized, and he hospitalized her again in 1957. Although he placed Sexton in a hospital where shock was the prominent approach to anything considered abnormal enough to cause hospitalization (depression, psychosis, violent rage, mania), Anne Sexton's treatment was the exception to the rule. Dr. Martin Orne proscribed shock and prescribed a five-times-a-week psychotherapy regime—an extreme exception for American psychiatry. At that time, Dr. Orne had been influenced by some education in psychoanalysis. Although not a trained psychoanalyst, Dr. Orne had knowledge of Freudian psychoanalytic theory and of some clinical theory, which enabled him to think in terms of the interaction of genetic history and transference. He also knew about the standard defense mechanisms.[2]

Dr. Orne's five-week engagement with Sexton during her early hospitalization allowed Sexton to experience his presence, no matter how closed off she was by her dissociated and unintegrated psychic state. It is unfortunate that during later hospitalizations Dr. Orne would not be with Sexton in this way. It appears that his countertransference anger had by then got the better of him, as he did not know how to use and process such reactions in order to enable him to understand Sexton's internal world and its compulsion to perpetually repeat its drama. It appears that Orne gradually, over time, began to use hospitalization as a punishment. Instead of having sessions with Sexton while she was in the hospital, as he once did, he seems to have later, several times, used the hospital as a place to remove himself from his patient, secluding her from him. One particular incidence of this will be described.

But, at this early stage of their contact, Orne was quite involved with observing Anne Sexton in all her manifold incarnations. She was a chameleon becoming whoever she conversed with. Viewing this as an hysterical dynamic, Dr. Orne was not totally out of his depth when Ms. Sexton began to speak schizophrenic language. Not believing that she had a thought disorder, Orne removed Sexton from the schizophrenic ward and found that her language transformed back to normal. He noted her schizophrenic language induced by imitating others, as she merged with others to find an identity. He viewed this as part of Sexton's "hysteria." Orne was astute enough to diagnose her as an hysteric, but it was descriptive traits, not psychic structure analysis, that informed this opinion. Anne Sexton's ability to so purely imitate, to model herself on others so quickly and thoroughly, can be related to a borderline hysterical dissociation, or to Helene Deutsch's (1942) view of the "as if" personality, not to a neurotic hysteric's mode of repression. Dr. Orne didn't make these distinctions. Sexton lacked a subjective "I." She was not in herself, not in her body. She was not, in Thomas Ogden's words (1986), an "interpreting subject." She inhabited the paranoid-schizoid state of mind most of the time, a state of mind in which reactive reflex and reenactive reflex dominate the scene, rather than reflective thought. What Dr. Orne did not understand was the core schizoid level of Sexton's hysteria, the borderline preoedipal condition, and its need for in-the-moment contact in treatment. He did not understand that Sexton's chameleon mode of identification with anyone nearby her indicated a core lack of subjective self-identity, and a borderline dissociation process, as differentiated from a neurotic hysteric's mode of repression that is founded on adequate preoedipal development. Psychic structure diagnosis was unknown to him, and a descriptive diagnosis of hysteria would have left him in the dark.

Following initial hospitalization, Anne Sexton became a patient of Dr. Orne's within his private practice. Seven years of intensive work was to following before Dr. Orne left his practice to take a research position in the psychiatric field. Within that time, Anne Sexton met with Orne on a twice-a-week and later on a three-times-a-week basis. Sexton would sit with Orne and discuss memories, transference, and her identity as it formed, yet to a very large degree, Sexton would remain sealed off and divided into parts. Her need for psychic internalization was never seen or addressed. Her body cravings, demanding that she take in what she needed in a libidinal form, would not be seen in the context of missing psychic structure. The failure to get beyond intellectual discussions in sessions to a level of emotional contact in which potential internalization could take place was never assessed by Orne, whose limited state of knowledge made such an evaluation nearly impossible.

Diane Middlebrook (1991), Anne Sexton's biographer, has included in her book a recorded session between Sexton and Dr. Orne. In addition, she writes her own narration of the treatment throughout a major portion of the book. The recorded session explicitly shows how Dr. Orne would speak to Sexton about her memories, thoughts, and psychodynamics, always apparently focusing on content, failing to enter into a moment of being with Sexton. It seems as if Sexton and Orne sat and chatted about her, about this third party named "Anne Sexton." From what we now know now about borderline character pathology (Kernberg, 1985, Masterson, 1976), this is the absolutely wrong approach. It is of necessity an intellectualized format. When penetration into painful split-off affect states is not made, no real trauma from the past can be mourned and healed. No mourning of painful guilt, and of regrets for past deeds, can be experienced in this format, no contact between the interpersonal object relationship field and the internal world can occur in this format. Consequently, no internalizations can take place. Grief must open space for internalization, but without emotional contact none of this work can be done (see Modell on the "cocoon stage," 1976). In Strachey's words (1934), interpretations must be mutative, meaning in this context that they must touch on a vulnerable emotional state in the patient so that penetrating internalization and psychic structure transformation can occur. Dr. Orne's interpretation was useless, precisely because it could not be mutative as Anne Sexton remained so sealed off. His attempts at uncovering work, in the mode of defense interpretation that could be done with neurotics, were bound to fail. He attempted to uncover her memories and history, as in sessions in which she reported incest and sexual abuse from her father. (Middlebrook, pp. 56–57). He helped her discuss her lies and distortions, in relation to her memories. Yet, the true memory lived in the moment, and he did not tune into this. There was no immediate moment in which Orne penetrated Sexton with awareness of how she was acting out the past in the moment with him. He never could see it in the session, how she had a shield up to avoid contact with him, and how her trance and body seductions were reenactments. Dr. Orne was an idealized extension for Sexton, as he fed her the intellectual concepts she hungered for. Orne mirrored her, and inflated her defensive grandiose self-structure, encouraging her to build an intellectual facade. Sexton also mirrored him—reflecting back to him his intellectual contributions to her psyche. Yet at the end of many sessions, she went into a trance. Her sealed-off yearnings for connection, often manifested by body cravings or by an incorporation process in her mind (as distinct form internalization), threatened to emerge through a pressured trance state, when they were warded off by emotional distancing during the therapy session. She became paralyzed at the end of each session, unable to leave and separate. She hadn't gotten what she needed in the session—the emotional contact and connection she required. The terror, the need, the blocked rage, the pain, were contained in that state of trance. The state of hysterical denial, of "Thou Shall Not Be Aware" (Alice Miller, 1984), was also part of the trance. Sexton's borderline separation trauma must have been inflamed as the limit of the end of the session was drawn. Her acute cravings for tactile contact must have been erupting from the sealed-off self most powerfully at that end moment in a dissociated trance.

Earlier in a session, Sexton seems to have split off parts of herself. During one session, this splitting process threatened to form a multiple personality. Unacquainted with borderline splitting, Dr. Orne was unequipped to deal with the phenomenology of a split-off personality appearing in a therapy session. Hoping to prevent Sexton's transition into a multiple personality, his response was to ignore the created personality, who Sexton called "Elizabeth." He said that when he ignored Elizabeth, "She went away." He thought he had stopped a pathological process. According to Sexton, however, Elizabeth was a "little bitch," the bitch-witch part of her that was erotically engaged in a sadomasochistic struggle with her father. Her father had become her demon lover, when he spanked her and aroused her erotically. She wrote a poem for Orne: "The royal strapping." Through the poem, Anne Sexton told him how her father had stripped her naked on his marriage bed, and beat her behind with her own riding crop, just after she had returned from horseback riding (McClatchy, 1978). But the poem was never consciously experienced in the session, either by Dr. Orne or by Anne Sexton. Orne was never directly experienced by Anne as the longed for and hated demon lover father. Instead, when Elizabeth came out, Dr. Orne, as indicated, ignored her. Elizabeth went away in the session, but that little bitch part of her had to reenact its inner scene somewhere! So, as Orne ignored that split-off bitch goddess part of her, it was taken out of Sexton's therapy, and acted out in her life again—in all her affairs. Dr. Orne never asked Anne, "Why is Elizabeth coming out now?," "Why at this moment?" He never interpreted, "You're splitting her off to get rid of a sense of badness, a bad self eroticized to ward off the terror and the need for your father, for your mother-father, Nana-father figure." He never asked, "What are you feeling towards me now that's making Elizabeth appear at this moment?" "Why do you have to split off into Elizabeth to feel erotic towards me? What are you afraid of?" "Is there an erotic feeling you're avoiding right now?" He never said, "Are you craving to be spanked by me right now?"

Instead Orne suggested that Sexton's teenage pimples, which used to be the subject of vicious attack from her father during her adolescence, could have reflected her attraction to her father (Middlebrook, p. 57). If he had known what we know today about the borderline psychic structure, he would have known this was too abstract, too detached. He asked her the question in relation to the content of the session, a discussion of her history, her memories, associations to her father as incestuous. He only spoke to the adult part of her. He didn't deal with what was potentially being aroused in the moment in her body. He didn't watch the nonverbal cues, the body level of enactment (Kernberg, 1985), so essential in the borderline. He tried to ignore her seductions, whereas her next therapist was to succumb to them. He didn't inquire into what her body was saying to him. During the session, Orne made conversation with Sexton's split-off mind. Then, at the end of the session her body got paralyzed, and she stared ghostlike. She went into trance, because she couldn't leave empty—with an "empty core self" (Seinfeld, 1990). She went into a passive clinging mode—holding on by holding back from leaving. One day he exploded at her. She wouldn't get out of his office! He slammed down a book to wake her out of her trance. She came back later that day for revenge (p. 175). She lay down on the couch in an adjoining office with a container of milk. She would nurse herself in front of him. He would pay! She would drink the milk and lie down with her internal Aunt Nana—nurturing herself—and leaving him out. She wouldn't take milk from him!—it was the contagion of semen—her father's incestuous desires mixed in with her Aunt Nana's maternal embraces. It was the fusion of her internal mother-father objects that was acted out in her melodrama. Orne responded to this melodrama by punishing Sexton with hospitalization. He didn't visit her daily in the hospital, like he once had. Later he apologized to her for pushing her too hard, for pushing her to remember her therapy sessions with tape-recordings. His apology missed the mark. She couldn't remember through tapes, when she expelled him as an internal object due to emotional reasons, due to powerful emotional needs, which created a dependence she could not bear. To punish her and apologize missed the experience of the dynamics.

INDUCED COUNTERTRANSFERENCE

If Orne had analyzed what happened in terms of induced countertransference, he would have seen that his rage was induced by Sexton's own split-off rage. He could have seen that parts of her that she put into him—through projective-identification—reflected an internal raging and overwhelmed child, and that this inner child was a communication of her childhood rage from incest trauma. Sexton's had been a childhood with no boundaries, which had condemned her to perpetual transgressions into bed with so many people she met (male and one female). She also put into her therapist the enraged bad-parent adult, who used her in an erotically exploitative manner to express a sexualized rage—her father's rage. She also put into him her sense of betrayal. In her mind, she had betrayed her Aunt Nana in adolescence—as she followed her developmental need to move towards heterosexual relationships with boys. Her guilt remained. She reenacted the betrayal repeatedly, rather than mourning her guilt over betrayal, as well as the related grief over the loss of her loved Nana.

Without a therapeutic holding environment, Sexton couldn't mourn. The reenactment of betrayal in her arrested pathological mourning state involved continual betrayals of Kayo for other men.

Sexton's guilt must have been experienced by Orne as induced countertransference. Instead of being aware of this, and processing its message to understand Sexton, Dr. Orne apologized. What message did this give Sexton? There was no room for her anger. His apology allowed him to repair his relationship with Sexton, but not to survive Sexton's infantile rage reactions. Orne and Sexton went back to their intellectualized conversations with one another. How would it have been different if Orne had consciously felt and analyzed his induced "damned if you do and damned if you don't" situation? Orne could have begun to know Sexton's internal world, her inner sense of entrapment. He could have felt it through his body—not just abstracted it though cogitations in his mind. He could have known her immediate and perpetuated dilemma firsthand.

It appears that Anne Sexton was internally imprisoned by her need to merge with her Aunt Nana and her incest father as combined figures, while simultaneously needing to escape to develop a separate self and to have adolescent relations with boys. Yet, in escaping, true separation could not take place. There was no sustained support for an affect contact that would be painful. Her escape also brought an unbearable guilt of betrayal. This is why Anne Sexton was trapped. Dr. Orne, coming from a Freudian orthodoxy, in which eroticism was always seen as oedipal-level desire, did not have the tools to realize that Anne Sexton was craving primary psychic internalization. Her libidinal incorporations through seductions and sexual intercourse were her way of trying to grasp the psychic structure she needed, a hopelessly doomed avenue to observing her need. If he had realized this, he would have seen her behavior in sessions in a psychological context. He would have seen the craving in her trance states, as well as the resistance. The major resistance of substituting sex for psychic internalization was not just an avoidance of memory and work, but was an urge to reenact a primary disruption in object-connected nurturance and a diffuse response to a psychic hunger that reached a traumatic level of psychic starvation.

TRANCES

Nana represented a primary symbiotic object. When Anne remembered Nana, she was relating to a present pressing need for a symbiotic mother. When Orne didn't help her experience her wishes in the moment with him, she stayed stuck in an intellectualized memory. Therefore, she could not sustain connection between sessions. She had not even connected within the session. Yet, Orne never seemed to see the trance as a compromise between expressing her intense yearnings and her compulsion to hold back. In her life, Sexton went into trance before every sexual affair. If "pleasure is the signpost towards the object" (Fairbairn, 1952), trance was Sexton's signpost. Speculations can be made as to what was being unconsciously experienced in these trance states. They appeared generally during critical times of separation and of wishes to merge. The trance was a barrier in itself to contact, but it expressed intense yearnings, yearnings for a symbiosis, later experienced with an erotically arousing father as an incestuous object. Once Sexton crossed the barrier into a love affair, she merged with the other, the idealized omnipotent part object.[3] She committed incest by grasping at the ghost of her father, and she merged with the symbiotic object, because the symbiotic mother and the oedipal erotic and incestuous father were combined. They had never separated in Anne Sexton's psyche.

The trance represented the failed separation, the trauma of separating from an early mother, whose abrupt loss was abortive to self-development. Sexton sought the lost object, first in her father, and later in her latency years with Nana. She sought the kind of "transformational object" that Bollas (1991) speaks of, the object that could provide the psychic structure and functions, as well as the contact of being, that was so necessary for self-development. Without the internalization of such an object, Sexton remained a perpetual addict, seeking idealized mirroring as a drug. She voraciously sought mirroring, when the true nourishment of object contact, of "going-on-being" (Winnicott, 1971) was unavailable.

To have the father created too much internal conflict. He was an intrusive, and thus incestuous, object, whether or not the actual physical molestation had taken place. Her father had used sexual hostility to cling to his daughter when she went out with boys, an act that threatened separation from him. In addition, his spankings were erotic. Sexton's trance could shield her from the direct contact with an incestuous father and with a symbiotic mother, as represented by Nana during Anne's latency and adolescent years. The earlier mother of toddler-age separation may have been emotionally unavailable and abandoning, compelling Sexton to be abandoned repeatedly in her life by all the lovers she merged with after trance, as well as by Nana and her father. However, the later symbiotic mother, Nana, was clinging and destructive to Sexton's developmental needs to separate and to have heterosexual relations. To act out sexually must have been Sexton's attempt to libidinally ingest, as well as to incorporate a symbiotic object that would remain with her. Yet it was also a betrayal of Kayo, who represented both Nana and her father. The trance protected her from the knowledge of her own intentions.

The trance was a hysterical way of denying knowledge, proclaiming "I am not aware" in relation to her own incestuous and symbiotic longings, her secret sin of betrayal as she attempted to separate. When these trances came at the end of the session, her wishes, her memories, her longings all pressured to emerge. She was arrested, starring into an abyss at the end of the session, when there was no contact within the session. Being intellectual in the session allowed Sexton to avoid direct contact with her internal exciting object, the feared and longed for mother-father demon—erotic, incestuous, and engulfing. But she needed a real object. Since Sexton's treatment didn't allow her the immediate emotional contact with her therapist that she needed for the necessary internalization to take place, she was arrested in a state of perpetual and addictive intellectual incorporation. She would have needed to open up to the rage, fear, and craving for her therapist as the incestuous lover or "demon lover" (Kavaler, 1986, 1988, 1989, 1990, 1991, 1992) in order to get past reenactment through repetitive love affairs. Only in this way could she have increasing levels of contact with the vulnerable, needy child in her, and as she opened to these areas of vulnerability with the therapist. She tried to control men, according to Middlebrook, referring to "the Female Con" (p. 250). Through the "female con," Sexton tried to get what she wanted without feeling the vulnerability of needing. She played the seductress.

To have a trance at the end of a session was to feel the unmet longings and needs pressing to make her cling to the therapist, even though she couldn't let her therapist emotionally touch her during the session. If Anne Sexton could have had an object-relations psychoanalyst, who could have confronted and eventually interpreted her seductive acting out, as well as her intellectual distancing—both forms of avoiding contact—her treatment might have become an active experience of her internal life.

Orne never helped Sexton to see the pattern of the session, the pattern he could not see himself, the pattern of trance at the end resulting from the patient not opening up to emotional contact during the session. To attend to the lack of emotional contact would have required opening to Anne Sexton's rage and fear, and to her deep grief for the lost symbiotic object. From Middlebrook's description, Sexton never mourned for Nana in treatment. She talked about her lost symbiotic object, her aunt. However, the mourning was not reached.

Dr. Orne may have been too optimistic about Sexton's capacity for object relationship. Although he believed her relationship with her Aunt Nana had provided her with capacities for current relationships, he did not seem to comprehend the need for mourning. Experiencing Nana in the transference with Dr. Orne was just part of the picture. Sexton needed to mourn Nana to open up to a new object—the therapist who could be there on a continuous basis, and who could also let her go. She couldn't take in a current object without first opening the psychic space for it—mourning the good symbiotic object. To accomplish this task she would have had to go though the rage of the traumatic separation from the original symbiotic object. Also, for Sexton, the incorporated and arrested symbiotic object was fused with the incestuous father.

Orne never believed that the incest scene described by Sexton, where both Nana and father were present, was a true representation of her past. He just saw it as the subjective experience of her historic past, but he did not visualize this subjective situation as a current internal-object situation. For the borderline in the paranoid-schizoid position (Ogen, 1986), there is no history. The history is in the present, in the moment—in the internal-object situation moment by moment. If Orne had seen Sexton's view of the incest scene recreated in Sexton's play, "Tell Me Your Answer True," as an internal situation, he could have seen how she was perpetually in a borderline "damned if you do" and "damned if you don't" situation, and he could have approached this situation in each therapy session. What was the "damned if you do" and "damned if you don't" situation, and how was this related to the trance? If the incest scene that Sexton described so often in her therapy with Dr. Orne as a memory can be seen as a subjective experience of an ongoing internal-object situation, then defining it becomes critical. The scene Sexton portrayed was of being in bed with Nana and having her father come in. Then, as the scene continued, her father begins to make sexual overtures to her, while drunk, indifferent to Nana's presence.[4] In this scene, Anne Sexton was seen as a child victim, who is "incested" by her father, with the erotic thrill of Nana watching, but also with the chilling element of her aunt's condemning judgment. Presumably, in the arms of her aunt, with her father's penis coming into her, Anne Sexton was psychically sealed off. In the incest scene, Anne Sexton had both her aunt and her father, or a fused father-mother. Yet, she had the libidinal part-object and eroticized bad-object form of this fused father-mother: i.e., the demon lover shadow side of the early mother and the oedipal father. She was behind the psychic screen, sealed off, similar to Emily Dickinson who sought her creativity through merging with a demon father in the dark of night (see Kavaler-Adler, 1991, 1993) and similar to Emily Brontë, who merged with her male muse in the night, as the "night wind" (Kavaler-Adler, 1993).

In this incest scene, as well as possibly in her actual history, Anne was damned if she did and damned if she didn't. To stay with Nana was to be suffocated in the oven of symbiosis, but to move forward to boys and men was to betray Nana and thus to endure an acute cut off, another traumatic separation. This separation would result in losing the contact that allows mourning, gradual disillusionment, and internalization to take place. To move forward developmentally or psychically would have meant traumatic abandonment for Sexton. Yet to psychically remain with Nana stifled her developmental need to form a separate identity and to have differentiated heterosexual relations. Then, she had to remain in a regressive symbiosis. This damned if you do, damned if you don't situation of Sexton's adolescence, as portrayed in the present, seems to mirror that of a borderline infancy, particularly a borderline rapprochement-separation phase trauma, the kind described by James Masterson (1979). The adolescent trauma may well have been a screen memory as well as a trauma in its own right, as the varying developmental levels merged in the internal object scene. Sexton's unconscious solution, which had its persistent pathology due to the lack of adequate development, was through an erotic addiction to an incestuous father. Whatever actually occurred in Sexton's history in terms of an actual incestuous incident, it is clear from Anne Sexton's memory, as well as from her mother's memory, that her father was engaged in frequent verbally aggressive assaults against Anne as she moved into her adolescence. This was the same period during which Anne was overwhelmed with guilt towards Nana because of her move towards boys and towards heterosexual sex and intimacy. Not only did Anne have to deal with the threat of overwhelming guilt and loss in relation to her good symbiotic mother, Nana—all without the emotional support of either parent—but she also had to deal with the threat she posed to her father, as she went through the awkward stage of becoming a woman, beginning to date boys, possibly entering a second realm of trauma. Her father is noted by Anne and her mother to have launched perpetual attacks against her at the dinner table at this stage of her life. He would first look at her acne, make sounds and motions of disgust, then refuse to look at her, and would viciously criticize her as well as withdraw from her and the whole family. It is no wonder that years later, when Anne Sexton was married, and had a family of her own, she warded off the pain of the dinner table scene by loading herself up with alcohol during pre-dinner cocktails with Kayo. While they had their drinks, she often incited Kayo to abuse her verbally—or often physically, reenacting being the victim of her father's erotic violence against her body. Once at the dinner table, Anne would start "headlighting." "Headlighting" was a term Kayo Sexton invented to describe his wife's trancelike behavior at the dinner table. According to Kayo and the children (as reported by Diane Middlebrook), Anne would sit staring at the wall at the dinner table. Her eyes would run up and down staring at the walls. She would obviously seem quite dissociated as in her other trances. One evening she actually passed out, and her head fell into her plate of mashed potatoes. What scenes was Anne reliving at the dinner table as an adult? Her father's shame-inducing, out-of-control, and perhaps terrifying assaults on her were probably being relived each time. This is made most plausible by her compulsion to incite Kayo against her by using her taunting voice as an irritant, according to Kayo, like "a needle on a Singer sewing machine" (Middlebrook, p. 370). Besides his dining room assaults, Anne Sexton's father is quoted as having made slurs against his daughter behind her back. Upon seeing her leave the house to go on a date with a boy, he commented to her mother, "She looks like she's going out to get fucked" (Middlebrook, p. 57). Anne's mother reported him as saying "She's going to get laid," but Anne remembered it as "She's going to get fucked." Either way it's pretty bad. Such behavior on her father's part (Harvey Gray) suggests a general overinvolvement with Anne that was intrusively incestuous as well as aggressively erotic. The sadomasochistic engagement between father and daughter seems to have become embedded in Sexton's psyche. How did Sexton's psyche unconsciously use this sadomasochistic father-daughter relationship? It seems that it may have been used, as instinctual intensity is often used by borderlines (and hysterics), to buffer her against the continuing tensions of her internal "damned if you do and damned if you don't" internal-self and object situation. The continuing tension of this internal situation was tearing Sexton apart. Moving forward would bring a sense of guilt and betrayal that she could not tolerate. Yet staying still meant she would be overwhelmed with her own paralyzed aggression, as her developmental need to move forward and out of sym-biosis with a primary mothering object was strangled. Supposedly, that's why Sexton sought affairs as a means to "action" to fight the inner paralysis. But also within a new erotic affair, she could try to capture the mir-roring father before he turned demon and possessive. She could try to control the other through inducing erotic desire. She could incorporate the other through the sexual act. Psychically, she may have been living out her early lust for her father, overwhelming in its intense need to incorporate him as a primary object, since the early mother had been inadequate. She could not connect to the new man. She would withdraw again into trance or else pursue him (e.g., Bill Wright) until he abandoned her (Legler). Then the man would turn demonic. She would try to create scenes like those in which her father beat her with his words, her riding crop, or his hand. With Kayo she lived this out, as she provoked him to beat her. When Kayo entered therapy and refused to let her provoke him into a physical rage, she began dreaming of being beaten. Her psyche was searching for her father's beatings. When she eroticized a beating, its object yearning, and its abandonment, she created a scene that could stimulate and arouse, buffering her from guilt, loss, and need, giving her an intensity that served as a temporary escape from the internal suffocation. The scene of erotic aggression with her father, the eroticized beatings, served to wipe out a sense of his injurious disgust. The scene also allowed Sexton to ward off intense loss and guilt or its alternative of paralyzing suffocation (experienced if she was alone in a supermarket and had to make a decision to buy something).

Dr. Orne never seemed to understand the psychodynamic role that Sexton's scenes with her "bad-object" (Fairbairn, 1952) father could play. He did see her masochistic tendencies to crave punishment as a way to evade guilt, which was obvious as in her marital relationship with Kayo. Orne was aware that Sexton wanted to get through Kayo's anger with a big explosion and then be loved again. She sought redemption in renewed love, through paying the price of a punishing beating, rather than facing the guilt of her own aggression towards Kayo. In avoiding her guilt, she perennially avoided repairing her marriage. She sent her husband off to therapy with an ultimatum of divorce. Eventually she carried out the threat, and divorced. Yet, Orne did not see the splitting and the bad self-object constellation within her, which that made guilt and grieving guilt intolerable. Orne's view of her seeking punishment was not enough to help her. In his view, she suffered from neurotic guilt, not borderline persecutory anxiety. He did not see that her punishment, especially when eroticized, was Sexton's way of using her internal relationship with her father (incestuous, aggressive, rejecting, and intrusive) to enact a bad self, not facing her aggression and the depressive despair behind it. Being beaten was also a way Sexton could buffer herself from the loss of her primary mothering object, experienced in the encapsulated memory of Nana. It was furthermore a way of not viewing the deeper betrayal, a betrayal of separating from both Nana and her father. In trance, as in the ongoing erotic affair, she found a compromise solution—a schizoid compromise (Guntrip, 1976). She avoided feeling either by anesthetizing herself in trance or by impulsive action that served as a manic defense against depressive despair. Her defenses were hysterical (fainting, trance, and erotic affairs), but they were used to ward off borderline developmental trauma (Balint's "basic fault," Winnicott's "breaks in bonding"). They were also used in the context of a borderline psychic structure, in which self and object, mother and father, were not fully separated, and a bad and eroticized self-object constellation, which she called her "witch self," was hidden behind a false idealized self-object constellation: the sleeping beauty princess and her self-perpetuated myth of the immaculate housewife, dressed in the best designer clothes (Middlebrook, p. 296).

POETRY AS SUBLIMATION AND AS DEFENSE

When Dr. Orne first met with Anne Sexton, he asked her what she could do to have an identity in the world. Sexton couldn't think of anything except possibly being a prostitute. She had been a high school graduate— no college education—and no interest in school. Yet, Anne Sexton was to become a sensationally received and publicized poet. She was to receive accolades from the most prestigious universities in the world—honorary doctorates and Phi Beta Kappa keys from Harvard, Radcliffe, Tufts, and many more. She was to receive accolades from myriad literary societies, the most notable of which was the Pulitzer prize. She received travel grants, Radcliffe fellowships, and eventually was a regular instructor at Boston University. She exhibited herself and her work in poetry readings all over America and England. She was one of an elite few poets who received high fees for a performance (up to $1000). She spoke before Auden in a British event and with the most noted poets of her day. She took workshops with Lowell, Snodgrass, and John Holmes, and had private tutoring from notable mentors. She had her own musical group backing up her rhymes, called "Anne Sexton and Her Kind."

How did it all begin? It all began the night she heard a lecture on TV about writing a sonnet. She propped up a typewriter and began to write. "I can do that," she thought, as she listened to the lecture on the sonnet. From then on, her therapist, Dr. Orne, saw the cultivation of her identity as a poet as a route to her mental health.

From an ego psychological perspective this was understandable. Ego psychologists were modern Freudians, who emphasized the need for auxiliary support in building a person's capacities for functioning in the world. They neglected the critical fact, emphasized by the British object-relation theorists, that the ego, as an authentic self (Winnicott on "the true self," 1971), was built from self and object internalizations, dependent on interpersonal relations.

The controversies in England between Anna Freud and Melanie Klein, since Sigmund Freud and his daughter Anna had left Austria and entered the English world of the British Psychoanalytic Society during the rise of Hitler, had contributed to the division between Freudian ego psychology in America and the object-relations schools of Melanie Klein and

Winnicott in England. The Kleinian view of the self as constituted from internal objects, the Fairbairnian view of the self being constituted by internal-self and object relations, and the Winnicottian emphasis on the internal good-enough mother as being essential to self-development were not yet significantly recognized in the United States, where the descendents of Freud and Anna Freud rejected Klein and Winnicott and knew little of Fairbairn. Within ego psychology in America there was the exception of Margaret Mahler (1975), when she spoke of necessary internalizations during separation-individuation, particularly at rapprochement, to promote object constancy. Yet, her studies had only begun in the 1950s. Edith Jacobson (1964) began to write about internalized introjects as critical to self-development, but always with an opposition to the idea of dynamic internal objects, like Fairbairn's bad objects and Klein's dynamic part objects. The general view of ego psychology in the 1950s did not address the difference between a true and false self and between ego strength and schizoid modes of compulsive functioning. Ego psychology focused on a person's capacity to function, and underemphasized Klein's, Fairbairn's and Winnicott's view of the self being constructed from internal objects. The focus was more on functioning than relating, and therefore a theoretical awareness of capacities for intimacy and authentic identity was minimal. Erick Erikson (1950, 1963) was an exception in America, when he wrote about intimacy and authenticity within a developmental and interpersonal framework.

Within the dominant ego-psychological perspective of the 1950s American psychoanalytic scene, Anne Sexton's phenomenal performance in the world, as she became a prolifically productive poet, would deceptively appear to constitute a fulfilled life. Defining criteria for identity in terms of functioning didn't allow an assessment of self-integration or a developmental view of mourning and internalization.

Besides having such a perspective, Dr. Orne may have also been a captive of the creative mystique. To see a distinguished poet emerge like a butterfly from a caterpillar, or from its crystallite cocoon, must have been quite a scintillating spectacle. To see a washed-out housewife, who had appeared inchoate, sealed off, underwater, terrified of reality, and always in the mode of escape, begin to articulate a broad inner life with an authentic inner voice, must have seemed like a miracle. To challenge anything about this much might have looked like sacrilege. In an ego-psychological sense, Dr. Orne can be said to have served as an auxiliary ego to his patient, Anne Sexton. As she began to use her formerly unseen capacities to spew forth vivid and authentic lyrics, her doctor was in the background, encouraging her, admiring her, listening to her struggles to enter the world through attending writing workshops. According to the tapes recorded from Sexton's therapy sessions, much time was spent with Sexton merely relating, in an ongoing saga, her activities, affairs, and performances in the poetry world.

It was in writing workshops, such as that of John Holmes and Robert Lowell, that Sexton shaped and re-shaped her evocative lines. Within two years, she had published a major work: "Double Image." It was one of her finest works, taking a disciplined attitude from that of the other auxiliary egos with whom she had participated in her creative process at that time—within the workshop environment. "Double Image" speaks of the core narcissistic tragedy in Anne Sexton's being. The poem begins "I made you to find me." She is speaking to her daughter, but it is also an imaginary monologue spoken from her mother to herself: it is her internal mother:

> And this was the cave of the mirror,
> That double woman who stares
> at herself, as if she were petrified... (Middlebrook, p. 86)

> I, who was never quite sure
> about being a girl, needed another
> life, an image to remind me. And this was my worse
> guilt; you could not cure
> nor soothe it. I made you to find me. (Middlebrook, p. 88)

As Diane Middlebrook remarks, within the mother who uses her child to mirror herself is an infant who has been cut off and traumatized by separation. The mother with an infant within had a real external mother who had used her as a mirror, a mother who never had given her what she needed in the way of her own mirroring, but more particularly in terms of contact for her inchoate self.

"Double Image" does not have the intensity of Sexton's later poetry, which often had a manic frenzy and lacked the form so regimented here. Similar to the trend of work of Sylvia Plath (see Silverman and Will, 1986), Sexton relinquished the psychologically containing element of form in order to pound out intensity. In the process, she lost the reflective "I" that existed in the "Double Image" poem. She lost a more advanced level of psychic integration in which she was an "interpreting subject" (1986). Instead she became more and more a victimized reactor, relishing the flamboyant language of an unconscious she had to seek in a trance. How much Sexton's "I" depended on the auxiliary egos of her fellow workshop participants can only be guessed. Her insight in "Double Image" is appealing and rich in resonance for readers. Yet, had she really experienced the effect of this trauma in her therapy sessions? It seems likely that she had not. Thus, her sealed-off, affective infant self remained unpenetrated. In her therapy sessions, Sexton must have mentioned looking to her daughter for a sense of herself, and perhaps Dr. Orne had inquired about her mother's mirroring of her. But had she experienced her yearning for a mirroring mother at any point in the immediate intensity of the transference with Dr. Orne? It is doubtful. He was actively providing a mirror, rather than allowing her to experience the loss and the need. Furthermore, the context of therapy sessions, as reported by Middlebrook, seems to have been made up of genetic reconstructions and questions which Anne Sexton may have responded to in an intellectualized manner. With neurotic patients, free associations may get to affect contact and true memories, but with borderlines, such as Anne Sexton, the sealed-off infantile self will not be touched by such associations and they become an intellectualized endeavor, lacking process.

How much was split off from the therapeutic process, abstracted, and put into Sexton's poetry? Within a year after writing "Double Image," Anne Sexton completed and published a book of her poetry, *To Bedlam and Part Way Back*. It was an open exposition of her mental illness: her hospitalizations and suicide attempts. John Holmes, one well-known poet who led a poetry workshop, warned her not to publish it. She faced him in a poem, declared that what was in her was in him, and implied that he himself was inhibited by shame.

By contrast, Dr. Orne was most probably extremely impressed by Sexton's rapid rise from an obscure and reticent hidden self into a major voice emerging for all the world to see through poetry. But was he so impressed that the creative mystique mesmerized him? Did he begin to believe that Anne Sexton's mental health was more dependent on her becoming a poet than on what happened within her psychotherapeutic treatment? Was he unaware that "themes" talked about in Sexton's sessions were being explored by Sexton in a state of solitude she employed to write poetry? Sexton's biographer notes that Sexton would go into a trance state during the act of writing a poem. The poet viewed this as an emersion in her unconscious. In this state, a panoply of images would emerge prolifically and richly. How many images were sensed in this state that were spin-offs of topics in therapy sessions? In her trance state, Sexton went into the area of the infantile self and produced images and words rich with the authenticity of felt inner experience. But the solitude of trance prevented Sexton from opening her feelings and her recessed feeling self to contact with her therapist. This trance writing could very well have served as a divergence from any contact in her treatment sessions. Her feeling self could go untapped indefinitely in treatment, remaining sealed off from contact with her therapist, and thus unable to develop and become integrated with the false outer shell of her narcissistic image self. Integration depended on affect contact, and affect process, a necessary mourning process that needed to take place within the containing presence of her therapist. Intense anguish needed to open up on the route to a developmental grieving process. Rage and terror needed to emerge too so she could reach a healing sadness. But because Sexton's sessions had intellectual themes that related to affective issues and affective memories, the experience of affect in the session—directly in the moment—seemed precluded. Dr. Orne would speak with Sexton about transference and other psychological concepts, and Sexton would use these concepts (Middlebrook, p. 54) to create poetry. In 1958, an early period in her poetry writing, she seemed especially preoccupied with psychological concepts learned from Dr. Orne (Middlebrook, p. 54). She took notes on her own therapy sessions in poetry (Middlebrook, p.55). In an era when borderline and narcissistic syndromes, and their split-off schizoid dynamics were unknown, poetry and other art forms of expression may have seemed adequate routes to affect expression, and even to cure. Dance therapy, music therapy, and with Ann Sexton's help, poetry therapy, were all beginning to be practiced in mental hospital settings.[5] Dr. Orne may very well have seen Sexton's poetry as curative in that it gave voice to her recessed inner self. What he did not seem to realize was that this inner self was split off, and was not just recessed or repressed. Interpersonal affect contact would be essential to open it up. When themes in treatment were converted into poetry, the craving for contact in the treatment session was bypassed, and the result was the perpetuation of a sealed-off (Fairbairn, 1952) or submerged self (Wolff and Kutash, 1991), which also seems to have been split into reflected images of idealized and demonic counterparts.

Perhaps the therapist's engagement with his patient in the poetry writing could be seen as a transitional phase of treatment. Such engagement could be a vehicle, like a mirroring self-object transference, to allow the therapist to become an object of desire, when frustrated cravings for object connection opened up. But this never seems to have happened in Sexton's treatment. Her cravings for merger, for object contact, for incest, were renamed and focused on men in her outside life, and later were acted out with a male therapist who succumbed to a sexual affair. Sexton's poetry writing gave her an identity in the world, but in her psychotherapeutic treatment it remained a major resistance. In Harry Guntrip's terms it served as a "schizoid compromise."

DR. ORNE'S USE OF RECORDING TAPES

Borderline patients disconnect from the basic object connection that they need so desperately. This terror of object loss, due to unmourned early abandonment trauma, makes them prone to disconnection from objects. Whereas some people can sustain a sense of an internalized other, having a good-enough internal object that can be contained, borderline personalities are like bulimics, psychically swallowing others who are at first viewed as idealized, and then spitting and vomiting them up. They cannot sustain the containment of an object ("object constancy") and therefore they are continually losing connection to others, no matter how intense the interaction with the other is in any one moment. Part of losing the other can extend to losing the memory of the other, or, less extremely, to losing the memory of the interaction with the other. When Dr. Orne encountered the phenomenon of forgetting in his patient, Anne Sexton, he had no psychic-structure perspective from which to see and understand the borderline personality. Therefore, Orne's approach to confronting Anne Sexton's "forgetting" of what transpired in her therapy sessions was rather naive. He decided to tape record the sessions, and asked Sexton to listen to the tapes in between the sessions. He wanted her to remember— the themes, the topics, the content of the sessions. However, with the borderline, the content of the sessions is hardly the issue! It's the process that is so critical. Remembering the content is related to the process and needs to come from the effectiveness of the process engagement in the session, and from the ability of the patient to sustain an internalization of that engagement. In asking Sexton to listen to her therapy session tapes, Dr. Orne was trying to circumvent the whole issue of memory related to an internalization process. He was unaware of the connection between memory and object internalization, and therefore did not realize that his intellectual approach to memory with Sexton was bound to fail. He did not understand that the psychic function of memory is based on the capacity to love an object and to sustain an internalization of it.

DR. ORNE'S FAILURE TO COMPREHEND THE PRIMITIVE NATURE OF SEXTON'S GUILT

As time went on in Sexton's treatment with Dr. Orne, it appears that Dr. Orne's countertransference began to lead to his increased distancing. Sexton's suicidal gestures and breakdowns may have begun to seem to him like a failure on his part, for which he punished her by removing her out of his sight to a hospital. When Sexton was offered a travel grant to tour Europe, while in her seventh year of treatment with Dr. Orne, he encouraged her to go, and took some pains to explain his optimistic view of her progress in treatment. The criteria he used for measuring her growth had nothing to do with psychic structure change. He explained to her that she was remembering more of her sessions, and she was therefore improving enough to take the risk of independence and self-reliance required by the trip. Sexton could never travel alone, even to the supermarket, but after finding a steady female companion, she set forth on the European venture.

At first, the poet did well on the trip. She was getting physical exercise in walking tours, quite unusual for her! Sexton had always resisted exercise. (Maxine Kumin reports that in her later life she used the excuse of a broken hip to totally vegetate.) However, on the European trip, Sexton was able to experience that her usual state of high anxiety dissipated (p. 206) when she had miles of walking and touring to do in a day. Unfortunately, she never subsequently used this knowledge about physical exercise to sustain her when in despair. Despite knowing the usefulness of physical exercise, she chose to withdraw into a despair which was enacted in suicidal gestures. But at the time of the European tour, necessity overrode her normal despair, and her body yielded to the physical exercise that temporarily dispelled her tensions. This, combined with the genuine excitement of the cultural adventure, and with love letters from Kayo which glorified her and portrayed her as an ideal "princess" (as absence made the heart grow fonder), gave Sexton an appearance of mental health. But then the new image of herself was shattered when her unintegrated libido was ignited. A Frenchman, named Louis, told her tales of his captivity by the Nazis during the second World War II, and his tragedy and manner enticed her. In the manner of her usual emotional starvation, Sexton converted her emotional hunger into a sexualized form, and greedily grasped at an opportunity for lovemaking with him. Afterwards, she was desolate, in a renewed despair that left no room in her psyche for anything else other than self-hate. She lost all interest in the tour, in her artistic purpose, and in any longterm goals. The inner accusations must have begun their powerful chorus in her mind as she reeled from puncturing the balloon she had been inflating with Kayo.

At the moment of entering the lustful, sex-hungry affair, Sexton may have lost all sense of time, of connections, of historical existence. Regression to a paranoid-schizoid position is a constant vulnerability of borderlines. In the paranoid-schizoid state of mind, there is no sense of oneself as an "historical subject" (Ogden, 1985). Therefore, every moment is a new beginning. In this mind state, a romantic fling can easily offer a circumscribed world of its own. With no past and no future, what's the harm? But after the lust, what would have happened in Anne Sexton's mind? From her behavior, it appears that she experienced a punitive form of guilt that compelled her to abruptly cut off from her new lover. She withdrew into trance and pervasive despair, returning to a suicidal state. She promptly returned to the United States and collapsed mentally and physically. Kayo's princess now was seen by him as his "bad" wife, the washed-out and depressed wife who, in Middlebrook's words, he wished was gone forever (Middlebrook, p. 210).

I will speculate about the intrapsychic dynamics of Anne Sexton's state of mind at this point, based on my knowledge of borderline psychic structure in terms of Mahler's, Klein's, and Fairbairn's theories. I believe that Anne Sexton's "morning after" reaction can be explained as a primitive superego response, which occurs in those who cannot contain the affects and conceptualizations related to guilt. Whether the primitive superego is called simply that, as it was by Klein, or whether it is called an "internal saboteur" or "anti-libidinal ego" in Fairbairn's terms, it operates as a relentless court in which accusations and attack are not modulated by a judge (as in the neurotic conscience) or jury, or by any defense attorney. Sexton could not contain the guilt of being disloyal to her husband by having an affair with another man. In her mind, it must have seemed a gross betrayal, at the level of black-and-white extreme thinking in which betrayal is murder. How could she contain the guilt of murderous betrayal, especially in light of the unmourned early guilt of her life? Throughout her life, Sexton had carried with her a childhood trauma sealed off from conscious thought and living connection, in which she had murderously betrayed her adopted symbiotic mother, her Aunt Nana. Her developmental need during adolescence to separate from a regressive symbiosis with Nana impelled her forward into yearning for boys. But no adequate separation could be made. Due to Nana's reaction when she attempted to separate, Nana could not be internalized as a good-holding object, and therefore separation and individuation could not take place. Nana could not be internalized because she turned cold with rage and withdrew from Anne Sexton just at the point when Anne needed her most for critical internalization during the transitional phase of adolescence. Nana reacted like a jilted lover. She not only withdrew her holding, hugging warmth—the old cuddling—but also seemed to have become ill, making implicit accusations against Anne as she was reduced to living in a mental hospital, following an initial breakdown. Her implicit accusations must have been spiked with poison, because Nana was obviously herself borderline, and Anne was serving the function of being her symbiotic mother. Perhaps Anne got the kind of holding from Nana that she never got from a detached, narcissistic mother during her infancy. Perhaps, she returned to an earlier symbiosis which was then aborted by developmental strivings of the toddler years, similar to the disruption due to developmental strivings in adolescence. In any case, the trauma with Nana during adolescence remained unmourned and therefore unhealed. It was a profound trauma in its own right, whatever its "screen memory" attributes in relation to Sexton's infancy. Carrying this trauma around with her, split off from the central self (Fairbairn's central ego), which engaged with the world as an "unthought known" (Bollas, 1987, Winnicott, 1971), the old trauma must have rumbled with tremors of self-fragmentation each time it was raised from detached slumber by a new trigger of association in the present.

Therefore, when Sexton slept with her Frenchman at the height of her renewed long distance love affair with her husband, Kayo, it must have caused an inner earthquake in the form of self-fragmentation, depletion, and unmourned detached despair. Sexton did not have a "depressive position" conscience which could contain and process guilt. She needed a therapist's emotional holding to help her contain grief affects so that guilt could become grief and be mourned. She needed the internalization of a holding therapist to allow her to develop the psychic structure of self- and object- internalization that would allow her to process the guilt in human and bearable terms. She was not getting this kind of holding from Dr. Orne. Without it she was left with her primitive, hostile, masochistic accuser—the inner voice and object that called her a murderous betrayer, the internal saboteur who could not forgive, who allowed her no compassion for herself. She was left with the bitch goddess-demon god accuser, turned against herself. She was left with the unrelenting assault by her inner grandiose judge calling her a murderer, over, and over, and over again. The sin of betrayal was upon her, and there was nowhere to run from her internal accuser. Thus, she shrunk within herself, shrunk from the sex that the day before had seemed so scintillating with life. Now the sex seemed poisoned. She would tell Anne Wilder, a female psychiatrist with whom she later precipitated a homosexual affair, that sex was a contagion that poisoned the purity of love. In her affair with the Frenchman, the theme of love must have undergone a borderline switch of split mind images in relation to the sex, with self-hate at seeing herself as a betrayer the result. At first her lover was an adoring idealized mirror. His gaze at her could make her feel pure and angelic, although lust rose to merge her with him. But the critical turn of the mirror inevitably came.

In the harsh light of day, following the sexual aura and trance, he would no longer shine his godlike light upon her, but instead could be seen to cast his demonic shadow. The sex then was a violation, a nerve gas poison and contagion which spread its dark shadow and enveloped her in its suffocating grip. Shrinking away from Louis and into herself, Sexton lost the connection with him which she hoped would strengthen her. Then there was the dark image of Kayo in her mind—reminding her of Nana and of her sinful nature. She could not control her body impulses. She was still compelled by manic energy into action. The theme of betrayal pervaded Sexton's work.

The several versions of her one play reflected this theme. Variously called "Tell Me Your Answer True" and "Daisy," her play focused on a female child protagonist who is guilty of a sin of murderous betrayal towards her whole family. She carries the sin with her and cannot exorcise it. Like the affliction in "Double Image," which could not be cured nor soothed, the sin of betrayal in her play could also not be cured or soothed. Sexton sought soothing from all her therapists but never found it. What she truly needed was an intimate understanding of her psychic phenomenon of primitive guilt and the emotional holding to contain her grief affects.

Even though Dr. Orne was Anne Sexton's best therapist, he failed his patient at a critical juncture, when she returned in a state of collapse from Europe. Dr. Orne's reaction must be considered in light of the limited framework of his clinical approach and the limited theory to which he had been exposed. It also needs to be considered in light of all therapists' tendencies to have countertransference reactions to their patients, and in light of the profound countertransference reactions incurred by borderline patients. It appears that Dr. Orne may have taken Anne Sexton's mode of return from the hoped-for triumph of her European journey as a blow to his own self-esteem as a therapist. His primitive response to her is a symptom and a clue. He placed her immediately in a hospital without any contact with her. She was denied the opportunity to talk to him. Furthermore, Sexton was particularly distressed by the type of hospital Dr. Orne placed her in. She petitioned for placement in another hospital, perhaps one in which there were more opportunities for therapeutic contact. Dr. Orne had surely not read about using countertransference responses, although such therapeutic work had been written about by Racker (1957) in England. Dr. Orne had surely not read Racker, given the American psychoanalytic scene, and he had surely not read about "induced countertransference," a concept that stemmed from the Kleinian analysts' clinical method of "processing projective-identifications."

Racker, as well as other followers of Melanie Klein, had developed a technique that was particularly critical to working with borderline patients.
Not having read these theorists, Dr. Orne would not have been equipped
to feel and analyze his own responses to Sexton at this time as part of the
treatment process. However, I can conjecture that his behavior reflected a
negative countertransference that became toxic when it couldn't be
processed, digested, and related to his patient's psychodynamics and psychic structure.

Dr. Orne had sent Sexton off to Europe with accolades. He confirmed
and validated her in an effort to infuse her with confidence to cross the
Atlantic. In applauding her progress, he was also confirming his own ade-
quacy as a psychotherapist. Although her memory was opened up more
from mental exercise then from affect contact (her abandonment depression was still sealed off), the hints of normal functioning had heartened
Orne after years of difficult work with his patient. So it is not surprising
that when Anne Sexton returned wrecked and bereft, returning to all her
former symptoms of schizoid depression, dissociation, trance, paralysis,
and helplessness, he was not thrilled. He must have felt that his belief in
his capacity to cure Sexton was mere illusion. As Sexton returned, in typical borderline fashion, to what appeared like point zero—devoid of a
capacity for self-reflection, insight, or self-integration—he may have felt at
the very least disillusioned, and at the worst, devastated. If he was unable
to face his reaction, because he did not wish to acknowledge his patient's
anger, and even more probably his own rage,[6] he could convert what
might have been hot frustration and rage into a cool and sophisticated
distancing response. His role of psychiatrist gave him an out that other
analysts, not hooked into mental hospital settings, do not have. As a psychiatrist, he could easily hospitalize Sexton and thus shield himself from
the knowledge that he was retaliating against her with a primitive countertransference. He could appear quite civilized—although the patients in
One Flew Over A Cuckoo's Nest might view him as a nurse Ratchet. He
was officious and efficient in his role of committing psychiatrist. He was
antiseptic, with sterilized psychic hands that never needed to touch his
patient without his gloves. He could hide behind this role if he wished to.
At this point, trying to repress his emotional rage reaction, hiding in his
role may have felt quite useful. But the cost of doing this was the psychic
and clinical price extracted from the treatment of Sexton. His emotional
distancing did not allow him to be with her at this moment of great crisis,
when her guilt anxiety was erupting into psychic fragmentation. It didn't
allow him to contain her. Without his presence, the hospital must have
seemed like a prison to her. Whereas formerly Dr. Orne had rendezvoused

with Sexton during her hospitalizations, initially seeing her five times a
week in the hospital, at this juncture he seems to have been all but absent.
Sexton must have felt this profoundly, but would have to have split off
the feelings from conscious awareness. There was no way she could have
contained them in her state of mind, and her feelings would have seemed
a threat to her relationship with her doctor. She wrote the poem, "Flee on
Your Donkey," during one such hospitalization, when she was left alone
in the hospital, without contact with Dr. Orne of any significant clinical
nature.

With Dr. Orne distancing in this manner from Sexton, he could not
have understood the kind of primitive guilt reaction that Sexton was having. On the other hand, with knowledge of his countertransference, he
could have felt a conscious sense of his own guilt in relation to her and
her treatment. He could have understood that if this was part of an
induced countertransference reaction, it reflected the intensity of the guilt,
as well as the rage and shame that Sexton herself was feeling. If he could
have become aware of her disowned guilt (and narcissistic rage) in this
manner, he might have embraced the opportunity to be with Sexton, and
to experience her guilt firsthand, so that he could have come to understand it. If he would have experienced the sensation of her guilt while with
her, he might have experienced her intense need to grieve. He might then
have discovered the triggering event of her breakdown: her affair with
Louis, and the context of the affair in relation to her long-distance honeymoon with her husband, Kayo. If he got this far, he might have connected her sense of betrayal in the present with that in the past with Nana.
However, with the lack of knowledge about the British object-relations
theorists by the American therapeutic community, this was not likely to
happen.

11)

ANNE SEXTON'S TREATMENT, PART II, AND ADDENDUM ON HER DEMON LOVER COMPLEX

Quite soon after this traumatic return from Europe, and the following hospitalization in Westwood Lodge, where Sexton was treated by Dr. Orne's mother, Dr. Brunner-Orne, rather than by Dr. Orne himself, Sexton was faced with another major disrupting event. Dr. Orne decided to leave his practice in Boston to accept a research and teaching professorship in Pennsylvania (Middlebrook, p. 213). After seven years of depending on Dr. Orne as her psychotherapist, Anne Sexton was faced with the end of her treatment. Dr. Orne was sensitive to the issue of termination, and worked with Sexton while she began treatment with another male psychiatrist, Dr. Zweizung. From this period of time, he had sessions concurrent and overlapping with sessions of Dr. Zweizung, so that Sexton could tolerate the transition. Following this transition period, he also continued to see Anne Sexton on a once-a-month basis for several years. By seeing her for as long as he did, Orne remained a continuous and solid figure of support in Sexton's life, an important addition to her husband, Kayo, whose relationship with her was intensely ambivalent. Orne's presence was particularly important, as Sexton had not yet been able to sufficiently internalize him, because of the limitations of his treatment. Sexton had consulted with several psychiatrists, probably referred by Dr. Orne, and had chosen Dr. Zweizung. The rest of the tale is infamous and very well known. Although Zweizung began treatment in a traditional manner, he eventually had Sexton lie on the couch and ended up on the couch with her. Having a borderline woman lie on the couch is questionable in itself, since observing nonverbal behavior is so important (although the body can speak more when on the couch as long as the analyst sees it), and also because the lack of a sustained internal object connection can create a sense of black void for the borderline person, which is terrifying, and often cannot be tolerated. It is likely that under these conditions Sexton redoubled her efforts to control things with her arts of seduction. A combination of body mannerism, preoccupation with sexualized thoughts, and the sensual seduction of her language and her poetry reading could all have played a part in her seductive acting out with Dr. Zweizung. Such behavior was a general hysteroid character defense against abandonment affects of rage, loss, and emptiness, as well as against the basic human vulnerability to loving and needing. However, in light of the enforced separation form Dr. Orne, Sexton's seductive behavior could have been employed to defend against separation grief in reaction to the loss of her doctor. In any case, it is likely that her seductive behavior was rather flamboyant and pervasive, especially considering Middlebrook's description of her ongoing seductive behavior with all who she met. Sexton's need to capture Dr. Zweizung, and win him over as a mother-father transference figure, must have been compelling. In fact, Sexton was known to call Dr. Zweizung "daddy doctor." Her pursuit of him, her efforts to control him, given how she had been so controlled by her narcissistic parents, would have been expected. However, unlike Dr. Orne, he was not a stable father figure. Dr. Zweizung seems to have been overwhelmed by his patient's language, talent, and fame. He seems to have been dazzled by her. At first he seems to have responded with counterseduction (and perhaps competition) with words. He began to write poems to her as she wrote them to him. According to Sexton, he was a "word-magic guy" (Middlebrook, p. 258). The word magic must have hypnotized Dr. Zweizung as much as Sexton. Sexton avoided the combination of current affect and symbolic communications, related to the yearnings sealed-off in her trance states, which pressured her from the sealed off part of her self, and gradually succeeded in sexually seducing Dr. Z. with words of poetry, until both were in a trance or "entranced." Sexton began bragging to her friends, one of whom was a female psychiatrist, of how she would tuck her "red nighty" into her purse prior to her sessions. She flaunted her sexual affair with her doctor before these women like one of her literary prizes or honorary doctorates. She must have sought their mirroring, reassurance, and perhaps outward controls. It would be a way for her to flaunt an incestuous oedipal victory before many transferential mother figures, hoping to stir up the envy in her "mother-sister" women friends, an envy that she herself was trying to rid herself of, living as she did in a perpetual state of emotional starvation. Her friends' reactions were various, but among them was concern for her. They felt protective, and wished to report Zweizung to a professional ethics committee, but they didn't. In the end, they left it all to fate with a cry of protest that Sexton was demeaning herself to the point of paying her doctor for sessions in which he was screwing her. Sexton's friends Maxine Kumin and Lois Ames commented: "Puritanical Yankees, what we couldn't stand was her paying him!" (Middlebrook, p. 314).

Meanwhile, Sexton colluded in a deceptive illusion propagated, apparently by himself, that "treatment" could be resumed at any time. They both chose to deceive themselves in this way, despite the fact that they had become literal lovers. Regardless of the input of Sexton's friends, such as Maxine Kumin, who had been through psychoanalysis, and Anne Wilder, who were encouraging Sexton to leave Dr. Z. and to seek help from an ethical psychotherapist, Anne Sexton never made any attempt to initiate a departure from him. Her self-sabotaging behavior can be taken as a sign of Sexton's masochism, of her degree of ego weakness, of her lack of individuation. Overall, lacking a good-enough separate and related internal object, her sense of self was bound to be impoverished. Her sense of power was likely to have been perverted by the impact of her seductive, intrusive, and abusive father. She sought power by being both the seductive father and the little girl who succumbed to seduction, and therefore controlled her seducer. She did not take the power she had to protect herself or to confront Dr. Z., nor to leave the scene of male prostitution in which she participated. Sexton was not only prone to be seduced by the arts of her own seduction and by any father figure—given the sado-masochistic sexualization of her own father's relationship with her, she also became addicted to Dr. Z., and separation appeared like dreaded abandonment. Earlier in the treatment, she wrote a poem, "Eighteen Days Without You," in which she counted out the days and the sensations of yearning and loss in a tolerable period of separation. It was this poem that Sexton read at a commencement celebration at Harvard University, when she was commemorated as an honorary Phi Beta Kappa scholar. Never having gone to college, this was quite an honor, and Kayo was beside her to share it. Ironically, she was speaking of her lover, with her husband as eyewitness. Poetry can present the illusion that translation through metaphor can result in spiritual transcendence, even while the realities of the concrete sexual act behind the poetry are having destructive consequences.

Sexton's affair with Dr. Z. was to become known to Dr. Orne in its earlier stages. In the many years that it ran its course, it was only Dr. Orne who would confront Zweizung, despite many friends of Sexton knowing of the affair from close to its inception. After the beginning of the therapy and affair in 1964, Dr. Orne first confronted Dr. Zweizung in 1966. Not wanting to damage Anne Sexton's positive view of the doctor (fearing the inducement of another traumatic loss), Dr. Orne was most genteel in his manner with the misanthropic healer. Nevertheless, he did confront the man. He told Dr. Z. that he could choose between an interview with him and a hearing before an ethics committee. Under such duress, Dr. Z. submitted to the interview. Dr. Orne praised him for his initial attempts to engage Sexton in a level of therapeutic intimacy that he himself was incapable of, and then preceded to chastise him for his transgression into the sexual enactment of the intimacy, which was inevitably followed by pulling back and defensive distancing on his part, as Sexton became more and more demanding. Orne told Dr. Z. that his withdrawal just repeated the abandonment trauma in Sexton's life, and undid any good work done on helping her trust and tolerate intimacy. Further, he castigated Dr. Z. for "using Sexton." He directly confronted Dr. Z.'s collecting payments when he was having sex with her rather than doing treatment. Orne demanded that Zweizung either return to analysis and deal with his countertransference or that he stop pretending to treat Sexton. Dr. Zweizung agreed but failed to follow through. In fact, according to Dr. Orne, Dr. Z. became more secretive about his behavior with Sexton, and Anne Sexton colluded by withholding information from Dr. Orne. According to Orne (Middlebrook, p. 315), Anne Sexton withheld the information about her treatment because Dr. Z. had not followed through on any of his promises to seek analytic help, or to discontinue seeing Sexton, and he was still charging her for treatment. In fact, according to Orne, the affair "got so complex" that Dr. Zweizung would control his involvement with Sexton by leaking information to his wife, when he wanted to have an excuse to distance from Sexton. It was at the point of Dr. Zweizung's distancing from Sexton in 1969 that Sexton once more beckoned Dr. Orne in to intervene in the affair, which led finally to a change of therapists.

In the face of such gross incompetence and exploitation by Dr. Zweizung, why does Diane Middlebrook emphasize rationalizing comments by people in Anne Sexton's life, attempting to excuse Dr. Zweizung's behavior and perhaps their lack of intervention in a tragic therapeutic situation? Diane Middlebrook states several times that in the years during which Anne Sexton remained in Dr. Z.'s "therapy," she had fewer hospitalizations and fewer suicide attempts. This is certainly a short-term view. What was the long-term result for Sexton of her acting out her demon lover addiction? Eventually, the result was a rupture of the one sustained and primary relationship in her life, followed by a blanket determination to exterminate herself. During the period when she was acting out her addiction, an addiction to an idealized daddy—she tried to fill up the void with libidinal gratification just as she did with pills and alcohol. As Mark Grunes (1984) has remarked about Ferenzi's experiments with gratifying patients as an attempt to cure, such behavior is like pouring liquid into a leaking container. In Sheldon Bach's study on *Narcissistic States and the Therapeutic Process* (1985), Bach speaks of the fallacy of thinking that anyone can build in psychic structure through libidinal routes, with libidinal supplies.

When people rationalize Dr. Zweizung's sexual, emotional, and financial exploitation of Sexton as some kind of temporary rescue effort which sustained her through this period, they are denying years of deterioration in her life given the stamp of approval—the phallic stamp—by a supposed professional clinician. The deterioration may not have been as overtly obvious as during other periods, because the acute abandonment stress was modified by Dr. Z.'s literal presence, and by the degree to which Sexton managed to contact him during that period. However, there was an accompanying psychic decay that went far beyond psychic stagnation. Anne Sexton's marriage was erupting into alcoholic brawls each night at dinner, and her alcoholism escalated daily. Her husband's feelings about her ongoing exclusion of him from her primary orbit—as she circled around Dr. Zweizung—were never addressed by anyone. Kayo Sexton tried to maintain his family, but viewed himself as a martyr subjected to Sexton's tyrannical provocations, to her entitled demands to support and rescue efforts, and to her continual exclusion of him from the intimate and pseudo-intimate sharing that she splurged on Dr. Zweizung. Kayo could not help feeling betrayed. The poignancy of his plight can ring the heart. Middlebrook reports a note he wrote to his wife, around the time of their nineteenth wedding anniversary, when he was too intimidated to speak to her:

> No matter what has been the matter, it is not like us to sleep in separate rooms [...] Tonight you asked me to cuddle you. It was so hard even to say maybe, 'cuz the stings of the cactus yesterday and today had made me leery of getting close to the cactus bush. [...]
>
> On the other side of the fence, [...] I am tired and short tempered. I overly react to what you do or say. [...] I am asking you to let me cuddle you—I don't want to play the game and hit you and let you feel there is one more in the world against you. I am for you—yet I am afraid of you. I can't fight or equal the mad hitting words. I can only write and say, I'm still Boots—maybe I have spurs on—but

then my Button still has the needle that sews her to me. [...]

I love you, want to make everything OK, but it's beyond my power. I'm just a jerk, tongue-tied, emotionally unable to keep up with you. Hear me—come to me—Kayo.

Middlebrook comments: "Looking back on that bitter time, Kayo recalled feeling a constant frustration. Aware of her infidelities—'Murder will out,' he said, laughing ruefully—he felt constrained by her illness from confronting her with the pain they gave him; I thought that if she ever got well, we could put that kind of thing behind us" (Middlebrook, p. 261).

SEXUAL CUDDLING VERSUS HOLDING

Winnicott's theories on the holding environment were banned from America by the tyrannical reign of psychiatrists from the New York Psychoanalytic, and their counterparts in Massachusetts, as well as elsewhere. His theories were abhorred, rather then read. The intense attention that he had garnered from members of the British Psychoanalytic Society was all but unknown in America. If Winnicott had been understood in the States, the function of psychic holding and its emotional mode of transformation might have been used and appreciated by therapists who were helpless in the attempting ethical and effective treatment with borderline patients. In Winnicott's book, *Holding and Interpretation* (1972, 1986), he emphasizes the significance of psychic holding for all patients even those with primarily neurotic conflicts. However, most of his other writing focuses on the critical role of the psychotherapeutic holding environment in treating what he called "false self" patients, patients who have schizoid detachment and borderline impulse enactment. Other theorists who have elaborated on the role of psychic holding are Mark Grunes (1984), who describes the "therapeutic object relationship" and Jeffrey Seinfeld (1989), who writes about developing the holding transference with borderline patients. Perhaps Anne Sexton's desires could have come together with her needs if she had a therapist who could have offered her psychic holding as a route to psychic structure internalization, and who could have dealt with Sexton's resistances to allowing someone to hold, enter, and penetrate her. Instead, she had a sham therapist, who gave her the sham hold and the sham thrust. Dr. Zweizung participated with Sexton in enacting the sealed-off drama that she used to anesthetize herself against her real terror of psychic penetration. Sexton's father seems to have been looked to, in fantasy, to gratify the vaginal modes of oral cravings, and Aunt Nana gratified the wish for cuddling. The father-daughter-aunt incest that Sexton depicted in her plays, the incest and seduction drama, could have had the immediate quick-fix quality of appeasing Sexton's true emotional needs and cravings, while simultaneously shielding her from the terror that was evident in her repeated trance states. Their enactment took her temporarily out of her trance and allowed a manic form of craved "action" (Middlebrook, p. 27), as Sexton expressed it. Sexton writes of her need for "action" in relation to early extramarital affairs, in which libidinal contact pushed her infantile cravings for psychic holding back into her unconscious, or split them off again. Sexton said that she was reluctant to give up "cuddling" with Dr. Z. in order to return to the hard "work" of therapy. This dichotomy was what she presented as providing her only alternatives. The two sides of this dichotomy should not have been her only alternatives. Another alternative was left out. It was left out in her doctors' minds as well as in her own—the alternative of psychic holding, the emotional embrace that can lead to psychic penetration into the "empty core" (Seinfeld, 1992), an area in the psyche cut off from interpersonal contact, that is Fairbairn's sealed-off area (1952). This empty core area, or sealed-off self, has been believed to be the result of early abandonment (Masterson 1979), or early disruptions in the needed environmental presence (Balint, 1979), environmental attunement (Mahler, 1975), or in the maternal matrix and it's capacity to "hold" (Winnicott, 1974).

When Sexton chose cuddling with Dr. Z.—a choice allowed by his sexual lust for her—she was reaching for some palliative that could soothe away her intense yearnings for infantile care and contact. But physical cuddling is not psychic holding. It foreshortens a distance between the therapist and his patient that does not allow the "transitional space" necessary for psychic transformation. Such space was described by D. W. Winnicott in terms of "play space," "transitional space," and "analytic space." Without this space, as Ogden (1985) so suggests, there is no room for the psychic illusion that creates the therapist in the patient's mind. There is no room for the patient to create a psychic space for penetration within her, a psychic space that, like vaginal space, can allow the entrance of the other, and also can lead to the germination of babies—psychic internal objects, as opposed to actual physical babies. Without analytic space, no transitional inner psychic space can be developed in the patient. For borderlines, whose inner space is totally aborted and foreshortened, not working at the creation of this inner psychic space can only end in tragedy.

Without the creation of inner psychic space, which is complementary to the analytic "play" or "transitional" space, there can be no developmental mourning process. For a borderline patient, this means that there is no possibility for a critical self-integration process to take place. It means remaining fragmented, with split-off self and object constellations that preserve the imprint of unmourned and unresolved trauma. It can mean, as in the case of Anne Sexton, that there is no space for rage to be expressed, so that the therapist can survive and contact can be made. It means that past objects, who are now persecutory internal objects—those Sexton revealed continuously in her poetry (see Kavaler, 1989)—cannot be felt enough to be grieved and let go of. Such grieving can only come about when there is love in the present, resonating with the lost love of the past. This love between analyst and patient can only be felt in an environment in which the patient's feelings and impulses can be contained and allowed to emerge, rather than pressured into arousal through the analyst's own need. When the patient can see her avoidance of her own will to surrender to love, both from within and from without, she can begin to feel the grief of the isolation and loss, a grief she is continuously creating. Contacting this regret, this grief, stimulated by a current loss, brings back the losses, regrets, wounds, and cut-off yearnings of the past. Rage is a weapon that opposes surrender. It can be a roadblock, but only if unexpressed. For the borderline person, this rage is connected to traumatic levels of frustration in the past—traumatic levels of unmet emotional needs for contact and understanding—for connection—for love. Cold rage must become hot rage. There must be space—interpersonal space—analytic space—and inner space—for this to happen. Once cold rage becomes hot, there can be a yielding to the grief of loss behind the hot hate. Always in the face of truly felt hate is the shadow face of love, waiting to appear, waiting to link the person to lost loves who still reside within as internal objects.

Anne Sexton went through none of this. She had a taped scene of incest preserved in her mind, similar to that of patients I have seen. Whether or not the scene actually took place in the manner preserved in her mind, the constellation had become a frozen psychic formulation that blocked, opposed, and/or engulfed potential contacts in the present. No matter who the potential new loves were, Sexton's psyche formulated them all into a salacious scene of seduction, in which she converted them into the mirror of the two-headed parent monster within her. One head of the parent was Norma who cuddled her, and the other head was the father who she imagined as molesting her and phallically compelling her into submission. This so-called memory, which Dr. Orne said was Sexton's subjective experience, due to its probable paucity of objective veracity, reflects the "a priori" psychic fantasy states described so vividly by Melanie Klein.

Such fantasy states Klein observed not only through her adult patients' associations, but also from her work with children in play therapy. Melanie Klein articulated the preoedipal (or pre-neurotic) child experience of the parents as a combined unit—as a fused mommy-daddy object. According to Klein (Segal, 1975) before the parents are experienced as separate and in a relationship, which inevitably stirs jealousy, they are experienced at a more primitive level as constantly engaged in sexual intercourse, and at an even more primitive level they are experienced as a merged unit, which can prompt intense envy. Still earlier, the mother's body contains the father and the father's penis. The father then seems to develop out of the mother, first as a merged extension and then as a separate partner in intercourse at the oedipal level.

Such predispositions in the psyche that Klein describes, like Chomsky's language grammar (Ogden, 1985), can be seen to become manifest in Anne Sexton's fantasy obsession, her memory collage and perseveration. As Dr. Orne had noted, it was probably impossible that Anne Sexton's report of incest with her father could have happened the way she described it to him, and the way she wrote about it in her play "Mercy Street." Sexton's repetitive version of the incest scene always merges her father's phallic intrusion with her Aunt Nana's cuddling of her. She is lying down in bed with Aunt Nana, and her father starts to fondle her. She cannot admit her wishes to go towards boys to Nana, but as Nana holds her, she can imagine her father forcing her into submission to his sexual desire, disowning her own desire, while indulging in it. Yet, her view of her father's role isn't just fantasy. Her father spanked her in a sexually aggressive manner, beating her on her bottom with her riding crop. He also called her stimulating and stinging names at other times, when spanking her. He called her a "little bitch" according to her taped sessions with Dr. Orne. He also glared at her across the dinner table, averting his eyes in disgust, during her adolescence. He was "into" her, staring at her, commenting on her pimples. She felt his salacious and rejecting attitude, reverberating from younger years in which her father had been both seductive and punitive.

The incest scene of motherly engulfment and paternal intrusion became a perseverated tape in Sexton's mind, which she was compelled to reenact as a defense against the painful affects of actual memory. Sexton became addicted to the arousal in the incest scene, but whatever terror she might have actually felt in the face of her father's aggression was warded off through eroticization. By sexualizing the aggression, she diverted the fear, but Sexton could never modify the fear as she defended against facing it. Prior to every eroticized reenactment of this mentally etched incest scene, prior to every impulsive affair in her life, Anne Sexton was overwhelmed by the unaddressed fear, and disappeared into a trance. Within the trance state, she must have warded off and yet resonated with the blocked arousal as well as the yearning for connection that was deadened into detachment by powerful guilt.

When the trance had come at the end of a session with Dr. Orne, it had signaled that the yearnings, which had been warded off during the session by intellectual discussions, were now threatening to emerge. My conjecture is that it was terror, as well as the aggressive force of blocked emotional needs, that caused Sexton to go into a trance. The trance would have allowed her to hold back from leaving the session. All that had not been reached during the session then would exert its pressure to free itself from within her, as she re-experienced abandonment in the threat of another separation and loss.

The trance seems to have been a compromise state, in between the opening of all that had not been expressed during the sessions—potential rage, need, grief—and the perpetual state of split-off intellectual defense. The trance state was not only the state that Sexton went into before an impulsive love affair, when her cravings to merge with some idealized god-muse-poet triggered the terror of engagement with her libidinal child self. The trance was also her mode of engagement with her creative process. When Sexton wrote poetry, she entered a dissociated trance state to find the split-off affect self, sealed off within her from childhood. Entering into trance to write did not bring Sexton into contact the other part of her self that intellectually performed for her male therapists, nor did it bring her into direct affect contact with the terrified, wounded, and enraged child within. When entering into a trance state to make love to Dr. Zweizung, Sexton was also performing the vicious cycle of acting out inside pressures, pressures that could not be converted into subjective desire without affect connection. She was acting out her internal world, and her internal objects' pressures on her, as their representations remained merged with split-off dynamic parts of her core self. It was as if she were in a cocoon, or behind glass. Consequently, she could not feel a subjective experience of contact that would heal her. To get beyond the cocoon or glass wall, to have navigated beyond the trance state, she would have needed a therapeutic holding environment to feel the anguish of her childhood loss and need for her mother, which remained sealed off within her. Thus, the trance was a compromise situation, which could lead to incestuous lovemaking, or to the "word-magic" of lovemaking through poetry. The cocoon glass wall remained a prison. She was perpetually condemned to reenactment, as her "exciting object" muse lover turned into a "rejecting object" demonic lover (see Fairbairn on "exciting" and "reject-ing" objects). Her entrapment led to wishes for suicide and death, to get out of the sealed-off state, to enter a world beyond in which the muse lover would be sought again, the muse lover who represented the early symbiotic mother prior to the time of preoedipal trauma (called "basic fault" trauma by Michael Balint [1979] and separation-individuation or abandonment depression trauma by James Masterson [1979]). The part of the symbiotic mother had been played by Sexton's Aunt Nana during her childhood (latency and early adolescence).

In trance, Sexton could act out the clinging to a mother that she enjoyed as a mode of cuddling with Nana, which became cuddling with Dr. Zweizung. As long as she went into an enactment of the incest scene that she carried with her, thus being compelled to repeat it, she was free of the paralyzing fear that came with the unleashed pressure of an intense need for touch, for connection, and for basic emotional contact. The enactment served to shield her from awareness of her fear. In the incest scene, she was in control, seducing daddy and letting him seduce her. The sex that followed cuddling with Dr. Zweizung could then become a drug used to keep the fear at bay, the fear of actual contact, the fear of the contact that was needed so much. If Anne Sexton would have allowed emotional con-tact with Dr. Orne, she could have gotten the psychic holding (as opposed to physical holding) she needed to internalize another presence and to build a core self (object constancy). However, she could not allow emo-tional contact because her need was so intense and it threatened to engulf her. Orne was not tuned into this. Dr. Zweizung not only failed to be tuned in, he was led by his own erotic desire (and its hidden emotional need), promoting Sexton's enactment, rather than memory, of the scene of cud-dling with Nana and having sex with daddy. Enactment assuaged the feel-ing of need in Sexton temporarily, but it warded off any true emotional contact, precluding the psychic holding that could come with analytic space (see Ogden, 1986, on potential space and analytic space). Sexton's hunger was insatiable as long as the deeper core self, sealed off by the incest enactment, remained untouched. This core self could only be reached by going through the fear, not by going around it. To really open herself emotionally, Sexton would have had to feel her fear, actually a deep core terror. It might have meant revealing deep shame. Only if Dr. Z. could have contained the fear with Sexton, letting him into the emotional place in which the fears were felt as terror, could she have truly opened herself. But opening brings the danger of acute loss for the borderline. To open emotionally, for a borderline person, as opposed to acting out the sealed off early trauma of disrupted maternal contact, is to open to the rage and grief of a primal loss. Sexton became addicted to Dr. Z., because she couldn't open to him at this central core place in her, where she needed to internalize him. There was no safe "holding environment" to allow it. The result was that early abandonments in her life—first with her mother—and then with her father at adolescence, were repeated with Dr. Z. Middlebrook alludes to letters written by Sexton that suggest that she had begged Dr. Zweizung never to leave her. Inscribed in his own omnipotence, Dr. Z. had promised not to. However, he inevitably did. When he decided to go back to his wife, "to work on his marriage," Anne Sexton responded by falling down a flight of stairs in her house, on her birthday, breaking her hip. She managed to permanently damage herself because her hip never fully healed. Perhaps this was her concrete way of expressing a broken heart, when poetry was no longer sufficient to contain her rage and symbolize it. Anne Sexton's rage was continuously turned against herself. Her self-punishment, part of which was her physical pain, warded off emotional feelings of loss which she had never learned to tolerate in psychotherapy—either with Dr. Orne or with Dr. Zweizung.

DR. CHASE'S TREATMENT

Dr. Zweizung broke off his pretence of treatment and his love affair with Sexton in 1969. What part did Dr. Zweizung play in Anne Sexton being referred to a doctor, Dr. Chase, who objected to the monthly sessions that Anne Sexton still sustained with Dr. Orne? Diane Middlebrook's biography suggests that Anne Sexton continued to write to Dr. Z. long after he ended their relationship. Perhaps his receiving these letters was his way of softening the separation, after he abandoned her, having promised he never would. Suddenly, he wanted to "work on his marriage." Anne was left out in the cold, because her relationship with Dr. Z. had already alienated her from her husband, Kayo.

Dr. Z. had tremendous power over Anne, maybe more than ever at the time of leaving her. He was such a potent force that she still clung to him through letter writing. Such conditions make it likely that Anne Sexton followed Dr. Z.'s recommendation for a referral when she sought a new therapist. She ended up going to a female therapist, a psychiatrist, Dr. Marian Chase. It is ironic that in choosing a female therapist to avoid the former pitfall of having a sexual affair with her therapist, she selected a woman who banned her relationship with Dr. Orne, the one stable and trustworthy figure in her life.

The reason that Dr. Chase gave for suggesting to Dr. Orne that he stop seeing Anne Sexton sounds reasonable enough on the surface. She told Dr. Orne that his continuing relationship with Sexton would divide her transference. Presumably Dr. Chase wanted to form a transference and work with it in treatment. However, it appears from the Middlebrook biography that Dr. Chase, like her predecessors, failed to work with the transference. It appears that she was at first idealized and then was devalued and made into a bad object. Dr. Chase doesn't seem to have dealt with any of this therapeutically, let alone analytically. Meanwhile, Anne Sexton lost Dr. Orne, a loss made greater because she had, as indicated, never successfully internalized him.

Middlebrook reports that Dr. Chase was seen as a mother figure by Anne Sexton, because she was female. There is no corroboration for this assumption through any clinical process. However, it does appear that in the opening months of her treatment, Anne Sexton brought Dr. Chase her poems and read her the fairytale themes of her new book, *Transformations*. Perhaps this was a stage of "mirroring transference," given Anne's narcissistic character dynamics (at a borderline level). Anne presented her poetry, rather than herself, to her new therapist. She played it safe in this way, demanding to be seen through her grandiose self alone, her molded feelings framed into poetry.

The presentation of her poetry, rather than herself, could have been challenged by Dr. Chase. Dr. Chase could have picked up on Sexton's substitution of a finished, molded, and refined piece of work for her uncontrived and unrehearsed self. For Sexton this might have aroused a similar terror to that which her father experienced, when he ran frantically up the stairs to escape as someone came to call spontaneously, and he had no preparation to "turn on the charm" (Middlebrook, p. 10). But this terror needed to be reached. Sexton's fears of exposure, her dark views of herself in the raw, views not yet chiseled into the lines of poetry, this was the core of her that needed to be reached by a therapist. Limits judicially imposed could have, in Michael Balint's terms (1979), changed a "malignant regression" into a "benign regression." Placing limits on the poetry presentation could have changed an acting out of a mirroring transference, designed to seduce the therapist, and to induce a sense of inferiority, into a true experiencing of need and of the terror of exposure. Conscious shame and conscious envy could have been felt by Sexton. Actual therapeutic work could then have begun!

Limits and confrontation for Sexton's terror about being in the moment with the therapist, and about being psychically penetrated, could have opened Sexton up to a real engagement with her therapist. Instead, Sexton continued to act out all her yearnings, needs, and fears with transient male lovers, and to continue her withdrawal from her husband, upon whom she projected her negative mother image.

Dr. Chase neither confronted Sexton, nor did she interpret the mirroring transference. Instead, she acted out a retaliatory negative countertransference against Sexton, the minute Sexton dropped her "performance" and started making demands. Also, Chase became intrusive and acted out a superego attitude of contempt towards Sexton, all of which made Sexton wall off and withdraw.

The first clash between Dr. Chase and Sexton seems to have come when Sexton told her therapist that she had shown a poem to her older daughter, Linda, in which she had written about her envy of Linda's youth, and of her own feelings of ugliness, contempt, and envious revenge. According to quote from a Sexton note in Middlebrook, Dr. Chase reacted by stating indignantly, "People come first" (p.349). Obviously, Chase's empathy for Linda Sexton was aroused, but her moral indignation seems to have created an immediate negative transference acting out, with Sexton indignantly retorting that Dr. Chase was trying to control her like her mother had. Sexton also proclaimed, in her own high-handed and offended manner, that Chase didn't understand what it was like to be a writer. She proclaimed that writing was her way of "mastering experience" (Middlebrook, p. 349), and that her daughter would understand because she was a writer. Anne Sexton obviously countered Chase's contempt with her own contempt. A wall divided them, and an intractable negative transference seems to have been instituted, with Sexton's idealization of Chase as her perfect mirror collapsing at the first sign of criticism. If Sexton reacted as if persecuted, Chase did nothing to repair the situation. She didn't seem to recognize her patient's profound narcissistic vulnerability and her inability to tolerate guilt and to face her own aggression. She didn't seem to understand how entrenched Sexton was in the splitting and persecutory projective-identification of the paranoid-schizoid position. In the role of the bad object, Dr. Chase was helpless without understanding the dynamics of primitive rage and aggression that lay latent beneath the initial narcissistic idealization of the mirroring transference.

Chase, now in the role of the contemptuous and controlling mother, seems to have turned cold in retaliation. The battle, once started, was a cold one. When Chase went away for an extended vacation, Sexton responded by complaining about being left with "babysitter" therapists. The symbolic significance of this reaction was never explored. Sexton was basically told to behave herself. Her guilt-provoking implication that Chase was abusing her by taking a vacation was probably warded off by Chase through a cold attitude that reflected her own defensive rage. Once again, the underlying vulnerability in Sexton was not addressed. All Middlebrook's evidence indicates that Sexton had terrifying fears of abandonment based on early borderline separation trauma, as well as on the ongoing separation trauma of having a detached narcissistic mother. Her manner of complaint would have covered her vulnerability as she exuded contempt from a manic defense stance. But an object relations therapist would have seen through this warding-off defense behavior to the vulnerability underneath. Knowledge of borderline and narcissistic conditions would have been necessary.

The cold war turned into a cold abandonment. Sexton managed to induce in Dr. Chase the very thing she feared the most, the abandoning mother who wanted to cut her off completely. In 1971, fights between Anne Sexton and her husband Kayo were becoming frequent again (p. 370). When Sexton started divorce proceedings against Kayo, Dr. Chase discovered that Sexton had more money than she claimed to have. Such a discovery seems to have quickly prompted Chase into her final retaliation—terminating Sexton without any period of separation in 1973 (Middlebrook, p. 381), after approximately three and a half years of attempted treatment. Sexton was now totally adrift. Dr. Orne, the one stable therapeutic influence, was out of the picture. She had cut herself off from Kayo, who had stood loyally beside her for over thirty years, despite her relentless betrayals. According to Middlebrook, she didn't even want the divorce after she filed for it. Her illusions that she could survive emotionally and function as well as when married, when on her own, were dashed repeatedly. At first Sexton stayed with numerous friends to avoid the isolation that she experienced when alone. However, as her incessant smoking, drinking, and drunken arrogance got on their nerves, even the best of her friends became worn out. Eventually, she had to risk returning home to an empty house. There, the anguish was unleashed. All the desperate tears, the crying in a vacuum, the loss, the rage, the horror of herself alone, all opened up. In the bathroom, she cried out her desperation, but without a good-enough separate internal object she couldn't process her pain into an active mourning process. Her crying merely left her empty. She then clung and clutched at some shred of self-coherence by running to her typewriter, but her words came out now in a jumble of pleas and plaints. She could see it herself. As Middlebrook comments (p. 395), "Deep down, Sexton knew these were no more poems than the senile ravings of an old woman were conversation."

Sexton tried to hold on to life by an heroic attempt to keep her connection with her friends in her mind. She told herself that she needed to feel all that she was grateful for. But she couldn't feel. Instead, she made her gratitude into a prayer: "But let me right now thank God for friends" (p. 381). Yet, then when her friends reached out to help her, she denied

them. One friend, Lois Ames, who had several times rescued her from suicide attempts, wanted to form a network with Anne Sexton's other
friends, so that someone would always be on duty to check in on Sexton.
Sexton rejected the offer with a bitter, flippant quip. Perhaps, she was
hurting people (Middlebrook, p. 395) because she was unconsciously propelled by shame over acknowledging the gravity of her need, and by envy
of those who had more health as well as the ability to help. Characteristic
of a manic stance of defensive contempt, and of the paranoid anxieties of
persecution that lay beneath such contempt, when at a level of punitive
denial and omnipotence, Sexton proclaimed that all her friends were
witches plotting against her. This left her without the support that she
needed desperately. But, as Middlebrook notes, Anne Sexton did not
resort to suicide immediately.

Bereft of husband and therapist, Sexton found a maternal social worker, Barbara Shwartz, to give her some support. This was within the same
year she was abandoned by Dr. Chase (1973). However, support was an
addiction, when her central self was still sealed off. It might get her
through one night, but it didn't open her to the kind of emotional contact
she needed to internalize an other as an ongoing core internal object, from
whom she could create an ongoing state of being.

Several suicide attempts proceeded Sexton's final and determined effort
at self-annihilation. Sexton spent one night dancing alone by a river, pop-
ping sleeping pills in her mouth. Rushed to the hospital by her friend, Lois
Ames, she survived! She had not taken her "killer" pills, only sleeping
pills. She had time to edit former work, and to give a smashing reading
from her book *Death Notebooks*, which she sardonically referred to as
her posthumous work. Her standing with the literary world was declining
as her ability to integrate and shape her thoughts failed, but her popular
appeal remained strong. When the spotlight was fully upon her, Sexton
organized herself from within. She could perform and charm to the very
end, and she did it through a medium that revealed her authentic self.
Here, her narcissistic character dynamics are most clearly seen. The mirroring audience could still enhance and congeal her. When poised before
the audience,[1] she could focus and formulate her passions and thoughts
into a vivid integration. Alas though, when the camera of the audience
was turned away to another locus, she was in pieces again—sensations,
instincts, thoughts jumbled, as the echo of an isolated central core within
bellowed.

The end came with a whimper rather than a bang. For perhaps the first
time in her life, this confessional poet, who indulged in expulsive projections of all her private thoughts, kept a secret deep inside her soul. On the

day she planned to end her life, she revealed no ripple in the pool of her interpersonal connections. She met with her social worker, and gave her a book that expressed simultaneously her gratitude and her lost hope at once—about the treatment of a schizophrenic girl. She met her friend, Maxine Kumin, and appeared more together than usual, as she shared the final edit of a poem. She was organizing herself, through her plans for her demise, but nobody knew. Not canceling her evening's date, she called to say she'd be late. Did she want her date to discover her? Was there some ambivalent wish here to be rescued? But, in saying she'd be late, she made sure the deed was done before she was discovered. Her ritual preparation can fill us all with excitement and horror, like the demon lover exciting object that still resided within Sexton, arousing her and punishing her.

Anne Sexton wrapped herself in her mother's old fur coat, and still nursing a second vodka martini, she headed towards her garage. She closed the door of the garage door to seal off air. Perhaps she was mimicking the sealing off of her internal self. She entered her automobile. There, inside that contained space, perhaps encapsulating the explosive fragments of self within (Hopper, 1991), she turned on the car radio. She removed her rings, and drank her vodka. Perhaps she hoped to drift off into a trance as she ignited the engine and inhaled the fatal fumes (Middlebrook, p. 397).

What unconscious fantasies led her to this point?

Middlebrook mentions that Sexton's most conscious fantasy of suicide was of entering an ocean that stood for a primitive mother or mothering womb environment. This seems to be one level of what Sexton was seeking in her withdrawal into a passive state as she actively suicided. Like Virginia Woolf and Virginia Woolf's mother (Panken, 1989), who viewed death as sinking into an ocean after being unable to keep up the "effort" of life, Sexton may have yearned for a death that would merge her with an early mothering environment, (see Balint, *The Basic Fault*, 1979). Yet, what other fantasies of death might have been operating within her?

So much of Sexton's poetry reveals a demon lover theme, as I have outlined in an earlier paper (Kavaler, 1989) that I speculate that Sexton was reaching for the oedipal father, as well as the benign oceanic mother in her death. For this woman poet, the oedipal father would be tainted with the incestuous dynamics of her father's intrusive aggressive eroticism. The oedipal father would also be joined with an early mother, combined in an undifferentiated fusion. Yet, the erotic desire for the oedipal father, tainted with overtones of aggressive eroticism, would be a compelling lure towards death, just as it was for Sylvia Plath (see Kavaler, 1986).

According to John Hale's studies on suicide, recently presented at the

Tavistock clinic in London (a conference sponsored by the Washington
School of Psychiatry July 1992), the trigger for suicide comes after a perceived act of betrayal, with the suicidal act itself being an act of murder
directed at another. Hale articulates that the person committing suicide
intends to kill off his/her own body, as a means to entering a merger with
an idealized spiritual and symbiotic mother, by cutting off the bad mother that resides in the body. The act of suicide is thus a vivid act of object
splitting. Thus, the act reveals the split consciousness of all those operating out of the paranoid-schizoid position dynamics. It is also, according to
Hale, an act of murderous rage. In striking against the internal bad object
in the body, one also strikes against the body that is the precious child of
the external object mother. The suicide aggressor is, therefore, trying to
drive the mother crazy, as he/she strikes against the precious child of the
hated part of mother.

How would this apply to Anne Sexton? Certainly, her self hatred in
destroying her body was a strike against the internal bad mother, as well
as a wish to join with some spiritual oceanic mother with whom she could
merge in death. Similarly, Sexton was most probably striking against her
demonic father, while seeking union with a god-father (as reflected in her
later poetry).[2] Her attack also could be a vindictive blow at Kayo, who
now represented her mother, as well as at her daughters, who had finally
refused to deliver the ceaseless attention and nurturance that she demanded. Although always betraying Kayo, at the borderline level of consciousness he would be perceived as betraying her, thus rekindling vindictive
wishes. Still, despite her wishes to seek revenge against Kayo and her
daughters, more consciously Anne Sexton could have been protecting her
family from herself, putting an end through death to her insatiability.

ADDENDUM TO ANNE SEXTON'S TREATMENT

ANNE SEXTON AND THE DEMONIC LOVER

The following addendum illustrates how Anne Sexton employed her
father as the demon lover figure, which perpetuates the demon lover
theme, of turning to father as a god-muse, experiencing the demonic side
of the god-muse figure, and having the demon then turn into an eroticized
image of death. All the women artists I studied who had preoedipal deprivation or trauma with their mothers employ the demon lover theme to
express their plight. The theme reveals the closed internal system of pathological mourning in which the father is looked to as a compensation for
the early omnipotent mother who is never mourned. The demon lover
becomes the image of the primal mother dressed in the father's personality, and although such a figure might be called a maternal father

(Masterson, 1994, personal communication), the eroticized nature of the longings reflects the tantalizing psychic input of oedipal stage desires as they color the masculinized father-mother object for the woman. Consciousness of psychic incest implies that there is already some boundary between the woman artist and her demon lover father. He is not just an extension of her. He is also an alien and desired masculine other. However, the female desire cannot be contained within her when she has not built in any adequate maternal container from the time of infancy. Her split-off desire is compounded by early primal (also oral and anal, but needs for basic connection as well) infant and toddler stage needs, and potential subjective desire is converted into the threat of alien rape. Ultimately, eroticized intensity replaces subjective desire, since subjective desire cannot be contained and thus sustained. As the demon lover becomes a dynamic internal object that serves as the fulcrum of the psyche, he haunts the woman in both her interpersonal world and within her creative work. For Anne Sexton, her compulsive multitude of sexual affairs demonstrated the demon lover of her internal world inhabiting her interpersonal domain. Her creative work became the land of her demon lover as well, and her obsession with the demon lover and with death became one overall obsession, leading to suicide. The path she tread in this vicious closed system of pathological mourning, with its creative mystique intensity that leads to the eroticization not only of creative work, but of death as well, can be seen as a mystique of merger with the demon lover daddy, with the creative work and death becoming scenes of marriage and childbirth with this demon.

Anne Sexton's story runs particularly in parallel with that of two other twentieth century women artists, Diane Arbus and Sylvia Plath. They all became addicted to creative work that became a manic mode of intensity, driven by split-off erotic desire. This creative work, with its mystique, displayed a manic defense used to ward off primal object loss that was repeated in later life with the loss of a spouse. In the following tale of Anne Sexton, the intertwining lives and spirits of Anne Sexton and Sylvia Plath become explicit (see "Lord of the Mirrors and the Demon Lover," Kavaler-Adler, 1986, and "Mirror on the Wall," Kavaler, 1985).

Anne Sexton's background was similar to Sylvia Plath's. She was born in the New England world of facade orientation—of manners and images—that children were to fit into. And when children were to be women, they were to remain in the mold. Yet Anne, like Sylvia, was to remain dormant only so long, before smashing the mold with her madness, and erupting into a creative passion that unsettled or embarrassed all those to whom she was tied. Like Sylvia, she became a confessional poet, and like Sylvia, it was through her own creative hand that she took her own life. Yet, in the whirlwind of those years, when she bled herself onto the pages of her manuscripts, seeking to keep her haunting delusions at bay by mastering and designing the images behind them, she made her madness into a craft.

Also, like Sylvia Plath. Anne Sexton had a father obsession! It drove her to create, and it drove her to destroy. Torn apart by the conflicting internal object themes, she crawled and rowed towards the idealized God father, only to be caught up each time in the web of he own devious journey. Ann Sexton's later poetry had themes of crawling and rowing towards a god-father from whom she desperately sought some form of redemption. She had a body of poetry entitled *The Awful Rowing Towards God*. The demonic shadow father—an eroticized dark devil—was the vivid afterimage of her own degenerated, alcoholic dad. Maxine Kumin writes, in an introduction to Anne Sexton's collected poetry (1981):

> It would be simplistic to suggest that the oedipal theme overrides all other considerations in Sexton's work, but a good case might be made for viewing her poems in terms of their quest for a male authority figure to love and trust...in Sexton's poetry the reader can find the poet again and again identifying herself through her relationship with the male other, whether in the person of a lover or, in the last, hasty, and often brilliant poems in *The Awful Rowing*, which make a final effort to end on 'the island called God'—in the person of the patriarchal final arbiter. (pp. xxix–xxx).

The cloak of disillusionment is swiftly thrown over the romantic oedipal themes. A whole work is devoted to *The Death of the Fathers*, and Sexton's father-daughter dance quickly dissolves into graphic themes of seduction:

> How we Danced
> and we danced, Father, we orbited,
> We moved like angels, washing themselves
> We moved like two birds on fire.
>
> You danced with me never saying a word.
> Instead the serpent spoke as you held me close.
> The serpent, that mocker, woke up

and pressed against me

like a great god and we bent together
like two lonely swans.

(*The Complete Poems,* 1981, pp. 322–324)

Here the poet retains some reverence for the phallic power, and some compassion for the lonely soul within the man. In "Angels of the Love Affair," the male other is more fully desecrated. He is the demon in the toilet bowl, who defiles her from behind:

I said, "The devil's down that
festering hole."
Then he bit me in the buttocks
and took over my soul.

(*Complete Poems,* p. 332)

Then later, in *The Awful Rowing Toward God,* the father is ultimately tarnished, turned into a demon, and devalued. The search for a powerful god ends ultimately in the image of a seedy and sleazy winner in a crooked poker game. Maxine Kumin writes, in her introduction to the *Complete Poems:* "God, the poker-player was the one living and constant Daddy left to Sexton out of the 'Death of the Father.' Of course he held the crooked, winning hand" (p. xxxi).

This view of God was the ultimate view for Sexton, seen through little girl eyes of her own father. This view of the devalued, power-hungry patriarch was turned into the demon and the demon lover through memories of seduction. Splitting is repeatedly used to appeal to a male figure for rescue from the devil father of seduction. However, Sexton can't retain the priest father without being devoured by the demon father, as seen in *The Awful Rowing:*

Occasionally the devil has crawled in and out of
me.

The priest understands when I tell him that I
want to pour gasoline over my evil body and
light it.

(*Complete Poems,* p. 446)

The image sense of her sullied body can then be traced back to the bit-

tersweet themes of childhood memories, fought off with denial and splitting. In *Death of the Fathers*, she tries to retain a good father, separate
form the bad, by calling him a stranger:

> Oh Father, Father,
> Who was that stranger
> Who knew mother too well?...
> He was beating me on the buttocks
> with a jump rope...
> I was stained with his red fingers
> and I cried out for you
> and Mother said you were gone on a trip.
>
> He was a stranger, Father,
> Oh God,
> he was a stranger,
> was he not?
>
> (*Complete Poems*, pp. 328–329)

In her autobiographical essays, as reported by McClatchy (1978),
Sexton writes of her trite lack of originality in revealing a memory to her
psychiatrist in a poem (p. 5). Her doctor had inquired about her memory
of any primal scene traces, and she came up with a poem in response. It
described her fantasy of her parents' sexual intercourse, through the images
of a spanking memory. In describing her parents' sex and the "royal strapping," she recalls having been laid on her parents' bed by her father, having
been stripped naked and then beaten with her own riding crop.

Yet in the 1972 *Death of the Fathers* collection (*Complete Poems*,
1981), she disowns the father who beat her on the buttocks, and entitles
the poem section "friends." Here she seeks to ally herself with a still idealized and untainted father, one devoid of the lustful aggression she
remembers so well.

Several years earlier (1960–1970), her anger was more open, more
flamboyantly present, rather than being denied with devaluation and
compounding idealization. In *Letters to Dr. Y*, she is full of accusations
towards her "father doctor" (*Complete Poems*, p. 160). In one of the
poems among the *Letters to Dr. Y.*, entitled "Speaking Bitterness," she
writes:

> When I was thirty-two
> the doctor kissed my withered limbs

and said he'd leave his wife and run
away with me. Oh, I remember the like of him,
his hand over my boots, up my skirts
like a corkscrew.
The next month he moved his
practice to Washington.
Not one man is forgiven! East, West, North, South!
I bite off their dingbats—Christ rots in my mouth.
I curse the seed of my father
that put me here
for when I die there'll be no one to
say: Oh No! Oh dear.

(*Complete Poems*, p. 584)

Stripped of all phallic glamour and idealism, the devalued image of her
father remains. Sexton displays the menagerie of her mind, and in it the
castrated father, shorn of all peacock feathers, a flabby demon:

Father,
an exact likeness,
his face bloated and pink
with black market scotch
sits out his monthly bender
in his custom-made pajamas
and shouts, his tongue as quick as
galloping horses,
shouts into the long distance telephone call.
His mouth is as wide as his kiss

(*Complete Poems*, p. 72)

Yet a few stanzas later, when seeing the painfully drawn image of herself
as victimized by the sexual aggression of "boys," it is her father that she
cried out to:

Father, father, I wish I were dead.

(*Complete Poems*, p. 74)

In "Cripples and Other Stories," she writes:

My father was fat on scotch
it leaked from every orifice..

> My father's cells clicked each night,
> intent on making money...

(*Complete Poems*, p. 160)

After daddy is drawn as demon, the demon turns into the visage of death. Death itself becomes the demon lover, and Sylvia Plath and Anne Sexton shared in this transformation.

The life paths of Sylvia Plath and Anne Sexton crossed, when they meet in Robert Lowell's writing workshop in Boston, prior to Plath's final move to England. After the writing workshop sessions, Plath and Sexton would meet for drinks and talk. Meeting in Boston, in cabs and cafes, the two women poets came together. Three dry martinis, and they'd talk about death—as the demon lover came to visit each of them. What had happened to the father turned demon? As with Emily Dickinson before them, he had been reinvented into Sexton's work, as death itself. The eroticization of death became a main theme in Sexton's work, as it did in Plath's. The two would sit and conspire—derisively plotting—their own stage sets for suicide.

Plath ultimately died in an oven, Sexton in a gas filled garage. Yet, their images and fantasies of death were much more abundant and varied than the stark reality of their actual demise. They could speak of death for hours. The topic was always hot!—Hot like an oven, or hot like the frayed wires of the electric chair. The displayed their pet deaths before them as the table of conversation was laid. Heat and sensuality combined, bringing electricity as one main image:

> Death,
> I need your hot breath

[perhaps a reference to her father's whiskey breath]

> my index finger in the flame,
> two cretins standing at my ears,
> listening for the cop car

> Death,
> I need my little addiction to you.

> To die whole,

> riddled with nothing but desire for it,

is like breakfast
after love

And then in parallel to the acrid oedipal theme in the psychiatrist
poem, and another, entitled "For My Lover, Returning to His Wife"
(*Complete Poems*, p. 188), Sexton expressed her oedipal rivalry toward
Plath, for running off with their shared lover, death. In a poem called
"Sylvia's Death," she writes:

Thief!
how did you crawl into,

crawl down alone
into the death I wanted so badly and
for so long

The death we said we both outgrew
The one we wore on our skinny breast,
The one we talked of so often each time
We downed three extra dry martinis in Boston.

The death that talked of analysts and cures,
The death that talked like brides with plots,
The deaths we drank to,
The motives and then the quiet deed?

(In Boston
the dying
ride in cabs,
yes death again
that ride home
with our boy.)

(*Complete Poems*, p. 126)

The split-off bad object in masculine form, eroticized in terms of the
father as demon lover, had now been transformed into death itself. How
interesting that one of Anne Sexton's later books was entitled
Transformations. For transformations are multiple or even infinite in a
transitional world (D. W. Winnicott), where metaphor is often mistaken
for life. So it was for Anne Sexton; and so it was that a poet was born,
and a woman died—by her own hand.

Winnicott (1960) tells us that a false self can attempt to kill itself to save its true self, but separation between the two is an illusion, and so death conquers both. Such a delusion seem to have haunted Anne Sexton. Did it prompt her suicidal hand, just as it may have prompted the suicidal hand of Sylvia Plath?

When one lies exclusively in a transitional world, with poetry as one's cradle and as one's tomb, such delusions are easy to come by. Anne Sexton's internal objects became real-life specters, and death was easily mistaken for her demon lover father, who lived like a tapeworm within her.

In 1974, Anne Sexton made her final suicide attempt and died in a gas-filled garage. Six months earlier she had made another attempt from which her friend saved her, and she raged at her friend for interrupting her death (introduction to *Complete Poems*, p. xxxiii). She was forty-five years old when she succeeded at killing herself.

Interviews with Sexton, as well as commentaries by those who knew of her (see McClatchy, 1978), reveal that her creative work was thriving at the time of her death, and that she had become increasingly well-known in both literary and academic circles. By the time of her death, she had won many awards, including a Pulitzer Prize in poetry (1967) and many honorary doctoral degrees. She was elected a Fellow of the Royal Society of Literature in Great Britain (1965) and three years later was named the Phi Beta Kappa poet at Harvard (1968). After teaching writing workshops at many colleges, she was eventually appointed a professor in literature at Boston University.

However, the outward mesh of the stable personal relationship in her life had deteriorated. With numerous mental breakdowns, she found herself unable to keep her children, and was forced to send them away for periods of time. Her shaky marriage, formerly enforced by her exclusive role as suburban housewife, wore itself into the ground, and she finally won a divorce. However, according to her close friend, Maxine Kumin, who wrote the introduction to her collected poems, divorce brought the terror of living alone, and Sexton sought refuge whenever she could. Yet she did not stop writing poetry. The eruption of her inner anguish made her dangerously prolific.

Kumin also reports how Sexton began to write poems in a "white heat" (*Complete Poems*, p. xxxi), at the rate of two, three, or even four a day. This was at the time when she was writing *An Awful Rowing*, a depiction of the vanquished and exhaustive struggle to find a male father-god. How reminiscent all this was of Sylvia Plath's early morning "blood-jets" of poetry, during the time of her "Daddy" poem and other poems collected for her book, *Ariel*, cannot be underestimated! For both authors, "daddy" was the fixation point of all the chaos in their minds.

There are similarities to the career of the nineteenth century poet, Emily Dickinson, who was known for her own self-characterization as a "soul at its white heat" (see Sewall, 1980). She too, had a demon lover god, with whom she was in constant battle. Yet, she could not break free of her addiction to him, and her "white heat" of prolific creative passion rose out of extreme depersonalization and even psychosis (see Cody, 1971). Cynthia Griffin Wolff (1986) has written a scholarly biography of Dickinson, and she depicts, over and over, the internal drama that was externalized as the nineteenth century poetic genius both wrestled with and adored her male father-god. When she couldn't defeat him, and the shattering of her mind brought a severance of the former hostile symbiosis with him, she began to become him. Cody recounts the transformation of Dickinson's identity as she took on a masculine persona in her later life, a persona enacted exclusively within her transitional world of poetry. Yet even more striking than the similarity of Dickinson's demon lover tale to that of both Sexton and Plath is the way in which the adored patriarchal god and villain takes on the metaphorical aspect of death in all these creative women. Emily Dickinson was courted by a fantasy gentleman lover who wooed her towards death, in the name of death.

Although Dickinson did not commit suicide, she spent the latter half of her life in increasing seclusion, and many believe she suffered a psychotic break (Cody, 1971, Kavaler-Adler, 1993). Like Sexton and Plath she was obsessed with images and themes of death. She had poems on the moment of death, the journey towards death, and the chasm of death, over which speculated fantasies of immortality rested uneasy for her. Her addiction to a father-god who becomes a demon lover, and who is eventually transformed into a personification of death is too resonant with the dynamics of Anne Sexton and Sylvia Plath to be dismissed. For all these women, intense bursts of creative expression alternated with intense death fears and yearnings, in a pattern that circulated around paternal, phallocentric fixation. We can also be reminded of Diane Arbus, another creative woman of prominent modes of prolific intensity, who though not a poet, showed similar cycles of creative work and dramatic mental disturbance.

There can be varying viewpoints from which to comment on this demon lover syndrome as I've portrayed it in the overlapping life themes of these distinguished creative women. From a feminist perspective, there are the obvious interpersonal dynamics of paternal and patriarchal dominance, which have been most clearly elaborated by Sandra Gilbert and

Susan Gubar (1979, 1984) in their book on women writers, entitled *The Madwoman in the Attic*. From a traditional psychoanalytic view, there are the overlapping incestuous and oedipal dynamics. However, from a developmental and object-relations point of view, we can see an integrative formulation of the internal world in regard to the pathological vicissitudes of its development.

In the demon lover syndrome, we can see a symbolic complex that is symptomatic of a fusion of preoedipal and oedipal strivings in women, which comes about with developmental arrest. The preoedipal cravings for an omnipotent mother, who can recognize and affirm true self-development, are displaced onto the oedipal father, who in turn becomes an eroticized ideal god, mirror, and judge. The ideal always has its dramatic demonic counterpart, related to preoedipal splitting. Also, the preoedipal mother's personality is subsumed in the personality of the father, who is given symbolic birth through the creative process.

Since the oedipal father is so important in instituting creative motivation into a daughter's ego ideal (see Kavaler-Adler, 1993), the father's power of preoedipal and oedipal level magnetism intensely galvanizes female tendencies to create. But the autonomous true self-strivings emerge with tragic consequences when preoedipal arrest causes the ego ideal to flood the female personality with the masculine instinct and image through profound paternal identification. In addition, since the primary feminine personality has not been supported by good-enough maternal identification and mirroring during the critical early period of self-development, the paternal mirroring becomes addictive. The daughter tries to fuse with the father, and a pervasive paternal symbiosis or a pervasive paternal identification become the daughter's only psychic alternatives. Cycles of creative compulsion and self-destructive impulses alternate out of the psychic alternatives.

Both masculine fusion through idealization and mirroring, and masculine identification through the imposition of a masculine persona upon the primary internal-object and self-structure, oppose the development of a separate and autonomous identity in a woman. No matter how creative she becomes, she will be cursed with a severe borderline personality disorder unless she undergoes the anguish of a therapeutic mourning process so that separation-individuation can proceed. This is also the Kleinian working through of the depressive position that is called for.

Unfortunately, none of the creative women mentioned, including Anne Sexton, could use the creative process alone to promote such therapeutic mourning. Although their internal true selves erupted through the use of the creative process, the eruption was erratic, and could not support a full developmental process of self-emergence and integration. Without an external holding environment (see Winnicott, 1965) to support the process, as generally provided by a therapist or analyst, Anne Sexton and many of her fellow female geniuses succumbed to the negative pole of the demon lover complex.

PART THREE

Clinical Cases

12)

THE CASE OF LOIS, PART I

Red Shoes Frenzy, Mystique, and Creative Compulsion

Lois is a single woman in her mid-twenties. She has been in object-relations psychoanalysis with me for two years. Lois has had many literary and artistic talents from an early age, and has pursued many forms of freelance writing.

The first time I saw Lois was when she entered my treatment room trailing behind her a blast of rage, anguish, and self-obsessed torment. It was not too long into our interview before she declared: "I have to be famous!" Her rising voice bemoaned her plummeting fortune: neither her first novel nor her second novel had found a publisher. She informed me that this failure had occurred despite her having the best literary agents in England and America. She was also unprepared for it because of her outstanding academic achievement, attested to by coveted honors and scholarships. She then railed against all those who said she should have studied pop art, or other unrelated areas of knowledge. She could not rid her head of this Greek chorus of advisors and critics. Every suggestion, I could see, became a persecutory object that seized her, similar to a snake she couldn't let go of, as indeed a later dream revealed. Lois portrayed herself as the victim of her parents' projections, which, by swallowing her up, enslaved her, forcing images and expectations upon her that I could see devastated any breathing internal presence. In those first interviews, she also revealed that she had become obsessed by snails. In her secret fantasy life, she was the king of the snails.

From the start, my response to Lois's alienating barrage of rageful accusations against therapists, parents, literary agents, and advice-givers was to powerfully engage the force of her opposition so it would become in contact with me. Simultaneously, I reached out to the helpless and whimpering being behind all this aggression. I was successful in my attempts to get through (partly through "deep interpretations" that touched the unconscious level of her anxiety), which made the chaos and darkness of Lois's world, as well as her whirling-dervish dance of compulsive creativity and self-obsessed manic activity a bit more bearable for both of us. It was not long before I glimpsed the vulnerable and extremely lovable inner child, the child that felt tiny enough to be a fetus.

Throughout the early phase, I told Lois that she was pushing me away and at the same time desperately pleading with me to help her. I said that I thought she was terribly ashamed of how much she needed me. If she didn't let me be with her, I predicted, her sense of desperation would escalate. I also told her that she had to deal with her own projections, not just her parents' projections onto her. And I said that her enraged protests about my being too powerful seemed to reflect her wish to be forced and enslaved. This interpretation hit some deep inner core. These direct ventures into her haunting and obsessive psychic fantasies brought some immediate relief.

For the first time, Lois was able to quiet down and to become reflective. She said that almost every other therapist she had seen was a handholder. I seemed different. But she also told me that I terrified her and that she felt nauseous in the session with me.

I suggested that her nausea might have to do with her present conflict about whether to take me in or spit me up. I stayed in the moment with her. She responded by allowing increasing affect contact and psychic connection with me. The relief in her being, and the sudden relaxation of the body she had seemed so disconnected from, was palpable.

Subsequent sessions dealt more with Lois's "need-fear" dilemma (Guntrip, 1976), in which her need for my help activated all of her paranoid terror about depending on anyone. Rather than continuing to make blanket accusations against others in her treatment sessions, she now assaulted me with self-righteous and arrogant accusations. This behavior seemed like a distancing maneuver combined with her own projected guilt in the form of emotional blackmail. She simultaneously attempted to push me away with her accusations, screaming for help through the implied demands for rescue that accompanied these accusations. Her own guilt about attacks on her internal objects, and on those in her external world who psychically clicked in with these internal others, was projected onto me as she declared that I had a hell of a nerve to say all these things about her, when I didn't even know her. Although this might be seen as a legitimate protest on her part, it was accompanied by a self-righteous air of condemnation that belied the way she used me as an external reflection of her internal Greek chorus and its internal attacks. She also used me as a scapegoat for her own unconscious crimes, when she was feeling filled with guilt about her critical and belligerent attacks on others. Later on in treatment, Lois would speak about this guilt in terms of a growing awareness of her compulsive cruelty towards those she felt dependent on. She would then speak of her condemning and devaluing attacks on others. During these first early sessions, however, I could only sense the compulsive nature of her accusatory attacks, and the sense of desperate craving for rescue from her persecutory internal world that seemed related to her focusing these attacks so immediately on me.

One of Lois's accusations was that I wanted her to submit to me. I suggested that perhaps she was fighting against her own wish to submit to me, which would be an enactment of an internal world situation that had been powerfully eroticized since early childhood. I asked if she might not have some desire to enslave herself. If so, she might experience me as trying to force her into submission. I asked if she had some desire to be a sex slave.

My questions brought an immediate response, a combination of interest and curiosity as Lois admitted that she did have such fantasies. She revealed her addiction to watching a porno cable TV channel.

All this came quickly and intuitively. There seemed to be an immediate resonance between us. Lois informed me that she came into treatment with me because I was tough. But she also said she was afraid I would turn out to be a "ruthless academic." During another session she readily laughed and seemed relieved, as she admitted that I had "de-fanged" her after one of her accusatory assaults. Her ability to let go of her tantrum rage and rigid mode of demands and accusations, shown when she laughed and said I "de-fanged" her seemed to indicate a positive prognosis. Lois was able to let go of her distancing maneuvers and was capable of play. Later on, during the second year of treatment, she could look back at this early period, in which she hallucinated about snails appearing in my lamp, and exclaim, "I was beserk when I first came to see you."

FAMILY DYNAMICS

Lois came from a nuclear family of five members. Her father was a history professor. Her mother was a freelance writer. Her brother, who was two years older than herself, was a journalist. She had a younger sister as well, still in college. Her parents had been divorced when she was twelve years old. During her childhood her father had frequently had extramarital affairs and her mother had stopped working, which had left the mother feeling quite depressed. The maternal grandfather was a concert pianist, who had oppressive standards of excellence, which he imposed on his daughter and her family. He was totally indifferent to his daughter's relationship and marital problems, and made it quite clear to his daughter that he was only interested in hearing about her career. Lois reported this to me with outrage, indicating that this attitude of her mother's father had dominated her entire upbringing.

Lois described her family as work-obsessed and terrified of emotional need. Every family member operated out of a Red Shoes mentality characterized by manic creativity, driven by the compulsion to create, achieve, and cultivate images of artistic success. Someone who stopped working even briefly threatened the entire family, because his or her exposure of emotional need terrified the others. Lois ended up conforming to the family system of nonstop work. Her way of coping was to work twice as hard as everyone else, because to allow any space not filled by work was to face the terror of having her emotional needs offered up into a vacuum (see Fairbairn, 1952). To not be working in Lois's family meant facing a darkness within that resembled an endless black hole. In Lois's earliest dreams, chaotic events occurred in dark undefined interiors without boundaries. In one dream, a scene of her riding in a dark van with her mother led into another in which Lois was covered with sheets of blood and was haunted by the image of an old boyfriend who committed suicide. The dream boyfriend appears with his naked penis protruding from his pants. In real life Lois warded off her terror of the darkness within by watching porno films on TV.

Another dream revealed Lois's sense of being unprotected and the terror this vulnerability elicited. In the dream, set in Yugoslavia, Lois told her family they had to escape the country. In commenting on the dream, she said that Yugoslavia was the place most under siege, the place that seemed the most unsafe in the world. All family members, she observed, acted as if they were under siege in a military dictatorship. They lived as if they might be invaded any moment by hostile forces.

At this early point in treatment, it was already clear to me that each isolated soul in this family lived in a compulsive state in which interpersonal contact was warded off at all costs, in order to avoid the dark terrors of feeling their unfulfilled emotional needs. This was played out in numerous ways. If Lois, for example, was invited to a cousin's summer house for the weekend, she was immediately warned to bring her work with her because everyone else was doing theirs. She explained: "Everyone in my family is writing a book!" Lois said that she felt behind in having neither of her novels published. "You have to write a book in my family to exist," she exclaimed emphatically. All internal object relations in this family, then, were poured into creative writing. Interpersonal love relations, and particularly intimacy and its nurturing internalizations, were minimal.

THE RED SHOES SYNDROME AND THE CREATIVE MYSTIQUE

In describing the Nazi part of herself that drove her—indeed the "Nazis" of her dreams, as we shall see, invading writing colonies—Lois quoted her maternal grandfather. Her grandfather said that everyone in the family, but Lois especially, was like a "white feather in a sea of black feathers." His remark demonstrated for her the "Nazi" standard of excellence that propelled her entire family. When she told me this she exclaimed, "See why I'm so crazy, so compelled to work and to ignore all my emotional needs, all my needs for contact and intimacy. I have to always live up to being that white feather in a population of black feathers. If I don't stand out, I don't exist. I have to be 'unforgetable.' I have to be famous to be loved. I'm only part of the family if I'm famous. I can't slow down. If I do I'll be beaten up internally."

Snakes, snails, and dinosaurs were split-off erotic intensities, without subjective passion, that inhabited her internal landscape, often appearing in her dreams. "When I'm not working," she reported, "when I simply read the paper, I feel like I'm disgusting, full of snail slime, that I'm haunted by snails, big, gray, and dripping. I can't stop thinking that if I'm not working I'm a disgusting creature, a snake or a snail. Sometimes I feel like a dinosaur." We began to speak of the myth of the Red Shoes as the theme of Lois's life. Sometimes I called it the "whirling dervish dance," for it swept her up, so that her entire being was driven, and she was disconnected from her body, and from all emotional contact. The theme of the Red Shoes, Lois felt, suited her perfectly because she could articulate how images of success, even artistic stardom, took her out of her body. To stop working in a manic manner, or in what could be called a Red Shoes frenzy, exposed her to the terror of a free fall into endless blackness. As long as Lois drove herself to work on a project, she escaped temporarily the terror of her plunge.

The speeded up manic state of the Red Shoes dance, in which she danced for the father demon within—such as the internalized grandfather who wanted her to be a white feather—always ended with obsessions about demon creatures inhabiting her inner world. Thus, after the project was completed she felt eviscerated, used up, and empty. She then became filled with haunting images of snails, dinosaurs, and snakes. Lois saw movies about dinosaurs, which she recounted, as if she had incorporated the biting teeth of the mammoth monsters inside of her. Now it

became clear why when Lois first came into treatment she had hallucinated that she was the King of the Snails. She had just finished a major
work project. Throughout this early phase of treatment, Lois continued to
speak incessantly of large biting creatures, such as dinosaurs. She said that
she had decorated her home with dinosaur motifs, collected pictures of
them and of clothes with their images.

Her dreams revealed her as feeling as if she were outside of her body,
like the women in her dreams whose uteruses hung in plastic bags in medical school exhibits. She associated uteruses with fetuses. This association
brought with it the snail image and the sense of being still unborn, inside
a cocoon. Her adult body, as symbolized by the woman's uterus, was foreign to her, outside of her, encased in plastic, and therefore emotionally
untouchable.

This dark inner world that conveyed the degree of Lois's disconnection
from her body awaited her the minute she slowed down. She was terrified of being engulfed by it, and thus felt threatened each time a work
project ended. The compulsion within her was, therefore, to keep "dancing"—that is to keep writing, to keep working, to keep up the manic frenzy of split-off erotic and aggressive intensities. Lois was dancing to the
tune of projected images, projected images from two halls of mirrors
within her. The first was her "star" hall of mirrors, with images of success. It reflected her images of her own work as a creative mystique. Such
success images drove her into a frenzy of work activity. But she also had a
"negative" hall of mirrors—with images of failure. She was addicted to
the images in her hall of mirrors. Just as she couldn't let go of the snake in
her dream, she couldn't let go of the images in her hall of mirrors. They
operated with snakelike intensity, wrapping themselves around her, encasing her in a cocoon of self reflections. They had a defensive purpose that
perpetuated her addiction: they warded off the affect life within her. In
the beginning of treatment, they also warded off the engulfing inner darkness.

Then, as she opened to me and to our therapeutic object relationship,
rage and darkness turned into powerful longings and grief. As Lois slowed
down from the whirling dervish dance of the Red Shoes and had moments
of contact and connection with me, she began to internalize a good-
enough object relationship to provide her with an inner container for
developmental mourning. Yet Lois's need to mourn was at the level of an
abandonment depression trauma. Sadness overwhelmed her as a primal
level of grief was reached. Once in the second year of treatment, just as a
session was about to end, she began to obsess about being a failure, fixating her attention on certain major magazines. I was able to point out to

her the critical timing of that obsession in relation to the ending of the session. I told her that she was using images of failure from her constructed hall of mirrors to ward off a feeling of loss because she had to say good-bye to me as the session was about to end. Immediately, then, Lois allowed herself to experience the loss and grief of saying good-bye. Able to contact these warded-off feelings in response to my interpretation, she was now able to experience me as a good object. She cried and said she did feel very sad to say "good-bye." The recognition freed her at least temporarily from her hall of mirrors obsession, in which images of failure, (and sometimes of success), were used to ward off the loss within. In crying with deep sadness, the grief of the core-self and separation trauma opened up. She could connect with me in the moment, and could therefore connect with her body and her entire inner life. When Lois left the session that day she had learned a very important lesson: that when she became obsessed with images of herself as a failure, she was psychically defending against feelings of object loss, often a loss related to a past or incipient separation. She was able to use this lesson later, while she was away for a week on a magazine assignment. On the trip, she again obsessed about fears of failure. But this time she was able to think of our previous session, and use what I said to interpret this addiction to her hall of mirrors. In other words, she saw that once again she was using these images to ward off her inner life. Specifically, she realized she was avoiding feelings of loss by thinking of herself as a failure. She had just written a story for a magazine about a past romance and now realized she was in the midst of Red Shoes manic activity, in obsessing about herself as a failure, and that she was using the Red Shoes dance of obsessions in her head to counteract preconscious feelings of missing a former lover, the former lover being the subject of the article that she was just writing. In connecting with her feelings of love and loss in relation to her former lover, Lois was then able, for the first time on her own, to connect with the grief affect in her body, and to gain the needed insight from the consciousness of this feeling. Her body came alive, her internal good object connections came alive, as her former lover, as well as myself, the analyst who had helped her, were felt though her feelings of love and loss. She no longer was trapped in split-off obsessive thoughts in her head, since she could separate from her internal hall of mirrors enough to be aware, with an observing-ego awareness, of her internal mirrors of self-reflection. Specifically, she could be aware of the failure images that became persecutory intruding internal objects (driven by a merger with split-off parts of the self), when she could not be separate from them. Through reaching a capacity to tolerate loss, Lois was able to slow down from the Red Shoes dance of obsession in her head. This compelled her to face grief and sadness, which allowed her to fill in the inner black hole. Preconsciously, she filled in the black hole with memory, grief-laden love, as well as with awareness of subjective desire as it emerged through connecting with the lost love object in her memory. Lois's internalization of me allowed her to make this developmental journey.

THE DREAM OF THE RED SHOES

After one and a half years of three times weekly object-relations psychoanalysis, Lois actually had a dream with the Red Shoes in it. She related the following dream:

> I was playing the youngest child in a play with other girls. There was this Don Juan figure, the other, who was like you, wanted to have sex with the man: But he had this young mistresslike person with him.
>
> It was suspenseful in the dream like a murder mystery. My mother had on really red shoes—like in the Wizard of Oz. She put on the shoes to get the man—Oh! The dance of the Red Shoes! You had them on, you monster!

In this dream, Lois cast me in the role of the split-off manic part of her, as symbolized by my wearing the Red Shoes. Lois consciously identified with the child in the dream. She showed this by enacting this child's position. That is, as soon as Lois reported the dream, she stopped talking. I asked her why she didn't respond to her dream. She said that she wanted me to tell her what it meant. I explained that we could find out what it meant together if she revealed her thoughts. Lois's passivity, then, represented the passive childlike role she took in the dream.

The following dialogue ensued:

Lois: I think the mother in the dream is eroticized—related to my mother's getting this grant to write a book. I connect success and sex. Now that she got this grant she's in a position to have sex with a man. The dream puts me in the position of being the youngest child in the play. I don't want to play this role anymore. I want to be an adult.

Analyst: Why do you have to be in the child role?

Lois: Because she's going to leave me for this man. Yeah! She has the red slippers on. But she's like the more adult part of me, I think. Woof! Woof! (animal sounds).

Analyst: Can you put that into English?

Lois: I feel scared—upset, longing and fear.

Analyst: I think it has to do with you going away next week.

Lois: Yes! You monster! I also feel rejected, angry, and mad. I feel mad at the *New Yorker*! (fictitious name)

Analyst: "You feel left by the *New Yorker* too, as well as by your mother who's going away with her grant. You're going away and you feel like everyone is leaving you.

The dream, and the dialogue about it, reveal significant aspects of how Lois employs the Red Shoes theme. Although Lois casts herself in a child role, she is aware that she eroticized success. She creates the image of a mother figure (in the transference, the analyst), whose sexuality is split off from her body, as symbolized by the Red Shoes. The Red Shoes mother is the part of Lois that runs away to wed herself to worldly success, in a manic flight away from her body and the body containment of true sexual desire and object-related longings. As the child, in relation to such a mother, Lois is afraid of being left. In fact, within her dream, another meaning for the Red Shoes appears, as her associations show. The Red Shoes symbolize a manic flight from both her internal world and her core body and interpersonal self. In addition, by making the Red Shoes in her dream like those in the *Wizard of Oz*, Lois implies that they can bring her home to mother—not just enable her to flee from herself into her hall of mirrors with images of success. The red shoes that Lois remembers from the *Wizard of Oz* take Dorothy back to her mother, who in the movie is her aunt. This is Lois's regressive defense against feelings of separation and loss in relation to her primal mother. In this dream, then, the Red Shoes symbolize both manic and regressive defenses. Lois is taking flight herself, yet she feels left. She puts the part of her that runs away to grasp at images of success into the mother figure, transferentially played by me, and into the prominent magazine that has recently rejected her work.

The feeling of loss underlies the defensive dance of the Red Shoes. In this session, we reached this feeling when Lois moved from feeling "mad" to feeling sad. When I suggested that she might want to be the smallest child in the play in order not to have to have such big feelings, she agreed. I then said: "Maybe you want to be little like the littlest child in the play in the dream in order to avoid having big feelings—maybe your feelings feel too big!"

Lois responded powerfully to my comment, saying, "They are! I'm sad!"

As an object-relations analyst, utilizing the containment of the therapeutic object relationship, just for the moment, I replied to this request rather than analyzing it. Therefore, I said, "You can feel the sadness while you're here with me rather than letting it hit you when you're alone. It's

good you can feel it now. Then you can stay connected to me this week."
This remark allowed Lois to repeat that she was sad. When it was time
for her to go, she looked at me sadly. Waving good-bye like a little kid,
she said, "I'll miss you!"

This session, in which the Red Shoes dream was presented, articulates
the resolution of the manic defense symbolized by the Red Shoes theme. As
I've described, the Red Shoes ballet and the movie built around it depicts
the female who wears the Red Shoes being driven into the regions of death,
in a suicidal flight towards achieving stardom, as reflected in the eyes of the
masculinized god-muse-demon. Yet the flight into death can be modified
by the capacity to mourn the primal mother, who lies under the masculine muse-demon image. The capacity to feel sadness is the capacity to
mourn the longed for primal mother from the time of core-self formation.
To feel the sadness is to open up the core self, which has been sealed off
due to a traumatic disconnection from the mother. In this session, Lois
was able to move from a rageful madness caused by a dark-hole emptiness within, to containing and expressing object loss. In accomplishing
this developmental task through the containing psychic structure of her
therapeutic object relationship with me, the intolerable anguish of primal
separation trauma and its intense abandonment depressive affect
(Masterson, 1976, 1981) can became a tolerable grief affect of sadness.
In feeling her sadness with me, Lois mobilized her loving capacity at the
core of her body self through the contact with me. This allowed her to
express sadness for the loss of the primal mother. The completion of this
process represents the only resolution to the vicious cycle of the manic
defense, with its narcissistic hall of mirrors. Unless the manic defense is
breached, it forms a closed internal system, which, because the self is sealed
off, isolates the person. Only by opening to grief and object-relations contact can this closed system be opened up. Through such mourning, separation is achieved. The regressive urge to go back home to mother, as well
as its opposite pull to take manic flight through a false narcissistic self-
sufficiency based on images, is modified. The key in this case to self-integration was Lois's capacity to feel her core-object loss the loss derived
from the trauma of early separation from her mother at the time when the
primary self was forming. Lois began this mourning process in the supporting context of the therapeutic object relationship, while also relating
to me as a transferential figure, i.e., mother, through the symbolism of the
dream.

The demon lover image in this dream was the Don Juan figure. In the
dream he is not yet a differentiated being. Rather, he is a part-object
extension of the Red Shoes mother, similar to the psychic blueprint of the

mother-father fused figure observed by Melanie Klein and Hanna Segal (1964). The Don Juan figure in the dreams is reminiscent of Klein's paternal phallus residing within the mother's body before the father becomes a differentiated figure. In keeping with Lois's associations to the dream, the Don Juan demon male is an extension of the mother in Red Shoes, who is driven by a manic intensity that can become a frenzy of work, which doesn't allow time and space for a real relationship with a whole-object male. The woman is driven by the reflection of her own image, possibly as reflected in the eyes of a tantalizing and seductive Don Juan figure, who encapsulates some split-off part of the woman's father (or father-mother), as in Lois's mother's father. This grandfather offered both her mother and herself narcissistic mirroring based on the implicit demand that they each use creative-work achievement to become "the white feather in the sea of black feathers." Thus, the woman in Lois's Red Shoes dream is driven by an image view of the self, which stands in the way of her achieving true object-related affect connection, which depends on core body-self connection. The mourning of primal loss allows the core self-and-body connection to develop so that interpersonal relationships, and the potential for intimacy, can supersede narcissistic image relations with their manic intensity and creative mystique. The Red Shoes mother, with her part-object demon lover male, lives in a hall of mirrors—images of success and failure haunting her. Her true sexuality can be split off in erotic intensities that block subjective passion, because they are not integrated with core internal-object relations. Annie Reich's essay on "Narcissistic Object Choice in Women" (1953) speaks about this phenomenon. According to Reich, the man is chosen as a reflection of the woman's own grandiose self or narcissistic-image self. This image self is used to defend against both underlying images of failure and inadequacy. The image self further defends against the darkness within, against instinctual aggression that kills off love, and against primal disconnection that disrupted primal object relations.

After Lois's Red Shoes dream, followed by her newly developed capacity to mourn the primal-object loss, she was able to have another dream in which body connection and its related fears emerged:

> This dream followed a moment with a man, in which she felt the intimacy of the man touching her on the cheek. Within the dream, Lois was aware of feeling intense sexual desire for this man, which she feared would overpower her. Immediately after sensing the intensity of the feeling, she turns away from the man, who she is with, and who is to become her boyfriend, to observe her girlfriend

and her boyfriend. She looks at her girlfriend's boyfriend, who is thin, and compares him to the man who aroused her, who is overweight. She feels intense envy of her girlfriend for having a thin boyfriend. She wipes out her feeling of sexual desire with her feeling of envy.

This dream was generated by her new relationship with a truly emotionally available man, who had recently entered her life. George was quite different than the more narcissistic men she had been attracted to, and she found herself distancing from him and from the feelings in her body that he aroused. For example, he touched her on the cheek, in a way that was "respectful but intimate," and she felt a surge of sexual feeling that became a powerful lustful desire in her dream. Lois felt compelled to cut off the power of this subjective passion, a phenomenon so different from the split-off erotic intensities symbolized by snakes and dinosaurs in her earlier dreams. She cut it off by turning it into a primitive impulse of envy. In the dream, she looked at her girlfriend's thin boyfriend and envied the girlfriend, while devaluing the man who has brought her body-self alive, engaging in obsessive mental criticisms of him as being overweight.

At the time of this dream, which occurred after a year and a half of treatment, Lois was able to analyze her own spoiling process. She became an interpreting subject (Ogden, 1986), who can experience thoughts and feelings as thoughts and feelings, rather than as primitive and impinging persecutory forces. She also no longer needed to inhabit a child's position in the session in which she presented the dream, as she did in presenting the Red Shoes dream. She now had a sense of initiative and agency. These enabled her to initiate her own free association and interpretation process. Thus, she volunteered that she was disrupting her sexual desire of this new man. She felt this was symbolized in the dream, by her envy of her girlfriend. Lois related this disruption to her fear of containing powerful body desires and subjective psychic passions. She next spoke of how she undercut her potential connection with George in her actual life. For example, she recalled suddenly thinking critically about his weight at a moment of potential intimacy and deep-feeling body contact. She then compared him to her former boyfriend, who encouraged her to live in her hall of mirrors, from where she was compelled to work all the time, enslaved to the mystique of success through creative work.

During a session following the dream, Lois continued to analyze her spoiling system. She observed that Steve, her former boyfriend, will love her if she does this "piece," while George, will love her even if she doesn't do the piece. She was aware of being loved by George for herself, rather than for her producing creative work. This terrified her! To be loved for herself, rather than for being "a white feather in a sea of black feathers," meant being responsible for being present with the other, with a man. It meant being responsible for being in her body and in a subjective experience of passion, which threatened to overwhelm her. When George was being maternal with her, she felt contained, but when he was "manly," showing his masculine and phallic side, she retreated into terror. For Lois, falling in love then was falling into darkness. She began to live in a world of snails again, regressing from body connection, into split-off erotic intensities that, as impinging part-object persecutors, threatened to annihilate any sense of self.

An earlier dream, which occurred during the first few months of treatment, shed light on this regression. This early dream featured a pile of tattered clothes Lois was discarding. She noted about the dream, "Someone must have undressed me," implying an erotic level to the dream, but experienced purely from the position of being a sex object or victim. Some alien man had undressed her. The tattered clothes symbolized her own self-fragmentation in the face of male penetration and male sexuality. Without a secure body container for her own subjective sexual passion, Lois experienced eroticism through projective-identification, as impinging on her from without. The impingement assaulted her through part-object phallic figures, such as snakes and dinosaurs or through alien and anonymous men who shattered her into bits with the force of their phallic power, as in the image of tattered clothes, which symbolized being undressed. To be undressed meant to be torn apart and so lose any body integrity.

The construction of a secure body container for subjective passion depends on internalizations of self and other connections from earliest infancy. Donald Stern refers to the internal blueprint from such internalizations as "rigs" (1985). The internalization of self and maternal other permits an internal body container to be developed within the internal representational world, so that all erotic and aggressive intensities can be felt as subjective feelings in relation to an "other," rather than as impinging dynamic persecutory objects (the uncontained split-off self parts merged with part-object representations—as internal objects are described by Ogden, 1986). But when there is early trauma, as in Lois's case, such a container is inadequately built into the psyche. This results in this Red Shoes phenomena of manic erotic intensities compelling the person towards images and away from interpersonal relations with external objects. However, with an object-relations psychotherapy, such as that between Lois and myself, a container for subjective passion may be built in. This is done through developmental mourning that opens inner space for new object connections. "Developmental mourning" (Kavaler-Adler, 1993) offers the only avenue to opening the sealed-off core self and its closed pathological system (see Fairbairn, 1952). When she had the dream of sexual desire disrupted by envy in the last half of the second year of treatment, Lois was at a midpoint in this developmental process. She had opened to some capacity for subjective passion, but could not sustain it. She began to experience George as too manly, as soon as his sexual desire showed. Some of Lois's terror could be traced to an oral rape trauma, to be discussed later. Another origin of the terror was the primal trauma of infancy and separation. Lois said that she was afraid to have sex with George, because she started to feel like she was falling down a dark hole and was back in snail land. Falling in love with George felt like falling down endlessly into darkness, a regression to the undifferentiated darkness that appeared in early dreams and daytime terrors.

Yet she was able to talk about these fears with George, and to "sob and sob" out the grief of loss and need within her. But she still needed to open in her treatment to the inner source of the pain and grief behind such sobbing. She needed to give her analyst access to the area of deep trauma and disconnection within. The cathartic grief spells in George's presence were not enough, although they allowed her to temporarily open herself to vulnerability and connection. Lois reported that she went home after seeing George one evening, and "cried like a maniac," the same way she had been able to cry when I was leaving her on the previous summer vacation.

Gradually, with her mourning of loss, often felt through separation experience in the transference, but stemming back to early disappointments with her father and mother, Lois could begin to open emotionally to George. She was able to let in his sexuality and to sustain a sense of her own sexuality, rather than to substitute compulsive creative work for sexuality and intimate interpersonal love relations. She began to "let go" and to enjoy her sexual desire, containing it, and inviting all phallic penetration, rather than experiencing it as an alien persecutory and annihilating force. (This is in contrast to Emily Dickinson's persistent and growing terror of male sexuality throughout her life. See Kavaler-Adler, 1993). As Lois's capacity to contain sexual desire in interpersonal love expanded, so did her capacity to sustain desire and contact with her creative work. Her creative work, less and less driven by compulsion and image addiction, was increasingly allowed to emerge as if she was giving birth. Lois, herself, spoke of creativity as pregnancy, as did Virginia Woolf (Panken, 1987). No longer tied to a compulsive, image mystique—less driven or addicted to a demon lover—Lois could allow free motivation based on subjective desire to propel her creative process. Simultaneously, she began to allow such free motivation in love relations and in sexual process.

LOIS'S EARLY CREATIVITY: BLOCKING AND COMPULSION

In the beginning of treatment we saw that Lois felt herself up against a wall in her efforts to publish her novels and short-story writing. At the same time, however, she complained, "I can't get inside the experience." Instead, as in sex, she felt like she was falling down a dark hole. She reported that her second novel had only one real character. This character created all the other counterpoint voices and images through her hallucinations. Lois questioned the solipsistic quality of her work at this time. She was distraught and self-hating when publishers described her novel to her agent as dark and depressing. Scared that the work she spent two years on would not get out into the world, because of a marketplace hostility to the darkness within her, Lois responded by trying to write more. She pushed herself, compelled by her hall of mirrors reflecting back her images of failure. But these very projections and introjections, as well as the more persecutory ones we discussed here, disrupted her process. She said she felt stuck, but couldn't let go! Lois thought she needed to allow herself a "free fall" in order to get inside her experience, but she couldn't.

I told her that she needed to allow me to be with her to enable her to tolerate going into the darkness within. She seemed to understand my suggestion and said that while she was away at a writing colony trying to write, she had missed me very much. As she let me in, she began to face the darkness and, gradually, the creatures within became differentiated as her own feelings. Also, the darkness itself assumed a more differentiated form. For example, in one memory, she waited in a dark apartment for her mother to come home.

She also had a dream about a dark work environment, another differentiated situation delimiting the darkness.

> In the dream, she entered her dark work environment, but was able to lead a woman who represented the inadequate and envious part of herself, out into the sunlight. The woman said to her: "You're lucky! You have your writing. I only have this job!"
>
> Lois led this alter-ego woman outside of the dark work environment, and attempted to comfort her by listening intently to her. She felt compassion and concern.

In her associations to this dream, Lois commented on her feeling of compassion, contrasting it with a former sense of contempt that she might have felt in the past. She also related her temporal and psychological move to compassion, and her capacity to listen to another, to the spatial move from darkness into light. The work environment was a defined interior dark space, rather than the infinite fall into the black hole of her past nightmares. Lois spoke of the envious woman as a part of herself that felt inadequate, but a part of herself that she was separating from by connecting emotionally with it through compassion, rather than being swallowed up and overwhelmed by it, as she was by psychic merger with self parts experienced as snails.

In guiding this woman out into the sunlight to comfort her, Lois, through her capacity for concern, showed herself to be opening up the darkness of her sealed-off, isolated self to the bright light of hope that she could now feel in letting another touch her, as she allowed me to emotionally touch her.

Lois began to have dreams of sunlit apartments as she allowed emotional touching between us. Through her treatment with me, she was able to sustain an internalization of me as a caring good object. The darkness, chaos, and blood of her early dreams thus began to change into differentiated apartments and work spaces with light. Simultaneously, her creative process changed from being characterized by compulsivity and blocking into a process of engagement with her internal objects in a fluid dialectic of interpersonal relations. Instead of being caught in a need-fear dilemma—in which need brought terror of persecution by the needed object or the envious other who didn't want her to have the needed object—Lois now owned a part of herself that could be in a position of need, while being responded to with compassion and empathy. Her primitive contempt for the needy parts of herself was softening, and turning into compassion and the capacity for concern, as her dreams foretold.

But regressions into contempt and self-hatred still followed rejections of her work. On being asked to write an article on self-mutilators, she overidentified with her subjects, seeing herself as one of them. She felt that the slightest rejection caused her to cut herself emotionally, with contemptuous and critical comments, and with reflected images from her "failure" hall of mirrors. She was, of course, terrified of acceptance as well, for that meant being the Red Shoes mother, and not the little girl who was afraid of possessing sexual desire, self-agency, and accountability. Lois admitted that she liked to fall apart so others could come and clean up after her. Her creative work also was stymied by her need to please the marketplace, because she was compelled to be famous, to be the white feather in a sea of black feathers. When she couldn't have an identity from within through body- and object-related connection in interpersonal relations, she sought a marketplace or outer-generated image identity. Nevertheless, she really did want to be an artist who conveyed her deepest interior life. She felt in a bind when magazines required her to write in a glossy popular style, rather than to confront readers with the darkness within herself.

When Lois wasn't true to her deeper self, she suffered agonies of regret. She beat herself up for not performing well enough. But she also was allowing herself to be comforted by my interpretations of the bind she found herself in, which caused her to postpone work until her writing fell far short of her own expectations and potential. I suggested that she delayed doing her work, thereby costing her a more complete creative process, because she was torn between writing for the commercial marketplace and writing to plumb her own artistic self-expression. Self-expression was definitely harder, requiring contact with her deeper self. Contacting her inner self was terrifying, while the marketplace image felt safe, but empty. My understanding of her dilemma helped Lois to stop emotionally mutilating herself. Yet she still had to integrate the compulsively driven part of herself that was addicted to images and the Red Shoes bitch-goddess "fame" with the part that wished to speak openly to others about her feelings and internal life. She needed to go beyond the mourning of early separation trauma, loss, and mourning of the primal object in abandonment-depression mourning. She had to mourn her regrets so that the working through of guilt in the depressive position could more fully integrate the now opened inner-core self (as opposed to a sealed-off or split-off core) with the concerns and response of the external interpersonal world. The fundamental antagonism between these two arenas in her internal world could be seen in her dreams of Nazis invading a writing colony.

FROM PROTOSYMBOLISM TO REPRESENTATIONAL SYMBOLISM THROUGH THE RECOVERY AND MOURNING OF ORAL RAPE TRAUMA

Lois was outside of herself in her earliest dreams. That is, she was an observer when the characters of her internal world emerged as part objects engaged in sadomasochistic scenes. These scenes were similar to those she watched on the porno cable TV station, as she tried to ward off an engulfing internal darkness.

> Lois's first dream was that of a man beating a woman. In the dream, there was a film of the scene between the man and woman. Lois thought to herself in the dream that if she could have stolen the film she would have figured out what was wrong with her and been cured.

At this beginning period of treatment, Lois was unable to associate symbolically to the dream, in contrast to her later prolific manner of association. At this stage, she reacted by enacting being beaten in her voice and behavior. In a whimpering anguish she exclaimed that if she could have taken the film of the man beating the woman she could have figured out what was wrong with her. Later sessions showed Lois and myself that the film in her dream was not only a kind of internal barrier within her that mimicked the porno films she watched on TV, but a symbolic screen memory of an adolescent trauma: her oral rape at the age of twelve by a strange man, who worked at Club Med, where she had been brought by her father on vacation. Because the trauma had been split off, Lois was placed in the position of an observer in this dream that reawakened the ghost of the trauma. With the distance of an observer she could avoid emotional connection with the mortifying trauma. For the same reason, the splitting off of the trauma from her central self (Fairbairn, 1952) and psyche also perpetually propelled her towards a violent reenactment, which she simulated in her analytic sessions.

Another dream from the first months of Lois's two-year treatment also revealed her disconnected state. The dream, as previously indicated, was of women in a medical school who had their uteruses displayed in plastic bags hanging on the classroom or laboratory wall. In this dream Lois was once again outside the internal world scene as an observer. But the split-off female parts of herself, the alter-ego women in medical school, were also outside their bodies, literally outside, looking at their insides from this vantage point. As Lois described the dream, she associated from uterus to fetus.

I conjectured that Lois's sense of herself as a fetus was continually projected into images of snails and protosymbolic sensory experiences of snails. Initially, when feeling like she was falling apart, she had psychotic delusions of living as their king in her own secret world. She next saw snails in a lamp in my office. When I suggested now that the snails might be like herself in fetus form, she reacted with a powerful affirmation: "Yes! Yes! Yes!" she cried, with her usual intensity and drama. The protosymbolic snail sensations, symbolized in the dream as a fetus, were soon to become, for Lois, symbols of oral rape. Later, they would return to her protosymbolic sensory level. However, connecting with the disconnected female fetus part of herself through this dream allowed her to enter into body connection and into symbolic associations within the therapeutic object relationship. Thus, by curling up in a fetal position on the couch, Lois enacted her fetal attachment to me as the analyst in the transference.

During her initial days in therapy, Lois had been a psychic bulimic, tak-

ing me in whole, spitting me out, and becoming nauseous in her first session because of the conflict between taking me in and spitting me up.
Gradually, she was able to take me in and sustain some connection,
digesting me a bit. But the urge to orally expel me was overwhelmingly
compulsive. When Lois's sensory level snail preoccupation began, therefore, to transform into a symbolic key to an oral rape trauma, her capacity to let me be with her as an ally was quite new and alluring. At the
moment she grasped the image of the snail in a totally novel way—as the
combined image of her lips and the male rapist's penis on which her lips
were forced—an important mystery yielded its story. Darkness had turned
to light through this deciphering of the snail symbol, just as her dreams
suggested, with dark places becoming bright, open, and sun-drenched
apartments.

However, for Lois to symbolize her experience in representational
images was to maintain a degree of separateness from her primal internal
objects that was hard to maintain. Throughout the course of the forward
and backward movement of emotional growth in treatment, and particularly within the first year of treatment, Lois was to regress from this parallel growth in symbolic capacity, free-associative capacity, and the
sustaining of a therapeutic alliance into a protosymbolic level of enactment, reflective of Hanna Segal's "symbolic equation," (see Segal, 1986).
Protosymbolic enactment is a concrete sensory, visceral, or behavioral
experience (Segal's "thing in itself"), without any representation of the
experience in the internal world (or secondary process). Losing the
metaphor and symbolism of transference, during the first year of treatment, Lois began to act like I actually was the demon lover rapist, forcing
her to submit to experiencing the pain and memory of the rape, to remember the inner scream that was choked off and locked within her, the kiss
forced into her, and the penis forced into her mouth.

Together, we traveled from the protosymbolic to the symbolic level and
back again. After the regression to enactment, compelled by the magnetic power of Lois's primal internal object attachments—the demon lover
enactment being related to an early combined mother-father figure, as
well as to the object internalization of the actual rapist—Lois moved forward again to new symbolism, as memories began to come alive in more
differentiated form. For example, Lois remembered standing in a hallway,
being carried over a shoulder, with a hand over her mouth, so that all the
screams inside imploded within her. She felt like a "screaming cloud of
pestilence," "clinging to an electrically charged fence."

Soon after this move forward to symbolic association and memory,
Lois regressed again to the protosymbolic level. Symbolic snail images

transformed backwards into snails in her mouth. She said that she had lost me inbetween sessions. While sitting alone in a room trying to write, she felt snails swimming in her mouth, erupting from symbolic containment into protosymbolic sensory impingement—engulfing and terrifying her.

Lois next had a dream of snakes and of holding onto one of them. In the dream she could not let go of the snake. Discussing the dream, she was able to ask why in a reflective manner. Her question illustrated how potential space had opened up through the intense grief and mourning of the rape trauma, allowing me to be better internalized as a good object. With this new psychic structure, Lois could look at the snake image in symbolic form in the dream, rather than turning me into the snake demon lover, as she had done during the early uncovering of the rape trauma. For Lois, snakes may have expressed erotic intensities without subjective passion, just as they do in the poetry of Emily Dickinson (see Kavaler-Adler, 1993). Lois had, as indicated, no adequate inner container to tolerate her own subjective desire. Only as she could reach the symbolic level and enter the depressive position mourning process could she make space to internalize her connection with me within the therapeutic object relationship. When this occurred, her split-off intensities, whether in the form of snails, snakes, or dinosaurs, could begin to integrate within her. In their split-off form, Lois's dynamic bad objects attacked her from within, and she expressed snakebite intensity towards others. The oral bites of the snakes and dinosaurs in her dreams were a part of her, a part she had felt and expressed towards her sister in childhood. She had torn up her sister's room reminiscent of Klein's tearing up the breast. Lois had also felt her teeth tingling from the fantastic urge to bite her sister's nose off.

MOVEMENTS TOWARDS THE LOVE-CREATIVITY DIALECTIC

Lois tended to talk over her feelings, racing past her internal self and past connection with an emotionally available external other, as shown with me as her analyst in treatment. However, once one level of the primal trauma was opened up, through symbolic articulation—as had occurred with the oral rape trauma—the earlier child level of experience could be reached and the primal separation trauma could be approached. But for this to happen, Lois needed the kind of containment in the therapeutic object relationship that she didn't have internally. In order to slow down from the manic St. Vitus dance of the Red Shoes, Lois needed a safe place where she could engage with her dark interior life.

In the first few months of treatment, Lois's dreams clearly showed that she didn't have an internal container adequate enough to allow her to feel and process the dark areas and demons of her internal world. In one dream, her father had a cat in his coat pocket which slipped away from him and ran off. Lois was quite upset when reporting this dream, asking how could her father let something so close to his heart slip away as she identified with the cat. Such a question was particularly poignant given that she had been on a vacation with her father at the time when she was abducted and raped at twelve. Her father had been preoccupied with his own social life, after his divorce from Lois's mother, and he encouraged Lois to go off on her own, during the evening, at Club Med. He was not there to protect Lois nor rescue her, when one of the men who worked at the resort literally picked her up and carried her away from returning to her room, forcing a kiss upon her, and then carried her down to the waterfront, after she had refused to go willingly on a boat ride with him. Lois's relationship with her father was consequently damaged for years, until she worked through the oral rape trauma within our treatment.

Lois was looking for a "maternal father" (Masterson, personal communication), because her maternal figure was, particularly at the time of the divorce, more of an absence than a presence. Even the consciousness of her mother's absence was a step forward into a subjective sense of self, supplanting a reflexive and reactive terror of the black-hole endless void. At an adult level, Lois saw her mother as preoccupied. Lois remembered incidents in childhood when she would come home from school and be invited to discuss her day at school with her mother, only to be sharply and abruptly interrupted the moment she began by her mother's hysterical cry: "Oh God, I have so much work to do!" This would promptly end any potential dialogue between them. Lois's urge to speak subsequently took the form of a compulsively prolonged monologue, as she sought to have a voice in the context of her invisibility and inaudibility in her mother's presence.

During the first months of treatment, Lois's father was represented in her internal world, not only as a faulty container but as an unbounded fluid semen force, leaking out in all directions. In one dream her father handed Lois a ski ticket sticky with fluid. This paternal dream image matched that of her own mucous soaked interior world, where snails, "big, grey, and dripping," inhabited and haunted her.

With failed maternal and paternal internal objects, Lois had split off from her central body core. She, like her parents, tried to live in her head. Also like her parents, she tried to live in her work! Lois's work was truly creative—full of images—but it was at first an externalization of her internal hall of mirrors, which, as noted, was filled with paralyzed part-object self fragments. These early, one-dimensional part-object images would

later change into rich three-dimensional images, but at this early treatment stage they were translucent with the transpersonal unconscious, as
well as truncated by inevitable sadomasochistic enactments that cut her
off from conscious self-ownership.

Her early dreams showed all this. One of the earliest dreams was of a
man beating a woman. The dream and our analysis of it led to the developmental journey that would heal and symbolize her twelve-year-old oral
rape trauma. However, the split-off masculine and feminine self parts in
the dream were also related to internal scenes of father and self from
childhood, as well as to later memories of her twelve-year-old oral rape.
Many levels of trauma, along with the sadomasochistic enactments stimulated by the trauma, entered these split-off self parts.

Lois reported her mother's memory of her father threatening to spank
Lois when he was diapering her at the age of two. She herself remembered
pestering her father at the age of six, while he was trying to work in his
study. He threatened her with a slap. Lois also remembered screaming
that she wanted more food at the Thanksgiving table and her father saying "no." Threatening to hit her, he then sent her to her room.

Lois also remembered her mother as never hugging her or touching her.
Through the dialogue between Lois and I about her memories, Lois con-
cluded that her cravings for touch got converted into screaming, biting,
tearing at, and psychically spitting up all those who tried to enter her
internal world through speech, a mode of psychic penetration that was
too painful when there was no support from a preverbal holding mother
from within. Without the internalization of a good-enough holding mother, intense frustration built up and erupted. Thus, there were the incidents
Lois reported of tearing up her sister's room in a fit, and of feeling the
compelling urge to bite her sister's nose off.

Lois's split-off masculine and feminine self parts, based on early modes
of imitating identifications with the sadism and unavailability of both her
father and mother, laid the seeds for a demon lover dynamic internal
object to develop within Lois, which continued to impinge on the higher
level symbolic representational world in her central self or ego. An oral
rape that really happened then could easily turn the interior primitive
father into the image of a male rapist. The snail image of the man's penis
and her own mouth, which couldn't contain the real semen forced into
her, became in her erotic fantasies, and in her dream, a man beating a
woman. In the same dream, there was "disgusting food" being served on
platters—a condensation of the semen and the penis that had been forced
into her mouth and the overflowing Thanksgiving dinner food that she
was prohibited from eating more than one portion of. It was interesting in

this context that Lois was then viewed by her parents as an insatiable child. Indeed, she tried to demand and extract with emotional blackmail what she felt had not been freely given to her. She had tried this with me in the first few months of therapy. My lack of intimidation and my capacity to "de-fang" her with my interpretations, so that the child within her could finally, as indicated, go beyond screaming to crying and needing, earned her gratitude.

We have already discussed the connection between Lois's fantasy of herself as a fetus and her oral rape. Disconnected from her body, in dreams, she experienced herself as a fetus, hiding in the snail's shell to avoid true vulnerability. She was able to gradually let me in as a containing presence, rather than spitting me up perpetually as she had done in the first session. She was able to digest me more and more as I saw the child within her and was not intimidated by her snakebite and her dinosaurlike exterior—an exterior that had unfortunately intimidated her family and played into the lack of containment she felt.

FROM OUTSIDE THE BODY TO CONTAINMENT WITHIN

In the first few months of treatment, dreams of being outside her self and body were vivid blueprints of the internal world disconnection that affected the realms of interpersonal love and creative-process love in her writing. Lois's dream of women in medical school, already described, vividly evoked the gut level of body disconnection that accompanied her into treatment with me. (The discussion of the Red Shoes theme and creative mystique theme grew from this.) The image of a uterus sealed off in plastic suggests the snail sealed off in its shell and the entire feminine self sealed off from contact with the outside world. As indicated, Lois associated from uterus to fetus in this dream, suggesting that her entire being was so sealed off in a maternal uterus that she had no contact with the outside interpersonal world. Lois was sealed off in her mother, sealed off from her feminine and maternal self. She was sealed off with a Red Shoes mother, who had split-off eroticism, an eroticized intellect, and a body cut off from its core moorings. This sealed-off state was Lois's plight. Yet now, she herself perpetuated the sealing off through defensive maneuvers.

With such body disconnection, and her experience as a fetus with the sealed-off uterus, Lois initially made such statements as "I need to be in a womb. I can't come out," "a novel is like a womb that totally encloses you," "I feel like the soft part of a man that will be annihilated by his sexuality," "I'm like the tattered clothes in my dream, a self in pieces, but the dream also suggests someone has undressed me." She implied that the penetration anxiety was at the level of annihilation anxiety, where the man's entrance into her, and perhaps even the essence of his attraction to her, shattered her into fragments, as symbolized by the tattered clothes.

To compensate for this sense of terror of her own vulnerability, and her relinquishment of fangs that could be felt like an evisceration, Lois danced the dance of the Red Shoes. She clung to an internal hall of mirrors that lent itself to the creative mystique, which left her eviscerated because the obsessional intensity and the accompanying creative compulsive behavior kept her sealed off from emotional contact with others in the external world. The lack of interpersonal contact and intimacy in turn drained her, drying up her creative resources. Sealed off from external objects, she was thrown back on her internal objects, which took on the aura of images in a hall of mirrors. These could be visualized consciously when the level of symbolic experience was reached.

When Lois was outside of her body, she was outside of her creative work. She was unable to connect emotionally with another, so she remained locked up in an internal system in which she operated out of projective-identification and introjective-identification. During her early treatment (1993), she was in a passive reactive position continuously. This position is reflective of body disconnection as seen in Lois in her dream of the sex slave with the man beating a woman. Lois's psychic life, as suggested, contained continual sadomasochistic scenes in which she was more consciously situated in the masochistic position. In these scenes, she would protest against a personified force, related to limits imposed on her for the completion of her work: "I am not going to bow down to this deadline!" Lois spoke as if the deadline in itself had a sadistic persona dynamically impinging on her from within, separate from any actual person, such as an editor, who might have set the deadline for her work through a publisher or magazine. Her protest was similar to that she made to me as she projected her sadistic aspect outside of herself and onto me. She cried: "How do you presume to know so much about me? Maybe you're not so smart! Maybe I'm smarter than you? Are you a ruthless academic? I'm scared of you!"

About her own relation to her work, she protested from a position of impotence, "I can't get inside of it!" "I need to drop down into a deep space, a deep level of consciousness." Gradually, Lois began to understand that letting me in to be with her in her internal darkness was the only way of allowing herself to drop down into a deep space, and the only way to "get inside of her creative work" (as well as to get inside of her body during sexual and interpersonal relations.) But if in her dreams, she was not in her body, how could she be inside of her work?

FROM PERSECUTORY OBJECTS TO TRANSITIONAL OBJECTS

This transformation occurred as Lois began to deal with her backlash reactions against her psychic internalization of me and of our therapeutic object relationship. In their split-off form, Lois's dynamic bad objects attacked her from within, and her external behavior reflected this as she expressed the snakebite intensity towards others. The oral bites of the snake and dinosaurs in her dreams were a part of her, a part of her that she had felt and expressed towards her sister in childhood.

After the first six months of treatment, persecutory objects began to transform into transitional objects. They were able to become transitional objects as erotic intensities became modified by symbolic transformations. Thus, in one dream the dinosaurs engaged in oral play—throwing their young back and forth into one another's mouths—rather than murderous biting. Lois also brought her stuffed dinosaur to a session one day, and curled up on the couch with him, showing by this how a persecutory object could transform into a transitional object. In addition, she teasingly called me "monster," including me in this play, thereby differentiating me from my persecutory aspect in the transference, in which I could be feared as a "ruthless academic" and a male rapist.

I too became a transitional object. Lois now saw me as the only person she could safely need and depend on. I was, in other words, a good object in a sea of bad, and frustrating, disappointing, and depriving objects. She said directly, "You're the only one." Everyone else is envious of me and abandons me." She now missed me terribly if I were going away and felt her grief in advance, "You go away too much. Sometimes I think it's bad for me to depend on you." She felt contained in the holding environment of the therapeutic object relationship because she cried out this form of grief. Now too she was able to move from an earlier rigid defensiveness, characteristic of persecution in the paranoid-schizoid position, to that of a "playing alliance" (Albert Brok, personal communication, 1993). She laughed with me, being both humorous and receiving humor from me at this time. For example, when Lois said that she was scared, I could tell her "You're scared because you're becoming a goddamn human being!" She laughed. I then said, "You're actually able to chat with people now, rather than lecturing in a monologue, or protesting about social injustice. You're actually feeling need and loss and laughing at yourself, rather than screaming and spitting up" My metamorphosis into a transitional object occurred in the second year of treatment, following Lois's psychic bulimic period, in which she spit me up.

GOOD OBJECTS

At the same time as I served as a critical transitional object, I also was internalized as a good-enough new real object. My being a good-enough real object allowed Lois's dreams of good mother figures to gradually emerge, particularly during the third phase of treatment, during the latter half of the second year. In one of these dreams, her mother offered to help Lois rent an apartment, which she could not afford. In this apartment was a fluffy yellow duck, a symbol of a softer, more vulnerable, and more feminine part of Lois, that was now being protected in a holding environment apartment, just as she was being emotionally held in therapy. Her associations to the dream showed that the duck also symbolized Lois's childhood, when she had a passion for ducks and would effervescently cry out: "Make way for ducklings!" This dream, then, showed that Lois's split part was changing into a positive image. No longer did she view herself as a impotent patsy, as the soft part of a man with whom she was fused, and who abused and annihilated her. Lois's new softness was quite different from the position she had felt herself in when she had cried, "I'm just waiting for some dick to come into my life and take it over, quite literally!"

Other good mother dreams emerged. In one, her new female agent dropped by at her apartment for cappuccino. I appeared in another dream as a landlady who offered to help her when her desk was so heavy with work that the floor caved in underneath it (in the dream her desk was in the bathroom). The landlady said, "We can fix it," offering reparative possibilities.

As the good object formed within her, Lois became capable in treatment of mourning object loss, which reflected early traumatic loss during infant and toddler core-self formation. Earlier she had said, "If I go and come back I'll be punished," reflecting her separation dilemma and bind. During the second year of treatment she mourned all our absences—not only my vacation—from one another. She also began to connect with feelings of loss when I interpreted all the ways she defended against them, including how she instantly hooked her mind into her failure hall of mirrors.

Surrendering to the deep core feeling of loss within transference, and within the mourning of the therapeutic object relationship, Lois could now use my words and images. She was not compelled to spit them up. She began to realize that she clung to an image of herself—often an image of failure—to avoid sinking into a feeling of loss in her body, a feeling thick with pain, but also open to love, when she experienced it with me, in the moment, within the context of the therapeutic holding environment.

13)

THE CASE OF LOIS, PART II

Healing and Movement Towards the Love-Creativity Dialectic

MOURNING, SEPARATION, AND SELF-AGENCY

The ultimate symbol in Lois's dreams of split-off aggression, which had been formed into a whole anti-libidinal psychic structure, was that of the Nazis. It was following the initial stage of treatment, during the beginning of the second year of treatment that Lois had her two dreams of Nazis invading the oasis of a writing colony. They reflected, as will be discussed, a significant developmental progression.

The first dream of the Nazis invading was as follows:

> Lois is feeling safe within a writing colony, when suddenly she is alerted to a forthcoming invasion by Nazis. She tells her girlfriend, and begs her to come with her to escape. They both start packing, and as they are packing, she hands a copy of the novel she is writing at the writing colony to her girlfriend. Her girlfriend continues her packing, and appears to be indifferent to Lois offering her Lois's book. Instantly, the room that she and her girlfriend are in becomes filled with rats. The threat of the Nazi invasion remains, but Lois is now preoccupied with the rats surrounding her and feels alienated from her girlfriend.

Lois was a subjective character in this dream. This is in contrast to her earlier dream, in which she remained outside the scene as she watched a man beating a woman. Parts of the man and woman's bodies also were outside the scene in the earlier dream. In the first Nazi dream, Lois enters into the sadomasochistic scene as the victim. Her affect state is thus externalized rather than internally integrated. The Nazis are feared as alien persecutory objects. Her girlfriend, to whom she clings in the dream, is an idealized sister-mother figure. In Melanie Klein's phenomenology, Lois's dream reveals her to be in the paranoid-schizoid position.

The Nazis, however, are not only external persecutors. They are also a part of Lois that persecuted her from within. Her psychic state then was similar to Ronald Fairbairn's anti-libidinal ego psychic structure, which he originally called an "internal saboteur" (1952). Indeed, recall that Lois had described herself as a Nazi at times, identifying with the fascist part of her that propelled her into compulsive cycles of manic work intensity.

In this dream, however, Lois clearly does not identify with the Nazis. She fears being their victim and wishes to escape with her girlfriend. The girlfriend is indifferent to Lois's pleas to escape with her. The friend is thus unwilling to play the role of the positive mirroring mother Lois desires, as the associations to the dream bear out. Lois had previously spoken of "losing it." Often, the phrase referred to losing her mother's attention. When in the dream, Lois offered the precious gift of her own novel, her girlfriend ignores it. Lois has created in her dream the reflection of her preoccupied internal mother. Suddenly, the room that she and her girlfriend are in fills with rats.

When Lois first reported this dream, she was unable to psychically connect with symbolic associations. Rather, she reacted, saying that she always had vile animals and Nazis in her dreams. She proclaimed that they lived inside of her. I then offered my own interpretation that linked together the rats with her own subjective self-experience. I said that the rats seemed to represent the rage she felt when her girlfriend rejected her novel, which she experienced as her essence. Lois agreed and was then able to follow with her own associations. She said she felt alone and ugly in the dream because of her rage. Also, she said that the Nazis represented a fascist standard of excellence and achievement that disrupted the creative process in her writing, because it took her away from her inner self. In this dream, Lois merged into her internal Nazis and rats, who operated like split-off self parts fused into persecutory part-object representations, creating the sensation of Fairbairnian dynamic demon objects. Internal affect is still externalized in this dream. Such externalization is characteristic of the paranoid-schizoid position and of protosymbolic communication through projective-identification. This contrasts with the depressive position dynamic of subjective feeling states, in which subjective rage can be experienced and contained, so that such hostile aggression need not be psychically converted into personified bad objects, split off from the conscious sense of self—persecutors external to the self. Such depressive-position containing of rage allows the instinctual aggression within the rage to transform into the depressive affects of grief and sadness. This, in turn, promotes interpersonal contact, renewed loving capacity, reparation of disrupted object relations, and overall self-integration through symbolic assimilation of subjective feeling states.

Lois's disconnection from her rage in this dream is less severe than her disconnection from entire body parts, as revealed in her first dreams. The disconnected rage was capable of paralyzing her. In the analytic session in which Lois presented the dreams, she is initially paralyzed in her abilities to symbolize. My initiation of the association process, through my interpretation of her externalized affect state, allowed Lois to begin to initiate from within by generating her own associations. This newfound capacity appeared in the session she brought her next Nazi dream to.

> In this second dream of Nazis invading a writing colony, Lois tells her girlfriend that she wants to travel and would like her friend to come with her. When her girlfriend sounds uninterested, Lois then tells her friend that they have to leave the writing colony to travel because the Nazis are coming. She starts to pack, and realizes that she will have to go alone, since her girlfriend is not coming with her. She leaves behind a book given to her by her father, a copy of the novel, *Anna Karenena*. She realizes that she doesn't need the book.

This second dream of Nazis invading a writing colony focussed more on Lois's desires than her persecutory terror. In the dream, Lois wants to travel with her girlfriend. When her girlfriend refuses to go with her, Lois tells her that the Nazis are coming and that she and her girlfriend must leave. Nevertheless, the Nazis seem like a more distant threat than in the earlier dream: in fact, they may just be an excuse to have her girlfriend travel with her. Lois's associations to this dream came easily within the session. Lois concluded through her associations that when her girlfriend finally declines to go with her in the dream, she feels a sense of strong personal initiative that allows her to believe that she can go on her own. When she does, she leaves behind a book given to her by her father, realizing she doesn't need it. The dream shows that Lois is essentially leaving behind her father's philosophy of life and finding her own way.

The mourning process is a separation process. In Lois's case it allowed her to begin to separate from the Nazi part of her. During the interval between these dreams, approximately several months, Lois has learned how to slow down from the manic whirling dervish dance of the Red Shoes. She had also traveled from rage and terror to deep states of sadness. She had begun to tolerate the pain of object loss related to her early separation traumas and sealed-off self core. Consequently, Lois had become increasingly able to let me be with her and to directly express her need for me to me. She had also been modifying the sadomasochistic aspects of her psychic structure. This opened her up to experiencing erotic fantasies, such as a man beating a woman, without acting them out in her life.

A dream following these dreams shows Lois's developmental growth next progressed into a depressive position capacity for concern. This development occurred as guilt and loss were felt and understood between us in the therapeutic mourning process. Lois was now able to have a dialogue with parts of herself that were formerly split-off and disowned, such as the part of her that felt inadequate. Her capacity for psychic structure dialectic is emerging here on an intrapsychic level. Such dialectic then can manifest as a growing capacity for interpersonal dialogue. As the psychic structure is built for dialectic, the intrapsychic range of creative process and mourning process relationships also interacts in its own dialectic with the interpersonal realm of love relationships.

DEPRESSIVE-POSITION MOURNING OF REGRET: PROCESSING GUILT AS GRIEF

Mourning of loss related to separation trauma and abandonment depression (Masterson, 1976, 1981) is only one aspect of the developmental mourning needed for self-integration and the evolution of the capacity for psychic dialectic, including the love-creativity dialectic. The other aspect of mourning is related to the role of our own aggression in creating loss, as written about by Melanie Klein in "Envy and Gratitude" (1957) and "Mourning and Manic Depressive States" (1940). Whatever early loss we may have, the repetition compulsion of our own reenactment of that loss causes us to perpetuate it like a self-fulfilling prophesy. In Fairbairn's terms (1952), we hold on to the bad object. In Melanie Klein's terms (1957), we kill off our loving capacity and thus kill our loving connections with those we also hate, due to the ambivalent nature of all love relations.

As Lois's bad objects became assimilated into her sense of self, she became able to own her aggression and to connect with "aggressive impulses" rather than being the victim of those impulses, which were merged with part-object personas that felt as if they were coming in at her as persecutors and demon lover rescuers ("Everything is coming in on me," "I'm waiting for someone to shove his dick into my life, quite literally"—first few months of treatment). With her psychic journey from black holes, ("energy demons," snails, and aborted fetuses), to rage and, finally, to the sadness of grief and loss, Lois became capable of psychic separation to the point where she could begin to own her own hate and destructiveness. Once she became capable of owning her hate and seeing how it destroyed love connections, she was able to feel regret and attempt reparation towards both her external and internal objects. She became capable of feeling the grief of her own guilt. When reparation could be received by the external other (see Klein, 1957, "Envy and Gratitude"), she could tolerate her hate without feeling she was all bad. This allowed her to mourn her regrets, rather than to perpetuate a splitting process in which she was all bad or all good, or where the other became all bad as she projected her badness into the other. With the owning and grieving of regrets, reparation could be made and mutuality between herself and the other could begin. This allowed for a dialectic of subjectivities and a dialectic of love with the external other, as well as for emerging creativity from interchange with the internal other.

Late in her second year of treatment, Lois demonstrated her new capacity for mourning regret and making reparation. She became familiar with her compulsion to attack those she felt dependent on, and came to realize how these attacks could make her feel alone, scared, and exquisitely sensitive to loss. She became increasingly aware of how she herself could create loss through her attacks on those she needed, even though she also carried with her an extreme vulnerability in relation to feeling loss when faced with separation.

She became even more aware of her spoiling process. Her dream of cutting off feelings of passionate sexual desire showed, as discussed, her use of spoiling. When she feared desire would overwhelm her with its intense arousal and multiple levels of yearning for the man, she converted it into criticism of the man she desired. This left her feeling empty and thus prone to envy, which in turn led to her destructive attacks on the object of her desire.

Once Lois split off the feeling of sexual desire and disconnected from her body self, she became a prisoner again of the hall of mirrors mystique. She would then see her boyfriend through the screen of her negative hall of mirrors, since he didn't fit into the type in her "star" hall of mirrors. She would then seek the narcissistic allure of the mystique within her creative work, where her own intensity would allure her, becoming a meaningful distraction from all the realities and limits involved with relating to her boyfriend. For example, when fearing George as big and so overwhelming her with his judgments, which reflected fears of her own projected judgments and of the projected power of her split-off sexual desire—Lois either attacked him or receded into the safe cocoon of her creative work. When she receded into her work, it was like diving into the ocean and hardly coming up for air. As she became aware of what she was doing, Lois observed: "I took a break from my writing and it was scary. Somehow I'm not equipped for regular life. I need to work intensely.... I've been going back to the intensity of work just like I used to when I was a workaholic nut case. I don't have to live then. I enjoy it! I don't have to deal with fears of George, or even see him in person, because I'm working. It's like being in suspended animation."

When not using the manic defense of compulsive creative work, Lois lashed out at her boyfriend, who had needs of his own. Within our psychotherapy sessions, Lois became quite aware of her hateful attacks on him. In Winnicott's terms ("The Development of the Capacity for Concern," 1963), she was beginning to be able to experience "held guilt" and a capacity for concern. But she still lashed out with hateful assaults when actually with George. She tried to contain the criticism of him that built up, but she often was unsuccessful. Frequently, she withdrew into sleep to escape her guilt over attacking him.

In her treatment, Lois allowed me to speak to her about her destructiveness and the grief she felt about it. She would exclaim, "Yes. I can be so cruel. I can be so mean." She openly demonstrated her wish for help from me in stopping her hostile aggression. She was in touch with the fear that she could drive her boyfriend away and in the process lose someone who had been nurturing and kind to her.

By the second half of the second year of treatment, Lois was no longer splitting her objects into good and bad. She did not turn her boyfriend into a bad object to justify her hate, as she would always have done during the earlier phase of treatment. She cried and felt the anguish of her own regret. As she did this in my presence, I was able to invite her to explore what was frightening her at the moment when she felt compelled to attack. Lois saw that she was terrified of the passionate part of the relationship with her boyfriend. She wanted him to be a parent, a mommy-daddy. She said the manly part of him scared her: he was too manly. She was afraid of letting him enter her, just as she was afraid of letting me "enter" her in our sessions. She pushed us away by attacks or distancing. At this time she generally no longer attacked me, but she fell asleep or distanced in other ways, which could be an unconscious attacks. However, she could now let me know that if she gave either of us her love, she was afraid she would lose all her power. I explained to her that loss of power lay in withholding her expression of love, not in expressing it. She, however, feared love as a submissive dependence on an object that would either be too powerful and would wipe her own sense of identity out ("I'm grey. I haven't been filled in yet."), or the object would fall apart

(I"m afraid if I depend on George, he'll fall apart."). She articulated these specific fears, which earlier had been merged in with a diffuse annihilation terror, during the second year of treatment.

As Lois began to understand the fears behind her attacks, she was able to have some compassion for herself. This softened her self-condemnation.[1] She now could tolerate the grief of her guilt, regret, and remorse. Although owning one's hate is essential for making reparation to both the internal object (the mother-father figure represented by George) and to the external object (to George himself), the ability to feel concern about one's hostile attacks requires an understanding of the anxieties that compel the vicious cycle of hate and spoiling in relation to love. Lois had paranoid-schizoid-position anxieties of persecution, in which she feared having her identity wiped out or needing an object that would disintegrate. She also had depressive-position anxieties, fearing that she had damaged her good object and fearing the experience of grief and sadness accompanying guilt and loss. She was afraid that allowing closeness with George, as well as passion, would open up endless realms of sadness within her. She feared her sadness, like many preoedipally traumatized characters fear it, as an ocean of undifferentiated feeling that would flood her and drown her (frequently referred to by patients as the opening of "Pandora's Box").

Lois expressed both regret and reparative strivings in other ways. Sometime during the second year of treatment, she was threatened by a misunderstanding between us over my agreement to lower her fee, due to extreme cutbacks in her income and major new expenses. (Her rent had been raised by $350 a month.) She began to scream at me. She had not shown such impulsivity and hysteria since the earliest stage of treatment. I interpreted both the hostility and fear behind her screams, and asked her why she had to resort to screaming, when it only prevented us from communicating. I asked her why she wanted to regress back to tantrums and accusations when she could contain the feelings better now. I also interpreted why she felt so threatened, suggesting that she feared losing me if we didn't come to an agreement about the fee. She could see that I was not intimidated by her screaming, but concerned about her defensive use of it to push me away, thereby obstructing contact and communication. She was able to stop the screaming, to hear what I said and to respond to it. She was then able to apologize, saying "I'm sorry I screamed at you." She could never have offered such an apology during her first year of treatment. She had become capable of making gestures of reparation, which acknowledged her destructive aggression and the mode of aggression that killed off object connection. She was now capable of softening her hatred and yielding to the reparative strivings within love, so that an object connection between us could be sustained. She did not need to break down into a state of terror, as she once might have done, when she surrendered her aggression. Now, she could acknowledge her hostility with an apology, while staying in contact, and could expand the rapport between us, rather than going into a panic state.

Another area of conscious regret, demonstrated by Lois, was related to her work. She couldn't tolerate the feelings that hit her when she could not sit down and fully engage with a piece of writing. Formerly, as discussed, she had approached the task of freelance magazine articles with a manic obsession, in which she totally merged with the subjective characters within the article and could not be separate from them. Otherwise, she would have withdrawm from the work and been unable to do it.

At this later point in treatment, however, Lois was able to approach the work with normal human failings and to tolerate some disillusionment about her own creative powers, surrendering her image of being a star. She was able to feel the pain of regret for having postponed her work to the point that she could not do her best. In writing one particular article, Lois could not penetrate to the depth she wished to in writing the article, because she did not go into her former trance. Moreover, her conscious confrontation with the themes of the article and with the magazine that was required it, brought up intense psychic conflict. Being conscious while in the struggle to do the work, Lois was able to recognize that her conflict between pleasing the marketplace and writing to plumb her own depths caused her to procrastinate. That is, feeling that she could not do both at once, she kept delaying her work. In telling me about this conflict, Lois was able to feel regret for her limitations. She felt this regret without attacking herself or another in order to expel the sense of regret. Now, there was no exorcism, discharge, or expulsion. She tolerated the symbolism of her own dilemma without enacting it in a sensory or visceral way at a protosymbolic level. In tolerating conscious symbolism related to the psychic conflict that inhibited her, Lois was able to feel the regret of her limitations in "becoming human." She became able to feel the grief of guilt that she couldn't perform up to the expectations of her ego ideal, which had formerly been assaultive, grandiose, and antilibidinal.

During one session, Lois spoke of this regret and then saw an expression of sadness on my face. She asked why I looked sad. I said that I was feeling some of her own sense of regret as well as perhaps some of my own. She was able to take in my emotional message and to re-own her own sadness a bit in the rest of the session, sensing that she was deflecting some of her own grief into me. She became quiet and sensitive to both me and herself, rather than whirling off in a Red Shoes mania. She connected to her feelings and to me and so was able to be in her body.

TOLERABLE DISILLUSIONMENT

Lois began to tolerate disappointments and rejections that she could never have tolerated in the beginning of treatment. She was able to mourn in treatment and let go of failed opportunities, whereas formerly she became perpetually enraged, thinking she would not survive.

Lois had to come up against the disillusioning truth that her wish to be famous was a symptom of insatiable cravings to fill up the emptiness within with narcissistically gratifying images (the star hall of mirrors). But narcissistic achievements could not fill up this inner emptiness. By herself, Lois began to come to the realization that she would have to deal with her capacity to love and how she could kill it off.

At the end of the second year of treatment, Lois lamented, "I don't feel happy, even though I have this major article to write. All I'm working on isn't making me happy." She said this, just after she had pushed her boyfriend once again away. She had also been pushing me away. Through these experiences she began to realize that being famous was no solution. She still needed to realize that she couldn't deny her destructive attacks on those she loved, and on her own loving capacity, whether through distancing or through overt hostility. This realization needed to strike Lois in many different forms and ways, for her to begin to truly understand the sabotaging route she had taken. Cycles of disillusionment occurred repeatedly, helping her along in this assimilation process. She bumped up again and again against the same truth: achievement in her work would not fill up the void within. In fact, she found herself outside of the work process, hung up on the images of achievement attached to it, whenever she couldn't sustain love and connection with those most intimate with her. The work process would become full and alive only when she sustained these connections, which she did as she moved closer to psychic health and its love-creativity dialectic.

HEALING OF SEPARATION TRAUMA THROUGH THE CAPACITY FOR PLAY

During the latter part of Lois's second year in treatment, a vacation of mine brought out a new capacity in Lois to negotiate separation, indicating the gradual resolution of her separation trauma—the wound within being healed by opening it up and grieving the pain of it. The new capacity was the capacity to play. In fact, Lois had formerly shown a capacity to play. She had, as described, brought her stuffed dinosaur into a session and curled up with it on the couch, showing a capacity to use a transitional object. But now, Lois was capable of an extremely interactive form of play, with me as a whole and separate object. Furthermore, she was capable of play prior to separations, which could easily have been traumatic for her. In the past, she experienced each of my vacations as an abandonment, and they, therefore, triggered disruptive phenomena indicative of early separation trauma. However, she had been able to mourn and feel the deep grieving sadness of separation before my summer vacation the previous year. This mourning seems to have enabled her to deal now with my one-week spring vacation in a sensual and playful manner, openly expressing her instinctual cravings to possess the object. But her cravings did not have the intensity of instinctual addiction. Rather, they were to be symbolized and contained through interactive play.

The last session before my vacation was playful from the beginning. Lois started out provocatively, by saying "No check. I don't want to pay. I hate you!" Responding to the playful element in this statement, I said, "Why does it sound like 'I love you?'" Lois burst out, "I do! I miss you! I'm angry you're going away! I felt horrible all day—felt like a loser!"

In this way, Lois acknowledged knowing that the return of her negative hall of mirrors (and the "anti-libidinal ego" internal saboteur) was elicited by her anticipation of loss because I was leaving her. She spoke of obsessions descending on her. She was obsessed with being rejected by a magazine she wrote for. Her obsession was her image addiction, her negative hall of mirrors. But then spontaneously she recovered in the session. She didn't remain stuck in her obsession. She spoke of being insatiable—shopping and shopping—trying to fill up the void she knew she would feel when I left. Then she experienced the oral cravings behind her insatiability and moved again into play:

"I felt like chewing on the tissue," she said. "I've felt a lot like biting recently. I imagined biting George, hanging onto him with my teeth."

I moved into the transference with her, "Maybe that's what you want to do with me," I responded. To which Lois replied: "I want to do it to everybody, to everybody I like." I then said, "So it's a love bite!"

Lois agreed, but then moved into an expression of annihilation anxiety concerning our impending separation, asking, "Did you ever have a patient who had to go into the hospital?" Next, she entered into her obsession about being rejected and being a failure. But, as we talked about the hatred she would feel towards me that got triggered whenever I was about to leave her, we discussed the hatred turning into self-hatred, and her obsession with her stereotypic failure image. As a result she recovered and reentered into the play mode, as illustrate in the following dialogue:

Lois: It's like if I chew on you you'll become more real.

Analyst: What would it be like to chew on me?

Lois: "Very squishy and real—solid, and if I bite down, you couldn't get away. I feel it would enable me to get close to you too, because it would be so real. (Here Lois is regressing to a protosymbolic rather than symbolic level, but she's able to put the oral craving into words. The "real" becomes the psychic fantasy.)

Analyst: So if you could grasp it with your teeth it's real, like a snakebite.

Lois: Hmm. Hmm. Yeah, and also it feels good! It feels good to have my teeth have something to work on. Because it feels good. It's real contact.

Analyst: It's time to go. We have to say good-bye.

Lois: I miss you. Don't forget me. When you come back you'll have a big check. That's why you'll come back.

Analyst: You set it up so I'll come back for your money. Why don't you think you're valuable enough for me to come back to you?

Klein's theory on the depressive position directly leads into D. W. Winnicott's theory on the capacity for play. As Lois came to tolerate her depressive feelings (sadness and grief) and anxieties, she became capable of playing. According to Klein's phenomenology, once depressive pain can be felt, loss due to separation pain can be assimilated and symbolized, increasing levels of self-integration. Self-integration allows the imagination to be used for play, as symbolism emerges. Also, when Lois created new losses by the expression of defensive and distancing aggression (critical attacks or withdrawals), she began to increasingly tolerate the depressive despair that her own behavior aroused, so that she could feel the consequences of her compulsive behavior, and then she could begin to try to understand what fears made her drive others away. At this point in treatment, Lois could experience depressive despair, rather than act it out in behavior, or in sensory and visceral enactments on the level of protosymbols. In our dialogue, Lois regressed back to self-persecutory obsessions, related to the paranoid-schizoid position, but she gets past this by imagining biting into me. Although she was clinging to a concrete image in her mind, it was a spontaneous one that emerged, not a static stereotypical image from her hall of mirrors. The spontaneity was a sign of her capacity to play, as was the loving and jovial feeling we shared together as she spoke about biting into me.

THE CAPACITY FOR SATIATION AND REGRESSIONS TO IMAGE OBSESSION AND ENVY

For Lois, every move forward into object-related contact brought its backlash reactions. She receded into obsessional self-imagery. She suffered intensely from envy. The split in her psyche had been only partially modified by her mourning, and her internalizations of my understanding as a loving "good-enough" object within her: she still had a deep sense of self-doubt that triggered her negative hall of mirrors, no matter how successful she was. Success only brought an insatiable craving for more success, because the narcissistic supplies she received could never fill up the interior void. Only a sustained loving connection with another (an external object), as indicated, could fill that void within; only a love connection could touch her core self, where mind and body joined. When she was obsessed with some real or psychically manufactured rejection, or was comparing herself to envied others on whom she projected her own grandiose images, she was totally in her head. The disconnection from her body left her overwhelmed with a constant sense of insatiability. This disconnection often took the form of not being able to emotionally sustain an awareness of loving connections that she had formerly internalized. The symbolization of internalized love relations could be disrupted by the defensive splitting and cutting off which continued to transpire, related to repetition of early psychic disruptions, as well as to fears of incestuous wishes, and of preoedipal wishes to merge with the other through oral incorporation. Without the sustaining of internal love relations through adequate symbolization, Lois was left overwhelmed with a constant sense of insatiability, which in part had always been responded to by manic drives for lustful intensity through protosymbolic sensory enactments. These could be enacted through a malignant nonstop drive to pursue her creative work, or could be seen in the demon lover themes in the work itself.

As the therapeutic object relationship could be more sustained and symbolized, Lois reacted less often with protosymbolic enactments. She less often was compelled to repeat and discharge the effects of re-experiencing past trauma, and the combination of such trauma with incestuous and other psychic fantasy wishes exorcised in modes of projective-identification and sadomasochistic impulse discharge. However, Lois's experience of conscious envy was a midpoint development between the raw discharge phenomena of the protosymbolic enactments and the psychic containment of object connections in symbolic form, a containment which could facilitate sustained "good-enough" interpersonal relations.

Lois spoke of being haunted by images of her girlfriend's job and boyfriend. She regressed into a constant state of envy, as we spoke of briefly before, in which she discounted and devalued everything she possessed. Lois split her hall of mirrors into the negative introjections applied to herself, and employed the star hall of mirrors, and the fundamental splitting behind it in projections onto her girlfriend. Behind her envy was a fear of loss. Lois spoke of being afraid she would lose her girlfriend to the man her friend had fallen in love with and who seemed to make her very happy. This fear caused Lois to envy everything about her girlfriend. She envied her girlfriend's job, which she saw as "fast-paced and high-powered." She daydreamed about having such a job herself at a time when she had quit a job to stay at home and write a major article. But sitting at home made Lois feel merged with her internal depressed mother, who had stayed at home when Lois was a child, while her husband went to work in an office.

Now the merger was experienced with the girlfriend, who could represent the preoedipal mother with whom Lois wished to merge through oral incorporation, felt at a higher symbolic level as envy of all that her girlfriend had.

The vicious cycle of envy took its toll. Lois killed off her love for her own boyfriend by comparing him to her girlfriend's boyfriend, as she herself knew from analyzing her own spoiling process, from the time of her first dream of sexual desire for her boyfriend. As she eradicated what she herself had, contaminating any loving internalization with her hate and envy, she felt worthless. Then she saw herself as without an identity: "I'm grey. I haven't been filled in yet!" Or she would see herself as containing disgusting stuff inside—garbage—even regressing back to feeling like snails—big, grey, and dripping, at times. Or she gave up on loving and said, "I can only love doggys, not people. I have conversations with doggys in my head."

When she emptied herself out with her envy and hate, she ended up fearing that if she did allow herself to love her boyfriend, and to own and experience what she did have, he would leave her. She was also propelled by fear of loss into a position of envy, as in fearing her girlfriend would leave her to be exclusively with her girlfriend's boyfriend. This only increased her envy. Her girlfriend and her boyfriend became the exclusive dyad (or parental couple in intercourse) she could not get into. She was on the outside looking in, and she couldn't value anything she had. The girlfriend became the mother in the Red Shoes dream. That is, the girlfriend was seen as the who wins the man through her achievements. The man was seen by Lois as a glamorized extension of the woman. Again, it was the woman Lois wanted, the mother figure, the star-image mother (who represents much more than a "phallic mother")—not the depleted and depressed mother of the negative hall of mirrors. But the Red Shoes mother dances away from Lois, as she goes off with her man.

Lois spoke of her envy: "If I heard that Carol and her boyfriend were having problems, I would feel much better. I would be able to enjoy myself more with George then. But knowing that Carol is having this happy time with her boyfriend makes me feel that what I have with George is worthless." Here we can see that on the level of psychic fantasy, Lois saw the penis inside the maternal body as perfect whereas the penis inside her was impaired. This psychic fantasy emerges at the level of primal oral oedipal psychic fantasy, as opposed to the differentiated oedipal level in which the man is valued for himself.

Lois: I start watching George for all his defects. He sent me flowers today, which was so sweet, but I wished they were from someone else. He already wants me.

Analyst: You feel you have him so he doesn't count.... You just want to be wanted. You can't sustain any wanting of him. The wanting to be wanted is an insatiable craving. You want to get more and more people to want you as an antidote to your deep self-doubt, but you'll never get rid of your sense of being defective that way. George has become contaminated by your sense of being defective. If he wants you, he becomes worthless and all you can see is what you see as his defects—his weight, his drinking. To love him and need him makes you fear that you'll want him more and more, and then he'll either fall apart or leave you. So you kill off your love and your desire for him. Then you can't take him in and sustain a sense of love inside of you. You kill off what you have, and then you're insatiable to be wanted, and you can't love or work. The Red Shoes dance is a dance of insatiability. You can't slow down.

The cure for this can never be attained in an intimate relationship, because all intimacy is wiped out by spoiling and devaluation. The only cure is within the therapeutic object relationship, in which where the moment-to-moment devaluation of object connection can be addressed. Lois needed to allow herself to need me and to deal with who I was to her in the transference. She imagined me to be on either side of her hall of mirrors split. She thought I had a husband who was either an impoverished academic or a husband who was a high-tech doctor. When I was in the star hall of mirrors, she envied me and excluded herself from having me connected to her. For example, she said: "You're well-known. You don't have any need for me." She made herself either defective or invisible, and she did the same damage to the image of her boyfriend in her mind. If he was not "the one," what was the point of going through all this to try and work things out? Finding the "one" could only be an insatiable quest.

This cycle of envy and image obsession affected Lois's creative work, as well as her love relations. Kohut (1971, 1977) has assumed that those who need narcissistic supplies in creative work can simultaneously have adequate interpersonal object relations. Kernberg (1975, 1980) has countered this view. The disruption and failing of internal object relations, Kernberg argues, always affects both love and work, because work is related to the sustaining of love for internal objects. When these internal objects split into idealized and bad or devalued forms, work is a problem.

For Lois, work could become caught up in the cycle of insatiability. When working on a major feature article, she kept gathering more and more material, never feeling she had enough. She would also sit alone trying to write, and be distracted by the isolation of her surroundings, feeling like her depressed mother sitting at home. When she connected to the work, however, she could start sailing into an active engagement with her internal objects. The work became alive. However, as soon as she stopped working, the image obsessions took over. She would feel the work losing value. She then obsessed about it. She began to fear that everything she was doing in her work was wrong or inadequate. She feared that she didn't have enough facts, or had too many facts. She feared her commentary on the facts were not enough, or she feared the commentary was too much. She was compelled to write more and more, and to gather more and more facts, but she also felt afraid to get into the work when she was disconnected from love relationships in her life.

Then, one day she discovered how profoundly she needed interpersonal love to fully embrace her work. This realization enabled her to replace her compulsion to create, and its accompanying block, with a freer motivation to work and to surrender to her creativity. After a weekend away from her boyfriend, when she had stayed with her family, she felt filled with love. This was a very new experience in relation to her family. It reflected how our object-relations analysis had helped her to detoxify the bad-object projections she had formerly placed on her family. Now she could both be with them and take them inside of her as good objects. On her return, she was able to open to grief and sadness. She sobbed when with her boyfriend. She let herself go and was able to open up to sex, love, and tenderness with him.

And then an amazing thing happened in relation to her work. Suddenly, for the first time, she felt that she had enough material to write the major story she had been engaged to do. Of course, this was only amazing to her. From an object-relations perspective, her new capacity for satiation was quite explanatory. When Lois sobbed out the grief of her need-fear dilemma (Guntrip, 1976), the dilemma of needing an object she was afraid of being abandoned by or engulfed by, she opened her core self to potential love relations in the present. She was then able to connect to others from deep within herself. Specifically, this allowed her to open to her boyfriend because she had the inner psychic space to internalize him. Then she no longer felt as if she was being engulfed or trapped by her boyfriend. She was able to willingly surrender to his entrance into her and her entrance into him. With such interpenetration she was able to take in enough contact to face her work with a hunger for engagement, which was no longer insatiable in nature. Her fear of abandonment lessened as she sobbed out the grief of former object loss and felt the guilt of regret in having killed off former relations. Then she could give herself to her boyfriend without fearing he would either fall apart or leave her. Feeling satiated with love, rather than insatiable, she could feel that she had enough in her work. She could stop her endless search for information, and could feel confident that she had enough to write a meaningful story. She says for the first time, "I just felt ready to write."

CAPACITY FOR GRATITUDE AND OBJECT SURVIVAL

Melanie Klein has juxtaposed a whole complex of psychic phenomenology in terms of envy versus gratitude (1957). From the time of Klein's major treatise on "Envy and Gratitude" (1957), a ratio of proportion between hate and loving capacity had been defined in interpersonal terms, as envy versus gratitude. The capacity for gratitude is the culmination of object-related experience. It signals the healing of the splits and self-isolation perpetuated by the vicious cycle of envy.

Although the spoiling dynamics of envy resurfaced in Lois even as she mourned and entered the world of object relations, this envy occurred as a backlash reaction against growing object-relations connections within her resulting from the therapeutic relationship.[2] When she could not face the fears of need and loving another or the fears of wanting another more and more, she disowned what she had and became envious.

As Lois tolerated these periods of envy and managed to open up new phases of grief and mourning by bringing the disruptive spoiling states into treatment, she became increasingly able to express gratitude. After our work within stages of powerful resistance, as in the second half of the second year of treatment, Lois would seem to suddenly connect with a deep loving core within her. Then she could say to me: "I am really grateful to you, not only for what you just said [I had been interpreting the self-sabotage of her loving connection to George], but also for how you've stuck with me throughout this whole intense period, when I've been pushing you away."

Lois offered me this heartfelt gratitude quite freely. It informed me that she was aware of her sabotaging maneuvers against me, and of my persistent involvement with her despite these maneuvers. In D. W. Winnicott's terms, I had "survived" her aggressive attacks on me as a subjective object, so that I could begin to be experienced and valued as a separate object. The connection between Lois and myself, with me as a separate object, had also been attacked by Lois. Bion speaks of "attacks on linking" (1959). Lois had become much less prone to launching aggressive assaults, characterized, as indicated, by accusations and emotional blackmail—during her transition from rage to the sadness of grief within the depressive position. But she had been pushing me away by many distancing maneuvers. Sometimes she just felt tired and couldn't speak in sessions. She then used up her time on the couch sleeping. This would often occur before some separation between us, when she didn't feel contained enough by the treatment, or when she had to cut down her sessions from three to twice a week due to a major reduction in her financial condition. When she did the same thing with her boyfriend, George became enraged, telling her that her sleeping was a way of slamming a door in his face. When she did it with me, I interpreted her fear of engagement with me and her inner world, but I stayed present emotionally with her while she withdrew. When she didn't want to get into anything, because she feared the dark places within her, including her sadness, I stayed with her emotionally. Only an analyst could stay through all her pushing away maneuvers. I survived by staying emotionally present with her, ready to relate to her whenever she showed a capacity for contact. In this way I survived as an object in Winnicott's terms, letting her kill me off as an object, when she used me as an environment only, and yet still being there. Lois could feel my connectedness, often expressing surprise that I remembered so much about her or that I understood her fears and motivations. It was a sign of her increasing self-integration, the diminishing of splitting and envy. It was accompanied by the increasing capacity to see me as a whole object from a position of separation and love. This new self-integration allowed Lois to consciously process my way of being with her, seeing me as a separate person—not just as an extension of herself—someone who was able to loyally attend to her. She had killed off the fantasy omnipotent object, and I had survived as a real human being. Her expression of gratitude said all this. She was now much more in the depressive position, in which losing another meant feeling regret for her hate, but not projecting her own aggression in order to distance from the other and from her own guilt. It meant being able to value the other's love throughout, not examining the object for defects.

CHANGE IN PSYCHIC STRUCTURE THROUGH THE TREATMENT

In order for Lois to move towards a love-creativity dialectic, in which she could freely move between interpersonal intimacy and her creative work, it was necessary that core aspects of her psychic structure change. Such change occurred throughout her object-relations analysis. Towards the end of her second year of treatment, she had a dream in which a wounded Nazi figure appeared. The parts of the dream Lois recalled were as follows:

> Lois saw herself lying on the couch in a therapist's office, an office like mine. Even though she was in the position of a patient, she was supposed to be doing rape counseling with a rape victim. This old man came into the office to be counseled. Instead of talking seriously with the rape victim, Lois, in the dream, was talking conversationally, like she was just shooting the breeze, for example, exclaiming in a jovial manner, "So how are you doing?"
>
> Then the old man, who is wearing a loose tunic, and is partly naked, turns around, and Lois sees that he has a wound in his anus, from which some puss is emerging. Lois suddenly sits up straight on the couch, realizing that this is a serious matter, and that "This man has really been raped!" Then she sees that the loose tunic that the man is wearing is a military tunic, and she then realizes that the tunic is part of the Nazi S.S. officer uniform. Even though this man has lived in the U.S. for a long time as an ordinary businessman, he is a Nazi S.S. officer from Germany.
>
> Lois runs out of the office to go and speak to her supervisor. She says that she can't counsel this man, because of his background. It would violate her ethics and be a conflict of interest.

Lois's associations revealed that Lois thought the wounded Nazi in the dream was a part of herself. What is so interesting about this man is that his wound was in his anus, where he was supposedly raped, and yet he wore a military tunic which turned out to be sign of his having been an S.S. officer in Germany as a young man. The Nazi theme had, as discussed, appeared in her dreams before, but never in such a visual and personal form. Lois had mentioned the Nazi part of herself, her fascist standard of excellence that she could not live up to, and so felt assaulted by. She also had spoken of identifying with this inner fascist operating like a split-off pathological psychic structure, as in Kernberg's (1975) pathological grandiose self. Lois's fascist was both grandiose and abusive, like Fairbairn's internal saboteur or anti-libidinal ego. The fusion of real self, idealized self, and idealized object existed, but it was joined with the aggression of an anti-libidinal ego (Fairbairn, 1952) or anti-dependent self (Seinfeld, 1990) force.

However, this psychic structure, as represented by this new Nazi figure was transforming. The Nazi was now wounded. Some integration had been effected between the sadistic part of Lois's psyche and the masochistic victim part. This new structure needs to be contrasted to the earliest figures that Lois had symbolized in her internal world, an "aborted fetus" and an "energy demon." Later, as discussed, she dreamed of a man beating a woman. When Lois first came into treatment, her view of herself as an aborted fetus was a part-object image split off from its counterpoint, "energy demon," another part-object image. Both of these figures were more human than the snail (which represented the aborted fetus). Yet they existed symbiotically joined in relation to one another only. Thus, the hostile demon part of Lois aborted all her object-connected experience, leaving her feeling like an aborted fetus, and totally disconnected from her body. Her whole being was wounded psychically and narcissistically injured.

Lois's dream of a man beating a woman came in a film version, like the porno movies she had been watching. Such blank silhouette figures could not be called whole objects, but they were closer to whole objects than the aborted fetus and energy demon. They were human, yet on film; because they were on film they lacked three-dimensional aliveness. The man beating the woman was joined to the woman *through the film*. The two lacked full autonomy and separation, but were partially separate, characteristic of all sadomasochistic human relations.

The wounded Nazi represented another advance. He needed help to reveal the puss running out of the wound in his anus. Thus, he was not omnipotent and split off from the body, like the far-off Nazi ghost figures in Lois's past dreams. The assaultive, raging, and grandiose anti-libidinal part of Lois had been softened into a wounded vulnerability. Lois had become human. She was no longer a fetus or a woman being beaten, although her erotic life might still be peopled by such fantasies. Lois was also no longer split off from her body in the form of an energy demon, or of a sadistic man beating up a woman. She was seeing herself as a male, her femininity visible only in her more conscious self—the woman on the therapist's couch, doing rape counseling. But the dream's important theme

was that of condensation of vulnerability and fascist violence. The Nazi in
her had become human through experiencing his vulnerability. Lois's
internalized Nazi was no longer a woman being beaten, but a man being
raped and seeking help. The whole object form, as Lois saw herself in this
figure, had surrendered his fascist sadistic origins, openly showing a need
for another. This dream image signaled the integration of the wounded
victim (her vulnerability) and the sadistic and grandiose abuser (her
aggressor). The depressive-position mourning process had allowed Lois
to integrate her vulnerability and aggression, and to be openly dependent
so that emotional contact can be made with the wounded emotional and
body self within.

SELF-INTEGRATION AND THE LOVE-CREATIVITY DIALECTIC

With self-integration, the healthy love-creativity psychic dialectic can be
realized. I have described the many phases of developmental growth in
Lois. She has moved from protosymbolic sensory and visceral enactments
to a level of more sustained symbolism in her emotional and intrapsychic
life. She has opened psychic space for new psychic structure internalization through opening the core wounded and rageful self. She has opened
to good internalizations through mourning critical abandonment-depression loss and depressive-position regrets and remorse. She has gained
insight into her repetitive modes of spoiling good experience and ending
up eviscerated from within, permitting envy and splitting to take over and
diminish all that she had. She has gained insight into her manic attempts
to work compulsively, seeking success and achievement, while running
from images of failure. She has begun to see how this Red Shoes mode of
racing away from her body, her emotional needs, and the love-object-
related connections within, left her depleted and fearing a loss of her sense
of self. She had seen how her inner split-off body parts and demons were
part of an arrested or pathological mourning process, in which her vulnerable self disowned its own aggression and remained a victim and a
child.

These developmental processes, along with insight into her intrapsychic dynamics, have allowed Lois to have times of self-integration, when
a free-flowing movement from love to creativity and back to love is possible. She still is blocked in the dialectic at times. But the opening up of
its possibilities is the result of moving past modes of splitting off from her
body and from interpersonal contact. She increasingly owns more of her
inner life, rather than expelling, discharging, or psychically warding it off
through projective-identification. She tolerates increasing degrees of grief
and sadness and allows me to be with her in the psychic places that used

to seem like voids or black holes. She no longer is in a perpetual state of insatiable craving, typified by sucking from another. She is able to truly take in another now, to receive and give back. She is able to repair disrupted object relations. She can make reparation through apology and is able to offer gratitude. This process enables her to take in the other as a good object. It is a sign that a good-object connection is being constructed within her through our treatment.

As treatment continues, it shows how Lois is moving towards even greater self-integration and thus towards a more complete love-creativity dialectic. I can now help her detoxify a bad object in one session, as indicated in the following example. One day she came in overwhelmed by hatred for a relative who had selfishly imposed on the solitude she had established at her father's country house where she was finishing an important article on deadline. This female relative had insisted at the last minute on coming to the house accompanied by two friends. Lois was beside herself with rage at this intruder, who ignored her pleas to be left in peace to finish the article. Once the relative showed up, she selfishly played loud music with her friends. Lois was forced to leave the premises with her boyfriend.

During our session, Lois said that she could not get this relative out of her mind. She was haunted by what she wished she had said to her. The relative had become a toxic internal object, (like the snake in her earlier dreams), which she couldn't let go of. Yet, even while acknowledging that she had turned this relative into an internal demon, Lois was able to salvage some psychic space for love of her boyfriend and me. She was able to tell me of her boyfriend's support during this episode, his quick and intelligent comprehension of her plight, and his continuing emotional support throughout. She was able also to trust me to help her disgorge her toxic object and, with this, the hatred she felt towards the relative, which kept the internal demon object alive. Lois realized that no matter how justified she might be in her anger, she was carrying a hatred that had nowhere to go. With my help she could see that it was inflamed by the painful disappointment caused by her father's inability to help her. He had "whimped out," when she asked him to deal with the woman who was assuming an entitlement to use his property, at the last minute, without any consultation with him. Her father had been sympathetic, that's all. In other words, he did not rescue nor protect his daughter, when he was the only one who had the power to do so. Lois realized, with my help, that she was re-experiencing the trauma of her father's inability to protect her as a child, particularly when she was raped. In the session we got past her hatred for this relative whom she had no hope of communicating with, past the help-

lessness caused by this incident, to the anguished pain of her injury in relation to her father's failing her in the past. Her pain was palpable, and I
told her so. She now had the psychic space to experience my empathy, for
she was no longer overwhelmed by the hate, which, with its conversion
into the image of the hated object, had formed a persecuting demon within. As a result, she also felt the grief of the loss of love for her father at
that moment, and for the new form of damage to her newly repaired relationship with him. She was able to understand that her pain came from a
deep place where she housed the love for her father, and the past disappointments and injuries to her idealized view of him. She was able to
mourn her own regret that she couldn't have more fully repaired her relationship with him, so that he could have understood her better. In this
way she could face her limitations and realize that she could only do so
much. Through such mourning in this single session, she realized that she
did have the choice to communicate again with her father, but that she
needn't until she was ready and wanted to. She also was able to realize
that it was her father who was important to her, not this female relative
who appeared to be beyond any accessibility to communication. She was
able to feel validated by my understanding of her responses to the relative and her father, without having her anxiety "reassured" away concerning the effects of her hatred towards the woman who had become a
bad object. Through connecting with me in the session, and through this
mourning of her father, Lois was able to feel love again. The next session
she said that she had left this session feeling close to me, feeling that I was
her friend, and feeling aware of her love for her boyfriend, whom she so
often devalued with unrelenting mental criticism. Moreover, she observed,
the female relative had lost her omnipotent and tyrannical demonic power
in her mind. The relative had resumed the stature of a distant and rather
unimportant person. This deflation was in keeping with the psychic reality of who she was for Lois, compared to the distorted psychic fantasy
that had so inflated the relative's importance, when hatred had overwhelmed love in Lois's intrapsychic economy. Working through the hatred
to the love, through mourning within the therapeutic object relationship
with me, had allowed Lois to increase her capacity to repair her internal
world and to sustain loving connections with those most important to her.
In this example, her boyfriend and I had become more securely installed in
her internal world as loved and loving objects, who assumed priority in
her intrapsychic and her external life. Her father was also reinstated as
an appropriately ambivalent love object, whom she could have a rapprochement communication with if she so chose. The urgency to reach
her walled-off father had subsided, as had her urgency to retaliate against

him and the female relative. Lois was able to discuss with me her impulse to retaliate, calling it a compulsion to punish them by treating them coldly. By articulating the symbolic expression of the retaliatory impulse, Lois could give it up, and move to a position of free motivation rather than compulsion. This affected her entire capacity to be freely motivated within her creative work and her external interpersonal relations. She was able to concentrate then on completing her article on deadline, because she could sustain internal connections to her creative work.

Additionally, in the realm of her interpersonal love relations, she was now able to carry forth her newfound appreciation of her boyfriend into action, by offering to rent a house for a month with him. She thus demonstrated her growing mutual capacities in creativity and love, in other words the psychic health of the love-creativity dialectic. In renting her own summer house, and, therefore, not being overly dependent on her father, Lois also freed herself from a position of helplessness to one of a realistic autonomy. Now she could allow a realistic adult dependency on her boyfriend to grow, and could allow the development of his dependence on her.

14)

THE CASE OF MS. C.

The following case was reported to me by a male analyst who was in private supervision with me for six years. He had already seen the patient for five years prior to our meetings. Pieces of Ms. C.'s history were disclosed to me over time. After I gained my colleagues's permission to write up the case (and after he received permission from the patient), I received the main dynamics of the treatment.

PRESENTING PROBLEMS

Ms. C. was an attractive woman in her early twenties when she entered treatment. In the middle of the break-up of her first marriage, which had lasted four years, she was searching for an ideal lover. She had become disillusioned about her husband, who she no longer saw as her ideal love. She also was seeking the father who she had lost in childhood, which partly explained her choice of a male analyst. At the beginning of treatment, Ms. C. had some superficial awareness of her underlying motives, which became a much deeper understanding as her sense of loss opened up over time. The patient's search for her father was linked to a search for an idealized self. This self was merged with her attachment to her father and his mirroring of her during early childhood.

Ms. C.'s presenting problem was related to her search for an ideal self. She was experiencing frustrations in her work as a fiction writer. Specifically, she was blocked by her own unique fantasy of the creative mystique. Ms. C. believed that if she could write a novel, it would be such a masterpiece that her life would be changed. So far, she had written short stories and poetry. But these pieces of writing she had proved capable of

producing did not carry for her the magic aura—the idealized self-projec-
tion—of the creative mystique. It was the idea of the novel that entranced
her, but it was also the idea that blocked her. For by focusing on the image
of her novel, she cut off the organic process of creativity, during which,
moment by moment, she could create the novel, just as she had created
her short stories. In addition, her preoccupation with the mystique of creativity and its product supported a fantasy of self-cure. According to this
fantasy, all her interpersonal difficulties would become irrelevant once she
was transformed into a famous author, arousing everyone around her into
an intense state of adoration and admiration. She had the fantasy that
after achieving fame through her novel, she would go off and live on a
mountain. There, she would not need anybody because everyone would
want her. She would receive tons of fan mail and could pick and choose
who she consented "to give an audience to." She would be "like royalty."

Ms. C. responded with coldness and distance to the analyst's first
attempts to question this fantasy and her related adamant belief that she
would not have to feel any need for anyone once she achieved fame. She
erected a wall against the analyst by withdrawing emotionally. She also
spoke in a monologue so that she couldn't be penetrated by any wounding
interpretations or questions.

MS. C.'S EARLY HISTORY

Ms. C. started life with some difficulty: she was a ten-month baby, whose
birth was induced. Her mother's ambivalence about having a second
child, after already having raised eight-year-old boy was evident from the
time of her daughter's birth. Ms. C.'s father was the one who desired a
second child. His wife went along with him without expressing any of her
own feelings. Perhaps the somatic effects of withholding such feelings
accounted for the rather difficult and delayed birth. In a sense, Ms. C.
came into the world after first having been held back and then having
been pushed out (induced) by drugs and doctors. Her own sense of agency
seems to have been thwarted from the start.

As Ms. C. grew up she played two notes: either she was the cute child
in the family, the special child of the father, or she was the mother's child
who was used by the mother as a container for her own badness. As the
special child of her father, she had to encounter the wrath of her mother.
Being bad was a way of bringing her mother and father together. Her
father punished her and her mother screamed at her. Both parents then
did not have to deal with their anger at each other. Eventually, Ms. C.
became the family scapegoat, for her brother also joined in the attacks,
accusing her of naughtiness and misdeeds. However, even while enacting

this role of black sheep, Ms. C. remained her father's adored and special little girl who was much applauded by him as she was brutally criticized by her mother. These encounters became highly eroticized during the oedipal period, when Ms. C. was alternately adored by her father through photographs he took of her and other intensely laudatory attentions, and also was spanked (at five) and later punished by him for being the bad kid who gave everyone so much trouble.

The two spankings she received when she was five became cemented in Ms. C.'s unconscious as highly eroticized events, in which she was the center of an intense engagement with her father. These episodes were later to form the essence of her most powerful erotic fantasy. The original repression of such a shame-ridden fantasy life caused blocks in sexual relations. Her sexual problems were another aspect of her original presenting symptoms. She compensated for them by her fantasy of ultimate arousal through the achievement of the creative mystique.

Ms. C.'s father died during her latency years from a heart attack. She was left alone with her mother for her brother was away at college. The period immediately following the father's death was characterized by intense involvement between Ms. C. and her mother, in which they may have reenacted dyadic mother-daughter dynamics from Ms. C.'s preoedipal years. During this period, Ms. C. regressed to babytalk and coy cuteness, which allowed her to be petted by her mother. This regressive behavior promised to satisfy her mother's cravings for touching, holding, and affection, which she could no longer share with her husband. Ms. C.'s double-binding mother actively seduced her daughter into regression, and then disowned her seduction. In fact, while disowning, Ms. C.'s mother expressed anxiety about her daughter's behavior, which provoked intense guilt in Ms. C. Consequently, Ms. C. received two contradictory messages from the mother. One message was that she should be cute and babyish. For example, she should talk baby talk to invite tender tones and caresses. The other message was that something was wrong with her for acting like a baby. After lulling Ms. C. into the cute baby behavior, the mother then suddenly pushed her away, exclaiming, "Why are you talking like that?" Repeatedly, Ms. C. experienced her mother as putting some part of herself into her, and then being targeted as the one with a problem. When her father was alive, she had been seen as the bad one. In the immediate period after his death, she was seen as the crazy one.

Ms. C. responded by feeling trapped and suffocated. The situation was exacerbated by the general manner in which Ms. C. had been treated by her entire family throughout her childhood. She was always talked about, never talked to. Nobody addressed her as a person with her own opinion or with her own voice. She was either adored as cute or criticized as bad. There was no opening for a dialogue between her and another.

During adolescence, Ms. C. escaped from her mother by falling in love with a teenage boy who provided a whole new crowd of friends for her. Then, in her early twenties, she escaped into marriage.

However, now that she had a husband of her own, Ms. C. had to contend with her mother's envious assaults. Internalizing these attacks, Ms. C. developed a hostile "internal saboteur" (Fairbairn, 1952). She also had to contend with her mother's attitude of "nauseous disdain" toward her. If she did poorly at anything, her mother attacked her for being inept and incompetent. Often, the attacks were expressed through criticism to others, behind Ms. C.'s back. For example, Ms. C. overheard her mother speaking on the phone about her, using this tone of nauseous disdain. At other times, her mother made snide but pointed comments to her face, belittling and shaming her daughter with her contempt. The mother's hostile aggression targeted Ms. C. where she was most vulnerable. Since she was young, assaults like these had sent Ms. C. running into the bathroom to cry. The bathroom became a refuge, a place where she could find temporary privacy and safety.

The attacks had no relation to Ms. C.'s behavior and achievements. Modes of opposite behavior drew the same fire. When Ms. C. received consistent 99s as grades in honors classes in high school—and a score of 100 on a math Regents—her mother was even more disdainful. She accused Ms. C. of "overdoing everything," of being unable to find a "happy medium." Fire seemed to escape the dragonlike nostrils of her mother as she bitterly articulated her disgust for her daughter. (As we will see, her mother became a "Chinese bulldog" in one of Ms. C.'s nightmares.) Once again, Ms. C. was viewed by her mother as a bad extension of herself, while her brother was viewed as the mother's good part. Ms. C. felt damned by her mother if she did and damned if she didn't, since failing a test or receiving a 100 on one occasioned the same hostile response. Always bad in her mother's eyes, Ms. C. internalized this vision. In a lofty attitude of supreme knowledge—something like Edith Sitwell's father's omnipotent and overriding assertion that "We happen to know!" (Kavaler-Adler, 1993)—her mother was always "right."

Tensions rose even higher when Ms. C. got involved with men. Not only did her mother sneer at her teenage daughter for her deep involvement with "a boy!," but after Ms. C. and her boyfriend broke up, her mother's contemptuous ridicule knew no bounds. Seeing Ms. C. in a deeply depressed state during the break-up, the mother perpetually attacked Ms. C. for being "so stupid" as to care so much about a mere boy, "when there are so many boys around!" (Her mother replaced lost objects rather than mourned them.) In her analysis, Ms. C. came to understand that her mother's own mother had been depressed and that her mother was quite anxious about seeing her own daughter in a depressed state. Her mother's attitude, as Ms. C. admitted later, was "what the hell does her daughter have to be depressed about!," since in her mother's envious eyes, her daughter had everything while she had nothing. This false perception caused Ms. C.'s mother to be totally incapable of understanding her daughter's depression and how it extended beyond the loss of her boyfriend to the loss of her dead father. The mother's own depression was covered over by her hostile contempt for her daughter. The hostile contempt served as a manic defense to avoid the guilt and depressive affect the mother was unable to tolerate.

After Ms. C. was married and divorced, her mother expressed her scorn even more strongly, but now her seductive attitude was operating in counterpoint. Near the beginning of Ms. C.'s psychotherapy with a male analyst, her mother made indirect and provocative comments to others in her daughter's presence, intended (perhaps only unconsciously) to arouse her daughter. This occurred during a dinner party at her mother's. Ms. C. was invited, along with her mother's friends, some relatives, and a bohemian cousin of her mother's who brought a Yugoslavian friend. The comment by her mother which stood out for Ms. C., and which seemed intended specifically for her was "Everyone's sleeping with their therapists these days!"

Ms. C. wondered if she was elected to be the tantalizing and scorned part of her mother who acted out her mother's repressed sexuality. Her mother's sexual needs had been more severely inhibited than ever after her husband's death. She claimed that for Ms. C.'s sake, she never dated men, as her daughter was still growing up. When Ms. C. was in her twenties, her mother did date one man. However, her mother's contempt obstructed any actual romantic involvement. Ms. C.'s mother barricaded herself with her attitudes of disdain, spreading the poison from Ms. C. to the man she herself was dating. She claimed to be too intellectually superior to him to take him seriously. Meanwhile, during Ms. C.'s early marriage, the mother made comments to Ms. C. about how "sexually dynamic" her husband seemed—unlike the men of the mother's age—and bemoaned her own anguish as her son-in-law "never brought her flowers anymore." She expressed envy and jealousy of Ms. C. with a complete lack of awareness. Her resentment was exuded in critical attacks on her daughter's marriage culminating in her encouragement of the couple's divorce. Soon after her divorce, Ms. C. had an affair with a foreign man—

a Latin lover. Her mother took a rather exaggerated interest in it, while also anxiously pushing Ms. C. to break up the relationship.

It was following these events that Ms. C. entered into a serious term of psychoanalysis with a male analyst. She had already developed her symptomatic syndrome of a compulsion to create, with its creative mystique. The syndrome had developed as she defended against the anguish of her incorporated internal mother by aligning with her adoring father and his validation of her as a creative and special person. Her creative work carried the projection of the adoring father and was, therefore, the intense focus of her merger with him, and with his narcissistic image of her. In her yearning to write a novel, Ms. C. combined a genuine creative motivation to express her inner voice with a profound compulsion to be reflected in the flattering gaze of her father's eyes. She sought displaced representatives of her father's adoring gaze, as a way of warding off the wounded and shame-ridden self that was tied to the sadistic part of her mother and to her mother's spoiling and devaluing view of her. Her bond with her father was also enacted in another way in her creative work. It was an erotic bond as well as a narcissistic bond. She needed to feel that she was special and beautiful to her father.

However, there was a dark side to her father's love for her and hers for him. Her father was both her muse and her erotic demon lover. After all, he had spanked and denigrated her to ease the jealous rage of his wife. He was, therefore, another source of her shame and deep humiliation. He was also the source of her incestuous desires, and her creative writing carried both the narcissistic mystique of these desires and the erotic impulses themselves in a sublimated and symbolic form. But, as discussed, symbolism cannot substitute for mourning, although symbolism of subjective desire may evolve from adequate mourning. The creative work could never substituted for the deep desire for a romantic love with the father, for a deep love between the father and daughter, which did exist, and which had been internalized. Ms. C.'s fantasy of self-reparation through some ultimate recognition that would come through writing a novel played into her illusion that the creative product, and the response of its audience, could substitute for a deep primary heterosexual love, a love which had been a resource for all intimate interpersonal relations in adult life.

COMPULSION TO CREATE AND CREATIVE WORK TRANSFORMATION

Given all this, Ms. C. clung to the mystique that she gained through her special role with the father—the father who sang show songs to her, took her on trips, put on her ice skates for her—the father who continuously snapped photographs of her. The mystique was like her father's adoring photographs, a shield against the conscious experience of a shame-ridden inadequate self. In other words, her idealized or grandiose self, reinforced by her father's positive mirroring, was the shield she held up in her conscious mind to keep out a deeply humiliating self view.

The negative view Ms. C. warded off was filled with both the psychic imprints of her father spanking her and of her dependent and needy self being scorned, rejected, and hated by her contemptuous mother. Through Ms. C.'s creative endeavors, and sometimes in the context of short romantic affairs with men, she permitted the counterpoint shield of the mystique its development in the world. As Ms. C. got older and became increasingly involved with the man who became her husband, she increasingly invested her modes of creative work with her self mystique, which became a creative mystique. Due to the need to defend against an awareness of the darker side of herself (which was connected to her negative mother and to the intensely arousing and humiliating erotic father of the two spankings), Ms. C.'s creative work became a prominent compensation that was weighted with her defensive needs. In her twenties, disillusioned with romances that never lasted, since they were based on childhood fantasies of being her father's little girl, she turned more and more to her work to express the pain of her repeated disappointments. She created female characters who had grand triumphs in winning men over. But her fictional women ended up either being enraged that the men didn't live up to her ideals, or being ashamed that they themselves didn't live up to their ideals. Sometimes the female characters were dropped and abandoned as their true personalities emerged. They lost their men as they emerged beyond the facade personas that, in an attempt to treat all men like personal photographers, they initially displayed. Ms. C.'s facade selves often appeared in her writing as female caricatures who perform novel and exotic roles in the world, but who are inevitably found out to be fakes.

As Ms. C. made progress in her treatment, and she began to contact all the split-off and hidden parts of her that she was ashamed of, her female characters changed. They were no longer only one-dimensional, reactive, and false. The new female characters were capable of feeling exposed, humiliated, and deeply confused by the eruption of the darker sides of themselves. And they were self-aware, self-revealing, and openly ashamed of their intense neediness. They were deeply involved with Ms. C.'s male characters. The male characters also changed. No longer naive romantics, who turned into sadistic villains, they were now integrated figures, with completely ambivalent emotions. As the individual female and male figures were transformed, so were their modes of interaction.

In the early stage of Ms.C.'s creative process, characters were either polarized in isolated internal or external monologues—frequently espousing their personal philosophies—or they merged with each other through shared romantic fantasies. After Ms. C. was able to mourn her genuine losses, and by this process, heal her psychic wounds, she achieved separation-individuation, integration, and internalization, and had worked through severe oedipal conflict. As Ms. C. mourned within her own treatment, she became capable of describing interactive behavior between her characters. She wrote dialogue that did not just reflect two alternate sides of a philosophical system, but revealed the emotions of authentic characters engaged in genuine interaction.

TRANSFERENCE WORK AND MOURNING

The two main transference dynamics in Ms. C.'s treatment were the idealized father and the negative or devaluing mother. In an object-relations context, the patient's positive father transference was not merely a resistance imposed from the past on the present: it was also a powerful striving for object connection that cultivates motivation for treatment. This transference was analyzed, understood, and allowed to transform from idealization to a more integrated positive object attachment. The intensely negative mother transference, which sometimes had an overlapping mother-father transference dynamic within it, was also a mode of object connection that was founded on intense sadomasochistic eroticism or eroticized longings for mothering combined with eroticized aggression. Each transference required the working through of mourning in order for the object-relations psychic structure to be transformed from childhood modes of relationship into more adult modes of relationship.

Early treatment was dominated by profoundly idealizing transference, hiding the negative mother transference, which could at times turn quite paranoid. Breaks in the early symbiotic bonding that fostered this idealized transference, at preoedipal and oedipal levels of dyadic relationship, caused acute disappointment reactions. Intense rage expressed through distancing contempt and criticalness—sometimes with an underlying terror and distrust that prompted threats of leaving—characterized these reactions. Ms. C. experienced sudden levels of distrust, when her idol toppled from his or her pedestal, prompting such intense panic that she wished to escape immediately from the presence of the analyst, who in those moments appeared to her as demonic. For here, all his motives became questionable. He seemed, she believed, to be out to control her totally and malevolently through acts of seduction. In her mind, this behavior on his part meant that he would keep her forever with him, and so prohibit her from any form of autonomy. Later, these projected, anticipated, or actually observed seductions would be analyzed by patient and analyst. They related these so-called seductions to the mother's crazy-making seductions, in which she actively pulled her young daughter back into a symbiotic mother-infant orbit, and afterwards cut Ms. C. off, making her feel abandoned and humiliated.

Each time the male analyst descended the pedestal from ideal father to demonic mother, the patient's rage challenged the analyst to survive without retaliation. When the analyst did become critical and retaliatory in response, Ms. C. went crazy with rage. She was then fearful that to escape her murderous impulses she would have to leave the analyst and leave her treatment. Faced with such fears, she became overwhelmed by anguish, acting out her need for support and holding, as well as her hostile provocative rage, outside of treatment.

When the analyst successfully survived Ms. C.'s rage, accepting the patient's criticisms without retaliating with coldness, cynicism, contempt, or reactive criticism, Ms. C. felt enormous relief. She immediately relaxed her entire body. The analyst's survival (Winnicott, 1974) allowed Ms. C. to begin a long, and initially intensely painful mourning process, related to the critical object loss of the beloved and idealized father. Grieving this loss, over the course of twelve years of treatment, Ms. C. connected her severance from the father, who had given her a more positive sense of identity than her mother, with the earlier loss of the mother that probably occurred whenever the mother had withdrawn into anger. In addition, there was an earlier critical rapprochement loss with the mother, reenacted with her current therapist, which earlier had forced Ms. C. to end a previous treatment. The patient had left her former therapist. She left this former therapist at the point when she felt that the therapist, onto whom she had projected the seductive rapprochement mother, or latency stage mother, severely threatened her autonomous strivings and needs for success.

The mourning process contained an intense abandonment depression, for the loss of the latency father also had meant being deprived of a critical self-extension (or subjective object). Earlier needs for positive mirroring and for tender emotional contact, which the alternately intrusive and distancing mother had frustrated, had attached to the father, particularly during the oedipal and postoedipal years, when he became the center of her romantic yearnings. However, these romantic yearnings were combined with earlier symbiotic yearnings for the mother, which had been traumatically frustrated during separation-individuation and especially during rapprochement. This sequence of events had followed the normal practicing stage grandiosity. Perhaps the mother could not deal with her daughter's neediness, and so saw the practicing stage as a relief. At rapprochement, the mother, if she couldn't have her cuddly symbiotic baby back, may have already wanted a totally autonomous child.

The patient's yearnings for the lost father overwhelmed her when the fragile narcissistic defenses of pseudo-self-sufficiency and grandiose autonomy broke down. Early in treatment, Ms. C. alternated sessions during which she would cry throughout the time with sessions in which she seemed walled off in a mode of backlash distancing after having felt vulnerable. One can compare these distancing sessions, characterized by much intellectualization, with the intellectual sessions of Anne Sexton, which frequently ended in trance states. During her distancing sessions, Ms. C. fended off all the intense vulnerability of the crying sessions by building a wall of detached monotone intellectualization. Her analyst interpreted this monotone to be a compromise between seeking the adoring eyes of the lost father and fending off (by closing off her emotions) the negative eyes or negative mirroring of the mother. In these sessions, Ms. C. parried the feared critical and contemptuous attacks of her mother by keeping herself emotionally sealed off, while secretly hoping for the adoring response of the father to her intellectual prowess. The analyst also observed oedipal dynamics at work. As painful as it was during the first several years of treatment, the mourning of the father also revived the patient's powerful and passionate love for him. As soon as she expressed these emotions, she experienced real closeness with her analyst, part of the affect contact of her grief and love. On these occasions, the backlash reaction to her expressions of love, and to her shared closeness with a man, was guilt and fear. These darker emotions caused Ms. C. to go into hiding, by becoming detached and intellectual. On an oedipal level, she feared the internal mother's retaliatory wrath for her closeness to the father (and for her secret passion, her erotic fantasies). This wrath she projected onto the analyst—as an intermittent mother transference. In the face of this transference, Ms. C. felt compelled to close off her vulnerability, and all feeling. Intellectualizing was a way of still holding on to the object, but without any true self-pathway to contact. On a preoedipal level, her backlash reactions to grief and love were understood in relation to a mother-child dyad, with a backlash against the exposure of symbiotic love, relating to fear of coming upon the hostile mother of separation, who is inevitably encountered after symbiosis.

This mother-child dyad was played out in the transference with the father. Ms. C. projected the preoedipal mother into him. The backlash that appeared after she expressed love for the father was seen as fears of the father leaving her again. Also, Ms. C.'s closeness with the analyst promoted erotic arousal accompanied by intense guilt. She had to defend against her arousal, for its incestuous nature, and, therefore, its threat to the bond with the mother, the latter manifesting as guilt-ridden obsessions about women being angry at her.

These two levels of fear surfaced in the process of sessions. In some sessions Ms. C. behaved with notable detachment and intellectualization after opening up to the grief of mourning. By contrast, in other sessions, Ms. C. seemed to be reliving oedipal stage spankings by her father, which were experienced as punishing and simultaneously intensely erotic. Ms. C. induced feelings of anger in the male analyst, which he began interpreting as Ms. C.'s projective-identification, as she put the spanking father into him, making him feel like spanking her. These spanking reenactments were interpreted as backlash reactions to the love within the mourning. They both extended and inflamed the love into eroticism, while also providing a punishment for the love and the erotic wishes. Thus, the patient acted out a masochistic appeasement of guilt towards the critical oedipal stage mother, and the same appeasement towards the father for her crime of trying to seduce him into incest. These transference dynamics became an intricate part of the mourning process.

The sadomasochistic internal relationship to the father, and the erotic fantasies related to it, operated as a repressed, but gradually emerging erotic transference within the treatment. With mourning in treatment, a separation process evolved. This evolution enabled Ms. C. to become more capable of working in an analytic fashion in treatment, that is, her free association became richer and her immediate body reactions had interpersonal meaning. She also grew more conscious of the fantasies her male analyst aroused in her and began to experience conscious erotic fantasies while making love. Previously, her sexual fantasies had been either intensely symbiotic and unconscious or rather constricted, especially when she had lived with her former husband who had the potential, because of her history, of becoming an incestuous object. In addition, she became aware that her most arousing fantasies were spanking fantasies that related back to her father's spankings. Her intense affect withdrawal, in response to the humiliating memories of spankings and fantasies of spankings gradually reduced, as she was able to articulate these fantasies to her male analyst and to thereby lessen her shame. With time, the erotic transference became a more overt part of her deepened connection with her analyst. Throughout treatment, grief and sadomasochism continued to be intricately interwoven phenomena for Ms. C. These reactions were traced to her father's death, after which they had generalized to all relationships that brought exquisite sensitivity to loss, along with love, making the sadomasochistic reenactment a distancing defense against object loss. The distancing defense is an inevitable backlash against the growing capacity to love. However, the analytic re-living and defining of the origin of the sadomasochistic dynamisms allowed psychic transformation.

DREAMS

The patient's dreams revealed some of the interplay between the significance of the object loss she experienced related to her father's death and the object loss caused by hostility. In one dream, reported during the fourth year of treatment, a small child is alone with a mother, who behaves coldly and with detachment. In the dream, the mother announces in a regal and imperious manner, "I have decided to die!" In response, the little girl—with whom Ms. C. felt consciously identified—starts crying and says "I need you." The more hysterical and upset the little girl becomes, the more the mother withdraws. A vicious cycle ensues, in which the more the mother withdraws and gets cold, the more the little girl cries and protests that she needs the mother. In response the mother detaches even more. The little girl becomes increasingly hysterical.

Another dream, reported in the fifth year of treatment, revealed the bind the patient felt herself to be in. This bind related to being trapped in a dyadic relationship with her mother, when the developmental time for such a dyad was past, and the need for a third party was obvious. The dream apparently depicted the state of Ms. C. after her father died during her latency and while her brother was away in college.

In the dream, Ms. C. is an adult interred in some kind of concentration camp. She fears that she is doomed. Ovens stand inside the camp, and she will be sent to them to suffocate. If the prisoner attempts to escape she will be stopped by tall wire-mesh fences, with huge Chinese bulldogs mounted on the top of them. The bulldogs have longpointed teeth and roar like lions. They have powerful tails like dinosaurs. Desperate to survive, Ms. C. makes an escape attempt. Exhausted from running towards the gates, she struggles to climb the wire fence, while trying to evade the grasp and teeth of a Chinese bulldog. Finally, she gets through a hole in the fence, one where no bulldogs are. Quickly, she scrambles down the other side.

Ms. C.'s associations to the dream revealed her rage to be projected and encapsulated in the Chinese bulldogs. She experienced this rage as coming at her. The analyst's attempt to interpret Ms. C.'s Chinese bull-dogs as symbolizing her own split-off rage were unsuccessful at this point. The patient was still experiencing herself as the victim-child self helpless in the face of a possessive, yet abandoning mother. Later in treatment, as she increasingly mourned her object loss, Ms. C. became aware of her own out-of-control rage—her rage was somewhat similar to Emily Dickinson's perspective: "But since we got a bomb and held it in our bosom" (*The Complete Poems*, #443, Kavaler-Adler, 1993, p. 229). Inbetween this ear-lier stage and the later stage, Ms. C. experienced the demonic mother as within her, as an internal object, which created fantasies of murder simi-lar to those in this nightmare.

Being seduced back into the mother-child dyad at this time must have put severe stress on Ms. C. in her efforts to develop autonomy and to workout a latency age resolution to earlier oedipal dynamics. In addi-tion, regressing back into this primal dyad seems to have prompted ear-lier separation stage trauma to reappear. Perhaps, however, the separation-individuation phase was actually less traumatic than the latency stage since Ms. C.'s father was at least present during the earlier phase. The mother's resistance to the daughter's separation, as appears in this dream of the initial fantasy mother, shows why Ms. C. was com-pelled to fuse with the father. When her symbiotic yearnings could not be resolved—often resulting in sickness and somatization—and when there was no adequate positive view of the self—due to failings in infant connection and internalization, she was compelled to use him as a nar-cissistic idealizing self-extension.

GROWTH IN INTERPERSONAL RELATIONS

Ms. C.'s original difficulties in interpersonal relations highlight the syn-drome of the "compulsion to create" and its accompanying creative mys-tique dynamic. If Ms. C. had not undertaken extensive object-relations psychoanalysis, she may have ended up driven to self-destruction, as the heroine of the *The Red Shoes* or the sculptor Camille Claudel. She could have withdrawn into seclusion as Emily Dickinson did or become emo-tionally isolated (see Kavaler-Adler, 1993). She could have been taken over by illness and despair, as was Katherine Mansfield. She could have fled into impulsive and short-lived sexual relations, as Anne Sexton did. Or she could have ended up as vengeful and retaliatory as Sylvia Plath was. In fact, at different times in her life, Ms. C. had tended in all these directions.

However, her early and extended entrance into object-relations psy-choanalysis enabled Ms. C. to express her extreme despair in her treat-ment. She was able to mourn deeply and to work through her mourning repeatedly and intricately during twelve years of treatment. In conjunction with the mourning of loss, she was also able to work through psychic conflict in erotic relations. Her self-deficits and self-losses were experienced in conjunction with this object-related mourning.

In addition, Ms. C. opened up to the full range of interpersonal relations she had closed off in defending against vulnerability to loss, disappointment, and oedipal psychic conflict. She saw how interpersonal growth expanded and deepened her creative-artistic work, while simultaneously freeing the work from the overpowering pressure of internal compulsion that dominated any freer motivation. Formerly, she had been compelled to compensate for profound lacks in interpersonal development and fulfillment with creative self-expression. Her mourning opened the way for interpersonal connection, contact, and fulfillment and this modified the compensatory role of the creative work, and allowed her to do progressive mourning within the work. The steady working-through of mourning was understood in treatment as it interacted with primary transference dynamics. These transference dynamics were not only resistance but primary strivings for object love and connection.

An object-relations focus responded to Ms. C.'s primal loss and its vicissitudes. Each session provided an opportunity for the analyst to see how Ms. C. avoided affect contact that would allow object connection. The primal yearning for an object, which had to be opened up in treatment, had been, as discussed, arrested—resulting in the sealing-off of self. This primal object need was at the time of disruption not yet at an interpersonal (or intersubjective) level when disruptions in developmental mothering had occurred. In regressing to early object relations during treatment, the patient returned to modes of relationship that were not yet mutual or interpenetrating. In cases like Ms. C.'s, the analyst may be viewed, at first, as a narcissistic self-extension (this view originating in symbiotic needs), or the analyst can be a transitional object from the separation-individuation phases.

Ms. C.'s early interpersonal relations were marred by the blocked psychic state she operated in because of unmourned loss. Ms. C. had left her husband because she felt alternately alienated from her husband or suffocated by his needs. Ms. C. had mainly been left alone by her first husband. Intensely involved in his own career, he had not objected to his wife's pursuit of an independent study, career, and friendships. However, this independence had come at a cost: Ms. C. experienced extreme disappointment concerning her original hopes for romance and intimacy. Moreover, as Ms. C. grew more invested in herself, and in her own creative and professional work, she no longer experienced her husband as an adequate self-extension. Because she discarded her narcissistic idealization of him, Ms. C. no longer hoped that they might share everything in the world. Some early rapprochement wish for sharing and intimacy seems to have been severely disappointed by the man she had picked for a first husband. He had been her teenage boyfriend, who while rescuing her from the regressive symbiotic orbit with her mother, revived her earlier oedipal desires for her father. From the start, they had both invested in creating a romantic love, which they had kept alive through a long-distance relationship, when Ms. C. was away at college. However, once they married and lived together, Ms. C.'s romantic dreams rapidly deflated. For she discovered little or no intimacy at the core of her marriage. Even before she entered treatment, she had started an early grieving process, crying for her lost teenage romance, which at sixteen had seemed sweeter than any sweet sixteen imaginable. Her ability, however, to grieve on her own was quite limited. She expressed some of this grief in creative dance, but mostly she handled the ensuing depression, brought on by her marital disappointment, in two other ways.

One way was to have affairs with other men, which later led her to a desire to leave the marriage and be single. Ms. C. had very little awareness at this time of her own difficulties in marriage, because in a new romance she found herself capable of an intimacy she had never experienced with her husband, even when their passion for each other had been alive and fresh. Her ability to be intimate in a short-term love affair was deceptive. Ms. C. didn't then understand how intimacy on an ongoing basis was quite different—that it required dealing with the losses and disappointments of the past that contributed to her alienation from anyone who did not continuously adore her. The incestuous dynamics in her marriage blocked Ms. C.'s sense of herself as sexually powerful and alive. In her unconscious, her husband had become an adoring father and a critical and angry mother. Once she felt that anger, Ms. C. lost the romantic love ideal that had previously inflamed her sexual passion.

The other way that Ms. C. dealt with her disappointment in marriage was to create a life separate from that of her husband. Having married quite young (at the age of nineteen), she had never really built a life with him prior to their marriage. During her adolescence, she wanted to remain in her husband's orbit. Therefore, she became the center of his crowd, no longer building relationships and activities outside of his sphere. The one exception was her dancing, which she continued to pursue. During the last years of her marriage, Ms. C. expanded her life increasingly beyond the circumference of her husband's world, especially in relation to her creative work. As Ms. C. experienced the loss of her earlier hopes for her marriage, she turned to her creative work to give her the emotional depth in her life that she was craved. And within the realm of the creative process, Ms. C. did find a transitional space in which to reveal her deepest feelings. Through dance improvisation, she expressed her heart, and she gradually became a successful choreographer. But Ms. C. seemed unable to bring this deep level of self-expression into the realm of her interpersonal relationships. She still could not communicate in an intimate way over time with anyone. In fact, even the initial intimacy she experienced in a new love affair was more fantasy than reality. The intense feelings of closeness she experienced in these love affairs, which she always hoped would last forever, and never did, were created by sharing her personal history and her fantasy life with a man. In a sense she created her own ideal self in how she related to the man and in the terms of what she told him about her. She only did so when the man clicked into an image that aroused her most intense erotic desires. At first, it was a man's flamboyance and exhibitionism that aroused her. Then it was his tenderness and his passion. With these ingredients she needed to see a protective quality and nurturing side. This combination of traits touched her deeply, because they were qualities she had identified with in her father. The problem was that genuine intimacy involves two people genuinely getting to know each other over time. Ms. C.'s projections of her father onto any new man, at the point when he was revealing his ideal self only obscured her seeing the real man. When she actually saw the real man, as she did finally acknowledge her husband, she felt profoundly disillusioned. She had not been able to navigate through this disillusionment to allow loving feelings between herself and any man to revive. She ended up criticizing and abandoning or being criticized and abandoned. She was unaware of how her earlier losses contributed to this disillusionment. Awareness came only with treatment.

As. Ms. C. drew further away from her husband and decided to divorce him, her sense of loneliness dramatically increased. She had one long-term love affair with a male dancer that lasted for two years, giving her the illusion of hope, but it too ended for her in dramatic disillusionment. With each blow to her naive faith in romantic love, she turned more deeply to the creative process. Her romantic fantasies took the shape of fantasies about being a famous dancer and choreographer (Red Shoes mystique). Although she had great gratification from expressing herself creatively, the gratification was short-lived, because the self she created in the nonverbal mode of dance remained split off from the rest of her life. This self-expression never reached the level of words that could be communicated to others in her life within daily, ongoing interpersonal relations. Therefore, the only times she felt seen was when she was on the stage. This put greater and greater pressure on her to be on the stage. No matter how hard she worked, she never felt like it was enough. She was never on stage enough. Even when she was, no matter how responsive the audience was, in the end it was composed of anonymous strangers. It did not include any one person whom she could know and be known by in a mutual and intimate fashion. To express the encroaching despair she felt in response, she wrote a short play about an aging ballerina who could not live, because she could no longer perform on stage and receive the audience's applause. In Ms. C.'s play, death came quickly when the ballerina lost the mirroring of an audience that served like a drug, which only temporarily compensated for the loss in her childhood of recognition and the lack of an internalized loving other in her childhood.

COMPULSION TO CREATE

As Ms. C. became increasingly disenchanted with love relations, she began to have only long-distance relationships with men. She withdrew more than ever from dating and from involvement with any one man. Even the men she might meet from out of town, who she might initially have a good time with, quickly turned disappointing. By their second encounter, she would frequently withdraw emotionally. As a result, her erotic desires, and her passionate desires to love and be loved by a man, were poured into her creative work.

Increasingly, Ms. C. developed themes in her dancing of victimized engagements with men. These male dance roles she choreographed showed men with enormous power over a woman because of her romantic desires and men who ultimately used and abused a woman. Often, they abused a woman by abandoning her after engaging in an intense mutual seduction. Both Ms. C. and her alter-ego female dance characters disclaimed their own seductiveness, and like her mother, they appeared to be child-waif victims of conniving men. As Ms. C. acted out her compulsion to submit to sadistic men—within the dance, and as she relinquished all her personal power to empower these male villains—she was simultaneously caught up in the manic erotic power of her creative urge. Her creativity began to feel more and more like a compelling drive, driven especially by the incestuous desires that went with her need for object connection. She not only placed her attachment needs in the creative process, but she also placed her narcissistic needs for the mirroring-back of an idealized or grandiose image into this process. The combination of the two forms of need-attachment and narcissistic attachment created the manic erotic intensity of the Red Shoes that could never let her rest. The symbolic shoes drove her to create and perform incessantly until she dropped. The creative self—the one viewed by the audience—became invested with the projection of the unmodified grandiose self,[1] the self symbolized by the Red Shoes.

In this way, the creative process itself, became invested with the hubris of the creative mystique. Sometimes Ms. C. experienced this as a star image. She yearned to glow, to remain forever a focus of fame, to glimmer perpetually in the eyes of her audience. This audience, although anonymous, was invested with the aura of her father's ideal self. The audience shined its radiance back to her as it took on the air of her father's intently adoring eyes, the eyes that told her that she was special. She, in turn, danced for "his eyes only" when she performed for the often too idiosyncratic and unpredictable audience. The Red Shoes syndrome I am describing might also be identified as the demon lover syndrome—as needs for a man and for a father-mother figure were re-focused on the creative process, becoming increasingly vicious in intensity over time. Therefore, when Ms. C. finally entered psychotherapeutic treatment with a male object-relations analyst, she was at a point where her emotional starvation had caused her to reach a breaking point. She was trying in vain to substitute creative self-expression for interpersonal intimacy and love. Frantic anxiety, obsessional thoughts of despair, and states of severe self-depletion resulted.

TREATMENT CHANGES IN INTERPERSONAL AREAS WITH PARALLEL CHANGE IN CREATIVE PROCESS

Ms. C. slowly surrendered herself (with regular backlash reactions of distancing) to facing the burden of loss she carried. It was a painful process. During the first year of treatment, tears poured out of her eyes in intense waves that echoed the rhythms of childbirth—as did her breathing at times, when she grieved so much that it seemed as if her cries were the primal cries of an infant. Years of increasingly refined mourning followed this initial intensity. Under all the intricate transference dynamics—idealizing, erotic, and aggressive—was the core experience of loss. Each time loss could be tolerated in the company of the analyst, love was renewed, and the terror of contact and connection was lessened by a degree. In between each step of mourning and of the memories accompanying the affects of grief—triggered by relations with the analyst in the present— were the backlash reactions of distancing. During the first five years (three sessions per week), Ms. C.'s movements between connection and backlash distancing, which originally had appeared in alternating sessions, gradually began to overlap within sessions, so that some chance for connection with her analyst, and with her inner self, was experienced within each session time. Ms. C. began to distance during only part of the session, rather than for an entire session. Then, towards the end of the session, she felt an intense anguish as the scales of her own walling off dropped from her eyes, and she realized that she was hungry for connection with her analyst. In other words, instead of remaining walled off throughout the entire session, she began to realize sometime during it that she not only felt alone but wished to connect with him. She realized that her intellectual monologue about herself did not encourage the paternal adoration she desired: in fact, it did the opposite. It was up to her to open herself so that the analyst's concern, understanding, and love might penetrate her, thereby forming in her its psychic internalization, which would then allow her to sustain the longevity of contact with her inner self. With more and more mourning, and the consequent self and other contact over the years, Ms. C. was able to more freely stop herself. She could now hear the compulsive course of her monologue—which mirrored the compulsive solo performance in her creative work. With the freedom to stop, breathe, and be aware of her actions, she reduced the compulsive monologue which hid secret wishes for mirroring and holding. The walling off from contact and emotion, while in the monologue, had numbed Ms. C. to an awareness of her sadomasochistic sexual fantasies, as well as warding off awareness of the preoedipal needs and trauma.

Then Ms. C. had a choice—one she never had prior to treatment—to let go of the monologue, and to open herself to whatever expression of self came from a deep feeling connection within her, which in turn held promise of inviting an inward response from the analyst. In this way, intimacy could truly begin. The difference here between the moment of contacting herself within the creative process, and that moment within the therapeutic process, is interesting. The unique benefit of the therapeutic process was that at the moment of Ms. C.'s contact with her inner self, the analyst was there to meet her, not only to hear her words, but to feel her feeling and her need, and to help define that need. The analyst's responsiveness encouraged a counter-responsiveness by Ms. C., which in turn elicited a new response from the analyst, ushering in a spiral of mutual responsiveness. The mode of dialectical responsiveness at this point was as important to Ms. C.'s cure as the understanding that they shared through the experience. They made connections together—in contrast to the analyst's simply interpreting. They made connections between past and present and between the sequence of events leading up to the present moment. The process of analyst and analysand making connections together was as important as the connections being made. This mutuality and interpersonal dialectic can be described in terms of what D. W. Winnicott called the "going-on-being" of the true self when it is supported. The moment responsive contact was made, which also depended on the affective presence and readiness of the analyst to connect, Ms. C.'s inner self felt a presence that could enliven it and could sustain its being in the world. This support of the inner self for its communication within the interpersonal matrix, allows interpersonal dynamics to develop and to be internalized, forming new structures or "rigs," which in turn allow contact with others.

THERAPEUTIC PROCESS IN ANALYSIS IN CONTRAST TO CREATIVE PROCESS
Unlike this epiphany of psychic response in the therapeutic environment, Ms. C.'s inner self in the creative process environment could remain sealed off, as it transferred its message to the dance floor or a sheet of paper. To the degree that affect contact and connection are formed, creative work depends on the reverberations and echoes of internal objects, since no external others are present. Internal others mirror, hold, and respond, but not in direct interaction as do external others. Often, internal others simply echo one another. For example, it would have been quite a different story for the choreographer George Ballanchine to have expressed his creative ideas to himself only, while choreographing from them, rather than having Suzanne Farrell there to be responsive to his thoughts and feelings in the moment.

Ms. C. could not form such creative collaboration in the way Ballanchine and Farrell did for many years. Prior to treatment, Ms. C. had been limited in the object relations of the creative process in parallel to her psychic limitations in the interpersonal process. Her mourning process in treatment was the critical variable that transformed these limitations.

LATER CHANGES IN INTERPERSONAL LIFE
How did Ms. C.'s life change with treatment? I have already delineated some of the changes that deepened, freed up, and enriched the creative process. What were additional changes in her range of interpersonal relations? As the mourning process in treatment moved forward, Ms. C. resolved her transference resistances, such as speaking in a monologue that demanded the transference father's mirroring. She transferred these addictions to her projected internal father, where they served as resistances to live desires for object connection. Ms. C.'s hunger for her mother, as well as her yearning for father, could begin to be felt through her love and desire for the analyst.

The stable holding environment of the treatment allowed Ms. C. to relax some of her hypervigilant anxiety. Her outside life could, therefore, move forward, as she began to date men again. Before too long she had found a man who she loved and decided to live with and then later marry. At the same time that she allowed this heterosexual relationship to develop, she also began to deepen the intimacy of her female friendships. Over the years, she became increasingly committed to her new husband, who was the most solid man she had ever been with. He was far more capable of intimacy and sharing than was her first husband, who had been extremely manic, competitive, provocative, and contemptuous, while still adoring her. Her new husband was not as adoring as her first, but he was far more capable of truly comprehending and loving Ms. C. for who she was than was her first husband. He did not alternate between naive adoration and contemptuous or mocking criticism—as her first husband had. The problem Ms. C. and her second husband had was that Ms. C. was very quick to feel intruded on by her husband's basic needs for her availability. It took up to ten years for this to significantly change.

Ms. C.'s addiction to the creative process was multidetermined. Ms. C. loved the creative process because it had always been her salvation, especially when she was starved for self-expression and recognition. However, the compulsive behavior attached to her creativity undermined the very joy that had originally led her to the process. Furthermore, her compulsions pressed in upon her, making her feel she never had enough time for creative work, which, in turn, made her react defensively to demands for her time and attention. This defensiveness caused the most difficulties in her new marriage, as her husband felt neglected and emotionally starved for time to be with her. Also, during some of the early years of this marriage, Ms. C. withdrew emotionally from the sexual part of her relationship with her husband, after having been passionately sexual with him during their dating and engagement periods. Scared of an ongoing intimacy that aroused incest guilt and fears of her internal hostile oedipal mother, she also feared the intimacy within commitment that arouses anxiety over losing the other. To ward off contact with her husband, she turned to her creative work. He responded with anger, either rageful, cold, or distancing. To defend herself against a profound guilt that evoked unconscious accusations from her critical and attacking internal mother (now experienced as a superego part of herself), Ms. C. became hostile.

With this cycle of anger and guilt generated in the marriage, Ms. C. was less likely than ever to turn to sexuality for love and intimacy. She automatically substituted her creativity for her sexuality, creating untoward stress on her creative life while starving herself of emotional life by depriving herself of the joys of both emotional and sexual intimacy. Again, as after her first marriage, Ms. C. began to deal with disillusionment of her initial hopes for an unending romance. She felt like withdrawing from men, as her husband was inevitably disappointing. The more her husband openly showed his need for her, the more disappointing he became for Ms. C. As she felt disappointed with her new husband, she turned away from her hopes for romance within the interpersonal space in her life, and turned with renewed intensity to her creative work.

During her engagement period both Ms. C.'s sexuality and her creativity had been more freely motivated. Then, her romantic fantasies were focused on a life with her husband, which she fantasized to include children.

However, once disappointed in love, she focused on the creative process with a vengeance. This phenomenon was reflected in her analysis by her continual retreat during the first five years of her treatment to self-constructed monologues, which, as discussed, warded off the analyst and her own needs for emotional and sexual intimacy that she projected onto him. When the analyst was silent, and therefore did not act out the idealized mirroring father whom she used as a defense, he was often perceived to be an intruding mother. In parallel, she experienced her husband as the intruding mother at home, particularly when he demanded more time and attention. When she asked the analyst why he wasn't responding to her, when she was engaged in a monologue, and he replied that she was allowing neither contact nor connection, Ms. C. perceived the analyst as demanding something from her that she couldn't deliver, just as she felt her husband was doing. Her perceptions of both analyst and husband were projections of an internal mother who was always intruding on her, demanding too much, a mother who was never satisfied, and who was always distracting her from herself and her own creativity. (For example, Ms. C. said that she remembered moments of potential creativity being abruptly closed down by the sound of her mother's voice, which became a haunting ghost within her.)

As we have seen, Ms. C. struggled to sustain her sense of self by turning to her creative work, which was invested with her fantasy of the idealized mirroring and adoring father. She used the creative work to try to keep the intrusive mother out. It served the same purpose in relation to her husband—who carried the mother projection and served as a transferential mother. She became so busy with her work that she hardly had any time for him. She used other tactics to keep her analyst out. These included operating self-sufficiently in the session, avoiding any feeling of need for him, and by creating an image of herself through a monologue, rather than being in the room and moment with him. As the situation changed within treatment, due to the successful containment of the painful affect experiences of the mourning process, the interpersonal dynamics of Ms. C.'s outside life changed as well. Without undermining the genuine love that Ms. C. felt for the creative process, Ms. C.'s analysis enabled her to let go of the process in a natural and organic way, allowing a fruitful flow back and forth (dialectical) with her interpersonal life.

Through her creativity, Ms. C. expressed deep internal voices within herself. The process of the creativity gave her the stage of contemplation and deep meditative concentration that she thrived on. Through it she could explore, talk to, and resonate with her internal object world. The analyst, through Ms. C.'s treatment, always understood the deep roots of her engagement with the creative process and respected her creative resources. Nevertheless, he clearly saw that the fantasies and wishes projected onto the creative process gave Ms. C.'s "use" of it a pathological dimension. He clearly saw that Ms. C. was compelled to use her creative work, as well as the time she set aside for it, in a defensive manner, distancing from the whole arena of interpersonal relations that so frightened her. This affected not only her marriage, but her friendships.

Ms. C.'s analyst put this all together and saw that Ms. C. was driven by the creative mystique. He understood the mystique that, in her mind, promised fame and fortune, but instead triggered the incestuous desires and narcissistic images associated with celebrity. In addition, he saw that Ms. C. was driven by her defensive need to use her work to stave off awareness of emotional starvation and to use up the time which she needed to face interpersonal relations. As the analyst became increasingly aware of Ms. C.'s fears of a realistic intimacy, as opposed to a romantic enactment, she was threatened by the internal impingement of unmourned trauma. The patient needed to unseal her inner self, through contact with the analyst, so that she could consciously feel the abandonment loss associated with her father's death. The analyst's growing awareness of her fears helped her to come to grips with her loss. The analyst also became aware that Ms. C. feared the overweening control of whomever she became intimate with due to her background with an intrusive, compulsive, and critical mother. As has been shown, this mother had continuously sought to seduce her and possess her, while also frequently abandoning her via a frigid anger when Ms. C. confronted her with her own emotional needs. The mother's rejection was particularly evident and painful when Ms. C. needed empathy with her love for a man and her wishes for success and autonomy.

Increments of change that evolved in Ms. C.'s treatment were, all along, accompanied by parallel changes in her interpersonal relations, and particularly in her marriage. As she allowed increased contact with her analyst, which did enable her to consciously feel the pain of loss, this helped her to renew her ability to love and feel her hunger for contact, and Ms. C. became progressively more available to her husband. She attempted to include him in her creative work, and she also voluntarily surrendered her work for periods of time to be with him. Also, as her mourning in treatment allowed her to open up to a powerful erotic transference—which she had formerly warded off with her compulsive monologues, just as she had warded off object loss—Ms. C. began to feel, express, and face her body desires as they occurred in the moment, rather than splitting them off.

Consequently, Ms. C. spent more time in sexual relations with her husband. At first, because she was quite frightened of being more receptive, Ms. C. needed to play an active sexual role. But, as she faced her feelings of vulnerability within treatment, healing the wounds caused her mother's attacks and as she faced her vulnerability due to the early loss of her beloved and erotically desired father, she became more open and receptive. Her behavior toward other people also changed. Formerly she had compulsively talked about herself, thereby cutting people off, without awareness that she did so out of fear of the emotional contact that aroused sensual feelings, the kind of feelings her mother's seductive over-stimulation had stirred up. People constantly saw her as self-absorbed. However, in analytic sessions, she became aware of how she was starving herself of people by not letting them in. Her seeming self-absorption was actually a wall she put up against contact and vulnerability: it protected her against tenderness, sensitivity, and sexual desires. When unable to listen and take others in, she did in fact become extremely self-absorbed, but this was a by-product of her defensiveness, not its original cause. However, when people rejected her because of her lack of receptivity, she was frequently hurt. Her isolation was reinforced, and her compulsion to hide in her creative work to avoid these re-traumatizing forms of injury was reinforced. It became a vicious cycle, making her overly dependent on the creative mystique from the creative process to restore her fragile sense of self-esteem. She was re-traumatized by the rejections of others, because the primary trauma with her mother, who never listened to her and who also never shared herself with her daughter (so Ms. C. had nothing to listen to), was being re-created and re-experienced. Ms. C. became capable of listening attentively and receptively to people, truly taking in their messages and their own unique point of view.

As Ms. C. opened to sustained contact in these interpersonal areas, she became less dependent on the creative process to provide her entire fulfillment. She felt that she could still desire to dance or to write while now more conscious of the powerful needs behind a compulsive drive to enter these activities. Consequently, she could relinquish her work for periods of time, without fearing that she would lose it, or the desire for it, forever. Previously, when she attempted to surrender her creative work for periods of time, she would panic. She feared she couldn't survive without it. She feared being empty, and even starved, without it. As she became more capable of opening up to internalizations in general, as seen when she formed new rigs (internal blueprints) in the interpersonal area, she could actually now internalize the creative process—as she was engaged within it. In this way, she could sustain a psychic sense of her creative capacities. This discovery gave her hope about pursuing future creative work, even when she was away from the work for extended periods of time. Also, with this new solid psychic foundation, in which her self-image of a woman possessing creative capacities was imprinted within her, she had less need to project infantile symbiotic fantasies and oedipal romantic fantasies onto the work and into her creative goals. Increasingly, Ms. C. began to enjoy the creative process for itself, lessening her intense need to make it the target for fantasies that would be disappointed.

Thus, Ms. C. experienced parallel growth in the creative and interpersonal areas of her life, as the compulsive, avoidant, and grandiose parts of each were modified. She created a true love-creativity dialectic. Now, she could freely desire both love and creativity and freely navigate back and forth (organically) between the two primary realms of human experience. In essence, she was flowing back and forth between external object relations in the interpersonal area and internal object relations in the creative process area—in what Winnicott called the "transitional" realm of experience (1974).

THEORY OF THE LOVE-CREATIVITY DIALECTIC

Ms. C. is a living example of Klein's and Kernberg's parallel dimensions between internal and external object relations. She also illustrates that Heinz Kohut's theories, as articulated in 1977 in *The Restoration of the Self,* fall far short of understanding human fulfillment and the in-depth treatment needed to allow human gratification. Kohut's cases focus exclusively on creative work, and totally disregard interpersonal object relations. Kohut makes the assumption that his patients have adequate relationships in their lives, when they are actually disturbed in parallel with the difficulties in creativity, as one would know when one understands object-relations theory, and how internalizations of self and object provide rigs for both interpersonal relations and creative work relations. Kohut attempts to shore up the creative work capacities of his patients, while all the while disregarding the underpinning of psychic structure, as formed from fundamental object relationships. He substitutes mirroring for object contact, thus confounding the pathology in the creative area of his patients as they become increasingly compulsive in efforts to use creative work as a compensation for interpersonal deficit. His mirroring of patients' grandiose fantasies in artistic areas feeds the creative compulsion, compounding its addictive aspects. Mirroring cannot provide the creative process with the necessary object-relations internalizations that make one confident of having and developing creative capacities. The mirroring fuels a compulsion to produce creatively so as to have a self-image. Since that self-image lacks grounding in object relations, or in self and object psychic structure, it becomes a grandiose self-image that must repeatedly and addictively be driven by external mirroring. This is particularly true since internal representations of a truly embodied mirroring other are not allowed without opening up interpersonal space for internalized object relations. Thus, Kohut's mentioning of creative process cycles (Kohut, 1978), in which the artist hardly finishes a cycle of creative work before his "self," in Kohut's terms, *hungers* for more. This "self" that Kohut is describing is a grandiose self, not an organic, body-based one. A body-based one is a self-image that is integrated with instinctual life, through and with the interpersonal relations that are internalized as psychic structure. Kohut's artists, instead, feed a grandiose self that addictively hungers for more and more creativity, because the basic creative needs for fulfillment through intercourse with internal objects has not been met. Also, the primary intercourse with external relations in the interpersonal world may be discounted by artists. Without alive interpersonal contact, such people can dry up, as in the case of Emily Dickinson, (Kavaler-Adler, 1993), who withdrew from interpersonal relations, and had a psychotic episode (Cody, 1971), followed by later schizoid developments that gradually dried up her creativity. Without adequate levels of interpersonal interaction, artists are compelled to look more and more voraciously to the creative process in their attempt to express all their frustrated cravings for contact and connection, and in their hope to fill themselves up with audience response to such expression. Eventually, such artists will fail in creative areas, suffering the drying up of creative imagination, because the creative inspiration is not being nurtured by alive interpersonal relations. This means that a vicious cycle of creativity is self-starving, and ultimately even starves the grandiose self of the mirroring of compulsive creative work, resulting in schizoid deterioration, as seen in such artists as Emily Dickinson, Edith Sitwell, Virginia Woolf, Emily Brontë, and in Anne Sexton.

NOTES)

CHAPTER 1

1   In *The Compulsion to Create* (1993), I demonstrate the demon lover theme and complex in literary myth and Jungian dynamics.

2   This psychic fantasy form can be seen as being related to a deep structure of the mind (see Ogden, 1986 on Chomsky's deep structure).

3   The term "projective-identification" is a Kleinian term referring to the split-off self parts that are intrapsychically put into another, while still being felt as part of the self. Projective-identification can also exert an interpersonal pressure on the other who is present to act out the projection.

4   In Fairbairn's, 1952, system, it is the object's attack on the self that is continually repeated, but the fusion of split off self parts and object parts makes this a moot point. The self is attacking itself and its object, as much as the object is attacking the self. The Kleinian perspective accounts for the attacks on the internal object, which perpetuates the bad-object experience, and sets up a wall against reparative interpersonal relations. Without loving interpersonal relations, healing and mourning are arrested or obstructed.

CHAPTER 2

1   This transitional period is related to Margaret Mahler's separation-individuation stage of development, but it is not merely a linear period of time. The transitional stage, referred to by Winnicott (as well as by Fairbairn), is not just a period in time, but is also a psychic state, similar to Klein's paranoid-schizoid and depressive positions. The transitional psychic state has transitional phenomena associated with it.

2   Such innate blueprints can be understood in terms of Chomsky's mode of "deep structure," as noted by Ogden (1986, 1993), and need not be viewed as a priori psychic fantasies. It is the grammatical shape of such presences that may be innate, not specific contents. The specific contents only develop through the lived experience with the actual parents.

3   I differ with Melanie Klein on her timetable of depressive-position

mourning, in which she claims an infant enters the depressive position at six months, through mourning. The child's mourning is a primitive form of mourning: its cognitive ideation in relation to the other is limited, as is its capacity to consciously associate to memories of the other.

4   Since I am writing mainly about women I will use the pronoun "she" when referring to all children.

5   This dialectic can also be related to other psychic dialectics, including that of masculinity and femininity (see Ogden, 1993), and the dialectic of self and other involved in the mourning process.

6   Entering into the depressive position is an ongoing state of psychic affairs from early life. As Ogden has noted (1986) there is no one linear demarcation line in development where this occurs.

7   Fairbairn (1952) has used the term "repression" to describe the aggressive activity of the antilibidinal ego towards the libidinal ego. I believe that the psychic processes of splitting and schizoid dynamics that he was dealing with can be described more adequately as dissociation than as repression. Higher level repression processes are not available to individuals with traumatic disruptions in core self-integration (what Fairbairn refers to as central ego integration). Fairbairn, however, freely used the terms repression and splitting as interactive events. But recent psychic structure theory has helped us to see that splitting results in projective-identification, as noted by Kleinians, and that when higher level repression processes operate there is less dissociative splitting and expelling of inner contents through projective-identification.

8   They are capable of loving and hating the same object.

9   These are "subjective objects," where the other is used as a prosthesis for a void in the self, the void created by the missing functions of the early environmental mother. The resulting dynamics in the interpersonal world manifest as part-object relations, where the subjectivity of the other is denied, or where it overrides the subjectivity of the self.

10 James Masterson uses the term "maternal father" to refer to the father who is needed as a primary object by those with developmental arrest in the separation-individuation period (personal communication).

CHAPTER 3

1   In Melanie Klein's mode of manic reparation, there is no true reparation without mourning.

2   This inability to mourn can be contrasted with the French writer,

Proust, who in *Remembrance of Things Past* is able to mourn his youth and the loss of his mother—remembering a time when he had his mother. He had the early mothering necessary to build in the psychic structure to mourn.

3　As in Fairbairn's view of the moral defense in which one blames oneself to protect the image of the parent, 1952.

CHAPTER 4

1　This is quite a contrast to Emily Dickinson who claimed "no" was the most exciting word in the human language upon being asked to marry. (Kavaler-Adler *Compulsion to Create*, 1993)

2　Farrell never stopped classes and daily dance exercises, similar to the heroine of *The Red Shoes*.

CHAPTER 5

1　D. W. Winnicott first coined the term "good-enough" mother, also called "good-enough" object, in his papers in the *The Maturational Processes and the Facilitating Environment* (1965).

2　Aunt Belle is referred to as aunt Beryl in her writing.

3　D. W. Winnicott (1967, 1971) was the first to write about the mother's mirroring role.

4　See Fairbairn's comments on the story of Christian, in his paper on "The repression and return of bad objects," in 1952 collection.

5　See Winnicott on "object usage" in "The Use of the Object and Relating Through Identifications" (1952).

6　D. H. Lawrence is reported to have turned venomously upon his friend Katherine, at one point, calling her a "reptile" and expressing his hopes to a male friend that she might "stew in her consumption."

7　The story ends with another oedipal abandonment theme, a theme which may have been reverberating through her consciousness since maternal abandonment in infancy.

8　D. W. Winnicott (1971) defines the "transitional world" as that psychic reality that exists inbetween the internal world and the external world, as the internal world emerges in play and creativity and in the artistic world of culture as a whole. The artist, like the transitional age child, does not consciously ask, who created the characters of their work, or whether they were created or they existed outside the self as an external reality. Just as the transitional age teddy bear is neither found nor created, but is some combination of finding the external other and re-creating it from within, so too with the artist's characters, the finding of the other and the creating of the other become one.

CHAPTER 6

1   *The Voyage Out* (1915), *Night and Day* (1919), *Jacob's Room* (1922), *Mrs. Dalloway* (1925), *To The Lighthouse* (1927), *Orlando* (1928), *The Waves* (1931), *The Years* (1937), and *Between the Acts* (1941).

2   Woolf immortalized Julia's enthrallment with Adrian, Virginia's younger brother, in *To the Lighthouse.*

3   This pertains to a description of Mrs. Ramsay in *To The Lighthouse.*

4   She rebelled with anorexia.

5   Essentially it is only the few erotic experiences with Vita that bring her body alive outside the creative process (see Panken, 1987).

CHAPTER 7

1   Rhoda must depend on shocks of factual reality, such as hitting herself against a wall, or hitting her feet against a bed post to survive.

2   Panken (1987) sees Percival as the symbolic representation of Woolf's brother, Thoby, who died in the first world war. Woolf struggles with her reaction to his death through the character of Rhoda.

3   As Edith Sitwell ended her life (Kavaler, 1993a).

4   Woolf had written in her letters that she had only twice in her life been physically attracted to a man.

5   Elma Bond proposes that Leonard told Virginia that these earlier affairs meant nothing.

6   The term "subjective object" was first used by Winnicott in his book, *Playing and Reality.* Later, Heinz Kohut converted the term into that of "selfobject" without acknowledging Winnicott's invention of the term and its conceptual view. When a mother mirrors her child during the preoedipal stages of self-formation, she aids development. When this mirroring is done for another in adulthood, it serves a compensatory function for those with arrested self-development, and it also feeds a psychic addiction.

7   Bond quotes Woolf: "I was looking at a plant with a spread of leaves, and it seemed suddenly plain that the flower itself was part of the earth; that a ring enclosed what was the flower, and that was the real flower; part earth, part flower." (Quoted in Bond, 1989, p.30). This view of the world is a sympton of Woolf's developmental arrest in the symbiotic stage, where separation has not taken place. Woolf's viewpoint does seem to reflect that of an arrest in self and other differentiation, symptomatic of borderline and narcissistic pathology. Differentiation exists, but the boundary of separation is not distinctly drawn.

8   I am referring here to the potential to internalize a more loving mode

of relatedness as defenses against such relatedness are dealt with. New and more loving internalizations can change the internal object situation so that ambivalence towards the object can be tolerated and the object can be consciously grieved.

9   Leslie Stephen's self-doubt seems to have been an obsessive rumination related to a narcissistic character structure, in which an internal omnipotent object persecuted him with expectations. His mother had viewed him as a genius, and he was obsessed that he wasn't living up to this image. He never seems to have separated from his mother and her narcissistic and mythic view of him.

10   She portrays Cam as doing this in *To The Lighthouse*.

11   Kelley comments on Woolf's effort in the face of life's impingements.

CHAPTER 8

1   Information on Diane Arbus's life is taken from *Diane Arbus, A Biography*, by Patricia Boswell, New York: Alfred A. Knopf, 1984.

CHAPTER 9

1   Masterson mentions the posssibility of transference cure in his article, "Reflections on Anna O.", in *Anna O., Fourteen Contemporary Reinterpretations*, ed. Rosenbaum, 1984.

2   The *Grief Tales* are mentioned by Pollock in "Bertha Pappenheim's pathological mourning: possible effects of childhood sibling loss" (1972).

3   see Schwartz-Salant, 1982.

4   Others, such as Bolosky (1982), remark on the borderline dynamics of Anna O.'s character, with Bolosky comparing such dynamics to Kernberg's criteria of preoedipal borderline pathology, p. 142.

5   Being the good mother that she wished to have when her actual mtoher's inadequacies promoted more hate than she could handle.

CHAPTER 10

1   Hanna Segal, Wilfred R. Bion, and Herbert Rosenfeld, as well as Melanie Klein herself, were all doing work with psychotic patients. They never excluded schizophrenics from their clinical theory.

2   As Anne Sexton became his patient, she took on the role of student, learning his terminology and interjecting it into her poetic work as it evolved.

3   This omnipotent part object is a remnant from the omnipotent fusion of the symbiotic era, and from the omnipotent other of the rapprochement stage, as Margaret Mahler (1975) describes it.

4   Dr. Orne believed that incest could not have taken place in this way

because "it wasn't the father's style when he was drinking," (Middlebrook, p. 58), and it would be impossible the way Sexton described it, i.e., with Aunt Nana lying there.

5 For example, Marian Chase began to practice dance therapy in a mental hospital in Washington, D.C. during the 1950s. This led to the pioneering work of Blanche Evan and others in the dance therapy field, who practiced outside of mental health settings.

6 Without access to the writings of the British object-relations theorists, Dr. Orne would not have had the opportunity to read D. W. Winnicott's "Hate in the Countertransference" (1947), which could have helped him accept and interpret his reactions.

CHAPTER 11

1 In the Kleinian theory of the unconscious, eyes are like breasts.

2 Anne Sexton's later poetry had themes of crawling and rowing towards a god-father from whom she desperately sought some form of redemption. She had a body of poetry entitled *The Awful Rowing Towards God.*

CHAPTER 13

1 This self-condemnation can be seen in terms of Ronald Fairbairn's dynamic psychic structure (1952), where the anti-libidinal ego attacks the libidinal self from within and self-criticism is clung to as one clings to an internal sadistic parent. The masochistic defense wards off contact with a current object, and so the fears of object contact need to be understood to help the patient let go of the addiction to the internal parental object.

2 The "backlash" can be seen as a "negative therapeutic reaction."

CHAPTER 14

1 This grandiose self exists prior to normal disillusionment that takes place as the "low keyedness" mode of mourning of Margaret Mahler's (1975) rapprochement period.

REFERENCES)

Alpers, A., 1982. *The Life of Katherine Mansfield*. New York: Penguin Books.

Bach, S., 1985. *Narcissistic States and the Therapeutic Process*. Newvale, New Jersey: Jason Aronson.

————,1994. *The Language of Perverson and the Language of Love*. Newvale, New Jersey: Jason Aronson.

Balint, M., 1979. *The Basic Fault*. New York: Brunner Mazel.

Barnhart, E. and Stein, J. eds., 1962. *American College Dictionary*. New York: Random House.

Bell, Q., 1972. *Virginia Woolf: A Biography*. New York: Harcourt Brace Jovanovich.

Bennet, P., 1990. *My Life a Loaded Gun...Dickinson, Plath, Rich, and Female Creativity*. Urbano: University of Illinois Press.

Bion, W., 1963. *Elements of Psychoanalysis*. London: Karnac.

————, 1967. "Attacks on linking," ch. 8, in *Second Thoughts*. London: Maresfield Library.

Bolkosky, S., 1982. "The Alpha and Omega of Psychoanalysis: Reflections on Anna O. and Freud's Vienna." *Psychoanalytic Review*, 69 (1).

Bollas, C., 1993. Interview with Christopher Bollas. *Psychoanalytic Dialogues*, Vol. 3 (3).

————, 1987. *The Shadow of the Object: Psychoanalysis of the Unthought Known*. London: Free Association Books.

Bond, E., 1988. *Who Killed Virginia Woolf?* New York: Human Sciences Press.

Boswell, P. A., 1984. *Diane Arbus, A Biography*. New York: Alfred A. Knopf.

Bowlby, 1969. *Attachment*. New York: Basic Books.

Bowlby, 1980. *Attachment and Loss*, vol. 1. New York: Basic Books.

Brenner, D., 1982. *The Mind in Conflict*. Madison, Connecticut: International Universities Press.

Breuer, J. and Freud, S. (1923–1925). *Studies in Hysteria*. Standard Edition of the Works of Sigmund Freud, vol. II.

Brok, A., 1993. Lecture at the Object Relations Institute of Psychotherapy and Psychoanalysis on the "playing alliance."

Brontë, E., 1965. *Wuthering Heights.* New York, and Harmonds, Middlesex, England: Penguin Press.

Butsher, E., 1976. *Sylvia Plath, Method and Madness.* New York: Simon and Schuster.

Cody, J., 1971. *After Great Pain, the Inner Life of Emily Dickinson.* Boston: Harvard University Press.

DeSalvo, L., 1989. *Virginia Woolf, the Impact of Childhood Sexual Abuse on her Life and Work.* New York: Ballantine Books.

Deutsch, H., 1942. "Some Forms of Emotional Disturbance and their Relationship to Schizophrenia." *Psychoanalytic Quarterly,* Vol. 11: 301–321.

Dickinson, E., 1960. *The complete poems of Emily Dickinson.* Edited by T. M. Johnson. Boston: Little, Brown and Company.

DO Productions (Bernard Artgues), 1988. *Camille Claudel.* France: Cannon Films Christian Fechner/Lilich Films Gaumont/A2 TV France/Films A2.

Ellenberger, H., 1970. *The Discovery of the Unconscious.* New York: Basic Books.

Ellman, S. J. (1991). *Freud's Technique Papers, a Contemporary Perspective.* Newvale, New Jersey: Jason Aronson.

Fairbairn, R. D., 1952. *Psychoanalytic Studies of the Personality.* London and New York: Routledge Press.

Farrell, S., 1990. *Holding on to the Air.* New York: Penguin Books.

Fogel, G. I., 1991. *The Work of Hans Loewald.* Newvale, New Jersey: Jason Aronson.

Freud, S., 1917. "Mourning and melancholia." In *Collected Papers,* Vol. IV, 30–59.

Garlandt, J. G., 1983. *An Interrupted Life, the Diaries of Etty Hillesum.* New York: Pantheon Books.

GB, Technicolor, 136m, 1948. *The Red Shoes.* GFD/The archers (Michael Powell, Emeric Pressburger, art direction, editing).

Gerin, W., 1971. *Emily Bronte.* New York and Oxford: Oxford University Press.

Gilber, S. and Gubar, S. [1979] 1984. *The Madwoman in the Attic.* New Haven: Yale University Press.

Glendinning, V., 1981. *A Lion among Unicorns.* New York: Alfred A. Knopf.

Gordon, L., 1984. *Virginia Woolf, a Writer's Life.* New York: W. W. Norton and Company, Inc.

Griffin-Wolff, C. 1986. *Emily Dickinson.* New York: Alfred A. Knopf.

Grotstein, J. S., 1989. "A revised psychoanalytic conception of schizophrenia: an interdisciplinary update." *Psychoanalytic Psychology*, Vol. 6 (3), 253–275.

Grunes, M., 1984. "The therapeutic object relationship." *Psychoanalytic Review*, Vol. 71 (1): 123–143.

Guntrip, H. (1976). *Schizoid Phenomena, Object Relations, and the Self.* Madison, Connecticut: International Universities Press.

Homans, M., 1980. *Women Writers and Poetic Identity.* New Jersey: Princeton University Press.

Johnson, T. H., [1890] 1960. *The Complete Poems of Emily Dickinson.* Boston and Toronto: Little, Brown, and Company.

Kavaler-Adler, S. A., 1985. "Mirror, Mirror on the Wall...." *Journal of Comprehensive Psychotherapy*, Vol. 5: 1–38.

Kavaler-Adler, S. A., 1986. "Lord of the Mirrors and the Demon Lover." *American Journal of Psychoanalysis,* Vol. 46 (4): 336–344.

Kavaler, S. A., 1987. "Nightmares and Object Relations Theory." In *Nightmares: Biological and Psychological Foundations*, ed. by Henry Kellerman. New York: Columbia University Press, 33–57.

———, 1988a. "Diane Arbus and the Demon Lover." *American Journal of Psychoanalysis,* Vol. 48 (4): 366–370.

Kavaler, S. A., 1988b. "The Father's role in the Self Developmnet of his Daughter." In *Critical Psychophysical Passages in the Lives of Women.* Edited by J. Zuckerberg. New York: Plenum Press, 49–65.

———, 1909. "Anne Sexton and the Demonic Lover." *American Journal of Psychoanalysis,* 49 (2): 105–114.

———, 1990. "Charlotte Brontë and the Feminine Self." *American Journal of Psychoanalysis*, 50 (1): 37–43.

Kavaler-Adler, S., 1991a. "Some More Speculations on Anna O." *The American Journal of Psychoanalysis*, Vol. 51 (2).

Kavaler-Adler, S., 1991b. "Emily Dickinson and the Subject of Seclusion." *American Journal of Psychoanalysis*, Vol. 51 (1): 21–38.

———, 1991c. "Object Relations Insights Concerning the Female as Artist." In *Psychoanaltyic Perspectives on Women.* Edited by Elaine Segal. Monograph no. 4 in *Current Issues in Psychoanalytic Practice.* New York: Brunner Mazel, 100–120.

———, 1991d. "A Theory of Creative Process Reparation and its Mode of Failure: the case of Katherine Mansfield." *Psychoanalysis and Psychotherapy* 9 (20): 134–150.

———, 1992a. "Anais Nin and the Developmental Use of the Creative Process." *Psychoanalytic Review*, Vol. 79 (1): 73–88.

———, 1992b. "The Aging Decline of Two Untreated Borderline Geniuses, Virginia Woolf and Edith Sitwell." *Psychoanalysis and*

Psychotherapy, Vol. 9 (2): 134–150.

———, 1992c. "The Conflict and Process Theory of Melanie Klein." *American Journal of Psychoanalysis,* vol. 53 (3): 187–204.

———, 1992d. "Mourning and Erotic Transference." *International Journal of Psychoanalysis,* vol. 73 (3), 527–539.

———, 1992e. "An Object Relations View of Creative Process and Group Process." *Group,* Vol. 16 (1): 47–58.

———, 1993a. *The Compulsion to Create; A Psychoanalytic Study of Female Artists.* New York and London: Routledge.

———, 1993b. "Object Relations issues in the Treatment of the Preoedipal Character." *American Journal of Psychoanalysis.* Vol. 53 (1): 19–34.

———, 1995. "Opening up Blocked Mourning in the Preoedipal Character." *American Journal of Psychoanalysis,* Vol. 55 (2): 145–168.

———, 1991. "The Vaginal Core in Women and the Demon Lover Part Object." Lecture at Object Relations Institute conference on "The Klein-Fairbairn Dialectic." Unpublished.

Kelley, A. van Buren, 1971. *The Novels of Virginia Woolf, Fact and Vision.* Chicago: University of Chicago Press.

Kernberg, O., 1975. *Borderline Conditions and Pathological Narcissism.* Newvale, New Jersey: Jason Aronson.

———, 1980. *Internal World and External Realtiy.* Newvale, New Jersey: Jason Aronson.

Klein, M. [1930] 1975. "The Importance of Symbol-formation in the Development of the Ego." In *Love, Guilt and Reparation and Other Works—1921–1945.* London: Hogarth: 219–233.

———, [1936] 1975. "Weaning." In *Love, Guilt and Reparation and Other Works—1925–1945.* London: Hogarth: 219–232.

———, [1940]. "Mourning and its Relation to Manic Depressive States." In *Love, Guilt and Reparation and Other Works—1921–1945.* London: Hogarth, 306–343.

———, [1957], 1975. "Envy and gratitude." In *Envy and Gratitude and Other Works—1946–1963.* London: Hogarth, 176–235.

Kohut, H., 1977. *The Restoration of the Self.* Madison, Connecticut: International Universities Press.

Lichtenberg, J.D., Lachmann, F. M. and Fosshage, J. L., 1992. *The Self and Motivational Systems.* New Jersey: Analytic Press.

Loewald, H., 1962. "Internalization, Separation, Mourning, and the Superego." *Psychoanalytic Quarterly.* Vol 31: 484–504.

Mahler, M. S. F., Pine, F., Bergman, A., 1975. *The Psychological Birth of the Human Infant.* New York: Jason Aronson.

Mansfield, K., 1956. *Stories (Selected) and with introduction by Elizabeth*

Bowen. New York: Alfred A. Knopf.

Masterson, J., 1976. *The Borderline Adult*. New York: Brunner Mazel.

———, 1981. *Narcissistic and Borderline Disorders*. New York: Brunner Mazel.

McClatchy, J. D., ed., 1978. *Anne Sexton, the Artist and her Critic*. Bloomington and London: Indiana University Press.

McDougall, J., 1980. *A Plea for a Measure of Abnormality*. Madison, Conn.: International Universities Press.

Meyers, J., 1978. *Katherine Mansfield, a Biography*. London: Hamish Hamilton.

Middlebrook, D. W., 1991. *Anne Sexton, a Biography*. Boston: Houghton Mifflin Company.

Miller, A., 1984. *Thou Shalt Not Be Aware*. New York: Farrar, Straus & Giroux.

Mitchell, S., 1993. *Hope and Dread in Psychoanalysis*. New York: Basic Books.

Modell, A., 1975. "A Narcissistic Defense against Affects and the Illusion of Self-sufficiency." *International Journal of of Psychoanalysis*. Vol. 56: 275–82.

———, 1976. "The Holding Environment and the Therapeutic Action of Psychoanalysis." *Journal of the American Psychoanalytic Association*. Vol. 24: 285–308.

Nashpitz, J. D., 1984. "Anna O., Seen by a Child Psychiatrist." In *Anna O., Fourteen Contemporary Interpretations*. Edited by M. Roenbaum and M. Muroff. New York: Free Press.

Ogden, T., 1986. *Matrix of the Mind*. Newvale, New Jersey: Jason Aronson.

———, 1993. *The Primitive Edge of Experience*. Newvale, New Jersey: Jason Aronson.

———, 1994. *Subjects of Analysis*. Northvale, New Jersey: Jason Aronson.

Orgel, S., 1981. "Fusion with the Victim. A Study of Sylvia Plath." In *Lives, Events and Other Players*. Edited by J. Coltrera. New York: Jason Aronson.

Panken, S., 1987. *Lust of Creation*. Albany, New York: State University of New York Press.

Paris, R-M, 1984. *Camille, the Life of Camlle Claudel*. New York: Arcade Publishing, Little, Brown and Company.

Pearson, J., 1930. *The Sitwells, a Family's Biography*. New York: Harcourt Brace Jovanovich.

Plath, S., 1961. *Ariel*. New York: Harcourt Brace Jovanovich.

———, 1968. *The Colossus*. New York: Vantage Books.

Pollack, G. K., 1968. "The Possible Significance of Childhood Object Loss in the Joseph Breuer—Bertha Pappenheim (Anna O.)—Sigmund Freud relationship." *Journal of the American Psychoanalytic Association.* 16: 711–739.

———, 1972. "Bertha Pappenheim's Pathological Mourning: Possible Effects of Childhood Sibling Loss." *Journal of the American Psychoanalytic. Association*, Vol. 20: 476–493.

———, 1973. "Bertha Pappenheim; Addenda to her Case History." *Journal of the American Psychoanalytic Association*, Vol. 21: 328–332.

———, 1975. "Mourning and Memoralization through Music." *Annual of Psychoanalysis*, Vol. 5, 423–436.

———, 1977. "The Mourning Process and Creative Organizational Change." *Journal of the American Psychoanalytic Association*, Vol. 25: 3–34.

Racker, 1968. *Transference and Countertransference.* New York: International Universities Press.

Reich, A., [1953], 1973. "Narcissistic Object Choice in Women." In *Psychoanalytic Contributions.* Madison, Connecticut: International Universities Press.

Rose, P., 1978. *Women of Letters.* New York: Oxford University Press.

Rosenbaum, M. and Muroff, M., eds., 1984. *Anna O., Fourteen Contemporary Reinterpretations.* New York: Free Press.

Salter, G. and Harper, A., 1956. *Edith Sitwell, Fire of the Mind.* New York: Vanguard Press.

Sandler, J., and Joffe, W. G., 1969. "Towards a Basic Psychoanalytic Model." *International Journal of Psychoanalysis*, Vol. 50: 79–90.

Sanford-Garard, D., 1994. Personal communication on the creative process.

Schwartz-Salant, N., 1982. *Narcissism and Character Transformation.* Tornonto: Inner City Books.

Segal, H., [1964], 1973. *Intrduction to the Work of Melanie Klein.* London: Hogarth Press.

———, 1986a. *The Work of Hanna Segal.* New York: Jason Aronson.

———, 1986b. "Notes on Symbol Formation." In *The work of Hanna Segal.* Newvale, New Jersey: Jason Aronson.

Seinfeld, J., 1990. *The Bad Object.* Newvale, New Jersey: Jason Aronson.

———, 1991. *The Empty Core.* Newvale, New Jersey: Jason Aronson.

———, 1993. *Holding and Interpreting.* Newvale, New Jersey: Jason Aronson.

Sexton, A., 1981. *The Complete Poems.* Boston: Houghton Mifflin.

Sewall, R. B., 1974. *The life of Emily Dickinson.* New York: Farrar, Straus & Giroux.

Silverman, M. A., and Will, N. P., 1986. "The Failure of Emotional Self-repair through Poetry." *Psychoanalytic Quarterly*. Vol. 55 (11): 99–129.

Stark, 1968. "On the Confounding of Creativity Contexts: Maslow's Psychology of Science." *Psychological Reports*, Vol. 23: 88–90.

Stern, D., 1985. *The Interpersonal World of the Infant*. New York: Jason Aronson.

Stevenson, A., 1989. *Bitter Fame*. New York: Houghton Mifflin.

Stolorow, R. and Lachmann, F., 1980. *Psychoanalysis of Developmental Arrests*. Madison, Connecticut: International Universities Press.

Tomalin, C., 1987. *Katherine Mansfield, a Secret Life*. New York: Alfred A. Knopf.

Winnicott, D. W., [1969], 1971. "The use of an object and relating through identifications." In *Playing and Reality*. New York: Penguin Books.

———, [1953], 1971. "Transitional Objects and Transitional Phenomena." Collected in *Playing and Reality*. Middlesex, England: Penguin Books.

———, [1963], 1982. "The Development of the Capacity for Concern." *The Maturational Processes and the Facilitating Environment*. Madison, Connecticut: International Universities Press.

———, [1967], 1971. "Mirror-role of Mother and Family in Child Development." Collected in *Playing and Reality*. Middlesex, England: Penguin Books.

———, 1971. *Playing and Reality*. Middlesex, England: Penguin Press.

———, 1974. "Fear of Breakdown." *International Review of Psycho-Analysis* 1: 103–107.

———, 1982. *The Maturational Processes and the Facilitating Environment*. Madison, Ct.: International Universities Press.

Wolff, C. G., 1986. *Emily Dickinson*. New York: Alfred A. Knopf.

Wolff, A. and Kutash, L., 1991. *The Submerged Personality*. Newvale, New Jersey: Jason Aronson.

Woodman, M., 1982. *Addiction to Perfection: the Still Unravished Bride*. Toronto: Inner City Books.

———, 1985. *The Pregnant Virgin: a Process of Psychological Transformation*. Toronto: Inner City Books.

———, 1993. *Leaving my Father's House, a Journey to Conscious Femininity*. Boston: Shambhala.

Woolf, V., 1927. *To the Lighthouse*. New York: Harvest Books.

———, 1928. *Orlando*.

———, 1931. *The Waves*. New York: Harcourt, Brace Jovanovich.

———, 1941. *Betweeen the Acts*. New York: Harvest Books.

INDEX)